Canary Islands

Lanzarote
p97

La Palma
p180

La Gomera
p164

Tenerife
p120

El Hierro
p202

Gran
Canaria
p42

Fuerteventura
p75

ON THE ROAD

SANTA CRUZ DE LA PALMA
P183

KAROL KOZLOWSKI / GETTY IMAGES ©

PUERTO DE MOGÁN P73

MICHAL SLEDECZEK / GETTY IMAGES ©

Contents

Welcome to the Canary Islands

Looming volcanoes, prehistoric sites, lush pine forests, lunar landscapes, sandy coves and miles of Sahara-style dunes. Yes, there is another world beyond the Canaries' seafront resorts.

A Dramatic Landscape

The Canary Islands boast near-perfect year-round temperatures, which means whether it's summer or winter you can enjoy the dramatic and varied landscape here that you usually have to cross continents to experience. Marvel at the subtropical greenery of La Gomera's national park, the pine-forested peaks in Gran Canaria's mountainous interior or the tumbling waterfalls of La Palma. Then contrast all this lushness with the extraordinary barren flatlands flanking Tenerife's El Teide, the surreal play of colours of Lanzarote's lava fields and Fuerteventura's endless plains, punctuated by cacti, scrub and lots (and lots) of goats.

Be a Good Sport

It is this very diversity of landscape, coupled with those predictable sunny days, that makes outdoor activities so accessible and varied. Hike the signposted footpaths that criss-cross the islands, ranging from meandering trails to mountains treks; scuba dive in enticing warm waters, marvelling at more than 350 species of fish (and the odd shipwreck); or pump up the adrenalin by riding the wind and the waves – kitesurfing, windsurfing and surfing are all big here. Slow down the pace with camel rides, rounds of golf, horse treks and boat rides.

Or Just Relax...

If your idea of a perfect holiday is that enticing combo of R&R, you're in the right place. The most obvious spot to relax is on a beach, and there are plenty of choices: from the soft rolling dunes in Fuerteventura to the wide arcs of golden sand in Tenerife. Others may like to up the self-pampering stakes by visiting a spa. Thalassotherapy centres are spouting forth everywhere and offer a tempting range of treatments and massages. There's also a tidal wave of ocean-front bars where you can enjoy a cocktail at sunset while contemplating the gently lapping sea.

Superb Art & Architecture

While the Canary Islands may not boast the grand-slam museums of Spain's big mainland cities, there is plenty to compel art and culture aficionados here. Surrealist fans should check out the spectacular canvases of world-acclaimed painter Óscar Domínguez in his Santa Cruz de Tenerife home town, while the huge abstract sculptures of locals Martín Chirino and César Manrique are impossible to miss on Gran Canaria and Lanzarote. If buildings are your thing, look for the emblematic wooden balconies, leafy internal patios and brightly painted facades that typify vernacular Canarian architecture.

Why I Love the Canary Islands

By Lucy Corne, Author

There are few destinations as underrated and maligned as the Canary Islands. My first real encounter, working in a Gran Canaria resort, wasn't the best introduction to the islands' scenic and cultural wealth. But on escaping I found dramatic mountains, quaint pueblos and charming seaside villages. I was enamoured with the underdog archipelago and moved there soon afterwards. For years I explored every island and was wowed – and wooed – over and over. On returning for this book I fell in love with the islands again. And when you hike through Tenerife's lava fields, drive Gran Canaria's central mountains or enjoy a plate of cheese in a hilltop pueblo, I suspect you might fall in love too.

For more about our authors, see page 288

Above: Charco de San Ginés (p100) in Arrecife, Lanzarote

Canary Islands

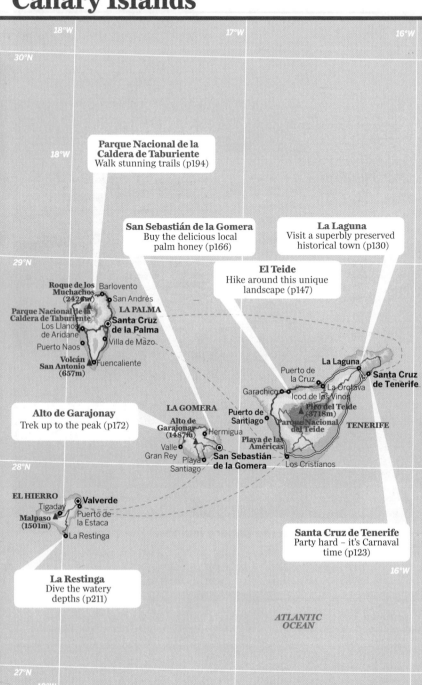

Parque Nacional de la Caldera de Taburiente
Walk stunning trails (p194)

San Sebastián de la Gomera
Buy the delicious local palm honey (p166)

La Laguna
Visit a superbly preserved historical town (p130)

El Teide
Hike around this unique landscape (p147)

Roque de los Muchachos (2426m)
Barlovento
San Andrés
LA PALMA
Parque Nacional de la Caldera de Taburiente
Los Llanos de Aridane
Santa Cruz de la Palma
Villa de Mazo
Puerto Naos
Volcán San Antonio (657m)
Fuencaliente

La Laguna
Puerto de la Cruz
Santa Cruz de Tenerife
Garachico
La Orotava
Icod de los Vinos
Pico del Teide (3718m)
Parque Nacional del Teide
TENERIFE

Alto de Garajonay
Trek up to the peak (p172)

LA GOMERA
Alto de Garajonay (1487m)
Hermigua
Valle Gran Rey
Playa Santiago
San Sebastián de la Gomera
Puerto de Santiago
Playa de las Américas
Los Cristianos

EL HIERRO
Tigaday
Valverde
Malpaso (1501m)
Puerto de la Estaca
La Restinga

Santa Cruz de Tenerife
Party hard – it's Carnaval time (p123)

La Restinga
Dive the watery depths (p211)

ATLANTIC OCEAN

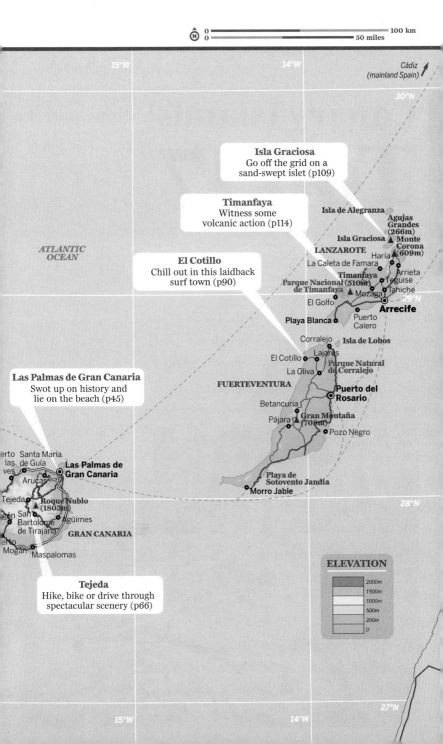

0 — 100 km
0 — 50 miles

15°W   14°W   Cádiz
(mainland Spain)

30°N

Isla Graciosa
Go off the grid on a
sand-swept islet (p109)

Timanfaya
Witness some
volcanic action (p114)

El Cotillo
Chill out in this laidback
surf town (p90)

ATLANTIC
OCEAN

Isla de Alegranza

Agujas
Grandes
(266m)

Isla Graciosa ▲ Monte
Corona
(609m)

LANZAROTE
Haría
La Caleta de Famara
Arrieta
Timanfaya (510m) Teguise
Parque Nacional ▲ Mozaga Tahíche
de Timanfaya
El Golfo   **Arrecife**
29°N
Playa Blanca Puerto
Calero

Corralejo   Isla de Lobos
Lajares
El Cotillo
Parque Natural
La Oliva   **de Corralejo**

Las Palmas de Gran Canaria
Swot up on history and
lie on the beach (p45)

FUERTEVENTURA   **Puerto del**
Rosario
Betancuria
Pájara   **Gran Montaña**
(708m)
Pozo Negro

erto Santa María
las de Guía
ves   **Las Palmas de**
Gran Canaria
Arucas

Tejeda   **Roque Nublo**
(1803m)
án San
Bartolomé Agüimes
de Tirajana   **GRAN CANARIA**
erto
Mogán
Maspalomas

Playa de
Sotovento Jandía
Morro Jable
28°N

Tejeda
Hike, bike or drive through
spectacular scenery (p66)

ELEVATION

	2000m
	1500m
	1000m
	500m
	200m
	0

27°N

15°W   14°W

Canary Islands'
Top 17

1

El Teide Magnificence

1 Start with a gentle hike around the base of Tenerife's El Teide (p147), kidding yourself that you are enjoying a stroll on the surface of the moon; it really is that extraordinary. The trails take you deep into an alien landscape with red, yellow and brown craters resembling giant prehistoric molehills, bizarre volcanic rock formations and pebble-like lapilli. If you have energy to spare you can hike to the summit, or take it easy on the cable car to the top. Wrap up warm, though; it can get pretty chilly up there in the clouds.

Carnaval

2 The Canarians love a good party and, in Santa Cruz de Tenerife, the fiesta spirit reaches its sequin-bedecked crescendo during the annual Carnaval (p128). Festivities generally high-kick off with a flourish in early February and last for around three weeks, featuring gala performances, fancy-dress competitions, fireworks and Rio-style parades. All the islands celebrate Carnaval with dawn-to-dusk frivolity and distinctive customs, so book your accommodation way ahead (if you intend to go to bed, that is). A contender for the title of Carnaval Queen

TIME WHITE / GETTY IMAGES ©

JUERGEN RICHTER / LOOK-FOTO / GETTY IMAGES ©

Driving Gran Canaria's Rugged Heart

3 While most people stick to Gran Canaria's coast, it is the mountains that hold the real appeal. Around every bend – and there are a lot of bends – you'll find another weird rock formation, or another view that will have you reaching for your camera and searching for a spot to pull over. Luckily, there are also plenty of pretty villages (p66) dotted around where you can take a break to sample hearty soups and sugary cakes without ever tearing your eyes away from it all.

Fuerteventura's Stunning Beaches

4 Some of the Canary Islands' most glorious beaches are in Fuerteventura. If you want to escape the rows of sunbeds topped by slowly roasting tourists, head for the northwest of the island and the wild beaches and thundering surf around El Cotillo. Windsurfers can catch the waves at Playa de Sotavento de Jandía (p93), while more watersports are on offer at Morro Jable's spectacular sandy arc. For kids' activities, check out family-friendly beaches like Costa Calma and Caleta de Fuste. Morro Jable beach (p94)

Hiking the Caldera de Taburiente

5 Put your best foot forward and discover the spectacular Parque Nacional de la Caldera de Taburiente (p194) by hiking one of the park's numerous trails. For many, the pine forests and curtains of clouds slipping over the side of the sheer caldera walls add up to what is the finest walking experience in the archipelago. Walks here range from simple hour-long strolls to demanding day-long feats of endurance. Don't forget to check out the informative displays at the park visitor centre. Barranco de las Angustias flows through Parque Nacional de la Caldera de Taburiente

La Laguna's Historic Old Quarter

6 Visit Tenerife's La Laguna (p130) for a stroll around one of the best-preserved historical quarters on the island: all cobbled alleys, merchants' houses and pine-balconied mansions. The unique vernacular architecture and layout was originally provided as a model for many colonial towns in the Americas. La Laguna may have an air of old-fashioned history about it, but it is far from dull and there is a tangible youthful energy about the place. It has a vigorous nightlife, and plenty of bars and cafes where you can kick back with a coffee or beer.

Farmers' Markets

7 Glossy blue-black aubergines, blood-red tomatoes, garlicky sausages, buttery almond biscuits, gigantic garlic bulbs, freshly baked bread... Who can resist a farmers' market? Throughout the islands, weekly markets concentrate on local produce. Look for regional specialities such as creamy *queso de flor* (cheese) from Gran Canaria, the sweet Malmsey wine from La Palma (p198) or Fuerteventura's famous Majorero goat's cheese – ask to try before you buy. Goat's cheese from a famers' market, Gran Canaria

TRAVELSTOCK44 – JUERGEN HELD / GETTY IMAGES ©

César Manrique Art & Architecture

8 A native of Lanzarote, the late César Manrique's lingering influence on the art and architecture of the island is special. That rich forest green you see is the specified colour of door and window frames everywhere here. Then there are those huge, zany steel sculptures decorating so many roundabouts. Visit Manrique's former home (p105), built around a cave and housing fabulous works by masters like Picasso, plus his other top sights: the Cueva de los Verdes and Jameos del Agua. Manrique's *Mirador del Río*, Lanzarote

Barranco de Guayadeque

9 The best time to visit this lush ravine (p57) in Gran Canaria is springtime, when the almond trees are in brilliant pink-and-white bloom. Year-round, however, it is leafy and lovely, flanked by steep mountains where caves have been dug out for restaurants, bars and even a chapel. Time your visit for a mealtime, when you can dine deep inside the rock. Walk off your lunch by following one of the trails, which will reward you with stunning views stretching right to the sea. Chapel carved out of rock in a settlement near Barranco de Guayadeque

Wrinkly Potatoes

10 They may not sound like the most appetising dish in the world, but the ubiquitous *papas arrugadas* (wrinkly potatoes) are a lot tastier in the flesh (skins and all). These small new potatoes are boiled and coated with coarse sea salt. The main treat here is the accompaniment: a choice of up to three sauces – *mojo picón*, *mojo verde* and *mojo de cilantro* (laced with chilli, parsley and coriander respectively). Wash down the quintessential Canarian tapa with a *caña* (draught beer) in Vegueta (p45), the historic heart of Las Palmas de Gran Canaria.

Isla Graciosa

11 There aren't many places in Europe that boast traffic-free roads, but diminutive Graciosa (p109) goes one better – it doesn't even have roads. Well, not paved ones anyway. Jump on the bumpy but blissfully short ferry from Lanzarote and spend a day or two indulging in some simple pleasures: cycling on sandy tracks, tanning on empty beaches or enjoying a beer with the locals. Once the last ferry departs, you'll feel like an extra on an empty Wild West movie set as the sand whips around Caleta de Sebo's deserted streets.

Surfing El Quemao

12 Known to surfers as the 'Hawaii of Europe', the Canary Islands are full of world-class surf spots, but none comes with a bigger rep than Lanzarote's radical left reef break, El Quemao (p111). For expert surfers able to snag a wave off the locals, these huge barrels promise the ultimate rush. For those not quite up to El Quemao standards, nearby La Caleta de Famara offers ideal conditions for learners to get on a board and get wet.

Alto de Garajonay

13 Peeking above the clouds that lie across La Gomera for much of the year, Alto de Garajonay (p171) is the island's highest peak (1487m). Ascending to its summit offers the chance to get to know the fascinating *laurisilva* (laurel) forests that sit like a bright green wig atop this small circular island. The walk is easy but the views from the summit, which take in these forests and (on clear days) snow-dusted El Teide on Tenerife, are anything but ordinary.

Wine Tasting in Lanzarote

14 La Geria (p114) is not your standard bucolic viticulture postcard of lush green vineyards, scenic rows of vines and verdant rolling hills. On Lanzarote, wine cultivation is, well, extraordinary, with vines grown in dimpled craters within volcanic stone semicircles called *zocos*. Wine tasting is made really easy here: you can visit most of the main bodegas on the same stretch of bumpy road in La Geria, including a taste of the famous *malvasía* sweet wine, once the tipple of the European aristocracy. Swot up first at the nearby wine museum.

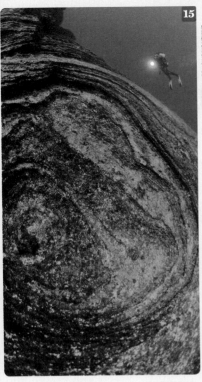

Diving El Hierro

15 Get in a tangled embrace with an octopus, blow kisses to a wrasse or make friends with an anemone. Under the waves of southern El Hierro (p211) is a hidden wonderland of weird and wonderful aquatic creatures, which, combined with warm waters and reliable diving conditions, make this one of the most exciting diving locations in all the North Atlantic. Getting underwater is also easy here with several dive schools offering everything from 'try dives' to full courses.

Gourmet San Sebastián

16 The western isles are known for their simple, down-to-earth cuisine and little La Gomera seems to have an excess of local delicacies. Get acquainted with some of them by buzzing around San Sebastián's market (p169) in search of the island's wonderfully tangy palm honey, made, as you might guess, from the sap of palm trees. Another local Gomeran speciality worth sniffing out is *almo-grote*, a spicy cheese pâté made with hard cheese, pepper and tomato, and spread on bread. Locally produced honey from San Sebastián de la Gomera

Searching For Moby Dick

17 Human tourists aren't the only ones who like swimming in the seas off the Canary Islands. Pods of whales and schools of dolphins also love a good splash in the warm waters. The channel between Tenerife and La Gomera is their favourite holiday destination, and if you're staying on either of these islands, a whale- and dolphin-watching boat tour (p151) is an absolute must.
Pilot whales

Need to Know

For more information, see Survival Guide (p257)

Currency
Euro (€)

Language
Spanish

Visas
Generally not required for stays of up to 90 days; some nationalities will need a Schengen visa.

Money
ATMs are widely available. Credit cards are accepted in most hotels, restaurants and shops.

Mobile Phones
Buy a pay-as-you-go mobile with credit from €30. Local SIM cards are widely available and can be used in unlocked GSM phones.

Time
Greenwich Mean Time (UTC+0), daylight savings time in summer

When to Go

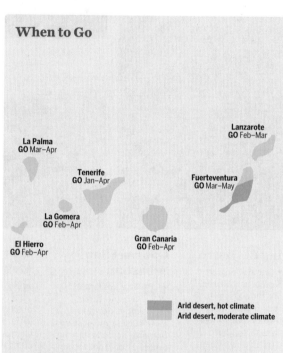

Lanzarote
GO Feb–Mar

La Palma
GO Mar–Apr

Tenerife
GO Jan–Apr

Fuerteventura
GO Mar–May

La Gomera
GO Feb–Apr

El Hierro
GO Feb–Apr

Gran Canaria
GO Feb–Apr

Arid desert, hot climate
Arid desert, moderate climate

High Season
(Dec–Apr & Jul–Aug)

➡ Coincides with Christmas, carnival season and Easter

➡ Accommodation prices are highest in January and February

➡ Mid-summer is holiday time on the Spanish mainland, so expect more tourists

➡ July and August are the hottest months of the year, but temperatures rarely hit higher than 38°C

➡ Rain is possible from January to March, especially in the mountains

Shoulder Season (May– Jun & Sep–Nov)

➡ Temperatures average around 28°C, nights are cooler

➡ Fewer tourists visit in the autumn overall

➡ Higher altitudes, particularly in Gran Canaria and Tenerife, can be far cooler with some fog

Useful Websites

Lonely Planet (www.lonely planet.com/canary-islands) Destination information, hotel bookings, travel forum and more.

Canary Islands Government (www.gobiernodecanarias.org) Local government information with plenty of details for tourists. In Spanish.

Official Tourism Office (www.turismodecanarias.com) Region-wide and island-specific information.

Daily English-language news (www.islandconnections.eu) Daily news.

Important Numbers

If you are calling within the Canaries, all numbers will have a total of nine digits beginning with 9 for landlines and 6 for mobile phones.

Country code	☏34
International access code	☏00
Ambulance	☏061
Police	☏112

Exchange Rates

Australia	A$1	€0.73
Canada	C$1	€0.75
Japan	¥100	€0.76
UK	£1	€1.39
New Zealand	NZ$1	€0.70
US	US$1	€ 0.90

For current exchange rates see www.xe.com.

Daily Costs

Budget:
Less than €60

➡ Budget hotel room (with shared bathroom): €25–35

➡ Excellent markets and supermarkets for self-caterers

➡ Check out museums with free entry, parks, churches and walks

Midrange:
€60–150

➡ Double room in midrange hotel: €55–80

➡ Three-course meal in midrange restaurant: €25, plus wine

➡ Top museums, galleries and sights: average €6

Top End:
Over €150

➡ Four-star hotel room: €100

➡ Fine dining for lunch and dinner

➡ Car rental from €20 per day

Opening Hours

The following standard opening hours are for high season only; hours tend to decrease outside that time.

Banks 8.30am to 2pm Monday to Friday

Bars 7pm to midnight

Post offices 8.30am to 8.30pm Monday to Friday, 9.30am to 1pm Saturday (large cities); 8.30am to 2.30pm Monday to Friday, 9.30am to 1pm Saturday (elsewhere)

Restaurants meals served 1pm to 4pm and 7pm until late

Shops 10am to 2pm and 5pm to 9pm Monday to Friday, 10am to 2pm Saturday

Supermarkets 9am to 9pm Monday to Saturday

Arriving in the Canary Islands

Gran Canaria Airport (p44) Regular buses to Las Palmas. Taxis €30; around 25 minutes.

Lanzarote Airport (p99) Regular buses to Arrecife. Taxis €12; around 15 minutes.

Tenerife South Airport (p121) Regular buses to Los Cristianos. Taxis €20; around 30 minutes.

Fuerteventura Airport (p92) Regular buses to Puerto del Rosario. Taxis €10; around 15 minutes.

Getting Around

Car While roads are winding, they are generally in excellent condition and driving is the best way to see the islands. Cars can be hired at airports and in resorts and larger towns, but book in advance for smaller islands. Drive on the right.

Bus All islands have a network that takes you to the main points of interest, though many rural lines are not too frequent. Discount cards are usually available.

Boat For hopping between adjacent islands, the fast ferries are superb. Many routes have frequent departures.

For much more on **getting around**, see p264

If You Like...

Scenic Landscapes

Gran Canaria The interior is fabulous and a bit like the Rockies, especially around the Cruz de Tejeda and Artenara. (p66)

Pico del Teide No hiking boots necessary to reach Spain's highest peak, accessible by cable car and offering suitably heady views. (p147)

Parque Nacional de Timanfaya For a moonscape of extraordinary rock formations, colours and atmosphere, head to Lanzarote's national park. (p114)

La Gomera One of the finest lookout spots here is the Alto de Garajonay, although the whole island is photographic heaven. (p171)

Mirador del Río The Manrique masterpiece hanging off a Lanzarote cliff offers sweeping views of the Chinijo Archipelago. (p110)

Beaches

The southern resorts have magnificent but crowded beaches, while the black-sand gems of El Hierro, La Palma and La Gomera are often deserted.

Playa de las Canteras This magnificent city beach is flanked by a wide promenade. (p50)

Playa de las Teresitas Head here for powder-soft sand, good seafood restaurants and a re-assuringly Spanish vibe. (p133)

Endless dunes Go the full Sahara and visit the extraordinary dunes in Fuerteventura and Gran Canaria. (p86)

Playa Mujeres, Lanzarote Drive along a dirt track to this rare pale-sand beach in a picturesque cove. (p119)

Playa de las Conchas, Isla Graciosa You'll likely have this gorgeous stretch of yellow sand to yourself, but take care in the water here. (p109)

Watersports

Fuerteventura and Lanzarote are known for wind and waves, while diving is best on El Hierro.

El Cotillo At the heart of Fuerteventura's surfing scene, surrounded by unspoilt wind-swept beaches. (p90)

La Caleta de Famara Lanzarote's hottest west-coast surf spot for kiteboards, windsurf boards and that original Malibu favourite: the bodyboard. (p111)

La Restinga Warm, clear waters make this coastal El Hierro village a diver's paradise. (p211)

Playa de Sotavento de Jandía Kite- and windsurfers of all levels flock to this wide golden beach that hosts the Windsurfing World Cup. (p93)

Pozo Izquierdo A quieter place to jump on a windsurfing board with a handful of well-trusted agencies offering classes and gear hire. (p71)

Southern resorts More commercial and crowded on shore, but once out at sea, the ocean is, well, the ocean. In Tenerife, check out the watersports in Los Cristianos; in Gran Canaria, visit Taurito. (p152)

Hiking

Aside from July and August, when the weather is at its hottest, the climate is sufficiently mild to enjoy some spectacular walking routes throughout the islands.

Parque Nacional del Teide, Tenerife Whether you attempt to tackle the summit or stick to the mountain's base, the lunar landscape offers some of the islands' best hikes. (p146)

Ruta de los Volcanes, La Palma This challenging 19km trek sees you shuffling over volcanic ash towards the site of the Canaries' most recent eruption. (p194)

Top: Dunas de Maspalomas, Gran Canaria (p68)
Bottom: Playa de las Canteras, Gran Canaria (p50)

Parque Nacional de Garajonay, La Gomera Plenty of well-sign-posted, shady walks criss-cross La Gomera's national park. (p171)

Parque Nacional de Timanfaya, Lanzarote Book well ahead to join a fabulous guided walk through Lanzarote's lava fields. (p114)

Parque Nacional de la Caldera de Taburiente, La Palma Follow the well-walked path through the Barranco de las Angustias or take the shorter trail to various lookout points. (p194)

Roque Nublo, Gran Canaria It takes just 30 minutes to reach Gran Canaria's iconic monolith from the roadside car park. (p67)

Barranco de Masca, Tenerife A demanding and dramatic descent through a ravine to the ocean, where you can catch a boat along the coast to save the strenuous return leg. (p150)

Camino de la Virgen, El Hierro Follow the 26km route taken by pilgrims during the island's most important fiesta. (p213)

Isla de Lobos You'll feel like the only person on Earth as you skirt the edge of this uninhabited island, a prime birdwatching site. (p89)

Wine & Cheese

La Geria Lanzarote's most famous vine-growing region, with several bodegas for tasting and buying. (p114)

Queso Majorero Try and buy your Fuerteventura cheese at a local *quesería* (cheese shop) where you can taste it first. (p82)

Malvasía wine The *malvasía* grape produces a sweet dessert wine, which you can taste at bodegas in Tenerife and La Palma. (p198)

Casa del Vino La Baranda, Tenerife Taste the region's robust red wines at this museum with attached restaurant. (p134)

Queso de Flor, Gran Canaria Sample creamy cheese blended with thistle flowers at the source in pretty Santa María de Guía. (p61)

Archaeology

The pre-Hispanic culture was virtually wiped out during the conquest, but a few fascinating Guanche sites remain.

Cueva Pintada, Gran Canaria The geometric designs at this cave are thought to be some sort of calendar. The attached museum offers insight into Guanche life. (p62)

Cenobio de Valerón, Gran Canaria An impressive set of caves and grain stores clinging to a cliffside. (p61)

Cuatro Puertas, Gran Canaria A manmade cave with four entrances sits atop a hill just outside Telde. (p56)

La Zarza, La Palma There's a small visitor centre close to the swirling rock engravings. (p201)

Los Letreros, El Hierro A long hike leads to these undeciphered petroglyphs. (p211)

Museums The Museo Canario in Las Palmas de Gran Canaria and the Museo de la Naturaleza y el Hombre in Tenerife have superb exhibits on pre-Hispanic culture. (p47)

Art & Architecture

Hotspots for arty travellers include Las Palmas de Gran Canaria, Santa Cruz de Tenerife and the entire island of Lanzarote.

César Manrique's designs Dotted throughout Lanzarote, the artist's modern sculptures and buildings contrast beautifully with the stark surrounds. (p105)

Tenerife Espacio de las Artes An exciting contemporary art centre with an emphasis on photography, modern art and edgy, socially conscious exhibits. (p123)

CAAM, Gran Canaria Along with its two satellite museums, the Centro Atlántico de Arte Moderno in Las Palmas showcases superb temporary exhibitions. (p48)

La Oliva Fuerteventura's one-time capital boasts interesting 18th-century architecture and a superb modern art gallery. (p85)

Traditional architecture Explore well-preserved old towns, including Teguise (Fuerteventura), Santa Cruz de La Palma, the Vegueta district of Las Palmas and, above all, La Laguna (Tenerife). (p130)

Off the Beaten Track

Cofete, Fuerteventura At the end of a vertiginous dirt road lies a minuscule hamlet and spectacular surf beach overlooked by a mysterious mansion... (p96)

Anaga Mountains, Tenerife Hike in verdant pine forests and discover unspoilt hamlets untouched by time. (p134)

Isla Graciosa, Lanzarote Camp on the beach and cycle a circuit of this tiny island, population 700. (p109)

Cala de Tacorón, El Hierro Pack a picnic and head to these idyllic rocky coves with crystal clear waters and a dramatic mountainous backdrop. (p211)

Charco Azul, La Palma Dine on the day's catch then take a dip in saltwater pools carved from volcanic rock. (p199)

Fortaleza de Ansite, Gran Canaria Hike to this spectacularly positioned Guanche site, where a tunnel is hollowed out through the mountainside. (p57)

Spa Therapy

The Canaries boast some superb spas allowing you to wallow in a day of self-pampering pleasure. Seek out a thalassotherapy centre, where the isles make use of something they have in abundance – seawater.

Aqua Club Termal Tenerife has many spas but this vast complex in Costa Adeje is the island's most impressive place to relax, with an array of beauty treatments, massages and a comprehensive thalassotherapy circuit. (p160)

Balneario Thalasso Visit Fuerteventura's impressive glass cube of a beachside thalassotherapy centre at Caleta de Fuste. (p83)

San Agustín Reputedly the largest thalassotherapy centre in Europe is in Gran Canaria. (p68)

Finca Argayall There's a chilled-out hippie vibe at this La Gomera lodge which offers yoga classes, meditation and various health therapies. (p231)

Hotel Balneario Pozo de La Salud The spring found next to Spain's westernmost hotel has been touted for its health benefits since the 1800s. Take a thermal bath in your room or choose from a host of treatments. (p234)

Month by Month

January

A popular month to visit as the southern resorts are generally still warm enough for beach days. Northern and inland regions are cooler and often rainy, while Tenerife's El Teide can be snow capped.

⚜ Kings' Day

Spanish children get their gifts in January, brought not by Santa Claus but by the three kings. The day is celebrated with regal parades and traditional eats.

⚜ Festival de Música de Canarias

This month sees the launch of the annual classical music festival (www.festival decanarias.com), which has been waving the baton for over 30 years.

February

Southern resorts are generally sunny, while cooler weather in the islands' interiors creates ideal conditions for walking. This is also carnival month, so book your bed early!

⚜ Carnaval

Second only to Rio in terms of sheer exuberance and party spirit, carnival here is at its biggest and best in Santa Cruz in Tenerife and Las Palmas de Gran Canaria. Santa Cruz de La Palma hosts a smaller but highly memorable party.

March

Enjoy springtime flowers, particularly on the hillsides of El Hierro, La Palma, La Gomera and Gran Canaria. During Easter week, expect tourist crowds.

⚜ Easter Parades

Easter bunnies and chocolate eggs take a back basket here during Easter week, when there are evocative parades with religious floats throughout the islands' towns and villages.

April

The sun still shines brightest on the southern beaches, although evenings are cooler and there can be showers, particularly on Tenerife.

✖ Deliciously Cheesy

Celebrate the delicious Gran Canaria *queso de flor* at its source – in Santa María de Guía at the annual cheese festival (www. santamariadeguia.es).

✖ Canarian Food Fair

Held over a weekend in Tenerife's Los Cristianos; taste and buy traditional goodies from all the islands here.

May

Another good month with plenty of towel space on the sand, plus warmer evenings, which make dining al fresco a delight.

☆ Gay Pride

Spain's second-largest gay pride event (after Madrid). Held mid-month in Maspalomas, Gran Canaria (www. gaypridemaspalomas.com).

June

You're still just ahead of the tourist onslaught, and the weather is perfect with an average of 10 hours of daily sunshine.

◉ Bonfire Night

Barbecues and dusk-to-dawn partying on the beach, plus big-bang fireworks and concerts. San Juan (23 to 24 June) is celebrated throughout the islands, but with particular gusto in Lanzarote and Las Palmas (Gran Canaria).

July

The mercury level is rising, with the average temperature in the southern resorts in the low 30s. Tourism numbers are up with the summer holiday crowd.

☆ Cool Jazz for Hot Days

The Festival Internacional Canarias Jazz & Más Heineken attracts big names from the international jazz world. Check out www.canariasjazz.com for names and venues.

🏃 Windsurfing World Championship

Like flocks of colourful butterflies, kiteboarders and windsurfers descend on Fuerteventura's Playa de Sotovento de Jandía early in the month to compete in this world-class competition.

August

This is the month you use your umbrella...as a sunshade: the weather is at its hottest. But it still rarely hits the 40°C norm of the southern Spain *costas*.

🎆 Rain Dance

The Fiesta de La Rama in Agaete is one of Gran Canaria's most important festivals. With origins in a pre-Hispanic rain dance, today it's part religious parade, part riotous night out.

🎆 Saint's Day

The Dia San Ginés on the 25th of the month is a mega-celebration in Lanzarote, with week-long celebrations that include concerts, football matches and beauty contests.

October

The average temperature is 23°C, with cooler nights. It's perfect weather for hiking in the mountains – or sitting on the beach.

🏃 Jog to the Music

Or walk, skate or spin those wheelchair wheels. The annual Music Marathon Festival (www.musicmarathon.com) in Puerto del Carmen, Lanzarote, is open to all, including four-year-old tots (½-mile race). Live music lines the route.

November

While evenings can be chilly, daytime temperatures are still conducive to beach visits and you're just before the tourist onslaught.

🏃 Kite Festival

The skies above Corralejo, Fuerteventura, are streaked with multicoloured tails for a weekend of kite-flying and family fun.

December

Christmas sees more tourists, particularly from northern Europe, seeking winter sun. Temperatures drop considerably at night and the northernmost island resorts can be cloudy, though seldom wet.

🎆 Street Party

El Hierro's Fiesta de la Virgen de la Concepción on the 8th is full of religious revelry while, on the previous evening, Valverde's streets are packed with jolly locals, eating, drinking and making merry.

Itineraries

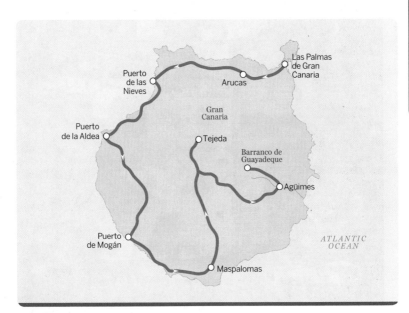

The Best of Gran Canaria

A week on Gran Canaria gives you enough time to explore the museums and restaurants of the capital, munch seafood along the coast, admire the mountains and even spend a little time on the beach.

Start in **Las Palmas de Gran Canaria** with a gentle stroll on Playa de las Canteras or a dip in the ultra-calm ocean – perfect for snorkelling. Pass the second day wandering the cobbles of historic Vegueta with its stellar museums. Day three, head to the lovely town of **Arucas** before hitting the north coast to sample seafood in **Puerto de las Nieves**. Day four, tackle the spectacular winding west coast road, grabbing lunch in quiet **Puerto de la Aldea**, then continue the magnificent drive to pretty **Puerto de Mogán**, with its Med-style yachting harbour. Day five, swing southeast to the shimmering sands of **Maspalomas** for a stroll or a swim, then take the GC-60 north to **Tejeda** for lunch with a view. Spend day six on a mountain hike or drive, drinking in the jaw-dropping scenery. To finish, wind your way down to **Agüimes** with its lovely pastel-painted buildings and historic charm, then veer back inland to the lush **Barranco de Guayadeque** for lunch in a cave.

Above: Valle Gran Rey (p178), La Gomera

Left: Harbour in Corralejo (p86), Fuerteventura

SABINE LUBENOW / LOOK-FOTO / GETTY IMAGES ©

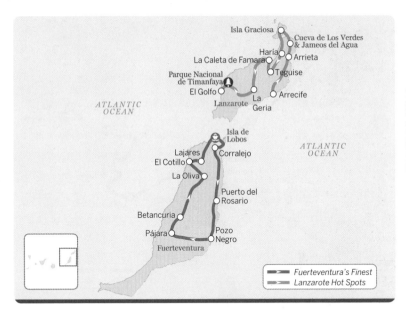

Fuerteventura's Finest
Lanzarote Hot Spots

6 DAYS Fuerteventura's Finest

The beaches here are brilliant, but there is more to the island. This route covers quaint fishing towns and inland villages as well as the famous dunes and beaches.

Start at **Corralejo's** pretty harbour for a little beach time or some watersports. Continuing in seaside mode, head southeast, past the endless shifting dunes on the FV-1 road. End the day with a stroll and dinner in **Puerto del Rosario**. Day two, continue south, stopping at pint-sized **Pozo Negro**, where simple seafood restaurants overlook the surf. It's time for a break from all those blues, so wend your way inland to pretty **Pájara**. Pop into the extraordinary church here and pray for a free room at the town's lovely *casa rural*. Day three, stop at **Betancuria's** eyecatching church and quirky museums then spend the afternoon exploring the art and architecture of **La Oliva**. Spend day five in the low-key beachside town of **El Cotillo**, sampling its fine cafes, eating seafood and watching the surfers. Day six, return to Corralejo via the hip surfing village of **Lajares**, ending with an afternoon ferry to unspoilt **Isla de Lobos** for a relaxing stroll on the sand.

6 DAYS Lanzarote Hot Spots

A touch of art, a splash of wine, a dash of seafood and a whole lot of spectacularly stark scenery.

Explore **Arrecife's** art and history, take a dip at the Playa del Reducto and have dinner and drinks at the smart new marina. Next day head north for the **Cueva de los Verdes** and **Jameos del Agua** before the tour buses arrive, then backtrack and take the rest of the day off in simple seaside **Arrieta**. Day three, head for overlooked Órzola, launchpad for ferries to **Isla Graciosa**. Spend the day on deserted beaches and the night in utter tranquillity. Back on Lanzarote, stop at postcard-pretty **Haría** to visit artist César Manrique's former home. Then head south to **Teguise**, a great little town that's a joy to wander. End in **La Caleta de Famara** for a seafood dinner as the sun sets. Watch dawn surfers in action before visiting the wineries of **La Geria**. Day six, explore the lava fields of the **Parque Nacional de Timanfaya**, joining the bus tour through the dramatic Ruta de los Volcanes. Stay over in unspoilt **El Golfo** and enjoy more seafood overlooking the waves.

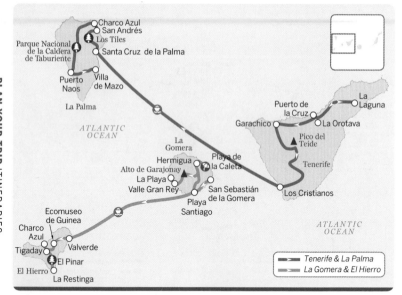

Tenerife & La Palma

La Gomera & El Hierro

10 DAYS Tenerife & La Palma

It's all perfectly preserved architecture and impressive mountain backdrops on this island-hopping adventure.

On Tenerife, stay two nights in **Puerto de la Cruz**, enjoying the shops, bars and beaches. Day three visit **La Orotava**, with its grand 17th-century mansions. Still in historical mode, continue on to **La Laguna's** traditional quarter for an overnight stay. Next day, retrace your steps to contrasting **Garachico** and its simple fishermen's cottages. Day five, head for **El Teide** for a day of walking, gawping and camera snapping. Day six, hightail it to **Los Cristianos** and catch the daily ferry to **La Palma**.

Spend a couple of nights in the capital **Santa Cruz**, exploring the old town, kicking back on the beach and taking a pilgrimage to the Santuario de la Virgen de las Nieves. Continue north to explore the hilly, cobbled streets of **San Andrés**. Day eight, visit the lush rainforest of **Los Tiles** before cooling off at the salt-water pools at **Charco Azul**. Day nine, hike through **Parque Nacional de la Caldera de Taburiente**. Continue south to lively **Puerto Naos** before visiting the handicraft museum at **Villa de Mazo**.

1 WEEK La Gomera & El Hierro

Simple pleasures reign on the smallest islands: rustic cuisine, forest hikes, ocean swims and plenty of winding roads.

Spend the first day on La Gomera exploring the backstreets, big streets and everything in between in **San Sebastián**. The next day recover from all that urban exhaustion with a dip at **Playa Santiago**. Day three, head to the verdant north, stopping at traditional **Hermigua** and postcard-pretty **Playa de la Caleta**. Next day, continue south for a trek through a fern-filled rainforest up to the lofty peaks (and views) of the **Alto de Garajonay**. Drive beside the stunning **Valle Gran Rey** gorge until it reaches the sea. Stay overnight at **La Playa** before returning to San Sebastián to catch the ferry to **El Hierro**.

Check out the low-key capital of **Valverde**, before heading south to the **Ecomuseo de Guinea**, a natural-cum-cultural treat. Dine on superb Canarian food at down-to-earth **Tigaday** and stay overnight. Next day, head for the natural pools at **Charco Azul**, before heading to the lush pines of **El Pinar**, the Centro Volcanicológico and the off-shore scuba diving at **La Restinga**.

Plan Your Trip

Outdoor Activities

Being outdoors is what the Canary Islands are all about. With year-round balmy temperatures, limited rain threatening to ruin your adventures, clear waters, wild waves and an astonishing variety of landscapes, you'd be forgiven for not wanting to spend any time inside at all.

Hiking

Hundreds of trails, many of them historic paths used before the days of cars and highways, criss-cross the islands. A good place to start is the national parks – the Parque Nacional del Teide on Tenerife, the Parque Nacional de Garajonay on La Gomera and the Parque Nacional de la Caldera de Taburiente on La Palma all have excellent hiking. Each of these parks offers a variety of walks and hikes, ranging from easy strolls ending at lookout points to multiday treks across mountains and gorges.

When to Go

You can walk in the Canary Islands any time of year, but some trails become dangerous or impossible in rainy weather, and others (like the trek up to the peak of El Teide) are harder to do in winter, when parts of the trail are covered in snow. Be aware that while along the coast and in the lowlands it's normally warm and sunny, as you head into higher altitudes, the wind, fog and air temperature can change drastically, so always carry warm and waterproof clothing. Don't forget to take water along with you, as there are few water sources or vendors out along the trails.

Best Island For...

Hiking

A question guaranteed to cause heated discussions among the walking fraternity. Tenerife, La Palma and La Gomera will have to fight it out for the hiking crown.

Kitesurfing & Windsurfing

The Canary Islands have some of the best kite- and windsurfing conditions in the world, but it's Fuerteventura that really gets the wind up people's sails.

Surfing

The Canaries aren't called the 'Hawaii of the Atlantic' for nothing. Most of the islands have great surf, but it's Lanzarote that's the centre of the scene.

Scuba Diving & Snorkelling

If you think tiny El Hierro looks good from dry land, just wait until you immerse yourself in its waters.

Cycling

Lanzarote and Fuerteventura appeal for their empty and comparatively flat roads, while hardcore cyclists flock to Gran Canaria's central mountains.

Hiking, Parque Nacional del Teide (p146), Tenerife

Hiking On...

➡ **Tenerife** The Parque Nacional del Teide is one of the finest walking areas in all of Spain. But there's more to Tenerife hiking than El Teide. The forested Anaga mountains in the northeast offer hikes through a mist-drenched forest filled with birdsong, and in the far northwest, the hamlet of Masca is the gateway to some stunning, and very challenging, hikes.

➡ **La Gomera** Thanks to a near-permanent mist (called horizontal rain), the green forest of Parque Nacional de Garajonay is dripping with life and moss. From the park's highest point, the Alto de Garajonay, you can see Tenerife and El Teide – if the clouds don't interrupt the view. There's excellent walking in and around this park for all hiking levels.

➡ **La Palma** Regarded by many as the finest island of all to walk on, La Palma's Parque Nacional de la Caldera de Taburiente offers a landscape somewhere between the verdant Garajonay and the stark Teide. You can hike along the rock walls of the park's interior or meander among the pine forests on the outer slopes of the park. Numerous other trails spin off across the island and walking these can

see you slipping in and out of rainforests or clambering up parched volcanic slopes.

➡ **El Hierro** The newbie on the walking scene, tiny El Hierro offers a real bonanza of trails, from family-friendly coastal hikes such as the easy walk between Las Puntas and La Maceta to shady ambles around the pine forests of El Pinar or the much longer Camino de Jinama.

➡ **Gran Canaria** Much less hiked than the western islands, Gran Canaria nevertheless

LOCAL MAPS

Some islands are better equipped than others when it comes to helping out hikers. La Palma and La Gomera in particular have well-signed paths and plentiful information. Elsewhere, if you're drawing a blank at the tourist information office you might have to head to the *cabildo* (island government). Hiking maps are generally available here, though having the patience and will to find the right person to help you can sometimes be as taxing as the trek itself.

HIKING BOOKS

There are loads of dedicated hiking guides to the Canary Islands (especially if you speak Spanish) that are easily available in all main bookshops across the islands. In English the best books for the general walker are those produced by Discovery Walking Guides, which publishes guidebooks and accompanying maps to Lanzarote, La Palma, La Gomera and Tenerife, and Sunflower Books, which has hiking guidebooks to all the islands.

offers superlative walking opportunities. The best trails are to be found radiating away from the Cruz de Tejeda, which sits close to the highest point of Gran Canaria, or in the verdant ravines on the east of the island.

➡ **Fuerteventura** If you want to walk but don't fancy too much of a climb, Fuerteventura has some pretty, gentle hikes. Mount Tindaya, near La Oliva, has plenty of archaeological interest and there are some scenic trails along the north coast.

➡ **Lanzarote** Walks in the national park have to be well planned, but there are other options for hiking here. You could walk between wineries in La Geria or take a gentle wander across Isla Graciosa – as long as you don't mind getting sand in your boots.

HIKING OFF THE BEATEN PATH

As well as the big-ticket walks mentioned here there are plenty of off-the-beaten-path hikes throughout the Canary Islands. Among our favourites are the walks around the Unesco-protected Los Tiles biosphere reserve on La Palma and the dunes of Maspalomas on Gran Canaria. For a truly spectacular walk, sign up for the Tremesana guided hike in the Parque Nacional de Timanfaya; you'll have to plan in advance, but the effort will be well rewarded.

Do seek local advice if you're tackling an offbeat path – some routes aren't well maintained and overgrown vegetation or absent signage can seriously hinder your progress.

Surfing, Fuerteventura (p75)

Watersports

Surfing, windsurfing and kitesurfing are popular on most of the islands, and schools offering classes and equipment rental are easy to find on the windier coasts. There are a variety of spots to choose from, ranging from the beginner-friendly sandy beaches of Fuerteventura to the heavy reef breaks of Lanzarote and Gran Canaria. You'll find diving schools in all the tourist resorts, though it is little El Hierro that's considered the top spot for underwater adventures.

Surfing

There's a wide variety of waves in the islands, from heart-in-the-mouth barrels breaking over super-shallow reef ledges to gentle sandbanks ideal for learners. The best season for surfing in the Canaries is from October through to April. At this time of year you will need a full 3mm wetsuit.

For more on surfing in the Canaries get hold of a copy of the excellent *Stormrider Guide: Atlantic Islands* published by

ATMN VICTOR / GETTY IMAGES ©

Above: Hiking near Alajeró (p177), La Gomera

Left: Playa Jardín (p138) in Puerto de la Cruz, Tenerife

BEST BEACHES

The Canary Islands have more than their fair share of beaches, and trying to pick the best is likely to lead to heated arguments, but in the cause of good arguments everywhere here's our list of the best of the best.

➡ **Playa de las Canteras** (Gran Canaria) This has to rate as one of the most enticing capital-city beaches in Europe; its 3km arc of golden sand fronted by a wide promenade is ideal for sunset strolls, while the reef ensures swimming-pool-like waters at low tide. (p69)

➡ **Parque Natural de Corralejo** (Fuerteventura) Backed by Sahara-style sand dunes with powder-soft sand, these pristine natural beaches are among the island's best. (p92)

➡ **La Caleta de Famara** (Lanzarote) A wonderful wild beach popular with kiteboarders and windsurfers, sporting a laid-back vibe and plenty of towel space on the sand. (p111)

➡ **Puerto de la Cruz** (Tenerife) The old dame of Tenerife tourism has the lot – stunning location, lots going on, safe swimming, all sorts of watersports and a wealth of places to stay and eat. (p135)

➡ **Playa Santiago** (La Gomera) OK, so it might be hard pebbles rather than soft sand, but with its shelter from the wind and cloud that can plague other beaches on the island, chilled-out hippy vibe, some good accommodation and great places to eat, we think you'll like this one. (p176)

➡ **Puerto Naos** (La Palma) It might be a purpose-built resort but it's low-key and easy on the eye. With soft black sand and generally safe bathing it's perfect for all the family. (p198)

➡ **Playa de las Arenas Blancas** (El Hierro) On the wild island of El Hierro this white-washed gem of a beach is utterly pristine but often wind and wave lashed (so swimming can be dangerous). Some great coastal walks fan out from it as well. (p214)

Low Pressure. And if going solo on a surf trip sounds a little daunting, Errant Surf Holidays (www.errantsurf.com) is a UK-based surf travel company that offers a number of surf holidays to the Canaries. Trips are suitable for learners.

Best Surf Breaks

SURF SPOT	WAVE TYPE
Los Lobos, Fuerteventura	Long, hollow right-point break
El Fronton, Gran Canaria	One of the world's heaviest waves – for bodyboarders only
Confital, Gran Canaria	Radical reef break offering huge tubes
El Quemao, Lanzarote	Very heavy and scary left barrel
San Juan, Lanzarote	Long, challenging left
Spanish Left, Tenerife	Long left with plenty of tube sections

Top Beginner Surf Spots

➡ **La Caleta de Famara** (Lanzarote) With its endless stretch of sand and plenty of surf schools, it's perfect for learners.

➡ **El Cotillo** (Fuerteventura) Offers perfect learner conditions.

➡ **Playa de las Américas** (Tenerife) Has a few mellow, learner-friendly waves and several surf schools.

Windsurfing & Kiteboarding

With constant winds, good waves and a perfect climate, the Canary Islands offer some of the best conditions in the world for windsurfing and kiteboarding.

International competitions are held here every year, and enthusiasts from all over the globe converge on the long, sandy beaches to test the waters. If you're new to the game, beginners' courses are easy to come by at all the main spots. Courses last between two

IAN AITKEN / GETTY IMAGES ©

Windsurfing in Pozo Izquierdo (p71), Gran Canaria

days and a week and prices vary widely according to how much you're aiming to learn.

The Kite & Windsurfing Guide Europe by Stoked Publications is a superb glossy guide to the continent's best kite and windsurf spots. It includes chapters on the Canary Islands.

Best Windsurfing & Kiteboarding Spots

ISLAND	BEACH
Fuerteventura	Playa de Sotavento de Jandía and Playa de Barlovento de Jandía
Gran Canaria	Pozo Izquierdo
Lanzarote	Costa Teguise
Tenerife	Las Galletas and El Médano

Swimming

Year-round sun and warm water (18°C to 26°C) makes swimming an obvious activity in the Canary Islands. From the golden beaches of the eastern islands to the volcanic pools of the western islands, there are plenty of splashing opportunities.

Beaches come in every shape and size – long and golden, intimate and calm, family friendly and action-packed, rocky and picturesque, solitary and lonely, windy and wavy.

You do need to be cautious, especially when swimming in the ocean. The first rule is never, ever swim alone. There can be very strong currents and undertows in the Atlantic, and rip currents can be so strong that they can carry you far from shore before you have time to react. If you're caught in a current, swim parallel to the shore (don't try to get to the beach) until you're released. Then make your way to shore.

The water quality around the Canary Islands is generally excellent. The only place you may find pollution is near ports (the occasional small oil spill is not unheard of) and on overcrowded tourist beaches. Smokers seem to think some beaches are a huge ashtray, so you may need to watch out for butts.

Scuba Diving & Snorkelling

The variety of marine life and the warm, relatively calm waters of the Canary Islands make them a great place for scuba diving or snorkelling. You won't experience the wild colours of Caribbean coral, but the volcanic coast is made up of beautiful rock formations and caves. As far as life underwater goes, you can spot around 350 species of fish and 600 different kinds of algae.

Scuba schools and outfitters are scattered across the islands, so you won't have trouble finding someone willing to take you out. Try El Hierro Taxi Diver (p212) in La Restinga, Atlantik Diving (p73) in Puerto de Mogán or the Los Gigantes Diving Centre (p151) in Tenerife. A standard dive, with equipment rental included, costs around €35 to €40, but a 'try dive' (a first-timer diving with an instructor) can be double that price. Certification classes start at €280 and generally last between three days and a week. Many scuba outfitters also offer snorkelling excursions for nondivers; prices tend to be about half the cost of a regular dive.

Cycling in Parque Nacional del Teide (p146), Tenerife

Best Diving Spots

➡ **La Restinga** A wealth of marine life and plenty of diving operators to show you the underwater wonders.

➡ **Puerto Calero** Visibility up to 20m and especially warm waters. You'll find marlin, barracuda and a host of other fish.

➡ **Los Gigantes & Puerto de Santiago** Wreck dives, cave dives and old-fashioned boat dives. Marine life ranges from eels to angel sharks and stingrays.

➡ **Puerto de Mogán** Dive in and around the caves and wrecks that lie not far offshore.

➡ **Playa de las Canteras** Not much of a scuba spot, but this is some of the most accessible snorkelling in the archipelago, just metres from the sand.

Whale-Watching & Boating

Around 30 species of whales and dolphins pass through Canarian seas; the most commonly seen are pilot whales and bottle-nosed dolphins.

The best area to see such creatures is in the waters between Tenerife and La Gomera, and a number of different operators run dolphin- and whale-spotting boat trips departing from the harbour at Los Cristianos.

Other whale-watching ports:

➡ **Los Gigantes & Puerto de Santiago** (Tenerife)

➡ **Valle Gran Rey** (La Gomera)

➡ **Puerto Rico** (Gran Canaria)

Whichever operator you choose it's worth taking note of their environmental credentials (we have tried to include only responsible operators) as it's not unknown for some boat operators to take their clients too close to the whales, which causes them undue distress and can eventually cause the whales and dolphins to completely change their behaviour or even leave an area altogether.

Away from whales and dolphins, virtually every tourist beach town in the archipelago offers some form of boat trip, but maybe the most impressive boat cruises on the islands are those running from Valle Gran Rey in La Gomera. The cruise boats (p178) float past kilometre after kilometre of impenetrable rock cliffs before arriving at one of the island's most unique sites, Los Órganos (the Organs), a rock formation seen only from the water that does indeed look just like an enormous pipe organ carved into the rock.

Golf

In the past decade, southern Tenerife has become the Canary Islands' golf hot spot. Golfers who love the balmy temperatures that let them play year-round have spawned the creation of a half-dozen courses in and around the Playa de las Américas alone. The courses are aimed at holiday golfers and are not known for being particularly challenging.

You'll also find several courses around Las Palmas de Gran Canaria and Maspalomas, one on La Gomera, and even a few on the arid islands of Lanzarote and Fuerteventura.

The lack of water on the islands makes golf rather environmentally unfriendly and a difficult sport to sustain. Golf-course owners say the water for those lush greens is sourced from runoff and local water-purification plants, but environmental groups say the golf courses take water from agriculture. The truth is in there

somewhere, and local politicians, golfers, environmentalists and farmers are still arguing about where the water comes from.

In winter, green fees hover around €100, but in midsummer they could be half that cost.

Cycling

If you've got strong legs, cycling may be the perfect way to see the Canary Islands. The price of renting a bike depends largely on what kind of bike you get – suspension and other extras will cost more. In general, a day's rental starts at about €15, and a guided excursion will be around €45.

Best Cycling Areas

ROUTE	LEVEL
El Teide (Tenerife)	Advanced
Alto de Garajonay (La Gomera)	Advanced
Valle Gran Rey (La Gomera)	Moderate
Los Llanos de Aridane (La Palma)	Moderate
Fataga Ravine (Gran Canaria)	Advanced
Timanfaya (Lanzarote)	Moderate
Isla Graciosa (Lanzarote)	Easy

Plan Your Trip
Travel with Children

The Canary Islands has something to satisfy even the most demanding mini traveller. Start with the natural canvas – wide beaches edged by shallow, calm water. Add to that a submarine trip or perhaps a kids' scuba diving class, throw in a museum focusing on the islands' nautical, pirate-plagued past and top it all off with a camel ride through sand dunes or a visit to one of the many theme parks.

Canary Islands for Kids

While plenty of attractions, including theme parks and zoos, have been designed specifically with children in mind, public spaces, such as town and village plazas, also morph into informal playgrounds with children kicking a ball around, riding bikes and playing, while parents enjoy a drink and tapa in one of the surrounding terrace bars. Indeed, many town squares actually have a kids' playground, something you'll stumble across with gleeful frequency. Local children tend to stay up late, and at fiestas it's common to see even tiny ones toddling the streets at midnight. Visiting children invariably warm to this idea, but can't always cope with it quite so readily.

Discounts

Discounts are available for children (usually under 12 years) on public transport and for admission to sights. Those aged under five generally go free.

Eating & Drinking

Whole families, often including several generations, sitting around a restaurant or bar table eating and chatting is a fundamental element of the lifestyle here and it

Best Regions for Kids

Tenerife
Parents may baulk, but the theme parks around Los Cristianos have undeniable appeal for children, while go-karting, whale-watching, beaches and boat rides should have the whole family smiling.

Fuerteventura
The sandy choice at Corralejo is superb. Older kids will love striding out on the dunes south of town, while tiny tots may prefer the small sheltered coves by the harbour. Splashier options include the massive Baku Water Park, plus boat rides and children's snorkelling courses.

Lanzarote
Parque Nacional de Timanfaya is something to impress the most blasé whippersnapper, with natural geysers, moonscape terrain, audiovisual presentations and camel rides. The restaurant's volcano-powered BBQ is pretty cool as well.

Gran Canaria
Las Palmas is not the most obvious region, but the city beach is magnificent, the Casa Museo de Colón's model galleon is awesome and the science museum should blow their little socks off.

is rare to find a restaurant where children are not made welcome. Even if restaurants do not advertise children's menus (and few do), they will still normally be willing to prepare a small portion for your child or suggest a suitable tapa or two. Baby-friendly extras like high chairs and changing tables are commonplace in resorts, though tend to be a little thin on the ground in more out-of-the-way spots.

Aside from the normal selection of soft drinks on offer, you might come across a *zumeria* (juice bar), where you'll find a healthy variety of fresh fruit juices. In bars, a popular choice for children is Cola Cao (chocolate drink) served hot or cold with milk.

Resources

Always make a point of asking staff at tourist offices for a list of family activities, including traditional fiestas, plus suggestions on hotels that cater for kids.

For further general information about travelling with children, see Lonely Planet's *Travel with Children* or visit the websites www.travelwithyourkids.com, www.oddizzi.com and www.familytravel-network.com.

Children's Highlights

Theme Parks

➡ **Guinate Tropical Park, Guinate, Lanzarote** Some 1300 exotic birds with aviaries, landscaped gardens and paths. (p110)

➡ **Siam Park, Costa Adeje, Tenerife** This massive water park has the works, including raft rides (on rapids), an artificial wave pool and even a white sandy stretch of beach. (p153)

➡ **Maroparque, Breña Alta, La Palma** A small zoo with spacious enclosures and pleasantly landscaped gardens. (p189)

➡ **Oasis Park, La Lajita, Fuerteventura** As well as an array of mammals, birds and sea life, there are camel rides on offer. (p92)

Watersports & Boat Rides

➡ **Dive Academy, Arguineguín, Gran Canaria** One-day bubble-maker course for children from eight to 10 years old. (p69)

➡ **Oceanarium Explorer, Calea de Fuste, Fuerteventura** Dolphin- and whale-spotting trips, kayak hire and sea lions at the harbour. (p83)

➡ **Submarine Safaris, Tenerife and Lanzarote** Underwater boat trips with diving opportunities for older, experienced children. (p117)

➡ **Canary Island Divers, Puerto Del Carmen, Lanzarote** Bubble-maker courses in the pool or ocean (over eight years) plus PADI courses for the over-10s. (p116)

➡ **Nashíra Uno, Los Gigantes, Tenerife** Daily two-hour whale- and dolphin-spotting boat trips. (p152)

➡ **Tina, Valle Gran Rey, La Gomera** Four-hour whale-watching excursions, including lunch. (p176)

Beaches

All the following beaches have shallow waters, fine sand (for sandcastles), various activities (pedalos, boat rides, volleyball or similar), plus family-friendly restaurants and ice-cream vendors within tottering distance of the sand.

➡ **Fuerteventura**: Corralejo Viejo, Muelle Chico (Corralejo), Caleta de Fuste, Costa Calma, Playa del Matorral (Morro Jable)

➡ **Lanzarote**: Playa Grande (Puerto del Carmen), Playa Blanca, Playa del Castillo (Caleta de Fuste)

➡ **Gran Canaria**: Playa de las Canteras, Playa del Inglés, Playa de Mogán

➡ **Tenerife**: Los Cristianos, Playa de las Américas, Costa Adeje, Playa de las Teresitas

La Palma, La Gomera and El Hierro have mainly black-sand beaches with, overall, fewer activities for children, aside from whale-watching cruises and the ubiquitous glass-bottom boat trips.

➡ **La Palma**: Puerto Naos, Puerto de Tazacorte, Charco Azul (natural pools cut out of the rock)

➡ **La Gomera**: Playa de las Vueltas and La Playa (Valle Gran Rey), Playa Santiago

➡ **El Hierro**: La Restinga

Museums

➡ **Museo de la Piratería, Teguise, Lanzarote** A swashbuckling museum about the history of piracy on the island. (p105)

➡ **Casa Santa María, Betancuria, Fuerteventura** Folklore and crafts, plus excellent underwater 3D film. (p80)

➡ **Ecomuseo La Alcogida, Tefía, Fuerteventura** Restored agricultural hamlet with plenty of outbuildings to explore (or play hide and seek in). (p84)

➡ **Museo Elder de la Ciencia y la Tecnología, Las Palmas de Gran Canaria** Fascinating science and technology museum with lots of hands-on exhibits for kids. (p50)

➡ **Casa-Museo de Colón, Las Palmas de Gran Canaria** Museum recounting Columbus' voyages with an impressive replica galleon. (p45)

➡ **Museo de la Naturaleza y el Hombre, Santa Cruz de Tenerife** Natural science and archaeology, including Guanche mummies. (p123)

➡ **Museo de la Ciencia y el Cosmos, La Laguna, Tenerife** Great science museum for children; includes a planetarium. (p132)

➡ **Artlandya Doll Museum, Icod de los Vinos, Tenerife** A fascinating doll museum with a vast collection of dolls from around the world. (p144)

Other Sights & Activities

➡ **Isla de Lobos, Fuerteventura** Children should enjoy the ferry ride and *Robinson Crusoe*–style novelty of landing on a tiny, uninhabited island. (p89)

➡ **Cueva de los Verdes & Jameos del Agua, Malpaís de la Corona, Lanzarote** Intriguing caves and caverns. (p107; p108)

➡ **Parque Nacional de Timanfaya, Lanzarote** Fascinating volcanic park with geyser displays and camel rides. (p114)

➡ **Lanzarote a Caballo, Puerto del Carmen, Lanzarote** Horse riding and short treks. (p116)

➡ **Pueblo Canario, Las Palmas de Gran Canaria** Mock Canarian village with nearby playground and folk-music displays. (p49)

➡ **Troglodyte caves, Artenara, Gran Canaria** Fascinating Flintstone-style prehistoric caves. (p65)

➡ **Lago Martiánez, Puerto de la Cruz, Tenerife** A fabulous watery playground. (p138)

➡ **La Caldera del Rey, Los Cristianos, Tenerife** Horse riding, plus petting farm, climbing wall and low rope course for kiddies. (☑648 65 04 41; www.tenerifehorses.com; San Eugenio Alto, Costa Adeje; 2hr trek €50)

Planning

This is an easy-going, child-friendly destination with precious little advance planning necessary. July and August can be very busy with Spanish families from the mainland, and hotels in the main tourist resorts are often block booked by tour companies. Early spring is a good time to travel with young children as the weather is still warm enough for beach days, without being too hot, and the theme parks and attractions are not too crowded – until the Easter holidays, that is.

You can buy baby formula in powder or liquid form, as well as sterilising solutions such as Milton, at *farmacias* (pharmacies). Disposable nappies (diapers) are widely available at supermarkets and *farmacias*.

Before You Go

➡ You can hire car seats for infants and children from most car-rental firms, but you should always book them in advance.

➡ Most hotels have cots for small children, but numbers may be limited so reserve one when booking your room.

➡ When selecting a hotel, check whether your hotel has a kids club, activities geared for youngsters and/or babysitting facilities.

➡ No particular health precautions are necessary, but don't forget the sun protection essentials, including sun block and sun hat, although they can also be purchased here.

➡ Avoid tears and tantrums by planning which activities, theme parks, museums and leisure pursuits you want to opt for and, more importantly, can afford early on in the holiday.

Regions at a Glance

The Canary Islands may share the same archipelago, but in every other way they are truly diverse. If you love the outdoors, there are some spectacular natural landscapes and scope for scenic strolls or more arduous hikes, particularly in Gran Canaria, La Palma, Tenerife and La Gomera. Beaches are on every island but Fuerteventura has, arguably, the best of the bunch, and is a hot and happening destination for water sports as well. Something darkly different? That has to be Lanzarote: its black volcanic lava fields form the ideal backdrop for some dramatic sculpture and architecture. History buffs have plenty to ponder here as well, particularly in Gran Canaria, which digs deep into its past with some truly extraordinary archaeological sites.

Gran Canaria

Mountains
Archaeology
Food & Drink

Dramatic Drives

The mountainous interior is ruggedly beautiful and fabulous to explore, either by car or by taking one of the hiking trails. Laurel and pine forests, volcanic craters and cool mountain reservoirs all contribute to this spectacular scenery, especially during spring.

Guanche Caves

The ancient Guanche history of the island is vividly brought to life at the excellent Cueva Pintada (Painted Cave) museum in Gáldar, the nearby Cenobio de Valerón, plus several fascinating museums and dozens of lesser-known cave sites including Cuatro Puertas in Telde.

Fine Dining

The northern coastal towns serve splendid seafood, while in the mountains you'll find hearty stews, fine local cheese and a wealth of traditional sweetmeats. But it is the Las Palmas culinary scene that really shines, with lengthy tapas lists, fusion bistros and menus that you'd otherwise only find in mainland Spain.

p42

Fuerteventura

Beaches
Surfing
Driving

Golden Sand

Fuerteventura's beaches are its major draw and justifiably so. They are magnificent and sufficiently varied to suit everyone's sandy choice, including secluded golden-sand coves, wild surf-thrashing beaches or darkly volcanic pebbles with a backdrop of cliffs.

Wind & Waves

Going hand-in-hand with the beautiful beaches are water sports. Surfing, windsurfing and kitesurfing are immensely popular throughout the island, particularly on the northwest coast. You can rent all the equipment necessary if your board doesn't fit in your baggage.

Straight & Narrow

If the neverending hairpin bends on the western islands have you reaching for the anti-nausea medicine, try the long, straight roads of Fuerteventura. Driving here is a pleasure but never boring – for something more challenging, drive from Betancuria to Pájara or, even better, along the winding dirt roads of the Jandía peninsula.

p75

Lanzarote

Volcanic Landscape
Art
Beaches

Lava Fields

Love it or not, the dark brooding volcanic landscape here has real drama, particularly at the Timanfaya core where a national park unfolds in undulating peaks, chasms and shifting colours. Driving through the interior of the island is an extraordinary experience with more than 300 volcanic cones.

Modern Sculptures

The whole island is like a giant piece of art, mainly thanks to César Manrique's influence. Open-air sculptures, art museums and some exceptional architecture and galleries contribute to the island's art lovers' appeal.

Pebble Coves

Although it is the black pebble beaches that are so emblematic of the island, there are plenty of golden sands here as well, such as the beautiful and remote beaches on Punta del Papagayo and tiny Isla Graciosa's sandy strips.

p97

Tenerife

Volcanic Landscape
Festivals
Traditional Villages

Mountain Peaks

Be impressed by the soaring volcanic peak of Mount Teide, Spain's highest mountain. The surrounding national park is fabulous for walking. Or you can stride out (or take the cable car) to the dizzy heights of the summit.

Colourful Fiestas

The *tinerfeños* love to party and scarcely a month passes without some festival here. The annual Carnaval is on the Rio-scale in terms of vivacity and fiesta spirit, while annual music festivals, food fairs and the extraordinary Corpus Christi festival in La Orotava can be equally memorable.

Rural Life

Traditional villages and towns with cobbled streets and typical architecture offer a low-key antithesis to the busy resorts. La Laguna and La Orotava provide a suitable taster, but explore further and you'll discover some real rural gems.

p120

La Gomera

Nature
Food
Walking

Dramatic Diversity

It's hard to find a road that doesn't pass through stunning scenery. From vast banana plantations to huge boulders, extraordinary rock formations, deep ravines, laurel forests and over 100,000 date palms, let's just say there are plenty of Kodak moments.

Traditional Dishes

Traditional culinary highlights include the delicious *miel de palma* honey made from the sap of palm trees, *sopa ranchero* (soup with vegetables), smoked goat's cheese and *almogrote* (pâté of goat's cheese, peppers, oil and garlic). Enjoy a fresh papaya juice on the side.

Mountain Hikes

It is only common sense that where there is wonderful natural scenery, there is going to be a real temptation to lace up those walking shoes and stride out. Fortunately, La Gomera has plenty of trails, particularly around Parque Nacional de Garajonay.

p164

La Palma

Nature
Adventure Sports
Walking

Green Scenes

Dense tropical forests, pine-clad mountains, rolling hills and rocky cliffs: La Palma has some sensationally verdant scenery, which contrasts beautifully with the starker, more arid south. There are no golden beaches, however – something has to give.

Fly, Climb, Paddle

Pump up that adrenalin and try something new. Paragliding, tandem glides, caving, sea kayaking and canoeing are all popular here, plus guided mountain biking, scuba diving and strenuous treks.

Volcanic Walks

The scenery certainly lends itself to walking and hiking and, appropriately enough, there are many kilometres of signposted trails, particularly around the pristine Parque Nacional de la Caldera de Taburiente. Walking trails criss-cross most of the island, giving you a chance to really get to know *La Isla Bonita*.

p180

El Hierro

Nature
Hiking
Diving

Pristine Scenery

The landscape here has a wonderfully remote feel with vast big-sky views, windswept groves of juniper trees, wild pine tree–clad terrain (often shrouded in mist), historic paths and, well, very few people: only around 11,000 folk live here year-round.

Demanding Hikes

Signposted, well-maintained trails criss-cross the island, including the famous Camino de la Virgen (26km), a historic trail stretching from Nuestra Señora de los Reyes to Valverde, and paths that pass through the cool pine forests of the south.

Marine Riches

There are some thrilling dive sites around the island. Head for La Restinga, where several outfits offer equipment hire and courses, and the surrounding waters have been officially designated a marine reserve. Water temperatures are a tad higher than other islands, which means some different fish species as well.

p202

On the Road

Lanzarote
p97

La Palma
p180

La Gomera
p164

Tenerife
p120

El Hierro
p202

Gran Canaria
p42

Fuerteventura
p75

Gran Canaria

📞 928 / POP 852,000

Best Places to Eat

➡ Deliciosa Marta (p51)

➡ Samsara (p70)

➡ Kitchen Lovers (p52)

Best Places to Stay

➡ Villa del Conde (p220)

➡ Fonda de la Tea (p219)

➡ Downtown House (p218)

Why Go?

Gran Canaria is the third-largest island in the Canaries' archipelago, but accounts for almost half the population. It lives up to its cliché as a continent in miniature, with a dramatic variation of terrain, ranging from the green and leafy north to the mountainous interior and desert south. To glean a sense of this impenetrable quality, head to the centre, where the sheer drama of the mountains more resembles the Tibetan highlands than a relatively small island.

Contrasting with these unspoilt peaks and valleys is a rugged coastline interspersed with white sandy beaches and, more famously (and depressingly), a garish tiara of purpose-built holiday resorts.

Beyond the sands, though, Gran Canaria can keep the adrenalin pumping, with scope for hiking, cycling and watersports, while culture-vultures can be similarly satiated, particularly in the historic cosmopolitan capital of Las Palmas.

When to Go

➡ Peak season here is spring (February to Easter): the weather is warm, rain is sporadic and the island's stunning interior is green, with the occasional visual blast of almond trees in blossom.

➡ Spring is also festival season, with the vivacious February Carnaval celebrations followed by the sombre ceremonies of Semana Santa (Easter).

➡ June sees one of the island's largest fiestas, San Juan, and temperatures are perfect, with an average of 24°C.

➡ July and August is a busy time, with Spaniards from the mainland and families from northern Europe on holiday.

➡ September and October are perfect: the weather is ideal and the crowds have headed home.

Santa Cruz de Tenerife;
Santa Cruz de la Palma

Cádiz (Spain)

Punta
Sardina

Punta de
la Vieja

Faro de
Sardina
Sardina

Gáldar 6 Santa María
de Guía

Playa de las
Canteras
Bahía del
Confital

La Isleta
Roque Negro
Isleta
(239m)

GC-2
GC-330

Pico del
Viento
(837m)

Moya Arucas

2 **Las Palmas de
Gran Canaria**

La Montaña
de Arucas

Agaete
**Puerto de
las Nieves** 4

San
Fernando

Firgas

GC-23

Jardín Botánico
Canario Viera
y Clavijo

Playa de
la Laja

GC-309
GC-21

Los
Berrazales

GC-75

Teror

Tafira

GC-110

Bandama

Vallesecco

**Santa
Brígida**

Tamadaba
(1444m)

Cruz de
Tejeda

GC-42

La Atalaya
**Vega de
San Mateo**

Caldera de
Bandama

Puerto del Rosario
(Fuerteventura);
Arrecife
(Lanzarote);
Morro Jable
(Fuereventura)

Artenara 7

GC-200

Puerto de
la Aldea

Todocomán

**Aldea de
San Nicolás**

Roque
Bentayga
(1404m)

GC-15

1 **Tejeda**

GC-100

Telde

GC-210

Roque Nublo
(1803m)

GC-41

Pozo de las
Nieves
(1949m)

Cuatro
Puertas

GC-130

Ayacata

**Barranco de
Guayadeque**

GC-1
GC-140

Montaña de las
Monjas (1468m)

GC-605

**San Bartolomé
de Tirajana**

3

GC-100

Airport

Los Azulejos

Presa de las
Cuevas de
las Niñas

Temisas

Ingenio

Mogarenes
(892m)

**Santa Lucía
de Tirajana**

5 **Agüimes**

Las Rosas

Mogán

Fataga

GC-551

GC-1

Guirre
(932m)

Palmitos
Park

Amurga
(1131m)

GC-65

GC-500

Arinaga

GC-200

GC-60

Vecindario

Puerto
de Mogán
Taurito

Mundo
Aborigen

El Doctoral

Playa del Cura

Juan Grande

Playa del Tauro

Puerto Rico

GC-500

**San
Agustín**

Playa de Tarajalillo
(Bahía Feliz)

Playa Aguila

ATLANTIC

GC-1

Maspalomas

Playa de las Burras

Arguineguín

Playa del Inglés

Playa de Triana

Costa Meloneras

Pasito
Bea

Dunas de Maspalomas

OCEAN

Playa de Carpinteras

Playa de
Maspalomas

0   10 km
0   5 miles

N

Gran Canaria Highlights

1 Drink in the incredible views from a restaurant terrace in mountaintop **Tejeda** (p66)

2 Stroll the sands of Playa de las Canteras then explore the historic Vegueta *barrio* in **Las Palmas** (p45)

3 Dig into lunch at a cave restaurant in the dramatic

Barranco de Guayadeque (p57)

4 Drive the spectacular west coast road to **Puerto de las Nieves** (p63) for a seafood lunch overlooking the harbour

5 Ponder the pastel-painted buildings in lovely **Agüimes** (p56), an aesthetically restored 15th-century village

6 Wonder at the ancient cave paintings at Gáldar's fascinating **Cueva Pintada Museum & Archaeological Park** (p62)

7 Explore cave culture in stuck-in-a-time-warp **Artenara** (p65)

History

Gran Canaria has an intriguing mix of nationalities and ethnic cultures, particularly in the capital, Las Palmas. This is nothing new. The island has historically been home to waves of settlers who have all had a lingering impact.

First on the scene, possibly as far back as 1000 BC, were the Guanches, who were most likely migrants from north Africa. They named the island Tamarán after the date palms *(tamar)* found here. In 1478, despite their plucky resistance, the Guanches' culture was largely obliterated by the Spanish. Gran Canaria was soon colonised by a ragtag assortment of adventurers and landless hopefuls from as far away as Galicia, Andalucía, Portugal, Italy, France, the Low Countries and even Britain and Ireland.

Las Palmas subsequently became the seat of the Canary Islands' bishopric and royal court, as well as a way station en route to the Americas. The economy was further boosted by sugar exports and transatlantic trade. But, as the demand for the Canary Islands' sugar fell and the fortunes of wine grew, the island declined before its main rival and superior vine-grower, Tenerife.

Many Canarians subsequently emigrated to South America, initiating a strong affinity between the two cultures that is still in evidence today. It was not until the late 19th century, however, that Gran Canaria recovered its position; the importance of the island as a refuelling port for steamships resulted in investment from foreign merchants, including the British.

It's an investment that continues to this day, only now in the form of tourism. The package-holiday boom of the mid-20th century has brought lasting prosperity to the island. However, there has been an environmental price to pay.

ROAD DISTANCES (KM)

	Maspalomas	Puerto de Mogán	Las Palmas de Gran Canaria	Teror
Maspalomas	68			
Puerto de Mogán	95	29		
Las Palmas de Gran Canaria	14	56	104	
Teror	13	66	35	21
	Arucas	Maspalomas	Puerto de Mogán	Las Palmas de Gran Canaria

Approximate distances only

Getting There & Away

AIR

Las Palmas airport is 25km south of the capital. **Binter Canarias** (✆ 902 391392; www.binter canarias.com) has direct flights to all six of the islands. **Canary Fly** (✆ 902 808065; www. canaryfly.es) offers direct flights to Lanzarote, Tenerife and La Palma.

BOAT

There are two passenger harbours on Gran Canaria that offer inter-island ferries. Boats from Las Palmas head to Tenerife, Fuerteventura, Lanzarote and, less frequently, to La Palma. There are also regular ferries from Puerto de las Nieves to Tenerife. Three companies operate on the island.

Fred Olsen (✆ 902 100107; www.fredolsen.es) Operates a fast ferry service from Las Palmas to Morro Jable (Fuerteventura; €45, two hours, twice daily) and from Puerto de las Nieves (Agaete) to Santa Cruz de Tenerife (€45, 1½ hours, six daily) from where there are onward connections to La Gomera and La Palma.

Naviera Armas (✆ 902 456500; www.navier aarmas.com) Runs direct ferry services from Las Palmas to Santa Cruz de Tenerife (€32, 2½ hours, four daily), Morro Jable (Fuerteventura; €43, three hours, daily), Puerto del Rosario (Fuerteventura; €35, 6½ hours, daily) and Arrecife (Lanzarote; €49, seven hours, Monday to Friday).

There are also regular services to Santa Cruz de la Palma and San Sebastián (La Gomera) via Santa Cruz de Tenerife, plus a daily service to Isla Graciosa via Arrecife (Lanzarote).

Trasmediterránea (✆ 902 454645; www. trasmediterranea.com) A weekly ferry leaves Las Palmas on Thursday stopping at Puerto del Rosario (Fuerteventura; €27, six hours) and Arrecife (Lanzarote; €27, 9½ hours). There is also a weekly service on Saturdays to Santa Cruz de Tenerife (€22, four hours) and Santa Cruz de la Palma (€28, 19 hours).

Getting Around

BUS

There is a comprehensive network of buses around the island, with Las Palmas and to a lesser extent, Maspalomas, serving as hubs. All corners of the island are covered by Global (p54). Smaller, more remote towns are often served by just one or two buses a day.

CAR

There are car-rental firms at the Las Palmas airport, ferry terminal and throughout the city's Santa Catalina district.

LAS PALMAS DE GRAN CANARIA

POP 382,200

Las Palmas has a mainland-Spain feel, spiced up with an eclectic mix of other cultures, including African, Chinese and Indian, plus the presence of container-ship crews, and the flotsam and jetsam that tend to drift around port cities. It's an intriguing place, with the sunny languor and energy you would normally associate with the Mediterranean or north Africa. The hooting taxis, bustling shopping districts, chatty bars and thriving port all give off the energy of this city, which is Spain's ninth-largest.

Vegueta, the oldest quarter, is both atmospheric and fashionable, with a fine selection of boutiques and cool bars. At the other end of town, the sweeping arc of Playa de las Canteras provides you with the tantalising possibility of taking a plunge in between sightseeing and shopping. Venture into the confusing maze of streets behind the beach and you'll find excellent restaurants serving more than the usual array of Canarian dishes. Las Palmas is an authentic Spanish working city and while there are areas you wouldn't walk at night with a camera slung round your neck, overall, you should feel perfectly safe here.

History

By the time Christopher Columbus passed by on his way to the Americas in 1492, the busy little historic centre had already been traced out by the Spanish. The city benefited greatly from the Spanish conquest of Latin America and subsequent transatlantic trade but, inevitably, became a favourite target for pirates and buccaneers. In 1595 Sir Francis Drake raided Las Palmas with particular gusto.

In 1822 Santa Cruz de Tenerife was declared capital of the single new Spanish province of Las Islas Canarias, which left the great and good of Las Palmas seriously disgruntled. Redress didn't arrive until 1927, when Las Palmas became capital of Gran Canaria, Fuerteventura and Lanzarote.

The fortunes of the port city continued to fluctuate until the end of the 19th century, when prosperity arrived thanks to the growing British presence in the city. In early 1936 General Franco was appointed General Commander of the Canaries – a significant demotion and a posting he considered to be a form of banishment. While staying in the

city – reportedly at the Hotel Madrid in Triana – Franco planned and launched the coup that sparked the Spanish Civil War.

Since the 1960s tourism boom, Las Palmas has grown from a middling port city of 70,000 to a bustling metropolis of close to 400,000 people. And, while it shares the status of regional capital evenly with Santa Cruz de Tenerife, there is no doubt that Las Palmas packs the bigger punch in terms of influence and size.

◎ Sights

The most interesting sights are concentrated in the narrow, cobbled lanes of Vegueta, while the heavier, more international action is around Santa Catalina. The 3km-long Playa de las Canteras is one of the loveliest city beaches in Europe. Ensure you make time for a leisurely stroll along the promenade or a dip in the calm waters of the Atlantic during your visit.

◉ Vegueta & Triana

This is the most historic and architecturally rich city district with traditional colonial buildings and enticing hidden courtyards. Take the time to stroll the streets, ducking into the atmospheric bars and restaurants along the way.

★**Casa-Museo de Colón** MUSEUM
(Map p46; ☎928 31 23 73; www.casadecolon.com; Calle Colón 1; adult/child €4/free; ◎10am-6pm Mon-Sat, to 3pm Sun; ◉) **FREE** This fascinating museum documents Columbus' voyages and features exhibits on the Canary Islands' historical role as a staging post for transatlantic shipping. Don't miss the model galleon on the ground floor, which particularly impresses children. The crucifix is said to have come from Columbus' ship. Upstairs there is an art gallery and some models of Las Palmas past and present. Travel geeks will love rooms five and six, which contain historical maps largely from the early 16th century.

Las Palmas (South)

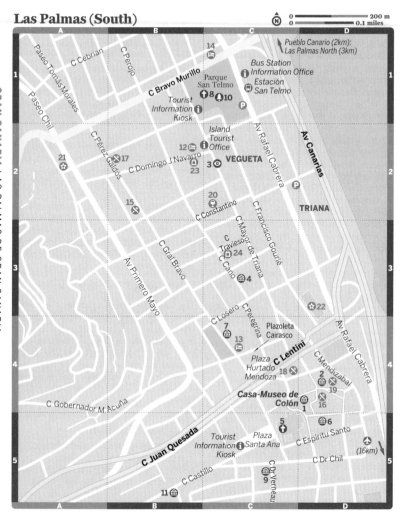

The building is a superb example of Canarian architecture, built around two balconied patios, complete with fountains, palm trees and parrots. The exterior is a work of art itself, with some showy *plateresque* (silversmith-like) elements, combined with traditional heavy wooden balconies.

Although called Columbus' House (it's possible he stopped here in 1492), most of what you see dates from the time this building was the opulent residence of Las Palmas' early governors.

Catedral de Santa Ana & Museo Diocesano de Arte Sacro

CATHEDRAL

(Map p46; ☎928 33 14 30; Calle Obispo Codina 13; adult/child €3/free; ⊙10am-5pm Mon-Fri, to 2pm Sun) The spiritual heart of the city, this brooding, grey cathedral was begun in the early 15th century, soon after the Spanish conquest, but took 350 years to complete. The neoclassical facade contrasts with the interior, which is a fine example of what some art historians have named Atlantic Gothic, with lofty columns that seem to mimic the palm trees outside. There are also

Las Palmas (South)

⊙ Top Sights
1 Casa-Museo de Colón D4

◎ Sights
2 CAAM San Antonio Abad D4
3 Calle Mayor de Triana C2
4 Casa-Museo de Pérez Galdós C3
5 Catedral de Santa Ana & Museo
   Diocesano de Arte Sacro C5
6 Centro Atlántico de Arte Moderno D5
7 Gabinete Literario C4
8 Iglesia de San Telmo C1
9 Museo Canario C5
10 Parque San Telmo C1
11 San Martín Centro de Cultura
    Contemporánea B5

⊟ Sleeping
12 Downtown House B2
13 Hotel Madrid C4

14 Hotel Parque C1

✪ Eating
15 Deliciosa Marta B2
16 La Dolce Vita D4
17 La Olivia B2
18 Latienza Gastro Bar C4
19 Restaurante Casa Montesdeoca D4

⊙ Drinking & Nightlife
20 Bodegón Lagunetas C2

⊙ Entertainment
21 El Escenario A2
22 Teatro Pérez Galdós D3

⊟ Shopping
23 Fedac B2
24 Librería del Cabildo Insular de
    Gran Canaria C3

several paintings by Juan de Miranda, the islands' most-respected 18th-century artist.

The ticket also includes entrance to the sacred art museum, set on two levels around the Patio de los Naranjos. It contains a fairly standard collection of religious art and memorabilia, including centuries-old manuscripts, wooden sculptures and other ornaments, but the setting is lovely – and fragrant, with the scent of orange blossom in springtime.

Once you've explored within, take the lift (admission €1.50) to the top of the bell tower for a stunning wide-angle view of the surrounding city and its coast.

Museo Canario   MUSEUM
(Map p46; ☑928 33 68 00; www.elmuseocanario. com; Calle Dr Verneau 2; adult/child €4/free; ⊙10am-8pm Mon-Fri, to 2pm Sat & Sun; ⏍) This slightly old fashioned yet still fascinating museum chronicles Gran Canaria's preconquest history. It claims the heady boast of having the largest collection of Cro-Magnon skulls in the world. There are also several mummies, plus a collection of pottery and other Guanche implements from across the island. The gift shop stocks some excellent children's educational material.

PLAIN SAILING

In the 1880s, when Puerto de la Luz (Las Palmas) was developing as a port, merchant and passenger ships had to moor some way from the docks. A quasi-rowing boat–cum-yacht was developed to ferry people and goods from ship to shore.

Like any business, these little *botes* (boats) suffered both busy and slack times. During the latter, their captains and crews organised regattas in the port area. This idea, born to ease the boredom of the long days before Facebook, eventually developed into a regular competition, and the tradition continues in a sport known as Vela Latina Canaria.

You can catch these curious craft in action on Saturday (usually from 5pm) and Sunday (around noon) from April to October. Crewed by eight to 12 people, each boat represents a district of Las Palmas.

Apart from the odd appearance of the participating vessels, the race itself is delightfully eccentric in that competitors race only *en bolina* (against the wind), but in such a way as to get maximum power from it. The fact that the prevailing wind remains pretty much the same off the east coast of Gran Canaria makes it the ideal spot for such races. The *botes* start at Playa de la Laja, a few kilometres south of the southern suburbs of Las Palmas, and finish at Playa de Alcaravaneras. Check out www.federacionvelalatinadebotes.org for more.

Las Palmas (North)

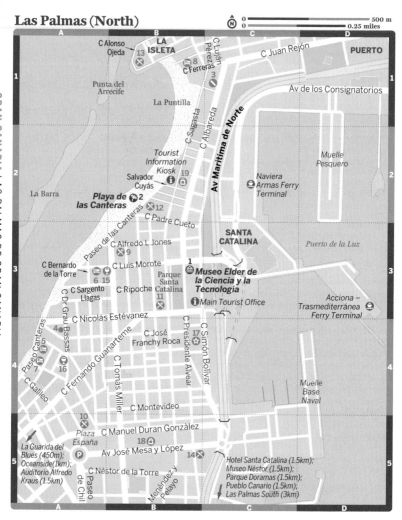

0 ——————— 500 m
0 ——————— 0.25 miles

C Alonso Ojeda
LA ISLETA
13
8
C Ferreras
C Luján Pérez
C Juan Rejón
PUERTO
3
Av de los Consignatorios
Punta del Arrecife
La Puntilla
C Sagasta
C Albareda
Av Marítima de Norte
Muelle Pesquero
Tourist Information Kiosk
19
Salvador Cuyás
Naviera Armas Ferry Terminal
La Barra
Playa de las Canteras
2
12
Paseo de las Canteras
C Padre Cueto
SANTA CATALINA
Puerto de la Luz
C Alfredo L Jones
9
C Bernardo de la Torre
6 15
C Luis Morote
Parque Santa Catalina
1
Museo Elder de la Ciencia y la Tecnología
C Sargento Llagas
C Ripoche
11
Main Tourist Office
Acciona – Trasmediterránea Ferry Terminal
C Nicolás Estévanez
C Dr Grau Bassas
4
Paseo Canteras
5
C José Franchy Roca
17
C Presidente Alvear
C Simón Bolívar
7
16
C Fernando Guanarteme
C Tomás Miller
Muelle Base Naval
C Galileo
C Montevideo
10
Plaza España
C Manuel Duran Gonzàlez
18
14
La Guarida del Blues (450m); Oceanside(1km); Auditorio Alfredo Kraus (1.5km);
Av José Mesa y López
C Néstor de la Torre
Paseo de Chil
Menéndez y Pelayo
Hotel Santa Catalina (1.5km); Museo Néstor (1.5km); Parque Doramas (1.5km); Pueblo Canario (1.5km); Las Palmas South (3km);

Centro Atlántico de Arte Moderno GALLERY
(CAAM, Atlantic Centre of Modern Art; Map p46; 928 31 18 00; www.caam.net; Calle Balcones 11; adult/child €5/free; 10am-9pm Tue-Sat, to 2pm Sun) The city's main modern art museum is housed in a tastefully rejuvenated 18th-century building. There are no permanent collections but the galleries, flooded with natural light, host some superb temporary exhibitions. There are two satellite galleries also featuring rotating exhibitions: **CAAM San Antonio Abad** (Map p46; Plaza San Antonio Abad; adult/child €2/free), near Casa de Colon, and the **San Martín Centro de Cultura**

Contemporánea (Map p46; www.sanmartincontemporaneo.com; Calle Ramon y Cajal 1; adult/child €5/free), based in a former hospital. A combined ticket to enter all three is €8 per adult.

Gabinete Literario HISTORIC BUILDING
(Library; Map p46; www.gabineteliterario.com; Plazoleta Cairasco) Dating from 1844, this ornate historical building is a national monument. It was the island's first theatre and retains an old-world display of faded elegance, with a gracious internal patio and rooms lined with bookcases. The place now functions as a private club, although the fancy terrace restaurant (O'Clock) is open to all.

Las Palmas (North)

Calle Mayor de Triana HISTORIC STREET
(Map p46) This pedestrianised street has long been the main shopping artery in Las Palmas. In between purchases, look skyward to enjoy some real architectural gems, including several striking examples from the modernism school of architecture.

Casa-Museo de Pérez Galdós MUSEUM
(Map p46; www.casamuseoperezgaldos.com; Calle Cano 6; adult/child €3/free; ⊙10am-6pm Tue-Fri, to 2pm Sat & Sun) In 1843 the Canary Islands' most famous writer, Benito Pérez Galdós, was born in this house in the heart of old Las Palmas. He spent the first 19 years of his life here before moving on to Madrid and literary greatness. Guided tours (in English and Spanish) explore the upstairs rooms, with a reconstruction of the author's study and various personal effects transported from his mainland Spain home following his death.

Parque San Telmo PARK
(Map p46) The Iglesia de San Telmo, on the southwestern side of this paved park, was one of the first religious buildings in town. Beside it is a tourist information kiosk and, in the northwestern corner, a beautiful modernist kiosk, which these days functions as a classy cafe for breakfast, sandwiches or a good cup of coffee served at the outdoor tables.

⊚ Ciudad Jardín

This leafy, upper-class suburb is an eclectic mix of architectural styles, ranging from British colonial to whitewashed Andalucian.

Also here is lovely Parque Doramas, with its fine *dragos* (dragon trees) and superlative children's play areas. The park was designed by the British towards the end of the 19th century, when the UK dominated the economic life of Las Palmas.

Pueblo Canario TOURIST VILLAGE
(⊙10am-8pm Tue-Sat, to 2.30pm Sun; ⊛) FREE
Designed by artist Néstor Martín Fernández de la Torre and built by his brother Miguel, this mock Canarian village borders the gardens of the Parque Doramas. It's a little unloved and the restaurant keeps sporadic hours, but it's worth a visit on Sunday mornings, when traditional folk music is played here at 11.30am. The *pueblo* is located on the south side of the Parque Doramas, accessed from Calle León y Castillo.

Museo Néstor MUSEUM
(☑928 24 51 35; Pueblo Canario; adult/child €0.50/free; ⊙10am-7pm Tue-Sat, 10.30am-2.30pm Sun) This art gallery is dedicated to the works of symbolist painter Néstor, who died in 1938, and also includes a modest collection of works by fellow Canarian artists. It's located within the Pueblo Canario.

⊚ Santa Catalina & Playa de las Canteras

The area between Las Canteras and Parque de Santa Catalina is an intriguing mix of city beach, multicultural melting pot, edgy port and business hub. At times you'll feel like you're in the developing world; at other times you're firmly in mainland Spain.

ℹ️ WALKING TOURS OF VEGUETA

Although most visitors to Las Palmas spend time in Vegueta, most stick to the main sights and fail to truly explore the pretty, narrow alleys of the old town. Get better acquainted on a **walking tour** (📞 674 128849; www.tripgrancanaria.com; adult/child €6/free; ⏰ noon Mon-Sat) of the historic quarter. Hour-long guided walks leave from Plaza Hurtado de Mendoza (known locally as Plaza de las Ranas), at the southern end of the Triana district. Advance bookings are essential.

Parque Santa Catalina is safe enough in daylight, though you can expect a fair number of down-and-outs, which increase after dark. On Saturdays at 11am, performances of traditional Canarian music and dancing take place in the park.

★ Museo Elder de la Ciencia y la Tecnología   MUSEUM

(Museum of Science & Technology; Map p48; www. museoelder.org; Parque Santa Catalina; adult/child €5/3.50, incl 3D film €8.50/€7; ⏰ 10am-8pm Tue-Sun; 👶) This 21st-century museum is full of things that whirr, clank and hum. In a revamped dockside warehouse in Parque Santa Catalina, it's a great space to spend a few hours. You can pilot a supersonic fighter plane, see how rockets send satellites into orbit or ride the Robocoaster where a robotic arm whizzes you through a series of programmable manoeuvres. Children will be rapt – the space pod and Van de Graaff generator are particularly popular.

There is also a small theatre showing a regularly changing programme of 3D films.

🏖️ Beaches

★ Playa de las Canteras   BEACH

(Map p48) The fine 3km stretch of yellow sand is magnificent, and considered by many to be one of the world's best city beaches. There's an attractive seaside promenade – the Paseo de las Canteras – which allows walkers, cyclists and joggers to cover the entire length of the beach, free from traffic. Perhaps the most marvellous part, though, is the reef, known as La Barra, which in low tide turns the waters of Las Canteras into a giant salty swimming pool that's perfect for snorkelling.

Further south, the restaurants and hotels peter out and the waves become a little bigger. It is here, near the auditorium in an area known as La Cicer, that surfers congregate in the water and footballers take to the sand.

🏃 Activities

There are 12 surf spots around Las Palmas, with the most popular being La Cicer at the southern end of Playa de las Canteras. It's a great place for beginners and there are a few surf schools to be found at this end of the beach.

7 Mares Las Canteras   DIVING

(Map p48; www.7mares.es; Calle Tenerife 12; dive with equipment rental €25, 2hr initiation dive €60) Has English-speaking diving instructors and offers courses at all levels, plus wreck dives and equipment rental.

Oceanside   SURFING

(www.grancanariasurf.es; Calle Numancia 47; 2hr course €25) A well-respected surf school offering a range of classes as well as board and wetsuit hire (€25 per day). Stand-up paddleboarding courses are also available for the same price. There are a dozen surf spots around the city, with La Cicer on Playa de las Canteras being the most popular.

📖 Courses

There are several language schools in Las Palmas where you can study Spanish.

Gran Canaria School of Languages   LANGUAGE COURSE

(Map p48; 📞 928 26 79 71; www.grancanariaschool. com; Calle Dr Grau Bassas 27; 1-week intensive course €170) Has been in business for more than 40 years and has an excellent reputation. Lodging can also be arranged.

🎉 Festivals & Events

Carnaval   CARNIVAL

(www.laspalmascarnaval.com; ⏰ 2-3 weeks before Lent) Two to three weeks of madness and fancy dress mark the first rupture with winter in February. The bulk of the action takes place around Parque de Santa Catalina, where there is a giant outdoor stage and a host of temporary bars.

Annual events include the crowning of both the Carnival and Drag Queens, and the Burial of the Sardine, when a huge effigy of a sardine is paraded through the streets to the beach at Las Canteras, where it is ceremoniously buried. An extravagant fireworks display is a fitting end to the celebrations. Celebrated throughout the island, but particularly in Las Palmas.

Corpus Christi RELIGIOUS
(⊙ Jun) This feast with movable dates is marked by the laying out of extraordinary floral 'carpets' in some of Las Palmas' historic streets.

Fiesta de San Juan RELIGIOUS
(⊙ 23 Jun) This Las Palmas festival honours the city's patron saint. Cultural events are staged across the city, while fireworks and concerts take place on Playa de las Canteras, along with the tradition of jumping over bonfires on the beach then plunging into the ocean at midnight. The following day is usually a public holiday.

🍴 Eating

The choice of restaurants in Las Palmas reflects its stylish big-city feel. For the most atmosphere, head to the Vegueta and Triana *barrios*. Over at the other end of the city, with a couple of exceptions, the restaurants on the beachfront tend to be multifarious places with multilingual menus and below-par food, but venture a street or two back and you'll find old-school Spanish restaurants and characterful tapas bars.

Vegueta & Triana

La Olivia CANARIAN €
(Map p46; Calle Pérez Galdós 32; menú del día €10; ⊙ 7am-5pm Mon-Sat) There is no fixed menu here. With everything homemade and freshly prepared, dishes depend on what is available at the market each morning. Expect traditional favourites like *ropa vieja* (chickpea stew) and plenty of fresh fish.

Latienza Gastro Bar TAPAS €
(Map p46; Calle Pelota 20; tapas €2.50-5; ⊙ 11am-late) By day this friendly place serves decent, well-priced tapas in its stone-walled dining room or outside on the cobbled street. By night it's a chilled-out spot for a beer or a glass of wine and a selection of light bites.

★ **Deliciosa Marta** SPANISH €€
(Map p46; ☑ 928 37 08 82; Calle Pérez Galdós 23; mains €15-20; ⊙ closed Tue evening & Sun) This chic place with its exposed stone wall and moody lighting has become one of the prime dining spots in town since it opened in 2007. The chef-cum-owner Pol trained in Barcelona at the famous El Bulli – and it shows,

with the ever-changing menu featuring ingredients like scallops, pork belly and truffles. Reservations recommended.

La Dolce Vita ITALIAN €€
(Map p46; Calle Agustín Millares 5; mains €11-15; ⊙ closed Wed evening & Sun; 🖉) Tucked down a narrow pedestrian street, the homemade pasta here is the real thing, with decadent sauces featuring caviar and black truffles. Gluten-free options are available. The decor is fun, with Italian film posters papering the walls, and there's a small shop selling Italian goodies out back.

Restaurante Casa Montesdeoca CANARIAN €€
(Map p46; ☑ 928 33 34 66; Calle Montesdeoca 16; mains €15-20; ⊙ 1-4pm & 7pm-late Mon-Sat) A romantic restaurant set in an exquisite 16th-century house. Dine in the gorgeous, leafy patio with its traditional wooden balconies and sunny yellow walls. The steaks are recommended.

Santa Catalina & Playa de las Canteras

De Cuchara CANARIAN €
(Map p48; Calle Alfredo L Jones 37; menú del día €12, tapas €4-9; ⊙ 1-4.30pm & 8pm-midnight Tue-Sun) As well as the usual three-course *menú del día*, there's a five-course tasting menu here, featuring all the favourite Canarian dishes. There's an interesting range of tapas too, served from 8pm. Try the *arroz negro de chipirones* (squid in ink with rice).

De Tapa en Tapa TAPAS €
(Map p48; Calle Diderot 23; tapas €3-8; ⊙ 1-4pm & 7pm-late Mon-Sat) The three-course *menú del día* (€9.50) at this long-standing tapas joint attracts lunching workers, while at night a youngish crowd descends to enjoy tapas and *cañas* (draught beer). The dates wrapped in bacon are a winner.

LOCAL KNOWLEDGE

RUTA DE LAS TAPAS

On Thursday evenings, Calle Mendizabal in Vegueta is a top spot for meeting locals (and other travellers) and partaking in a bit of a tapas crawl. You can enjoy a small beer and a tapa for €2 in a number of bars along this strip. You will need follow-on food plans as portions are tiny; it's more about socialising than eating, but it's a great way to get a feel for the Canarian al fresco lifestyle. The fun starts at 8pm.

Natural Burguer BURGERS €
(Map p48; Avenida José Mesa y López 3; mains €2.50-3.50; ☺1-4pm & 7pm-late; ☑) South of Santa Catalina, this eco-burger joint is justifiably popular with budget-seekers and students. Veggie burgers with a choice of toppings are on the menu, as well as regular beef burgers. Extras include watercress salad, corn on the cob and *papas del abuelo* (thick-cut potato chips).

★ **Kitchen Lovers** MEDITERRANEAN €€
(Map p48; ☑928 98 76 10; Paseo de las Canteras 16; mains €10-18; ☺1-4pm & 7pm-late Tue-Sun) Wade through the myriad tourist menus along the promenade to this airy, stylish restaurant – a real treat. Spanish and Italian cuisines come together to produce delicious, beautifully presented yet unfussy dishes served with a phenomenal view. Try to get a window table. Reservations essential.

El Cid Casa Pablo SPANISH €€
(Map p48; ☑928 22 46 31; Calle Nicolás Estévenez 10; mains €12-20; ☺1-4pm & 7pm-late) A grand old restaurant with a knight in armour lording it over the front door. Plenty of Spanish celebrity pics adorn the walls to leave you in no doubt that this is *the* place to come in Las Palmas for solid traditional cuisine – particularly seafood. The lunchtime *menú del día* is a very reasonable €10. Dinner reservations recommended.

La Marinera SEAFOOD €€
(Map p48; ☑928 46 88 02; Paseo de las Canteras; mains €12-18; ☺1-4pm & 7pm-late) Dine within earshot of thundering surf at this long-standing seafront favourite. The menu is predominantly fishy, with fresh fish sold by the kilo (keep an eye on the price to avoid nasty shocks). Solid choices include paella, *pescado al la sal* (fish coated in salt) and *sopa de mariscos* (seafood soup).

Drinking

There is no shortage of watering holes in Las Palmas. The Vegueta area, with its low-key ambience, is perfect for chilled drinks and a handy pub crawl – Calle La Pelota and Calle Mendizabal have the highest concentrations of bars. If you're looking for live music, head to the southern end of the Paseo de Las Canteras, near the auditorium. The north end of the city is where you'll find most of the banging clubs, though there are also plenty of more relaxed drinking options, particularly the *terrazas* (terraces) on Plaza España and lining Parque Santa Catalina.

Bodegón Lagunetas BAR
(Map p46; Calle Constantino 16; ☺7pm-midnight Mon-Sat) One of several tapas bars on this street, this one also has a restaurant. Hang out in the bar with a *caña* and enjoy the fascinating sepia photo exhibition of late-19th-century Las Palmas.

Pachichi BAR
(Map p48; Calle Los Martínez de Escobar 51; ☺7pm-midnight) It's a poky little place and not much effort has gone into the decor, but Bodega Don Juan Pachichi – generally shortened to just Pachichi – is a local institution serving cheap rum and cokes to start the evening. It's two blocks back from the beach.

Disco 3x1 CLUB
(Map p48; Calle Luis Morote 51; ☺midnight-5am Wed-Sat) A late, late disco playing mainstream music. A cover charge usually applies, but you get a drink voucher on entry so it evens out.

Entertainment

El Escenario LIVE MUSIC
(Map p46; Avenida Primero Mayo 57; ☺8pm-2am Wed-Sat) There's a small cover fee here, but it's well worth it for the chilled-out performances of live jazz and flamenco.

La Guarida del Blues LIVE MUSIC
(Calle Portugal 68; ☺6pm-midnight Thu-Sat, 5pm-10pm Sun) Live jazz, rock and, above all, blues concerts happen at 8pm on Thursday and Friday, 6.30pm on Saturday and 5.30pm on Sunday.

Auditorio Alfredo Kraus LIVE MUSIC
(☑928 49 17 70; www.auditorioteatrolaspalmasgc.es; Avenida Principe de Asturias) Designed by Catalan architect Óscar Tusquets, this spectacular auditorium is striking in its geometric modernity. Constructed partly of volcanic

rock, with a huge window and panoramic ocean views, it is the dominant feature of the southern end of Playa de las Canteras. This is one of the venues for the annual summer Jazz Festival (www.canariasjazz.com).

Casino Las Palmas CASINO
(Map p48; www.casinolaspalmas.com; Calle Simón Bolívar 3; ⊙8pm-4am) If you feel like a flutter, don the glad rags, grab your passport and head for the casino in the northern part of the city, near Parque Santa Catalina.

Teatro Pérez Galdós THEATRE
(Map p46; ☑928 43 33 34; www.auditorioteatro-laspalmasgc.es; Plaza Stagno) Stages theatrical performances and music recitals.

Unión Deportiva Las Palmas FOOTBALL
(www.udlaspalmas.net) Better known as UD Las Palmas, this is Gran Canaria's premier football team. To see them in action, join the throngs heading for the 31,000-seat Estadio Gran Canaria. The stadium is located around 4.5km from Vegueta, heading southwest via the GC-23 and GC-1 highways (direction Teror).

🛍 Shopping

The long-time traditional shoppers' street is Calle Mayor de Triana, which is as interesting for its architecture as its idiosyncratic shops. Other recommended shopping strips include Calle Cano, Calle Viera y Clavijo and the surrounding streets, all in the southern part of the city.

Las Palmas' super-chic shoppers' hang-out is Avenida José Mesa y López. Here you'll find two branches of the mammoth department store El Corte Inglés (Map p48; www.elcorteingles.es; Avenida Mesa y López 15 & 18) facing off across the busy road, as well as numerous shops and boutiques. Nearby, around Parque Santa Catalina, there are plenty of cheap electronic goods and discount shops with great deals on cameras, watches, computer equipment and mobile phones.

Fedac HANDICRAFTS
(Foundation for Ethnography & the Development of Canarian Handicrafts; Map p46; www.fedac.org; Calle Domingo J Navarro 7; ⊙10am-2pm & 5-9pm Mon-Fri, 10am-2pm Sat) Head to these two adjacent government-sponsored, non-profit stores for handicrafts. One specialises in modern design, including exquisite hand-painted silk scarves, woven shawls and modern jewellery, while next door the emphasis is more traditional and includes pottery and basketware.

ℹ FOLLOW THE SHOPPING BASKETS

For the freshest and cheapest produce, including everything you might need for a picnic, check out the covered markets: the best are located between Calles Barcelona and Néstor de la Torre and on the corner of Calles Mendizabal and Juan de Quesada in Vegueta.

Librería del Cabildo Insular de Gran Canaria BOOKS
(Map p46; Calle Travieso 15; ⊙10am-2pm & 5-9pm Mon-Fri, 10am-2pm Sat) Stocks lots of titles about the Canary Islands. Most are in Spanish but there are a few shelves of English guides, including Lonely Planet.

La Casa de los Quesos FOOD & DRINK
(Map p48; www.lacasadelosquesos.com; Calle Sagasta 32; ⊙10am-2pm & 5-9pm Mon-Fri, 10am-2pm Sat) There are a whopping 150 varieties of cheese from mainland Spain and elsewhere on sale here. It's a great place to pick up a gourmet picnic – they also stock locally made sauces, jams and cakes and have a superb selection of Canarian wines.

ℹ Information

INTERNET ACCESS

Although internet cafes are not as abundant as they once were, you'll still find access in the city's *locutorios* (telephone call centres), which also offer cheap international calls.

Wi-fi is widespread – most hotels, cafes and restaurants offer access and there is even a plan to launch wi-fi hotspots on the beach.

MONEY

For the highest concentration of banks with 24-hour ATM machines head for Calle José Franchy Roca, just south of Parque Santa Catalina.

TOURIST INFORMATION

The city's tourism authority website is www.lpavisit.com. It is an excellent resource with information on activities, attractions, accommodation and restaurants across the city.

Main Tourist Office (Map p48; www.lpavisit.com; Parque Santa Catalina; ⊙9am-6pm Mon-Fri, 10am-2pm Sat & Sun) In a neo-Canarian building designed by local artist Néstor Martín Fernández de la Torre, this office has iPads loaded with Las Palmas apps as well as the more traditional array of pamphlets.

Island Tourist Office (Map p46; ☑928 21 96 00; www.grancanaria.com; Calle Triana 93;

ⓘ PEDAL POWER

You can cycle around the city for free by registering with **By Bike LPA** (p265). There are 11 pick-up locations around town and you can borrow a bike for three hours at a time. To register, you'll need ID and you'll have to buy an LPA Movilidad card (€1.50, available from the Santa Catalina municipal bus office). For more information, check the website.

⊙8am-3pm Mon-Fri) Has a variety of maps and brochures covering the whole island. Ask for the series of hiking maps.

Bus Station Information Office (Map p46; Estación San Telmo, Parque San Telmo; ⊙6.30am-8.30pm Mon-Fri, 7.30am-1pm Sat & Sun) Covers island-wide transport and has some info on other towns around Gran Canaria. There's also a smaller office in Parque Santa Catalina.

Tourist Information Kiosk (Map p46; Plaza de Santa Ana; ⊙9am-6pm Mon-Fri, 10am-2pm Sat) Other kiosks are located at Parque San Telmo (Map p46; Parque San Telmo; ⊙10am-8pm Mon-Fri, to 3pm Sat) and Playa de la Canteras (Map p48; Paseo de las Canteras; ⊙10am-7pm Mon-Sat).

ⓘ Getting There & Away

BUS

Global (☑928 25 26 30; www.globalsu.net) operates buses to all points around the island, leaving from **Estación San Telmo** (Map p46; Parque San Telmo), at the northern end of the Triana district.

Frequent main bus routes include the following:
➡ Buses 30 and 50 express to Maspalomas (€6.15, one hour)
➡ Bus 1 to Puerto de Mogán (€8.75, 1½ hours)
➡ Buses 12 and 80 to Telde (€1.65, about 20 minutes)
➡ Bus 105 to Gáldar (€3.10, one hour).

The night-owl bus 5 links the capital and Maspalomas. It leaves on the hour from 8pm to 3am from Estación San Telmo in Las Palmas, and on the half-hour from 9.30pm to 4.30am from Maspalomas.

ⓘ Getting Around

TO/FROM THE AIRPORT
Bus

Bus 60 runs between the airport and Estación San Telmo twice-hourly between 6am and 7pm and hourly thereafter (€2.30, 25 minutes), continuing on to Santa Catalina (€2.95, 35 minutes).

Taxi

A taxi between the airport and central Las Palmas costs about €30.

BUS

Yellow Buses (www.guaguas.com) Yellow buses (guaguas municipales) serve the metropolitan area. Pick up a route map from the tourist office, kiosks or the bus station. Individual journeys are all €1.40 but if you plan to take the bus more than a few times, it's worth investing in a 10-trip bono de guagua (€8.50), on sale at bus stations and newsagents. One bono de guagua can be shared between a number of travellers.

Yellow buses 1, 12, 13 and 17 all run from Triana northwards as far as the port and the northern end of Playa de las Canteras, calling by the bus station and Parque Santa Catalina.

City Sightseeing Bus (☑902 70 20 71; adult/child €15/7.50; ⊙9.30am-7pm) The hop-on, hop-off City Sightseeing Bus is good way of getting an initial overview of the city. The main departure point is Parque Santa Catalina, but you can jump on at any of the 10 stops between there and Vegueta.

CAR

Driving in Las Palmas is a pain, with the normal big-city rush-hour traffic jams and a baffling one-way street system. Most of the centre operates meter parking (coins only), but finding a space is challenging. Otherwise, there are several underground car parks, where you pay around €2 per hour. The most central are at Parque Santa Catalina, Plaza de España and at Parque San Telmo, opposite the main bus station.

TAXI

If you need a **taxi** (☑928 15 47 77, 928 46 90 00, 928 46 00 00), you can call, flag one down or head for one of the plentiful taxi stands across the city.

THE EAST

Charming as Las Palmas is, it is still a noisy and chaotic city. Thankfully, if you are seeking some more mellow, albeit dramatic, surroundings, you won't have far to travel. Within a short drive you'll find picturesque historic towns, misty mountain villages and the soaring sides of the verdant Barranco de Guayadeque, a ravine that's rightly popular with both locals and tourists.

Tafira Alta

Jardín Botánico Canario

Viera y Clavijo   BOTANICAL GARDEN

(Botanical Garden; www.jardincanario.org; ⊘9am-6pm; P) FREE About 9km southwest of Las Palmas, this vast botanical garden – Spain's largest, encompassing 27 hectares – hosts a broad range of Macronesian flora from across the Canary Islands, including many species on the verge of extinction. The garden clings to the walls of the Guiniguada Ravine and has plenty of information boards in English and Spanish. There's a restaurant at the upper entrance (on the GC-110 road).

Buses 301, 302 and 303 pass by the garden's upper entrance. The lower entrance is on the GC-310.

Caldera de Bandama & Santa Brígida

South of Tafira Alta is the impressive Caldera de Bandama, one of the largest extinct volcanic craters on the island, 200m deep and 1km in diameter. You can drive to the top for superb views into the crater and beyond. If you're fairly fit, the hike down to the crater floor is worthwhile. In the base you'll find farming and winemaking equipment; until fairly recently, Bandama was inhabited. The hike leaves from the cluster of buildings on the GC-802, where you'll find a cosy local restaurant and a winery. Close by is La Atalaya, the prime pottery-producing village on the island, where you can buy lovely ceramics, then stress about transporting them home.

The road continues to climb towards Santa Brígida, about 5km west of La Atalaya. A rather drab place, it's lifted by a pretty park and narrow tree-lined streets at its heart. There are sweeping views from the parish church over fields and palm groves to the central mountains. Stop at the Casa del Vino (Calle Calvo Sotelo 26; mains €10-18; ⊘closed Sun dinner & Mon), a pleasant restaurant at the edge of the park. There are some Canarian specialities on the menu, plus plenty of grilled meat dishes. The wine list is excellent, and every bottle on it originates in Gran Canaria. Tastings are available. There's a small museum (⊘10am-3pm Mon-Fri) FREE here with a modest display of wine-making implements.

Bus 311 (€1.55, 30 minutes) leaves hourly from Las Palmas to Santa Brígida, stopping at Bandama and La Atalaya en route.

Vega de San Mateo

As with most of the northern part of the island (especially the northeast), the area around San Mateo is heavily cultivated and agriculturally rich; it's an important vine-growing region.

Most of the island's population lives in the north, and this area is fairly densely populated. The town is memorable mainly for its dramatic setting, along with the excellent farmers market held every Saturday and Sunday in a large building behind the free car park. If you fancy sticking around, leave the hectic main road and head instead for the quiet, cobbled streets of the *casco histórico* (old town). If you are here in September, try to come on the 21st for the *romería* (pilgrimage) and celebrations of the patron saint, St Matthew.

Bus 303 (€2.55, 30 minutes) comes up from Las Palmas every 30 minutes.

Telde

POP 19,400

Telde is the island's second-largest city and, although relatively devoid of notable museums and sights, the historic centre is well worth exploring.

The town dates back prior to the Spanish conquest and is known for its production of stringed instruments, above all the *timple* (a kind of ukulele) – the islands' musical emblem.

⊙ Sights

Look beyond the city's drab industrial shell and head for the historic centre that comprises three distinct neighbourhoods: San Juan, San Francisco, and a little further afield, San Gregorio. Start with San Juan, where it's fairly easy to park and wander the narrow cobbled streets towards San Francisco, stopping for photographs of simple whitewashed houses punctuated by the brilliant dazzle of crimson bougainvillea.

Iglesia de San Francisco   CHURCH

(Plaza San Francisco; ⊘sporadic) To reach the church from the central Plaza de San Juan Bautista, take cobbled Calle Ynes Chimida due west. This tranquil street runs alongside

GRAN CANARIA AGÜIMES

PRE-HISPANIC SITE: CUATRO PUERTAS

Although it's only 5km south of Telde, this impressive pre-Hispanic site is seldom visited, even by locals. Cuatro Puertas means 'four doors' and takes its name from the multiple entrances carved into the rock face of this man-made cave complex. There are information panels here but no visitor centre, meaning you can visit whenever you like. It's just off the GC-100 road in the minute hamlet of Cuatro Puertas. Bus 36 from Telde (€1.40, 10 minutes) passes by hourly en route to Maspalomas.

an old aqueduct with orange and banana groves below. In the church, note the three polychrome stone altars on the northern-most of the twin naves and the fine *artesonado* (coffered) ceiling.

Basílica de San Juan Bautista   CHURCH
(Plaza San Juan Bautista; ⊙9.30am-12.30pm & 5-8pm) Among the grand old buildings of the San Juan area is this neo-Gothic church. You can't miss the gloriously kitsch 16th-century altarpiece, all gilt and gold, with a crucifixion at its heart. The Christ figure was made by the Tarasco Indians in Mexico.

Museo León y Castillo   MUSEUM
(www.fernandoleonycastillo.com; Calle León y Castillo 43; adult/child €2/1; ⊙10am-6pm Tue-Sun) This museum is devoted to the city's most famous resident, a late-19th-century politician. The building, his former home, is lovely with its galleried wooden balconies; in contrast, the exhibits, ambassadorial credentials and the like may fail to thrill.

ⓘ TELDE WALKING TOUR

If you happen to be in town on a Friday, take a free walking tour (www.discovertelde.com; ⊙noon) of Telde with an audioguide. Bookings are essential. You can also book the tour for other days and times, when it costs €10. Tours usually depart from Plaza San Juan Bautista.

Beaches

Playa de Melenara   BEACH
This decent beach is 5km from Telde and frequented by townsfolk rather than tourists. The wide arc of dark sand is fronted by apartments and several good, inexpensive seafood restaurants. A footpath follows the rocky coast to Playa de la Garita, another popular local beach, located 3km to the north. There are some good surf spots en route.

ⓘ Information

Tourist Office (www.telde.es; Calle Conde de la Vega Grande 9; ⊙8am-3pm Mon-Fri) One street north of the Basílica de San Juan.

ⓘ Getting There & Away

Buses 12 and 80 run to/from Las Palmas (€1.65, about 20 minutes, every 20 minutes).

Agüimes

A short bus ride (or drive) south of Telde brings you to Agüimes, with its perfectly restored historic centre. The church here was the inspiration for the ostentatious lobby building at the mega-luxury hotel Villa del Conde in Maspalomas. Agüimes is often overlooked by tourists, but this is one of the prettiest towns on the island and definitely deserves a wander.

◉ Sights

The pedestrian streets are lined with lovely buildings that reflect vernacular Canarian architecture, especially surrounding shady Plaza del Rosario.

Iglesia de San Sebastián   CHURCH
(⊙9.30am-12.30pm & 5-7pm Tue, Thu, Sat & Sun) The vast church, with its dome of 12 large windows (symbolising the 12 apostles), is considered one of the best examples of Canarian neoclassicism. Construction started in the late 18th century but the church wasn't completed until the 1940s.

Museo de Historia de Agüimes   MUSEUM
(Calle Juan Alvarado y Saz 42; adult/child €3/free; ⊙9am-5pm Tue-Sun) Covering more than just the history of the town, the well-presented exhibits here give a good insight into Canarian history, covering everything from pre-Hispanic customs and the conquest to agriculture, folklore and witchcraft.

SCENIC DRIVE: AGÜIMES

The narrow and winding GC-550 road climbs northwest from Agüimes offering views of the mountains and, far beneath you, the Atlantic Ocean. After 10km you reach the tiny village of **Temisas**, set on a natural balcony. It's a sleepy but atmospheric place, with original stone houses and cottages, plus a restaurant if you want to stop for refreshments.

The road meanders another 10km to Santa Lucía, home to two castles (of sorts). You can't miss the quirky **Castillo de la Fortaleza** (admission €2; ☉9.30am-3pm; 🚻), a grey-turreted private museum at the southern entrance to the town. The one-time home of local archaeologist, writer, artist and collector Vicente Sanchez Araña, it has 16 rooms displaying everything from old weapons to mammalian skeletons, paintings and a collection of Guanche artefacts found in nearby caves.

Heading south on the GC-65 you'll pass a turnoff for **La Sorrueda**, a breathtaking reservoir backed by verdant mountains and fringed with palm trees. A little further south is Santa Lucía's second castle, a much more natural affair. The **Fortaleza de Ansite** could be just another mountain, but this natural fortress is one of Gran Canaria's most important pre-Hispanic sites. It was here that the Guanches' last stand took place, with many opting to hurl themselves into the ravine rather than face a life of slavery. Break out the hiking boots to explore the 'fortress', with its caves and tunnel cutting through 34m of mountain.

As the road descends, look out for the GC-551 turning to your left, an even narrower road that makes its way slowly back to Agüimes.

Centro de Interpretación del Casco Histórico MUSEUM
(Old Town Interpretation Centre; Plaza San Antón 1; ☉8am-3pm Mon-Fri) **FREE** There are some well-documented exhibits on the evolution of the town's urban structure through the centuries. Don't forget to peep into the old chapel. It's in the same building as the tourist office.

🍴 Eating

El Populacho CANARIAN €
(Plaza del Rosario 17; tapas €2.50-6; ☉1-4pm & 7pm-late; 🚻) On the corner of the main square, this welcoming tapas joint with its zinc bar and art deco lights is housed in a former grocer's shop (1933), as depicted in the lively murals that cover the walls. Rumbling tummies should opt for a generous tapas portion of *garbanzada* (chickpea stew with bacon). There's live music on Friday nights.

ℹ️ Information

Tourist Office (www.aguimes.es; Plaza de San Antón 1; ☉8am-3pm Mon-Fri) You can pick up a brochure here with mapped-out walks around town.

ℹ️ Getting There & Around

BUS
Buses 11 and 21 connect Las Palmas with Agüimes (€3.40, 45 minutes, hourly). Bus 22 heads southeast to Arinaga (€1.40, 20 minutes, hourly), a popular coastal swimming spot even though it lacks a real beach.

CAR
There is a paying car park on Calle Acebuche, just outside the historic centre.

Barranco de Guayadeque

The Barranco de Guayadeque (Guayadeque Ravine) rises up into central Gran Canaria in a majestic sweep of crumpled ridges. For most of the year the vegetation here is lush and green; if you can, visit in early spring when the almond trees are in blossom and the landscape is remarkably verdant and beautiful. Start your visit at the **Centro de Interpretación** (admission €2.50; ☉9am-5pm Tue-Sat, 10am-3pm Sun), occupying a cave at the entrance of the *barranco*. Exhibits explain the geology of the ravine and cover its fascinating history, from the pre-Hispanic inhabitants to the troglodytes of today. Probably most interesting is the mummy found in a local cave in the 19th century.

Around 4km from here, stretch your legs at Cuevas Bermejas, a small settlement of cave homes carved out of the mountainside. Be sure to peek into the tiny chapel, where the pulpit, altar and confessional are all hewn from rock.

The road continues to wind upwards until you reach Montaña de las Tierras, with its cave restaurants and smattering of homes. If you want to continue from here you'll need sturdy hiking boots. There are a couple of trails with stunning views that stretch right to the sea; ask at the interpretation centre for information.

The ravine is really at its best once the lunchtime crowd has left. If you'd like to spend the night, check out www.casasru ralesdeguayadeque.com for rural accommodation in the *barranco* – much of it, of course, in caves.

✖ Eating

A short way past Cuevas Bermejas is a pleasant and very popular picnic site if you prefer to self-cater.

Bar Guayadeque   TAPAS €
(Cueva Bermeja 23; tapas €4-9; ⊙1-4pm & 7pm-late) With hams hanging from the ceiling and an interesting tapas menu, this is a quieter place to stop for lunch than the restaurants higher up the ravine. It's next door to the chapel.

Restaurant Tagoror   CANARIAN €€
(www.restaurantetagoror.com; Montaña de las Tierras; mains €8-16; ⊙1-4pm & 7pm-late) There's not much to choose between the numerous cave restaurants in the ravine, but Tagoror is a long-standing place with consistently good reviews. Hearty stews are the order of the day and there's no shortage of *papas arrugadas* (wrinkly potatoes) with spicy *mojo* (salsa).

THE NORTH

Gran Canaria's fertile north presents a gently shifting picture from its rugged, mountainous interior to the southern beach resorts and dunes. Dramatic ravines, intensively tilled fields and terraces, and forests of pine trees, covered with mossy lichen, typify the landscape as you wind along twisting roads, passing myriad villages and hamlets. Only as you reach the west does the green give way to a more austere, although no less captivating, landscape: the west coast is the most dramatic on the island.

Teror

POP 6650 / ELEV 543M

In spite of its name, Teror does anything but inspire fear. The central Plaza Nuestra Señora del Pino and Calle Real are lined with picturesque old houses, painted in bright colours with leaning walls and wooden balconies. The only jarring building is the modern Auditorio de Teror, just west of the basilica. Aesthetics aside, it has admirably provided the town with a welcome cultural venue. There's a small farmers market in the plaza on Saturday mornings, with stalls selling local goodies like the deliciously garlic-laden *chorizo de Teror* (sausage), which should scare off those vampires for a while. The Sunday market is larger and more commercial. It's located 20km southwest of Las Palmas.

FROM PARROT FISH TO PIGS' TAILS

Local cuisine is renowned for making use of every part of the *cochino* (pig). That cute, curly *templero* (tail) was traditionally hung from the kitchen doorway to be periodically dipped into the cooking pot for stock. A typical *tapa* here, generally accompanied by the traditional rum aperitif, is *caracajas* (pieces of fried pork liver doused in a spicy sauce). Goat is also popular, along with rabbit, while seafood is, naturally enough, always a good bet – this is an island, after all. Try the much-prized *vieja* (parrot fish), a member of the sea-bream family.

Goat's cheese is produced on several islands, though one of the best-known soft cheeses, Gran Canaria's *queso de flor*, is made from a combination of cows' and sheep's milk. The cheese, which is produced exclusively in the northern Guía area, is then infused with the aroma of flowers from the *cardo alcausí* thistle. Another scrumptious winner is the similar-tasting *pastor* cheese, produced in the Arucas region. Pick up the booklet *La Ruta de los Quesos* (in English) at larger tourist offices for more cheesy information.

Almonds are a favourite ingredient of many traditional desserts, including the must-try *bienmesabe* (literally translated as 'it tastes good to me') made from ground almonds, lemon rind, sugar and eggs.

Among the outstanding Gran Canaria wines is the fruity Del Monte, a perfect, if tiddly, accompaniment to meat dishes, with an alcohol content over 11.5%. Aside from *ron miel* (honey rum), which is more liqueur than rum, the island produces a decent drop of golden rum – head to the distillery in Arucas to taste the full range. *!Salud!*

◎ Sights

The main joy in this town is just wandering around the historic centre snapping photos, but it's still worth checking out a few of the sights.

Basílica de la Virgen del Pino   CHURCH
(Plaza Nuestra Señora del Pino 3; ⊙ church 8am-noon & 2-6pm, treasure room 1-3pm Mon-Fri, 11am-2pm & 3.30-5.45pm Sun) Dominating the square is this neoclassical 18th-century church, home to Gran Canaria's patron saint. According to legend, the Virgin was spied atop a pine tree in the nearby forest in the 15th century, which turned Teror into a quasi-Fatima pilgrimage site. The church interior, a lavishly gilt-laden affair, sees the enthroned Virgin illuminated in her place of honour at the heart of a lavishly ornate altarpiece, surrounded by angels.

Don't miss the 'treasure room', accessed from the rear of the church. Here you can get a closer view of the Virgin and see the armfuls of weird items gifted by the devout. There's also a room displaying the outfits she's worn through the ages – a new dress gets premiered each year during the fiesta held in her honour.

Casa de los Patronos de la Virgen   MUSEUM
(Plaza Nuestra Señora del Pino 3; admission €3; ⊙ 11am-4pm Mon-Fri, 10am-2pm Sun) One of the loveliest buildings here houses this modest museum. Pleasantly musty, it's devoted to preserving 18th-century life and is full of intriguing odds and ends, mostly from the Las Palmas family, who used it as a second home.

✰ Festivals & Events

Fiesta de la Virgen del Pino   RELIGIOUS
(⊙ 1st week of Sep) The Virgen del Pino is the patron of the island and Teror is the religious capital. This festival is not only a big event in town, it's the most important religious feast day on the island's calendar. Events include processions, a livestock fair and plenty of music and dancing.

✖ Eating

El Rincón de Magüi   PIZZA €€
(Calle Diputación 6; mains €9-15; ⊙ 1-4pm) Very popular pizzeria and restaurant with outside tables, plus a brick-clad dining room decorated with ceramic plates and photos of well-fed celeb diners like former Spanish PM Aznar.

CISTERCIAN COOKIES

A sort of divine aura hangs over Teror, so it seems fitting that any snacks you purchase should be handmade by nuns. Puff and pant your way up steep Calle Herrería, next to the museum until you reach Calle del Castaño. Here you'll find a **Cistercian convent** (⊙ 10am-1pm & 3-6pm) where the nuns produce some tasty biscuits. If there's no-one around, ring the bell and have your cash ready – transactions are carried out by a speedy, unseen sister.

El Encuentro   CANARIAN €€
(Plaza Nuestra Señora del Pino 7; mains €8-16; ⊙ 1-4pm & 7pm-late Tue-Sun) Right on the square, this cheery place has a fine selection of steaks as well as a traditional *potaje* (stew) of the day (€4) – perfect in winter when Teror can be bitterly cold.

❶ Information

Tourist Office (Calle Padre Cueto 2; ⊙ 9.30am-4pm Mon-Fri) Located behind the church in the corner of the square.

❶ Getting There & Away

Buses 216, 220 and 229 connect with Las Palmas (€2.30, 30 minutes, hourly); bus 215 with Arucas (€1.40, 20 minutes, hourly).

Arucas

POP 10,400
A visit to Arucas makes a great day trip from Las Palmas. It is a handsome, compact town with pedestrian streets lined with elegant historic buildings and a lovely flower-filled park.

◎ Sights

The town is a delight to just stroll around. From the Iglesia de San Juan, walk down Calle Gourié to Calle León y Castillo, flanked by colourful colonial-style buildings. Turn right into Plaza Constitución, situated across from the lovely town gardens and home of the late-19th-century modernist *ayuntamiento* (town hall) and a couple of pleasant terrace bars.

MARKET TIME

The towns and villages are the scene of some interesting small markets, most of which sell local cheeses, cold meats and bakery goods, as well as some souvenirs and trinkets. They make for an easy-going morning away from the bustle of the resorts. Markets generally last from 9am to 2pm and include the following:

Puerto de Mogán (Friday) One of the most touristy.

San Fernando (Wednesday and Saturday)

Arguineguín (Tuesday and Thursday)

Santa Brígida (Saturday)

Teror (Saturday and Sunday)

Vega de San Mateo (Saturday and Sunday)

★ **Iglesia de San Juan Bautista**   CHURCH
(⊙9.30am-12.30pm & 4.30-7.15pm) The extraordinary, neo-Gothic church stands sullen watch over the bright white houses of Arucas in a striking display of disproportion. The church has a Sagrada Familia (Gaudí) look with elaborate pointed spires and was, fittingly, designed by a Catalan architect. Construction started in 1909 on the site of a former *ermita* (chapel) and was completed 70 years later. Treasures within include a nude, reclining image of Christ carved by local sculptor Manolo Ramos and three magnificent rose windows.

Jardines Municipales   GARDENS
(Calle Heredad; ⊙9am-10pm) **FREE** The municipal gardens are laid out in French style with fountains, pavilions, sculptures and tropical trees, including the rare evergreen soap bark tree *(Quillaja saponaria)* and several magnificent dragon palm trees. Calle Heredad flanks the gardens on the southern side of the plaza, dominated by the beautiful neoclassical **Heredad de Aguas de Arucas y Firgas** building, completed in 1908 and now housing the local water board.

Jardín de la Marquésa   GARDENS
(www.jardindelamarquesa.com; adult/child €6/3; ⊙9am-1pm & 2-6pm Mon-Sat; P) Northwest of town, on the road to Bañaderos, this lovely botanical garden is owned by the Marquésa de Arucas (along with the Hacienda del Buen Suceso). Lushly planted with more than 2500 different perennials, trees and cacti, there are ponds, places to sit and a greenhouse with banana trees. The admission fee includes a detailed guide identifying the plants on display.

Museo La Cantera   MUSEUM
(Camino los Callejones; ⊙9am-5pm Mon-Fri) **FREE** Based above a former quarry, this small, well-presented museum pays homage to the town's long-running stone masonry industry.

Destilerías Arehucas   RUM DISTILLERY
(www.arehucas.com; ⊙10am-2pm Mon-Fri; P) **FREE** The free guided tour of this rum distillery culminates in a tasting of five rums plus up to 11 liqueurs and the opportunity to buy a few bottles to take back home.

Municipal Museum   MUSEUM
(Jardines Municipales; ⊙10am-6pm Mon-Fri, to 1pm Sat) **FREE** The gardens house the town's main museum, which has a permanent exhibition by Canarian painters and sculptors, plus temporary shows.

✖ Eating & Drinking

★ **El Belingo**   TAPAS €
(www.elbelingo.com; Calle León y Castillo 3; tapas €4-10; ⊙closed Sun dinner, Mon; ☞) The menu at this friendly pavement cafe offers traditional Canarian fare without being too touristy. The *ropa vieja* (chickpea stew) is superb. There is live music on Saturday afternoons.

Tasca Jamón Jamón   TAPAS €
(Calle Gourié 5; tapas €3.50-8; ⊙1-4pm & 7pm-late Tue-Sun) Boasts an ace position on this narrow pedestrian street with soul-stirring views of the church from the outside tables. Enjoy good basic tapas like wedges of crumbly Manchego cheese with crusty white bread.

La Dolorosa BAR
(Calle Párroco Cárdenes 5; ⊙ 7pm-midnight Wed-
Mon; ⊛) The most stylish place in town with
a trendy cocktail bar and light tapas. The
outdoor tables are no more than 5m from
the imposing facade of the church.

ℹ Information

Tourist Office (Calle León y Castillo 10;
⊙ 8.30am-5pm Mon-Fri, 10am-2pm Sat) Can
assist with accommodation bookings and has
public toilets.

ℹ Getting There & Away

Buses 205 and 210 connect Arucas with Las
Palmas (€2.10, 25 minutes) every 30 minutes.
Bus 215 runs hourly to Teror (€1.40, 15 minutes).

Around Arucas

If you have wheels (preferably four), take the
steep, well-signposted route to La Montaña
de Arucas, 2.5km north of town. From here
there's a splendid panorama of Las Palmas,
the northern coast of the island, orchards,
banana groves and the less-photogenic sight
of hectare upon hectare of plastic greenhouses. The restaurant here, La Corona de
Arucas (www.lacoronadearucas.com; mains €10-
25), has fabulous views and is touristy but
good. The main menu includes enough meat
to keep a caveman happy, plus several fish
dishes and a couple of token salads. There is
also a tapas menu with some fine Canarian
choices. Try the grilled goat cheese with *bienmesabe* (a sweet sauce made of almonds,
lemon rind and a *lot* of sugar).

Moya

POP 1320 / ELEV 490M

The spectacular 20km drive between Arucas
and Moya hugs the flank of the mountain,
providing gee-whiz views of the northern
coast. Moya is an unpretentious working town
with some traditional Canarian architecture,
including the lovely Casa-Museo Tomás
Morales (www.tomasmorales.com; adult/child €2/
free; ⊙ 10am-6pm Tue-Sun) **FREE**. Once home to
the Canarian poet, who died in 1922 aged just
37, the museum includes a music room with a
170-year-old clavichord, a small hall used for
classical concerts and a pretty walled garden
with grapefruit trees and cacti. More impressive though is the vista across the *barranco*
(ravine) from the back of the 16th-century
church. It's bettered only by the view of the

JUST A SPOONFUL OF RUM

Generally associated with dancing barefoot on a Caribbean beach, rum has also
long been produced here, dating back
to the days of the sugar plantations. The
local product has a superb international
reputation, being famed for both its
heart-warming flavour and, yes, even
the medicinal properties. Feeling a tad
feverish? Then have a glug of *ron miel*
(a honey-infused white rum) – it sure
beats an aspirin.

church itself from the other side of the ravine,
clinging precariously to the mountainside.
Buses 116 and 117 run hourly to/from Las
Palmas (€2.95, one hour).

Santa María de Guía

POP 4900

Just off the main GC-2 highway, 25km west
of Las Palmas, Santa María de Guía (or just
Guía) is an atmospheric small town that was
temporarily home to the French composer
Camille Saint-Saëns (1835–1921), who used to
tickle the ivories in the town's 17th-century
neoclassical church. The church overlooks a
spacious square which is a pleasant place to
stretch your legs.

In the 18th century, the town and surrounding area were devastated by a plague
of locusts. To rid themselves of this blight,
the locals implored the Virgin Mary for
help. This remains a tradition and on the
third Sunday of September the townsfolk
celebrate La Rama de las Marías by dancing
their way to the doors of the church to make
offerings of fruit. The town is also known for
its *queso de flor* (cheese). You can find it at
the local supermarkets, or try Casa Arturo
on Calle Lomo Gullén (the main road as you
enter from the GC-2).

Buses 103, 105 and 150 (€2.85, 50 minutes) pass by roughly every half hour on
their way from Las Palmas.

Around Santa María de Guía

About 3km east of town lies the Cenobio de
Valerón (www.arqueologiacanaria.com; Cuesta
Silva s/n; adult/child €3/free; ⊙ 10am-6pm Tue-
Sun), a fascinating ancient site consisting
of over 350 caves, silos and cavities of var-
ious sizes that were used to store grain in

pre-Hispanic times. Located on deep slopes, separated by steps and walkways, there are informative plaques throughout explaining the history and archaeology of the site, as well as the volcanic geology of the area.

Gáldar

POP 10,780 / ELEV 124M

This charming town was the capital of the *guanartemato* (kingdom) in pre-Hispanic times and is justifiably famous for its extraordinary archaeological sights. It has a bustling and attractive historic core centred around the gracious Plaza de Santiago with its neoclassical Santiago de Gáldar church. The square is also home to one of the oldest *drago* trees on the island, dating back to 1718. It's located in the patio of the 19th-century Casas Consistoriales, where the **tourist office** (www.ciudaddegaldar.com; Plaza de Santiago 1; ⊙9am-3.30pm Mon-Fri) is situated.

Sights

★ **Cueva Pintada Museum & Archaeological Park** ARCHAEOLOGICAL SITE
(⊉902 40 55 04, 928 89 54 46; www.cuevapin tada.com; Calle Audiencia 2; adult/child €6/free; ⊙10am-6pm Tue-Sat, from 11am Sun, guided tours 12.30pm in English, 2.30pm in German, 3pm in French; ⬛) Discovered by a local farmer in the late 19th-century, this is one of Gran Canaria's most important pre-Hispanic sites: a cave adorned with geometric shapes, thought to relate to the lunar and solar calendars. It is also the most accessible of the island's archaeological sites, situated not halfway up a cliff but right in the heart of the town (it is wheelchair-friendly).

The museum complex features videos and reconstructions shedding light onto local life before the conquistadors arrived, and showcases the 5000-sq-metre excavated site where the remains of cave houses have been dug out from the volcanic rock. The highlight is the painted cave itself. While you can visit independently, the guided 90-minute tour is highly recommended. Try to book in advance via the website – there is a limit of 20 people on each tour so you might end up disappointed if you just show up.

In order to prevent further deterioration to the paintings, the cave is open at set times (too many to list here!) and you can only view the paintings for up to four minutes, from behind a window. In the decade after 1972 the colours of the pigments were reduced by a shocking 50% due to the constant stream of visitors.

Casa Museo Antonio Padrón MUSEUM
(Calle Capitán Quesada 3; adult/child €2/free; ⊙10am-6pm Tue-Sun) Locals are justifiably proud of native son Antonio Padrón who, in the 1960s, was just starting to gain serious recognition in the European art world when he tragically died of an allergic reaction to penicillin at just 48 years old. His paintings are wonderfully colourful and distinctive, many inspired by the geometric motifs of the Guanches. The museum is located at the artist's former studio.

Getting There & Around

BUS

Bus 105 (€3.10, one hour) heads east for Las Palmas roughly every half hour. Southbound, bus 103 (€1.40, 20 minutes, hourly) links Gáldar with Agaete and Puerto de las Nieves.

CAR

The town is confusing to drive around, with narrow one-way roads and virtually no street parking. There are two free car parks on Calle Real de San Sebastián as you approach town from the direction of Las Palmas.

DOGS, BIRDS OR BERBERS?

So how did the Canary Islands get their name? From the trilling native canary birds perhaps? Or maybe they were named after the Latin word for dog (*canus*), because members of an early expedition discovered what they considered unusually large dogs? (Still others held that the natives of the island were dog eaters. Nice...)

A more plausible theory claims that the people of Canaria, who arrived several hundred years before Christ, were in fact Berbers of the Canarii tribe living in Morocco. The tribal name was simply applied to the island and later accepted by Pliny. How Canaria came to be Gran (Big) has a couple of predictably feeble explanations: either because the islanders put up a big fight while resisting conquest, or the island was thought to be the biggest in the archipelago. Evidently, they didn't have great tape measures in those days – as we know all too well – Tenerife and Fuerteventura are larger.

Agaete & Puerto de las Nieves

POP 4660

The leafy town of Agaete, 10km southwest of Gáldar, is well worth a visit. The pretty main street, Calle de la Concepción, is flanked by typical Canarian buildings, some with the traditional wooden balconies, while in the centre of town stands the handsome main church.

Situated just 1km away is Puerto de las Nieves, the island's principal port until the 19th century but now better known as the terminal for fast ferries linking Gran Canaria with Tenerife. It's a small place with black pebbly beaches, but the mountainous setting is lovely with stunning views south along the Andén Verde. The place has a tangible fishing-village feel and the buildings, with their brilliant blue trim against dazzling white stucco, look as though they have been transplanted from some Greek island. The port is well known for its excellent seafood restaurants and fills up with locals at weekends.

From the jetty you can see the stump of the Dedo de Dios (God's Finger), a basalt monolithic rock that was the town's icon and a low-key tourist attraction until it took a tumble in a 2005 hurricane. Take a look at the photos outside the namesake restaurant to see what the rock looked like in its full skyward-pointing glory.

○ Sights

Iglesia de Nuestra Señora de la Concepción   CHURCH
(Plaza Constitución, Agaete; ○sporadic) Built in 1874, this handsome church is strikingly Mediterranean in style. Smaller but of equal interest is the Ermita de las Nieves (○11am-1pm Mon-Sat, 9-11am Sun), a tiny chapel just back from the water in Puerto de las Nieves. Here you can see a renowned 16th-century Flemish triptych painted by Joos van Cleve and dedicated to the Virgen de las Nieves.

Museo de la Rama   MUSEUM
(☑928 55 43 82; Calle Párroco Alonso Luján 5; adult/child €2/free; ○by appointment) Next to the main church, this small museum honours the town's most important annual festival: La Rama. It has explanations, history and displays, including the quaint papier-mâché figures with their giant heads who supposedly represent popular characters in the town.

CANARIAN COFFEE

A pretty, reasonably straight drive takes you from the town of Agaete 6km into the fertile valley of the same name, where you can seek out one of several coffee plantations. Finca La Laja (www.bodegalosberrazales.com; Calle de los Romeros; ○10am-5pm Mon-Fri, to 2pm Sat) cultivates tropical fruit and grapes alongside the beans and a tour includes wine tastings and a cup of the fine, rich coffee. High above the valley, the Tamadaba pine forest is also a prime hiking area.

Huerto de las Flores   BOTANICAL GARDENS
(Calle Huertas; adult/child €1.50/1; ○10am-4pm Tue-Sat; **P**) This 19th-century garden has more than 300 tropical plants and is a leafy retreat on a hot day. The cafe here serves coffee produced in the nearby Agaete Valley.

✦ Festivals & Events

Fiesta de la Rama   FESTIVAL
(○4 Aug) An extraordinary festival with origins that lie in an obscure Guanche rain dance. Nowadays, locals accompanied by marching bands parade into town brandishing tree branches and then get down to the serious business of having a good time.

✗ Eating

Aside from one indifferent pizzeria, seafood takes pride of place on the restaurant menus in Puerto de las Nieves.

Bar Angor   SEAFOOD €
(Avenida de los Poetas 2; mains €8-12; ○1-4pm & 7pm-late) Based in a pretty blue-and-white building, Angor is popular with locals and visitors, largely for its excellent value, three-course *menú del día* (€7).

★ Cofradía de Pescadores   SEAFOOD €€
(Muelle Puerto Nieves; mains €9-16; ○1-4pm & 7pm-late) Next to the port, with an outdoor terrace, you can dine on the catch of the day along with the fisherfolk – and there's no better recommendation than that. Try the *parrilla de pescado y marisco* (seafood mixed grill) or the marvellous paella. There are three token meat dishes but precious little for vegetarians.

ECO-TOURISM IN EL ROQUE

The waters off the coast of Puerto de la Aldea are part of a pilot project to attract ecotourism to the area. The El Roque Micro Área (www.microareas. org) encompasses a small stretch of spectacular virgin coastline and local authorities hope to entice hikers, divers, snorkellers and kayakers in a sustainable initiative that seeks to raise awareness – and funds – in this forgotten corner of the island. At present, facilities are thin on the ground so you need to be self sufficient, but the canvas is certainly an impressive one. There is no admission fee for the time being.

Restaurante Las Nasas　SEAFOOD €€
(Calle Nuestra Señora Nieves 7; mains €8-10; ⊙1-4pm & 7pm-late Wed-Mon) There's a great atmosphere in this former warehouse with its old-fashioned black-and-white interior, jolly model boats, high ceilings and a small open-air terrace overlooking the ocean.

Restaurante Dedo de Dios　SEAFOOD €€
(Carretera Puerto Nieves; mains €8-10; ⊙1-4pm & 7pm-late Wed-Mon) A cavernous restaurant hung with ferns in a lovely old building overlooking the beach and the rocky remains of the poor old Dedo. It fills up with large, boisterous families at weekends and has a vast menu of mainly fish and seafood dishes, plus a solid selection of desserts.

❶ Information

Tourist Office (www.agaete.es; Calle Nuestra Señora Nieves 1, Puerto de las Nieves; ⊙9am-5pm Mon-Fri, 9am-2.30pm Sat) Next to Restaurante Dedo de Dios.

❶ Getting There & Away

BUS

Bus 103 links the town and port with Las Palmas (€4.30, 1¼ hours) at least hourly. Bus 101 heads south for Aldea de San Nicolás (€3.95, one hour, four daily).

BOAT

From Puerto Nieves, **Fred Olsen** (☐ 902 10 01 07; www.fredolsen.es) operates six fast ferries daily (adult/child €42/25) for the hour-long trip to Santa Cruz de Tenerife. There is a free bus connection to Las Palmas (Parque Santa Catalina).

Returning, the bus leaves Las Palmas an hour before the ferry is due to depart.

CAR

There's a free car park in Agaete, opposite the botanical gardens on Calle Huertas. It's fairly easy to find street parking in Puerto de las Nieves, especially on weekdays.

Aldea de San Nicolás

POPULATION 2575

Sometimes referred to as San Nicolás de Tolentino, but more often known simply as 'La Aldea' (the hamlet), this rather scruffy town has little to excite the senses – it's the sort of place you only hang around because the arse has fallen off your car. The lure here is the travelling, not the arriving. The road between Agaete and San Nicolás takes you on a magnificent cliffside journey. If you head southwest in the late afternoon, the setting sun provides a soft-light display, marking out each successive ridge in an ever-darker shadowy mantle. There aren't many places to stop, so pull over at every opportunity. Vertigo sufferers might want to tackle the 40km journey, which can take anything up to two hours, in the opposite direction. If you drive from south to north, you get to hug the mountain rather than tackling the countless curves with the steep drop directly beneath you.

The approach from Mogán and the south, though lacking the seascapes, is almost as awesome.

Bus 38 (€3.85, one hour, five daily) runs between Puerto de Mogán and Aldea de San Nicolás. Bus 101 (€3.95, one hour, four daily) runs between Agaete and San Nicolas.

Around Aldea de San Nicolás

Heading north out of town, take a detour to Puerto de la Aldea, with its small harbour and smattering of seafood restaurants – the local speciality is *ropa vieja de pulpo* (chickpea stew with octopus). For self-caterers, the shady Parque Ruben Día, with its stone tables and benches set under the pine trees, is a nice spot for a picnic. After lunch, enjoy a stroll along the promenade and check out the small black stony beach and the Charco (puddle), where each September an odd festival sees revellers from across the island sloshing around, attempting to catch fish with their hands.

GRAN CANARIA FOR CHILDREN

Gran Canaria is a kiddie wonderland with plenty of natural, manufactured and theme-parked stuff to do. The **beaches** are the most obvious attraction and those in the southern resorts come complete with all variety of boat rides. In Puerto Rico you can go dolphin-spotting with **Spirit of the Sea** (p72). Further west is **Taurito**, which resembles a family-themed park with several pools (and pool tables) plus an abundance of amusements geared towards children and accommodating grown-ups. Theme parks are prolific in these parts, particularly around **Playa del Inglés**, where you can choose from camel rides, zoos, water parks, Wild West shows and a few more things besides. **Cocodrilo Park** (www.cocodriloparkzoo.com; adults/child €10/7; ⊙ 10am-5pm Sun-Fri), near Agüimes, is part zoo, part sanctuary, with the majority of its animals being abandoned exotic pets. On a more highbrow note, even the most museum-jaded tot cannot fail to be impressed by the model galleons at the **Casa-Museo de Colón** (p45) in Las Palmas, with its colourful Columbus history. For a more hands-on, how-the-hell-does-it-work experience, tag after the school trips at the superb **Museo Elder de la Ciencia y la Tecnología** (p50) science museum, also in the island's capital.

Also just out of town, in the hamlet of Tocodomán, is the well-signposted **Cactualdea** (www.cactualdea.com; adult/child €6/3; ⊙ 10am-6pm), which claims to be the largest cactus park in Europe, with over 1200 species of the prickly plant, plus a replica Guanche cave. Expect the usual insipid theme-park eating options; take a picnic if you can.

CENTRAL MOUNTAINS

Artenara

POP 920 / ELEV 1270M

Dramatically positioned Artenara is the highest village in Gran Canaria. The views of a huge volcanic crater from Mirador de Unamuno are truly astounding; this is one of several signposted miradors. On the other side of the village, Mirador de la Atalaya overlooks several troglodyte caves, some still inhabited, as well as the distant peak of El Teide in Tenerife.

In Artenara, it is all about caves. People live in caves, the restaurants are in caves, the town museum occupies a series of caves and if you want to spend the night in the area, you can even sleep in a *casa rural* based – you guessed it – in a cave. Check out www.artenatur.com for accommodation options. The sleepy town is overlooked by the **Corazón de Jesus**, a Rio-style (albeit much smaller) statue of Christ, arms outstretched.

☉ Sights

Santuario de la Cuevita   CHURCH
(Calle Camino de la Cuevita) Dating back to the early 19th century, this is one of Gran Canaria's smallest and most endearing chapels. Everything here – the altar, confessional, pulpit – has been carved straight from the rock; it's like a small-scale version of a Lalibela church. It houses the Virgen de la Cuevita, the patron saint, bizarrely, of both Canarian folklore and cycling.

Iglesia de San Matías   CHURCH
(Plaza San Matías) A delightful late-18th-century church with a carved wooden ceiling, frescoed altar and art nouveau stained-glass windows.

Museo Etnografico Casas Cuevas   MUSEUM
(Calle Pàrroco Domingo Bàez; admission by donation; ⊙ 11.30am-4.30pm) Once inhabited by locals, this cave complex is now home to the village museum, a likable place that focuses on village life in times gone by. You could see why someone would want to live here: the cave homes, now decorated with period furniture, are surprisingly roomy and have to-die-for views.

✖ Eating

Restaurante Mirador La Cilla   BARBECUE €€
(☏ 609 163944; Camino de la Cilla 9; mains €8-16; ⊙ 1-4pm & 7pm-late) A tunnel carved through the mountainside serves as the entrance to this long-standing restaurant. Book ahead to guarantee a table on the expansive terrace with marvellous views of Roque Nublo in the distance (and plenty more in the fore-

ground). The menu is meaty, with steaks cooked over an open fire on weekends.

ℹ️ Getting There & Away

Bus 220 runs hourly to/from Teror (€2.95, 1¼ hours), from where you can easily connect to Las Palmas.

There's a spectacularly vertiginous road (GC-210) connecting Artenara with Aldea de San Nicolás, but no buses brave this route.

Tejeda

POP 1485 / ELEV 1050M

Sitting in the centre of the island, Tejeda is a lovely hill village with a handsome church and steep, winding streets lined with balconied houses. Whichever route you take to get here, you drive through splendidly rugged scenery of looming cliffs and deep gorges. Although pretty at any time of year, the town is simply gorgeous in February when the almond trees are blossoming. A fiesta celebrates all things almondy once the trees have bloomed.

◉ Sights

This region is ideal for both hardcore hiking and less arduous walks. The tourist office has detailed brochures of surrounding trails.

Centro de Plantas Medicinales GARDENS
(📞 928 66 60 96; Calle Párroco Rodriguez Vega 10; adult/child €3/free; ⊙10am-4pm Mon-Fri, 10am-3pm Sat & Sun) An appealing garden that showcases medicinal plants with explanations (in English). There is a small interpretation centre and a cafe where you can fittingly end your visit with a cup of curative herbal tea.

Museo de las Tradiciones MUSEUM
(Calle Párroco Rodríguez Vega; adult/child €3/free; ⊙10am-4pm Mon-Fri, 10am-3pm Sat & Sun) Based in one of the town's most charming buildings, this museum gives a good overview of local life, starting with the Guanche era and covering the conquest, plus some interesting exhibits on agriculture in the mountains.

🍴 Eating

⭐ **Dulceria Nublo Tejeda** BAKERY €
(Calle Hernández Guerra 15; ⊙9.30am-10pm) The gastronomic highlight in town is this sublime pastry shop with delicious local treats freshly baked on the premises. Try the al-

mond cakes coated in chocolate and take home a jar of delicious *bienmesabe* (a sickly-sweet almond spread).

⭐ **Déjate Llevar** BISTRO €€
(📞637 083694; www.letmetakeu.com; Calle Doctor Domingo Hernández Guerra 25; mains €6-12; ⊙1-4pm & 7pm-late Wed-Sun; 🎤🍴) With its arty, minimalist decor and bistro-style menu awash with vegetarian options, this place is an unexpected gem. The inventive salads offer a healthy alternative to all the rabbit and goat stews around, and there is a range of freshly squeezed juices or, for those not tackling the winding roads after lunch, a selection of local wines. Reservations recommended.

ℹ️ Information

Tourist Office (www.tejedaturistica.com; Avenida de los Almendros; ⊙10am-5pm Mon-Fri, to 4pm Sat & Sun) In a kiosk near the petrol station at the south entrance of town.

ℹ️ Getting There & Away

Bus 305 (€2.55, one hour, six daily) connects Tejeda to San Mateo, from where there are frequent connections to Las Palmas.

Around Tejeda

Cruz de Tejeda

The greenish-grey stone cross from which this spot takes its name marks the centre of Gran Canaria and its historic *caminos reales* (king's highways), along which it is still possible to cross the entire island. The site is one of the most popular coach-tour destinations from the resorts, so is usually swarming with tourists – hence the souvenir stalls and donkey rides.

From the lookouts here you can contemplate the island's greatest natural wonders: to the west is the sacred mountain Roque Bentayga and, in clear weather, you can see the towering volcanic pyramid of Teide on neighbouring Tenerife; to the southeast is the island's highest peak, Pozo de las Nieves, and the extraordinary emblem of the island, Roque Nublo, often enveloped in cloud as its name suggests. Dropping away to the northeast is Vega de San Mateo.

From here there are walks of all levels, from half-hour strolls on paved paths to five-hour treks through the mountains. The

12.5km circular route from Cruz de Tejeda to Roque Nublo is especially recommended. Allow about 3½ hours and take warm clothing, however hot the day might appear. You can get information and tips from Hotel El Refugio or the **tourist office** (⊙10am-5pm) next to the large, free car park. If you prefer to join a group, try **Walk in Gran Canaria** (ww.walkingrancanaria.com; day hikes per person from €40), who have scheduled hikes throughout the mountains on weekdays. There are a couple of very touristy restaurants in Cruz de Tejeda, or for something a little fancier try the Parador.

Bus 305 (€1.45; one hour, six daily) from San Mateo passes by on its way to Tejeda.

Roque Bentayga

A few kilometres west of Tejeda village rises Roque Bentayga (1404m). It's signposted but you will need your own transport. There are various reminders of the Guanche presence here – from rock inscriptions to granaries and a sacred ritual site. Don't miss the **Centro de Interpretación** (⊙10am-4pm Mon-Fri, to 5pm Sat & Sun) FREE at the base of the rock. It offers excellent insight into the pre-Hispanic settlement of Gran Canaria's central mountains. Ask about walking trails to visit the caves that would once have housed Guanche families.

Pozo de las Nieves

Those with their own wheels can drive 15km southeast of Tejeda to the highest peak on the island (1949m). Follow the signs for Los Pechos and keep an eye out for the military communications post that sits atop the rise. On a clear day the views are breathtaking. Due northwest of here stands the distinctive Roque Nublo.

Roque Nublo

The island's icon is an impressive monolith (1803m), jutting skywards 80m out of the surrounding volcanic landscape. It sneaks into the background of virtually every photo you take in the area, but it's worth approaching to get an up-close shot as well. The half-hour walk from the roadside has a few steep sections, but isn't too challenging and the views are wonderful.

San Bartolomé de Tirajana

POP 5800 / ELEV 890M

San Bartolomé is a pretty town with a number of lookout points offering awesome views over the Tirajana Valley. If you're looking for something to do, the 17th-century **church** with its striking stained-glass windows is worth a look. This is a grape-growing region and in the upper part of town, near the hotel, you'll find **Bodega Las Tirajanas** (www.bodegaslastirajanas.com; Calle Las Lagunas; tastings per wine €1; ⊙10am-4pm Mon-Fri, to 2pm Sat & Sun). You can drop by for a casual tasting, but book ahead for a tour and a sampler of local cheese, olives and *mojo* with your wine. San Bartolomé makes a good base for hiking and exploring the surrounding mountainous countryside; there are several signposted trails.

There is a small free car park on Calle Los Naranjos at the north entrance of the town.

✖ Eating

La Panera de Tunte   BAKERY
(Calle Reyes Católicos; ⊙7.30am-8pm Mon-Sat, to 3pm Sun) Whether you're hiking or driving, the mountains surrounding San Bartolomé are definitely picnic worthy. Stop at this long-running cafe-bakery to put together an al fresco lunch of cured meat, fresh bread and local cheese. With tables out in the square, it's also a nice spot to stop for coffee and a slice of cake.

Fataga

The 7km drive from San Bartolomé south to Fataga is as drop-dead gorgeous as the hamlet itself, sitting squat on a small knoll humbled by lofty cliffs to the west. Its cobbled lanes are a joy to roam, especially as there are at least three bodegas in this vine-growing centre – all are well signposted but, less happily, all have sporadic opening hours.

About 1.5km north of the village, parts of **El Molino del Agua** (☑928 17 23 03; Ctra Fataga; mains €10-15; ⊙1-4pm & 7pm-late) hacienda date back to the 16th century. The historic mill is hidden among a grove of around 1000 palm trees, and also offers accommodation. The restaurant has tables under the orange trees and a reasonable Canarian menu.

Located on the main road in Fataga, **Bar Restaurante La Albaricoque** (Calle Nestor

Álamo 4; mains €7-12; ⊙1-4pm & 7pm-late Wed-Mon; 🗟) is good for tapas and has sound local fare, including croquettes with a range of fillings, *ropa vieja* and *carne de cabra* (goat meat stew). The main draw, however, is the outside terrace with its wall-to-wall mountain views.

Bus 18 (€2.65, 50 minutes, four times daily) from Maspalomas to San Bartolomé stops here.

THE SOUTH

Playa Del Inglés & Maspalomas

POP AROUND 30,000

This is Gran Canaria's most famous holiday resort and a sun-splashed party place for a mainly Northern European crowd. That said, during the day (and out of season) it has a more upmarket appearance than you might expect. This is not Benidorm, nor even Los Cristianos in Tenerife. In the centre you are more likely to stumble across expensive hotels or smart apartment blocks than Dot-and-Alf-style English pubs. On the downside, there is virtually nothing that is even halfway Spanish here; everything is tourist-driven and the only languages you'll need are German or English. The town plan is also undeniably soulless, with the neatly traced boulevards and roundabouts betraying all the town-design spontaneity of a five-year plan.

At night, most of the action takes place in and around the Yumbo Centrum, with the leather handbags and wallets in the stores replaced by leather gear in steamy gay bars. The vaguely wholesome, bustling family atmosphere evaporates as the discos (both straight and gay) swing until dawn, barrels and bottles are drained by the dozen in bars, and the drag shows, saunas and sex shops all do a roaring trade.

The only natural items of genuine interest are the impressive dunes of Maspalomas, which are also home to some of Gran Canaria's most luxurious hotels and the island's largest golf course. The dunes fold back from the beach and cover 400 hectares, and their inland heart has been declared a nature reserve with restricted access.

There are bus stops all over the resort, including a couple beside Yumbo.

◉ Sights & Activities

Dunas de Maspalomas   NATURE RESERVE

These fabulous dunes were designated a nature reserve back in the 1990s, ensuring that the rapidly multiplying hotels would never encroach on their golden sand. The best view of the dunes is from the bottom of Avenida Tirajana. Stroll through the arches of the Hotel Riu Palace Maspalomas to the balcony, which is surrounded by a botanical garden displaying many shrubs and plants native to the Canaries. There is a small information office here with sporadic opening hours.

Although the dunes look too pristine to blight with footprints, you *can* walk on the sand, but do respect the signs and keep to the designated trails. Alternatively, you can go the full Sahara and opt for a camel trip with **Camello Safari** (☑928 76 07 81; www.camellosafari.com; adult/child €12/8; ⊙9am-4.30pm).

Centro de Talasoterapia   SPA

(Thalassotherapy Centre; ☑928 77 64 04; www.gloriapalaceth.com; Hotel Gloria Palace, Calle Las Margaritas, San Agustín; 2hr circuit €23; ⊙10am-9pm) Massive and luxurious, this is Europe's largest centre for thalassotherapy – a relaxing spa therapy that uses heated seawater. The standard treatment at the 7000-sq-metre complex is a circuit featuring a variety of jacuzzi-type treatments, saunas and an ice cave. Massages, facials and the like are also available.

Theme Parks

There are a multitude of theme parks with brochures and advertising everywhere. The following are some popular, long-standing choices. The tourist office can advise on appropriate bus routes and times – some parks offer a free bus service from the resorts.

Palmitos Park   ZOO

(www.palmitospark.es; adult/child €30/22; ⊙10am-6pm; 🔄) Palmitos is a subtropical park crammed with exotic flora and 1500 species of birds, along with an aquarium, orchid exhibit, petting farm and animals such as wallabies and orang-utans. There is a discount for online bookings. Note that the park also runs dolphin shows, which may sound lovely but dolphin performances have received criticism from animal welfare groups who claim the captivity of marine life is debilitating and stressful for the animals, and that this is exacerbated by human interaction.

The park is located a few kilometres north of the Playa Del Inglés resort area.

GAY GRAN CANARIA

Gran Canaria is the gay honeypot of the Canaries, and Playa del Inglés is Europe's winter escape playground. There are several hotels and apartment blocks that cater towards gay and lesbian guests. A seemingly endless string of bars, discos and clubs are crammed into the Yumbo Centrum, which is predominantly a gay scene, although this doesn't stop small numbers of lesbians and straights from wading in. Little happens before midnight. From then until about 3am the bars on the 4th level of the Yumbo Centrum bear the brunt of the fun, after which the nightclubs on the 2nd level take over.

At dawn, people stagger out for some rest. Some make for the beach at Maspalomas, across the dunes, which are themselves a busy gay cruising area.

Maspalomas Pride (www.gaypridemaspalomas.com; ☺May) consists of 10 days of parades, concerts, excursions and parties.

For more information about gay clubs, events, accommodation and personal classifieds, check the following websites: www.gaygrancanaria.com, www.gaymap.info and www.grancanariagay.com.

Mundo Aborigen   AMUSEMENT PARK
(www.mundoaborigen.es; Carretera Playa del Inglés-Fataga; adult/child €10/5; ☺9am-6pm; 🚍) Situated 6km along the road north to Fataga, around 100 model Guanches stand in various ancient poses designed to give you an idea of what life was like before the conquistadors turned up to build theme parks.

Aqualand   WATER PARK
(www.aqualand.es; Carretera Palmitos Park; adult/child €26/18.50; ☺10am-5pm; 🚍) An enormous water park with miles of rides and slides.

Camel Safari Park La Baranda   CAMEL RIDES
(www.camelsafarigrancanaria.com; Carretera Playa del Inglés-Fataga; 1hr ride €25; ☺9am-6pm; 🚍) Has 70 camels and is located in a lush property with palm, avocado and citrus trees 13km north of Playa del Inglés. There is also a restaurant, bar and small zoo.

Watersports

Although surfing is possible here (the best waves tend to break off the western end of Maspalomas by the lighthouse), this is not mind-blowing territory. Windsurfers are better off heading east, beyond the resorts to Bahía Feliz, Playa Aguila and, best of all, **Pozo Izquierdo**, 25km along the coast.

Club Mistral   WINDSURFING
(☎928 15 71 58; www.club-mistral.com; Carretera General del Sur, Km 47, Playa de Tarajalillo; 6hr beginner's windsurfing course €140) Rents bodyboards, surfboards, ocean kayaks, windsurfing boards and equipment in Bahía Feliz. It also organises windsurf safaris.

Dive Academy Gran Canaria   DIVING
(☎928 73 61 96; www.diveacademy-grancanaria.com; Calle La Lajilla, Arguineguín; initiation dives from €46, advanced open-water course €270) Has a free minibus to pick up plungers from their hotels and take them to the dive academy, due west of town. Both boat and shore dives are available.

Prosurfing Company   SURFING
(☎628 104025; www.prosurfingcompany.com; Avenida de Moya 6, CC Eurocenter; 1-day surf course €49, board & wetsuit rental per day €30) A well-regarded company offering surfing, kitesurfing, windsurfing and stand-up paddleboarding (SUP) lessons, as well as board and wetsuit hire.

Canaries Extreme   KAYAKING
(☎675 911923; www.canariasextreme.com; Calle Alféreces Provisionales 33; 3hr kayak tour €49) If you are looking for a watery pursuit more adrenalin-boosting than a glass-bottom boat, this outfit organises single- and double-kayak tours along the coast.

Other Sports

To enjoy an exhilarating (and free) 5km walk, simply follow the promenade that extends eastwards from Playa del Inglés. The path follows a track that is sometimes at shore level and sometimes above it.

★Free Motion   CYCLING
(☎928 77 74 79; www.free-motion.net; Hotel Sandy Beach, Avenida Alféreces Provisionales; bike hire per day from €14, tours per day from €49) This slickly run company offers a range of tours for small groups, and has mountain, road and city bikes for rental. The company will

arrange transport to/from various resorts on the coast, including Puerto Rico and Puerto de Mogán, for a small fee.

Happy Biking
CYCLING

(✆ 828 12 57 95; www.happy-biking.com; Avenida de Gran Canaria 30, Centro Comercial Gran Chaparral; bike hire per day from €10; ⊙ 9-11am & 5-7pm Mon-Sat) Rents out a range of cycles and also organises serious cycling trips, starting at 60km, which include bike hire, transport and refreshments (€60).

Happy Horse
HORSE RIDING

(✆ 658 925286; www.happy-horse.org; 3hr trek €65) Organises one-, two- and three-hour horse treks in the hinterland southeast of town. Pickup from your hotel is included in the price.

🏊 Beaches

Playa del Inglés
BEACH

Aside from the magnificent Maspalomas dunes, the main attraction for the thousands of annual visitors to the island's quintessential package-tour destination is the resort's beach, a magnificent and vast sandy beach stretching 2.7km. Beaches, from east to west, are **Playa de las Burras** (San Agustín), **Playa del Corralillo**, **Playa del Inglés** and **Playa de Maspalomas**. They all link up to form one long, spectacular beach.

🍴 Eating

The resort is predictably swarming with restaurants, with the normal mix of Chinese buffets, Argentinean grills, bland international and that increasingly rare breed – authentic Spanish.

El Salsete
MODERN CANARIAN €€

(✆ 928 77 82 55; www.elsalsete.com; edificio Jovimar Bloque 1, Calle Secundino Delgado,; mains €12-

---

> ### ℹ️ IT'S A LONG WALK FOR A SWIM
>
> The abundant apartments and hotels stretch from the shoreline to the San Fernando area, some 2km inland. Although there are buses that head to and from the beach, they may not coincide with your timetable. If you have booked a room somewhere here and it is suspiciously cheap, be sure to check the exact location; there are far pleasanter parts of the island to stretch your legs.

18; ⊙ 1-4pm & 7pm-late Mon-Sat) Off the beaten tourist path in the north of the San Fernando district, the unassuming facade conceals a welcoming dining room offering food that wouldn't be out of place at a cutting-edge restaurant in Barcelona. Dishes are creative in taste and presentation, and use only market-fresh ingredients. Reservations recommended.

Mundo
FUSION €€

(✆ 928 76 10 63; Apartamentos Tenesor, Avenida Tirajana 9; mains €10-18; ⊙ closed Sat lunch, Sun; 🌱) An oasis of fashionable sophistication, Mundo has seriously raised the culinary game in these parts. Think American-diner-meets-Japanese, with a spruce-minimalist dining room, retro black-and-white tiles and cherry-red chairs. Try the black pasta with king prawns. Reservations recommended.

Casa Vieja
CANARIAN €€

(Calle El Lomo 139, Carretera de Fataga; mains €8-15; ⊙ 1-4pm & 7pm-late) Just north of the GC-1 motorway along the road to Fataga, this restaurant is run with passion. The 'Old House' has a real *campo* (countryside) feel. Plants festoon the low roof, canaries trill and the menu is pretty authentic; try the grilled meats. There is live traditional music from 8pm most nights.

⭐ Samsara
FUSION €€€

(✆ 928 14 27 36; www.samsara-gc.com; Avenida Oasis 30; mains €18-25; ⊙ 7pm-late Tue-Sat) Located across from the Palm Beach Hotel, a giant Buddha statue sets an appropriate tone. Dishes blend Canarian and Spanish ingredients with Asian flavours – think smoked goats' cheese with wasabi or seafood pasta spiced with lemongrass. Reservations recommended.

Restaurante La Toja
MEDITERRANEAN €€€

(✆ 928 76 11 96; edificio Barbados II, cnr Avenidas Tirajana & EE UU; mains €15-25; ⊙ 1-4pm & 7pm-late) A quality establishment blending the best of cuisines from France and Galicia. Try the veal in Marsala wine or troubling-sounding elephant's ear with chips (actually a thin fillet of steak). There is also a range of rice dishes designed to feed two.

🍷 Drinking & Entertainment

The Yumbo Centrum transforms into a pulsating clubbers' scene at night. There are straight and gay places in the centre and you could stagger around Yumbo Centrum – as many do – for weeks and not sample all the nightlife options.

WORLD CLASS WINDSURFING

The windswept but likeable town of **Pozo Izquierdo**, 25km northeast of Playa del Inglés, has just one reason for being – windsurfing. In June and July, the town fills up with enthusiasts when it stages a leg of the Windsurfing World Cup. The rest of the year it's a quiet place, but the conditions for windsurfing are always fine.

There are a number of companies offering equipment rental and classes. Try **Cutre Windsurf School** (📷 928 79 13 04; www.cutre.com; equipment hire with insurance per day €75, 10hr beginner course €150), who conduct their lessons via radio-connected helmets, or **Pozo Winds** (📷 928 15 50 09; www.pozowinds.com; 10hr beginner course €140), who also offer windsurfing, kitesurfing and stand-up paddleboarding (SUP) lessons. The schools can organise accommodation or there's a large hostel at the **Centro Internacional de Windsurfing** (📷 928 12 14 00; www.pozo-ciw.com; Calle Centro Internacional de Windsurfing; dm/d with shared bathroom €18/32; 🅿 🛜 ✼), right on the beachfront with ocean views from the dorms.

Live music can be hit or miss. A long-running place with Irish music and Guinness on tap is **Dunes & Tunes** (www.dunesandtunes.com; Beach Blvd, Playa del Inglés; ◷8.30pm-late). If you're looking for a club with big name DJs, head to upmarket **Pacha** (www.pachagrancanaria.com; Avenida Sargentos Provisionales 10; ◷11pm-5am).

🛍 Shopping

The main shopping centres are north of the centre in San Fernando and Bellavista. In them you can buy everything from children's wear to electronics.

Fedac   CRAFTS
(Centro Insular del Turismo, cnr Avenidas España & EE UU; ◷10am-2pm & 4-7.30pm Mon-Fri) If you're after local handicrafts, visit the small Fedac shop located within the main tourist office. Fedac is a government-sponsored nonprofit store, with prices and quality that are a good standard by which to measure those of products sold elsewhere. You'll also get a guarantee with your purchase.

Yumbo Centrum   SHOPPING CENTRE
(www.cc-yumbo.com; Avenida EE UU; ◷24hr) There are more than 200 businesses in this four-level commercial centre. You can buy tax-free shoes, leather goods, perfume and anything else you fancy, although the quality should be checked. There are also supermarkets on the premises.

❶ Information

Main Tourist Office (www.grancanaria.com; cnr Avenidas España & EE UU; ◷9am-6pm Mon-Fri, to 1pm Sat) Just outside the Yumbo Centrum, with maps, helpful staff and public toilets.

Playa del Inglés Tourist Office (Commercial Centre Anexo 11, Local 20; ◷9am-6pm Mon-Fri, to 1pm Sat) Smaller tourist office with a convenient location on the main beach.

❶ Getting There & Away

Buses link regularly with points along the coast, westwards as far as Puerto de Mogán (€4.15, 45 minutes) and eastwards to the capital. For Las Palmas (€6.15, one hour), take express lines 30 or 50 (nonstop). There is also a night bus (line 5) if you're seeking *marcha* (nightlife) at the other end of the island. The tourist office has timetables covering both the southern and northern routes.

❶ Getting Around

TO/FROM THE AIRPORT
Bus 66 runs to/from the airport (€3.75, 30 minutes, hourly) until about 8pm. For a taxi, budget for about €35 for Playa del Inglés and €40 for Maspalomas.

BUS
Global (www.globalsu.net) runs buses to many of the theme parks. The fare for a standard run within town is €1.40.

CAR
If you must take your car down to the beach, there's a large paying car park beside Playa del Inglés. Street parking costs from €0.50 for 30 minutes.

TAXI
Taxi stands abound and are reliable; otherwise, you can call for a **taxi** (📷 928 76 67 67). From Playa del Inglés, no destination within the urban area should cost more than €10.

SCENIC DRIVE: BEACH DETOUR

If you want more space on the sand, there are several choice beaches on the coast hugging the GC-500 road, west of Playa del Inglés. Follow the signs to the town hospital and Puerto de Mogán from the centre (top of Avenida Tirajana), passing Holiday World on your left. The road climbs past palm plantations and the golf course, Meloneras Golf. At Km 7 watch for the **Pasito Bea** sign, turning left on the rough approach that leads to a small black sandy cove secluded by rocks, which is mixed nude and clothed.

After a quick dip continue along the road, which winds around arid hills and, after 1.2km, comes to **Playa de Carpinteras**. Follow the track east of the main beach here, park on the cliffs and you will discover an idyllic, little-known (until now!) broad arc of sand with shallow water backed by sloping dunes. Known as the **Playa de Montaña Arenas**, you can clamber around the rocks due east of here to reach the beach, which, again, is mixed nude and clothed. The third beach worth recommending is at Km 9.2. **Playa de Triana** is a black pebbly beach, with parking on the main road; note that you will be expected to wear your clothes here!

Follow the road a further 4km to a roundabout, where it rejoins the GC-1 heading towards the vastly more commercial beaches of Puerto Rico and beyond.

Puerto Rico & Arguineguín

While Maspalomas has redeeming features – the shape of its natural dunes and its superbly unnatural nightlife – its resort cousins further west are a good example of how greedy developers can destroy a coastline that shares a similar setting to Italy's Amalfi Coast. Around every corner it seems there is yet another resort surrounded by steep banks of apartment blocks stretching into the hinterland.

Parts of the port area of Arguineguín still remain true to its roots as a small, active fishing settlement, but overall it's a nondescript town with a couple of rather scrubby beaches. If you are here at lunchtime, check out the **Cofradía de Pescadores** (Muelle Pesquero de Arguineguin; mains €8-15; ⊘ closed Wed & Sep), which, despite the plastic tablecloths and disarming six-language menu, buys its catch of the day directly from the fishing boats. Arguineguín is also home to a well-respected diving school.

Puerto Rico is a fine example of appalling town planning: the original fishing village has disappeared under a sea of concrete, with the apartment blocks stacked up like stadium seats against the mountains. The beach is pleasant but certainly not large enough to cater for the number of beds here. The only escape is the multitude of boat trips that depart from the harbour, including the dolphin-spotting **Spirit of the Sea** (☑928 56 22 29; www.dolphin-whale.com; adult/child €27/14), offering two-hour trips in glass-bottom catamarans, with a complimentary second trip offered if you don't spot any cetaceans the first time around.

The resorts further west, including Playa del Cura, Playa del Tauro and **Taurito**, are of a similar ilk. At least the latter has made an effort to gear itself to families, with a vast landscaped lido with lagoon-style pools, tennis courts, minigolf, gym equipment, bars and sun beds on a grey sandy beach. The waters here are flat, smooth as glass and safe for swimming.

Half-hourly buses connect Puerto Rico and Arguineguín with Maspalomas and Playa del Inglés (€2, 30 minutes) and with Puerto de Mogán (€1.55, 15 minutes) and Las Palmas (€7.55, one hour 45 minutes). If you prefer to travel by boat, **Lineas Blue Bird** (☑629 989633; www.lineasbluebird.com) offers an hourly service to Puerto de Mogán from Arguineguín (adult/child €6.50, 70 minutes) and Puerto Rico (adult/child €6.50/3.50, 30 minutes).

Puerto de Mogán

West of Taurito, a couple of kilometres of rugged coastline recall what this whole southern stretch of the island must have been like 50 years ago, before mass tourism descended on the Canaries.

Finally you round a bend; below you is a tempting crescent of sandy beach and, next to it, a busy little yacht harbour and fishing port. Puerto de Mogán, although now largely given over to the tourist trade, is light years from its garish counterparts to the east. Thankfully, even the recent construction inland is more aesthetically pleasing than in other resorts along this coast.

Although its nickname 'Venice of the Canaries' may be a tad exaggerated, the architecture and bridged waterways are as pretty as a chocolate box, and the whole place exudes an air of opulence and charm. In the heart of the port, low-rise apartments have wrought-iron balconies, brightly coloured trim and are covered in dazzling bougainvillea.

On the downside, the place gets packed during the day with envious tourists from the other resorts, particularly on Friday morning when a street market takes over part of the town. Stalls sell the usual over-priced belts, bags and shell jewellery; if you are staying here, it's a good day to leave.

☉ Sights & Activities

Tucked among the restaurants and bars on the Calle Los Pescadores, the simple **Ermita de San Fernando** church dates back to 1936. You can take a peek inside during mass at 6pm on Tuesday and Saturday.

The waters here are a little calm for the likes of surfing or windsurfing, but it's a great place for scuba diving and snorkelling, with caves and wrecks just offshore.

Atlantik Diving   DIVING
(☑ 689 352049; www.grancanariadiveresort.com; Hotel Puerto de Mogán, Playa de Mogán; single dive with equipment hire €40) Offers courses at all levels, from a Discover Scuba experience (three hours, €90) to Dive Master (minimum 20 days, €720).

Canary Diving Adventures   DIVING
(☑ 928 56 54 28; www.canary-diving.com; Hotel Taurito Princess, Playa de Taurito) Offers guided boat dives (€40 including equipment hire), four-day PADI certification courses (€340) and one-day beginner courses in their pool (€75).

✕ Eating

There are plenty of cafes and restaurants offering fresh fish on pleasant *terrazas*.

La Cucina   ITALIAN €
(Calle Corriente 8; pizzas €6-9; ⏱1-4pm & 7pm-late) Run by Italians, this tiny place is predominantly a takeaway but has a few outside tables. The pizzas come highly recommended, and there is also a good range of pasta dishes and salads, plus the obligatory creamy tiramisu. It's set back from the main complex in the old part of town.

Jack El Negro   BARBECUE €€
(Pasaje Pescadores 6; mains €12-16; ⏱1-4pm & 7pm-late) Housed in one of precious few original fishermen's cottages, this restaurant has carafe-loads of earthy atmosphere. It is named after a legendary Caribbean pirate and run by Italian owner Claudio since 1970 (hence the Chianti bottle candleholders). A speciality is the steaks cooked to a tee on a *parilla* (open grill). The pizzas also come recommended.

La Bodeguilla Juananá   MEDITERRANEAN €€
(Plaza Mayor; mains €8-22; ⏱1-4pm & 7pm-late) Tucked into the corner of grandly named Plaza Mayor in front of the yacht harbour, this restaurant is run with passion. The decor has an African theme and the gastro-flair dishes include daily specials like black pudding fried with an avocado and garlic sauce. There are a dozen cheese-based dishes on the menu, showcasing Canarian *queso*.

Patio Canario   SEAFOOD €€
(www.restaurantemogan.com; Urbanización Puerto de Mogán; mains €15-20; ⏱1-4pm & 7pm-late) This popular place enjoys an ace position with two sprawling terraces overlooking the small harbour. The menu includes such dishes as oven-baked king prawns with fresh coriander; there are meaty options as well as

GRAN CANARIA PUERTO DE MOGÁN

PACK A PICNIC

Consider substituting sand in your sandwiches and sunbeds on the beach for a picnic with civilised tables and benches, coupled with idyllic lakeside surroundings. Head 2.5km beyond Mogán and take the GC-605, surrounded by truly bucolic scenery with massive rocks, lofty mountains and clusters of palm and pine trees. About 10km after the turnoff you come to the **Cruz de San Antonio** mirador, from where there are dramatic views of the lake and snaking road below. There is a lovely signposted walk to Inagua from here (10km). The road continues winding through the Pinar de Pajonales pine woods until you reach your destination: the **Presa de las Cuevas de las Niñas** lake and those strategically positioned picnic tables by the water. The journey from Mogán will take just under an hour. From here you could turn back or continue on to Tejeda and the highest peaks on the island.

fish. The food is good though the service is a little lacking.

★ **Qué Tal by Stena**   MODERN SPANISH €€€
(928 56 55 34; www.quetalbystena.com; Urbanización de Puerto de Mogan; 5-course menu €60; 7pm-late) With contemporary paintings from local artists hanging on the walls, white tablecloths and an exquisite set menu that changes regularly, Qué Tal is the place to come for a special dinner. Opt for the wine pairing option (€45) to sample some special vintages from the cellar. There is one sitting daily at 7.30pm. Reservations highly recommended.

ℹ **Getting There & Around**

BUS

There is no shortage of buses heading east to Puerto Rico (€1.55, 15 minutes) and Playa del Inglés (€2, 45 minutes). Bus 1 (€8.75, two hours) departs hourly for Las Palmas. Ferries also run between the port and Puerto Rico (adult/child €6.50/3.50, 30 minutes).

CAR

There are two underground car parks; the cheapest is on Calle La Mina, signposted as you come into town, and there are generally spaces. There is blue-zone street parking throughout the centre (€1.80 per hour).

Mogán

POP 1415

Just as Puerto de Mogán is a relief from the south coast's relentless armies of apartments, bungalows and Guinness on tap, so the GC-200 road north from the port is another leap away from the crowds. As it ascends gradually up a wide valley towards Mogán, just 8km away, you pass craggy mountains and orchards of avocados, the main crop in these parts.

Mogán is a relaxed, unspoilt small town in a lovely mountainous setting. Although there are no real attractions, it's a lovely, relaxing spot for lunch or a stroll.

✖ **Eating**

Most of the town's restaurants and bars are on the winding main street of Calle San José.

El Tomate   CANARIAN €
(Calle San José; mains €8-10; closed lunch Sun) The most stylish restaurant in town serves traditional dishes like goat stew and *ropa vieja* alongside a fairly standard tapas menu.

Restaurante Acaymo   CANARIAN €€
(www.restauranteacaymo.com; Carretera General Km 15; mains €12-18, menú del día €12.50; 1-4pm & 7pm-late; ℗) Don't let the flags fluttering outside put you off – longstanding Acaymo is as popular with locals as it is with tourists. It's best known for meat, with veal, lamb, rabbit and steaks on the menu. You'll also find Canarian classics like *gofio escaldado de pescado* (a thick stew of gofio and fish broth). Self-catering accommodation is available.

Casa Enrique   CANARIAN €€
(Calle San José 7; mains €9-15; 1-4pm & 7pm-late) Serves up sound Canarian dishes, superb coffee and cakes.

Mogán to Aldea de San Nicolás

From Mogán, the GC-200 winds off to the northwest, travelling 26km through some spectacularly craggy mountains to Aldea de San Nicolás, though the final approach is sadly blighted by the surrounding sea of plastic greenhouses. Stop for a glass of fresh papaya juice at **Las Cañadas** (tapas €4-7; 9am-7pm Fri-Wed), around 8km from Mogán on your left-hand side. This is an agreeably quirky restaurant and bar with stunning views plus the added appeal of turtles, a chameleon and a small museum with old agricultural equipment, radios and the like. You can also buy local honey and the largest avocados you have ever seen (when in season).

The winding road continues through **Los Azulejos**, a colourful rock formation created by different-coloured minerals of brilliant greens, yellows and ochres. To avoid a head-on collision, take your photos from the signposted **Fuente de los Azulejos Mirador** lookout, where you'll find a fabulous juice stand.

Fuerteventura

♪928 / POP 107,000

Best Beaches

➡ Playa de Cofete (p96)
➡ Parque Natural de Corralejo (p86)
➡ Playa de la Barca (p93)
➡ Playa de la Mujer (p85)

Best Places to Stay

➡ Casa Isaítas (p222)
➡ Hotel Rural Mahoh (p222)
➡ Soulsurfer Hotel (p222)

Why Go?

Fuerteventura lies just 100km from the African coast, and there are striking similarities not only with the landscape, but also the houses, with their North African–style flat roofs for collecting rainfall. In other ways, Fuerteventura emulates its neighbour Lanzarote, only with more colours. Its volcanoes resemble piles of saffron, chilli and coriander, surreal triangles of exotic spices.

Most visitors, however, are more interested in mastering the waves and the wind than contemplating the abstract aesthetics of the scenery. The second-largest island in the archipelago (after Tenerife), Fuerteventura has year-round sunshine and the biggest and best beaches in the Canaries.

The main tourist resorts lie at opposite ends of the island. At the northern tip is Corralejo, beloved by British sun-seekers, while deep down south lies Morro Jable, largely frequented by Germans and a markedly staider place.

The island was declared a Unesco Biosphere Reserve in 2009.

When to Go

➡ High season runs from December to February, with accommodation filling up well in advance; temperatures are slightly cooler with prevailing winds, but still pleasant.

➡ Late spring (April to May) is perfect temperature-wise, although Easter can mean crowded beaches.

➡ Spanish holidaymakers favour the islands in July and August, along with families travelling with school-age children. Temperatures often surpass 30°C, though it rarely gets stiflingly hot. The Windsurfing World Cup takes place in July.

➡ Autumn is a great time for festivals, including Corralejo's Kite Festival and the Fiesta de la Virgen del Rosario in the capital. Average daytime temperatures hover around the agreeable 20°C mark, while nights gradually become cooler.

History

Fuerteventura has had several names in history, ranging from the Roman's unimaginative Planaria ('Plains', due to the island's overall flatness), to the considerably more exciting Fuerteventura (Strong Adventure), which dates from the first European conquerors. Ruled by the Norman nobleman Jean de Béthencourt, the conquerors turned up in 1405 to find the island divided into two tribal kingdoms separated by a low 6km-long wall. Jandía occupied the southern peninsula, as far north as La Pared; Maxorata controlled the rest of the island.

Béthencourt established a permanent base, including a chapel, in the mountainous zone of what came to be known as Betancuria, with Santa María de Betancuria evolving as the island's capital. The choice of location was determined by the natural water supply that is still in evidence: this is one of the lushest regions on the island. The mountainous location also created a measure of natural defence against those dastardly pirate raids.

New settlements spread slowly across the island and, in the 17th century, Europeans occupied El Cotillo, once the seat of the Guanche Maxorata kingdom. At this time, the Arias and Saavedra families took control of the *señorío* (the island government deputising for the Spanish crown). By the following century, however, officers of the island militia had established themselves as a rival power base in La Oliva. Los Coroneles (the Colonels) gradually took virtual control of the island's affairs, enriching themselves at the expense of the hard-pressed peasantry. You can learn more about their reign by visiting their extraordinary former home: Casa de los Coroneles in La Oliva.

The militia was disbanded in 1834 and, in 1912, the island, along with others in the archipelago, was granted a degree of self-administration with the installation of the *cabildo* (local authority).

ⓘ Getting There & Away

AIR

Fuerteventura airport (☑ 902 40 47 04; www.aena.es) is 6km south of Puerto del Rosario in El Matorral. **Binter Canarias** (www.binternet.com) has direct flights to Gran Canaria and Tenerife, from where you can fly on to the other islands.

ROAD DISTANCES (KM)

	Puerto del Rosario	Corralejo	El Cotillo	Caleta de Fuste
Corralejo	32			
El Cotillo	58	20		
Caleta de Fuste	10	36	56	
Costa Calma	64	90	87	56

Approximate distances only

BOAT

Fred Olsen (☑ 902 10 01 07; www.fredolsen.es) Ferries leave seven times daily from Corralejo for Playa Blanca (€27, 25 minutes) in Lanzarote. You can buy tickets at the port in Corralejo. There's also a service from Morro Jable to Las Palmas de Gran Canaria (€45, two hours, twice daily).

Naviera Armas (☑ 928 54 21 13, in Corralejo & Morro Jable 902 45 65 00; www.navieraarmas.com) Six daily ferries leave Corralejo for Playa Blanca (€26, 35 minutes) in Lanzarote. From Morro Jable, daily ferries leave for Las Palmas de Gran Canaria (€41, three hours) and to Santa Cruz de Tenerife (€70, 6½ hours). From Puerto del Rosario there are ferries to Las Palmas de Gran Canaria (€35, 6½ hours) and Santa Cruz de Tenerife (€62, 11 hours) at 11am from Tuesday to Saturday.

Trasmediterránea (☑ in Puerto del Rosario 902 45 46 45; www.trasmediterranea.es) Operates a weekly service to Puerto del Rosario from Las Palmas de Gran Canaria (€33, six hours) on Saturdays. There are also indirect boats from Santa Cruz de Tenerife and Santa Cruz de La Palma, but journeys are long and you'd be better on a plane.

ⓘ Getting Around

BUS

Tiadhe has 17 bus routes covering the main destinations across the island.

CAR

Driving is a pleasure here; the terrain is largely flat and the roads excellent. Cicar is a reliable local car-rental choice, with offices at the airport, Puerto del Rosario and all the main resorts.

Map Labels

Playa Blanca
(Lanzarote)

Isla de
Lobos

Majanicho

The Bubble

Corralejo

Faro de
Tostón

Parque Natural
de Corralejo
(Grandes Playas)

Los Lagos

El Burro

El Cotillo

Lajares

FV-101

FV-10

FV-1

Montaña de
Tindaya
(401m)

Villaverde

Esquinzo

La Oliva

Playa de la Mujer

Tindaya

La Matilla

ATLANTIC
OCEAN

Los Molinos

FV-211

Tefía

Tetir

FV-10

FV-207

Arrecife
(Lanzarote)

Ecomuseo la Alcogida

Puerto del
Rosario

Los Llanos de
la Concepción

Casillas del
Ángel

Playa
Blanca

Valle de
Santa Inés

La Ampuyenta

Parque Natural
de Betancuria

FV-20

Mirador Morro Velosa

Betancuria

Antigua

Calete
de Fuste

Ajuy & Puerto
de la Peña

FV-621

Gran
Montaña
(708m)

Vega de
Río Palmas

FV-30

FV-2

Tiscamanita

Las
Salinas

Pájara

Tuineje

FV-605

Pozo Negro

FV-20

FV-2

Playa de
la Pared

Las Playitas

Faro de la
Entallada

La Pared

El Brasero

Giniginamar

Playa del
Gran Tarajal

Playa de
Barlovento de
Jandía

Costa
Calma

La Lajita

Tarajalejo

Gran
Tarajal

Pico de la
Zarza (807m)

Cofete

Playa de Sotavento
de Jandía

Puerto de
la Cruz

Península de Jandía

FV-2

ATLANTIC
OCEAN

Faro de Jandía

Morro
Jable

Punta de
Jandía

Playa del
Matorral

Las Palmas de
Gran Canaria

Las Palmas de
Gran Canaria

Fuerteventura Highlights

1 Surf, windsurf or just enjoy coffee and cake in the laid-back coastal town of **El Cotillo** (p90)

2 Kick off your shoes and do cartwheels in the soft, powdery sand at **Parque Natural de Corralejo** (p86)

3 Catch the waves at **Isla de Lobos** (p89), just one of

Fuerteventura's super-cool surfing spots

4 Eat seafood at the end of the world in the **Punta de Jandía** (p96)

5 Be dazzled by the verdant valley location of lovely **Betancuria** (p80)

6 Sample the famous Majorero cheese at the **Museo del Queso Majorero** (p82) in Antigua

7 Treat yourself to a session of aromatic thalassotherapy at the beachside **Balneario Thalasso** (p83) in Caleta de Fuste

PUERTO DEL ROSARIO

POP 29,012

Puerto del Rosario, the island's capital, is home to more than half the island's population. It's a relatively modern little port town that only really took off in the 19th century. If you fly to the island, or use the buses, you may find yourself passing through. It can appear as a confusing city with sprawling suburbs, but head to the old town behind the promenade to find the majority of the shops, bars and restaurants.

Long-overlooked, the capital is making efforts to attract a few tourists, with sculptures and street art dotted around. There are no major attractions here, but it's still worth a stroll and a lunch stop.

History

Puerto del Rosario, once little more than a handful of fishermen's cottages, became the island's capital in 1860 as a result of its strategic position as a harbour.

Until 1956 it was known as Puerto de las Cabras, named after the goats who used to come here for water (and later becoming the main departure point for their export in the form of chops). In an early rebranding exercise, it was renamed the more dignified Puerto del Rosario (Port of the Rosary).

When Spain pulled out of the Sahara in 1975, it sent some 5000 Legión Extranjera (Foreign Legion) troops to Fuerteventura to keep a watch on North Africa. The huge barracks in Puerto del Rosario is still in use, although troops now number less than 1000.

◉ Sights

Pick up a *Puerto on Foot* guide from the tourist office; it has an easy-to-follow map showing 16 of the most centrally located sculptures. There's also a map detailing the city's street murals. The pedestrianised Avenida 1 de Mayo leads west from the main church and is lined with shops and bars.

Casa Museo Unamuno   MUSEUM
(Calle Rosario 11; ⊙9am-2pm Mon-Fri) FREE
This small museum honours the philosopher Miguel de Unamuno, who stayed here in 1924 after being exiled from Spain. His crime was criticising the dictatorship of Primo de Rivera, both verbally and in writing. He later escaped to France before returning to his position as lecturer and rector at Salamanca University in Spain when the Republicans came to power in 1931.

The ground-floor house has been turned into a period piece, with four rooms furnished from Unamuno's day, including the bedroom (complete with chamber pot) and his study with original desk. There are brochures available in English.

Centro de Arte Juan Ismael   ARTS CENTRE
(Calle Almirante Lallermand 30; ⊙10am-1pm & 5-9pm Tue-Sat) FREE Named for a Fuerteventura-born artist, there are rotating exhibitions on display here. None of Ismael's paintings are on show, though you can buy souvenirs and replicas of his surrealist works.

★✿ Festivals

Fiesta de la Virgen del Rosario   RELIGIOUS
(⊙7 Oct) Puerto del Rosario dons its party threads to honour the Virgen del Rosario, the capital's patron. Processions accompany the image of the Virgin as she is paraded around town.

✗ Eating

Eating out can be rewarding, with some good choices and modest prices. The local **mercado** (market; Calle Teófilo Martínez Escobar) is tiny, but a good place to sample (and buy) some of the island's famed goat's cheese.

★ Casa Toño   SPANISH €€
(☎928 34 47 36; Calle Alcalde Alonso Patallo 8; mains €12-20; ⊙1-4pm & 7pm-late Mon-Sat) Book ahead to get a table at this popular restaurant that brings a little cutting-edge cuisine to Puerto del Rosario's dining scene. The speciality is lightly seared red tuna; also expect plenty of tapas utilising fresh, local ingredients. There's an impressive gin menu with close to 50 different varieties.

Mar y Monte   SPANISH €€
(Carretera a los Pozos 6; mains €12-16; ⊙1-4pm & 7pm-late) One of a number of terrace restaurants overlooking Playa Chica at the southern end of the city. The varied menu includes a good selection of tapas and plenty of seafood.

El Cangrejo Colorao   SPANISH €€€
(☎928 85 84 77; Calle Juan Ramón Jiménez 1; mains €14-24; ⊙1-4pm & 7pm-late) There's a pleasing old-fashioned elegance about this seafront restaurant with its bow-tied, white-tablecloth ambience. The menu mainstays include meaty stews, though locals recommend the seafood platters and fresh fish. Dinner bookings recommended.

Drinking

Puerto del Rosario has a modest nightlife scene geared for the locals. The bars are clustered in the narrow alleys of the old town, opposite the tourist office, and leading off Calle León y Castillo.

Pub La Tierra   BAR
(Calle Eustaquio Gopar; ⊗7pm-midnight) Tucked away in a narrow cobbled lane, La Tierra is a fine place for drinks at the outdoor tables. Rock, jazz and blues tend to dominate the playlist.

Camelot   CLUB
(Calle Ayose 6; ⊗11pm-3am Thu-Sat) This bar has a medieval theme and a bank of music-video screens mixed in with local DJs. You can catch live music performances here too, although the quality can be patchy.

Information

Tourist Office (www.turismo-puertodelrosario. org; Avenida Marítimo; ⊗9am-7pm Mon-Fri, 10am-1pm Sat) A hugely helpful office with enthusiastic staff offering island-wide info. It's on the promenade opposite Hotel Roquemar.
Provincial Tourist Office (www.visitfuerteventura.es; Almirante Lallermand 1; ⊗7am-3pm Mon-Fri)

Getting There & Away

Tiadhe (☑650 53 28 66; www.tiadhe.com) buses leave from the main bus stop just past the corner of Avenidas León y Castillo and Constitución. The following are some of the more popular bus services from Puerto del Rosario:

Bus 1 Morro Jable via Costa Calma (€10, two hours, at least 12 daily)
Bus 2 Vega de Río Palmas via Betancuria (€3.30, 50 minutes, three daily)
Bus 3 Caleta de Fuste via the airport (€1.50, 30 minutes, at least 18 daily)
Bus 6 Corralejo (€3.40, 40 minutes, at least 16 daily)
Bus 7 El Cotillo (€4.35, 45 minutes, three daily)

Getting Around

Despite the sprawling nature of the town, the grid system of streets makes navigating reasonably easy. There's a large, free car park just beyond the market heading eastwards on Avenida Marítimo.

  One municipal bus does the rounds of the city every hour. You'll need to call for a **taxi** (☑928 85 02 16, 928 85 00 59).

TO/FROM THE AIRPORT
Bus 3 makes the trip to the airport. It takes 10 to 15 minutes and costs €1.30. A taxi will run about €10.

FUERTEVENTURA PUERTO DEL ROSARIO

FOR CHEESE LOVERS...

More than any other Canary island, Fuerteventura's traditional cuisine is simple and essentially the result of poverty. One of the keys remains the quality and freshness of the ingredients.

  Given that there are more goats than people on Fuerteventura (honest!), goat stew is a popular dish. But it is the goat's cheese that is the real winner. In fact, so renowned is the Majorero cheese that, just like a fine wine, it bears a *denominación de origen* (proof of origin) label, certifying that it is indeed from the island and the genuine product. It's the first Canary Island cheese to receive this accolade, and the first goat's cheese in Spain to bear the label.

  At the heart of the process is the Majorero goat, a high-yielding hybrid of goat originally imported from the Spanish mainland. The cheese is ideally purchased young and soft, with a powdery white rind that becomes yellow with age. One of Europe's top goat cheeses, Majorero is rich and buttery with a nutty flavour that goes particularly well with fruit. The wheels are often sold with a coating of oil, corn meal (*gofio*) or paprika to preserve them. The best place to buy your wheel of *queso* is at a local produce market, where there will always be several cheese stalls. Ask for a taste.

  To learn more about cheese – and goats – check out the Museo del Queso Majorero (p82) in Antigua.

THE CENTRE

Central Fuerteventura offers the most geographically diverse landscapes on this overwhelmingly desert-covered island. The soaring mountains of the Parque Natural de Betancuria are contrasted in the south with the wadi-style, palm-tree oasis of the Vega de Río Palmas. The west and east coasts are characterised by rocky cliffs interspersed with small black-pebble beaches and simple fishing hamlets.

In further contrast, the central copper-coloured plains around Antigua are dotted with old windmills dating back a couple of centuries. It is the sort of landscape that makes you wish you had invested in that wide-angle camera lens. This area has some of the most scenic drives on the island, particularly around Betancuria and Tefía.

Betancuria

POP 800

Wonderfully lush, this pretty hamlet is tucked into the protective folds of the basalt hills and is a patchwork of dry-stone walls, palm trees and simple, whitewashed cottages. Lording over it all is a magnificent 17th-century church and courtyard.

Jean de Béthencourt thought this the ideal spot to set up house in 1405, so he had living quarters and a chapel built. To this modest settlement he perhaps rather immodestly gave his own name, which, with time, was corrupted to Betancuria. During the course of the 15th century, Franciscan friars moved in and expanded the town. Amazingly, given its size, it remained the island's capital until 1834. Fuerteventura's proximity to the North African coast made it easy prey for Moroccan and European pirates who, on numerous occasions, managed to defy Betancuria's natural mountain defences and sack it.

Today Betancuria is fairly touristy, with multilanguage menus, souvenir shops and museum staff dressed in traditional garb. It is still very much worth a visit, though you might want to get here first thing in the morning, before any tour buses arrive.

○ Sights

If you approach from the north, look for the ruins of the island's first **monastery** on your left, built by the Franciscans. For such a small place, there is plenty to see here.

Casa Santa María MUSEUM

(adult/child €6/3; ⊙10am-4pm Mon-Sat;) This place is unabashedly tourist-orientated but still worth visiting. The German owner, Reiner Loos, bought the original rambling building in the 1990s and spent several years collecting traditional handicrafts and ancient agricultural tools, as well as lushly landscaping the garden. Inside you can see craftspeople at work, sample local cheese and *mojo* (spicy salsa) and even visit the 'virtual goat stable'. The highlight, however, is an expertly produced 3D underwater film of the local coastal sea life, including the rare green turtle.

Museo Arqueológico de Betancuria MUSEUM

(Calle Roberto Roldán; adult/child €2/free; ⊙10am-6pm Tue-Sat) Archaeology buffs should check out this modest but interesting museum. It concentrates on the indigenous Guanche tribes and includes a skeleton that was found in a local tomb and is thought to be between 600 and 1000 years old. There are also some artefacts from the Roman occupation. The admission includes an excellent brochure in English.

Iglesia de Santa María CHURCH

(Calle Alcalde Carmelo Silvera; admission €1.50; ⊙10am-4pm Mon-Sat) This church dates from 1620 and has a magnificent stone floor, wooden ceiling and elaborate baroque altar. Don't miss the sacristy with its display of vestments, altar ware and carved wooden ceiling in shades of gold and red. Pirates destroyed the church's Gothic predecessor in 1593. The entrance ticket also covers the adjacent **Museo de Arte Sacro**, which has the usual selection of religious paintings and statues.

★ Festivals

Día de San Buenaventura RELIGIOUS

(⊙14 Jul) Locals honour the patron saint on Día de San Buenaventura, in a fiesta dating to the 15th century.

✕ Eating

Valtarajal CANARIAN €

(Calle Juan de Béthencourt; raciónes €6-8; ⊙1-4pm & 7pm-late Mon-Sat) This cosy place has an authentic local feel and a good choice of *raciónes* (large portions of tapas).

Casa Santa María MODERN CANARIAN €€€

(☑928 87 82 82; www.restaurantecasasantamaria.com; Plaza Santa María de Betancuria 1; mains €20-25; ⊙noon-5pm Mon-Sat) Adjoining the museum complex, this restaurant looks like it was

A SPORTING CHANCE

Fuerteventura is a superb year-round destination for the sports enthusiast. Although surfing the waves or sailing the breeze are the most famous sports here, there are less adrenalin-spiked activities available. Fuerteventura's peaceful but stark landscape offers some great walking opportunities, with oases, volcanic craters, abandoned haciendas and rugged coastlines awaiting the intrepid. The Isla de Lobos nature reserve is also excellent for walkers; turning right as you hop off the ferry will take you on a circular tour of the island. There's also a climb up Caldera de la Montaña here – well worth it for the dizzying views.

Leaving behind those hiking trails, mountain biking in Fuerteventura is a completely different experience. 'Cycling in the interior is a bit like cycling on the moon', one enthusiast was heard remarking. Most resorts have bicycle-rental outfits. Ask at the tourist information offices for a copy of the Eco-Fuerteventura map, which details hiking and biking routes across the island.

If you fancy swinging a golf club, Caleta de Fuste is home to the island's first PGA championship–rated golf course, the Fuerteventura Golf Club. Or just make use of the blustery climate by flying a kite. If you're in Corralejo in early November you may catch the three-day festival on the beach, when hundreds of kites speckle the blue sky like a flock of brilliantly coloured butterflies.

transplanted from Andalucía. Try to get a table in the flower-lined courtyards. The menu includes all manner of goaty offerings – from roasted to fried with cheese and chutney, as well as colourful salads where goat's cheese, once again, takes pride of place. Pricey but worth the splurge.

ℹ Getting There & Around

Bus 2 (€2.80, 50 minutes) passes through here three times daily on its way between Puerto del Rosario and Vega de Río Palmas, a short distance south.

There's a small, free car park south of the centre.

Around Betancuria

This area encompasses some great scenery and superb far-reaching vistas. For a start, a couple of kilometres north of Betancuria on the FV-30, there's a handy lookout (on both sides of the road) that explains the various mountain peaks looming on the horizon. The immense statues here are of the island's two pre-Hispanic kings, Ayose and Guize. Further on, the Mirador de Morro Velosa (www.artesaniaymuseosdefuerteventura. org; ⊙10am-6pm Mon-Sat) FREE offers mesmerising views across the island's weird, disconsolate moonscape. You can stop at the bar located here, with its large picture windows and exhibition space for subjects related to the landscape and environment.

The view is almost as spectacular at the pass over which the FV-30 highway climbs before it twists its way north through Valle de Santa Inés, a hiccup of a village.

In pretty Casillas del Ángel, on the FV-20, the petite Iglesia de Santa Ana contains an 18th-century wooden carving of St Anne. For a superb meal, try La Era (🕿633 113888; Carretera General de Casillas del Ángel; mains €14-22; ⊙1-4pm & 7pm-late Tue-Sun) at the western end of the town. A long, low ochre building, the elegant dining room attracts business bods from all around with its menu of traditional, superbly prepared local dishes. Advance reservations essential.

Heading south of Betancuria for Pájara, you soon hit the small oasis of Vega de Río Palmas (Fertile Plain of the Palma River). As you proceed, the reason for the name becomes clear – the road follows a near-dry watercourse still sufficiently wet below the surface to keep alive a stand of palms.

Antigua

POP 1800

In the 18th century, sleepy Antigua held the title of capital, albeit for just a year. Today it's a pleasant enough place for a wander before visiting the excellent museum. There is an ATM and a petrol station here should you need to refuel your wallet or car.

◉ Sights

★ Museo del Queso Majorero   MUSEUM

(☑646 972202; artesaniaymuseosdefuerteventura.org; adult/child €2/free; ⊙10am-6pm Tue-Sat; P 🚻) This new museum is one of the island's best, with lots of interactive displays including a 'virtual milking' activity! Kids will enjoy all the touch-button exhibits with information on the island's flora and fauna, while adults can get an education on Majorero cheese production, plus tips on tasting the finished product. There is a shop selling a range of cheeses though, sadly, at present, no tasting facility.

There is also a restored windmill here, which you can climb up before exploring the cacti garden and craft shop. All proceeds from the shop go directly to the craftspeople.

Iglesia de Nuestra Señora de Antigua   CHURCH

(⊙10am-2pm) One of the island's oldest churches, built on the site of a 16th-century chapel. Set in a pleasant square, the most interesting feature is the pretty pink-and-green painted altar.

ⓘ Getting There & Away

Bus 1 (€2.15, 30 minutes) passes through en route between Puerto del Rosario and Morro Jable.

Around Antigua

You'll require your own transport to access the towns of La Ampuyenta and Tiscamanita.

◉ Sights

Ermita de San Pedro de Alcántara   CHAPEL

Located in tiny La Ampuyenta is the 17th-century Ermita de San Pedro de Alcántara. The *ermita* (chapel) is surrounded by a stout protective wall built by the French from the Normandy area. Within, the walls of the nave are decorated with large, engagingly naive frescoes that date from 1760. Although the Sistine Chapel comparisons are a trifle far fetched, the murals are undeniably stunning in their pastel colours and simple execution.

The best way to visit is on a free guided walk leaving from the Centro de Interpretación de Las Ermitas de Fuerteventura (⊙guided tours 10.30am, 12.30pm, 2.30pm & 4.30pm Tue-Sat) FREE. As well as the chapel, the walks take in the 19th-century Casa Museo Doctor Mena and the birthplace of Fray Andresito, a Franciscan monk born in La Ampuyenta in 1800.

Los Molinos Centro de Interpretación   MUSEUM

(www.artesaniaymuseosdefuerteventura.org; adult/child €2/free; ⊙10am-6pm Mon-Sat) This fully functioning windmill has a small information centre with all the information about windmills you could possibly want to know; there's a free guide in English. When we visited, the mill was lacking a miller, though you could still sample *gofio* (ground, roasted grain traditionally used in place of bread in Canarian cuisine). It's located in Tiscamanita, 9km south of Antigua.

Pájara

POP 2000

Pájara is a leafy oasis set amid a desert landscape. But what has really put the place on the map is its unique 17th-century Iglesia de Nuestra Señora de Regla. The exterior is Aztec-inspired with its animal motifs. The simple retables behind the altar also have influences flowing back to Mexico and are more subdued than the baroque excesses of mainland Spain (stick a coin in the machine on the right at the entrance to light them up). Don't forget to look up; there's a magnificent carved wooden ceiling.

✗ Eating

There are several reasonable restaurants and one exceptional place to stay (p222) in town.

Ca'Luisa   CREPERIE €

(Calle Nuestra Señora de Regla 19; crepes €3-5; ⊙1-4pm & 7pm-late Tue-Sun) If you're getting tired of tapas, the sweet and savoury crepes on sale at this friendly cafe make a pleasant change.

Casa Isaítas   CANARIAN €€

(☑928 16 14 02; www.casaisaitas.com; Calle Guize 7; mains €10; ⊙10am-4.30pm; 🖉) Based in the hotel of the same name, this is the best place to eat in town. The varied menu includes lots of hearty soups and stews, some interesting tapas and a good selection for vegetarians.

ⓘ Getting There & Around

Bus 18 (€3.30, 30 minutes, three daily) runs between Pájara and Gran Tarajal, from where you can take onward buses to Puerto del Rosario and Morro Jable.

Street parking is fairly abundant and there's a free car park just south of the church, opposite the Casa Isaítas rural hotel.

AJUY & PUERTO DE LA PEÑA

If you have your own wheels, a 9km side trip from Pájara takes you northwest to Ajuy and contiguous Puerto de la Peña. A blink-and-you'll-miss-it fishing settlement, its black-sand beach makes a change from its illustrious golden neighbours to the south on the Península de Jandía. The locals and fishing boats take pride of place here, and the strand is fronted by a couple of simple seafood eateries serving up the day's catch.

Once you've filled up on fresh fish, walk it off on a 40-minute round-trip wander along the coast. The path starts at the north end of the beach and passes an old limestone kiln before eventually leading you to some impressive caves in the cliff face.

Caleta de Fuste & Around

This smart, well-landscaped resort exudes an opulent southern-California feel, particularly around the sprawling Barceló mini-village, which fronts the main beach. Caleta is often referred to as El Castillo (particularly on road signs) for the squat 18th-century Martello tower in the harbour. It is close to the airport and, if you're travelling with a young family, the wide arc of sand and shallow waters are ideal. However, if you are seeking somewhere intrinsically Canarian, look elsewhere; this is a purpose-developed tourist resort. In all fairness, though, it is a relaxing place with some good hotels and decent restaurants.

Beaches

Playa del Castillo BEACH
The resort is fronted by a white sandy beach, complete with volleyball net and **camel rides** (30min ride for 2 people €12). It is ideal for families, although a poor relation compared to the rolling dunes and endless sands of Corralejo and Jandía.

Sights & Activities

Museo de la Sal MUSEUM
(Salt Museum; Las Salinas; adult/child €5/free; ⊙10am-6pm Tue-Sat) Just south of Caleta, this museum has audiovisual displays that explain the history of salt and demonstrate how it is extracted from the sea. It's perched on the ocean right next to the still-operational salt pans.

Watersports
Deep Blue DIVING
(☑606 275468; www.deep-blue-diving.com; orientation dive €23, open-water diver course €390; 🚐) Conveniently situated beside the port, this long-running outfit offers courses, dives for the already qualified (from €30), children's courses (€45) and snorkelling trips (€20).

Fuerte Fun Center WINDSURFING
(www.fuerte-surf.com; Playa de Caleta de Fuste; equipment per hr/day/week €25/60/220; ⊙10am-5pm Sun-Fri) On the far side of the beach, this reliable choice offers four-hour beginner windsurfing courses for €90, including equipment hire. They also rent stand-up paddleboards (€15/40 per hour/day).

Boat Trips
Oceanarium Explorer BOAT TRIPS
(☑928 54 76 87; Puerto Castillo Yacht Harbour; 🚐) This outfit runs a range of family-friendly activities, including half-day fishing trips (from €70), kayak and jet-ski hire (from €6 per hour), sea lion encounters and boat trips (adult/child €40/20) where you might catch sight of dolphins and whales.

Golf
Fuerteventura Golf Club GOLF
(www.fuerteventuragolfclub.com; Carretera de Jandía; 18 holes €75) This club has top-whack facilities, including a pro shop and resident PGA professional, and covers a vast 1.5 sq km.

Cycling
Caleta Cycles CYCLING
(☑676 600190; Hotel Los Geranios; tours €30-50) A British-run place that organises guided bike tours and also rents bikes (€10 per day).

Thalassotherapy
Balneario Thalasso SPA
(☑928 16 09 61; www.barcelo.com; Calle Savila 2; spa circuit €25, 1hr massage from €60) You can't miss the glass building behind the beach with its giant 'Thalasso' sign. There is a range of treatments on offer – try the 'total aloe' (€99), a peel, wrap and massage combo that uses aloe from the island, or just enjoy the various bubbles and jets of the spa circuit. Guests staying at the Barceló get reduced rates.

SCENIC DRIVES: FUERTEVENTURA

The drive between Betancuria and Pájara on the FV-30 is one of the most spectacular on the island, although possibly not for those suffering from vertigo. The narrow road twists and turns steeply between a flowing landscape of volcano peaks and lava fields, with the sea visible (at times) in the far distance. In spring, the peaks are surprisingly lush; a vivid green contrasting with the rich ochres and reds of the soil.

The journey via La Pared south towards Península de Jandía is almost as dramatic. Fuerteventura is relatively flat when compared to Lanzarote and the other islands to the west, but you would never know it as you wend your way through this lonely and spectacularly harsh terrain.

✗ Eating & Drinking

★ Frasquita   SEAFOOD €€

(☑928 56 69 98; Playa de Caleta de Fuste; mains €15; ☺1-4pm & 7pm-late Tue-Sun; ℗) This is one of the best restaurants on the island to come to for fresh seafood, despite its very plain appearance and plastic tables and chairs. There's no menu, just a plate of freshly caught fish and seafood to point at. Book ahead to get a seat in the glassed-in dining room overlooking the beach.

Los Caracolitos   SEAFOOD €€

(☑928 17 42 42; Salinas del Carmen 22; mains €10-15; ☺closed dinner Sun; ℗) On the coast overlooking the salt pans, this is a fine alternative to the resort's multifarious tourist menus. Fish and seafood feature heavily and travellers rave about the shellfish soup. It's 2km south of Caleta de Fuste; if you don't fancy the coastal walk, the restaurant offers a free shuttle service.

El Faro   BAR

(Puerto Castillo; ☺7pm-midnight) On a jetty jutting out into the ocean, this swanky glass-walled bar is the top spot for a sunset cocktail. There's also a good beer menu and light snacks are served. It's part of the Barceló complex but open to all.

ⓘ Information

Tourist Office (Centro Comercial Castillo; ☺9am-3pm Mon-Fri) You can pick up pamphlets here, but there's rarely anybody manning the stand.

THE NORTH

Road to La Oliva

The FV-10 highway travelling westwards away from Puerto del Rosario to the interior of the island takes you through a landscape that typifies Fuerteventura. Ochre-coloured soil and distant volcanoes create a barren landscape of shifting colours and shapes, depending on the position of the sun. Before crossing the ridge that forms the island's spine, the road passes through the sleepy hamlets of Tetir and La Matilla. The tiny 1902 chapel in the latter is a good example of the simple, bucolic buildings of the Canaries – functional, relatively unadorned and aesthetically pleasing.

About 7km south of La Matilla and 1km beyond the village of Tefía along the FV-207 is the Ecomuseo la Alcogida (adult/child €5/free; ☺10am-6pm Tue-Sat; ⓐ), a restored agricultural hamlet complete with furnished houses, outbuildings and domestic animals (though the chained-up dogs have a troubling un-eco feel). Overall, it's an interesting glimpse into the tough rural life of the not-too-distant past, with local artisans working in some of the settlement's buildings making lace and wicker baskets. There are explanations in English, plus a gift shop and bar.

West on the FV-211 from Tefía leads to Los Molinos. This is another lovely drive with the road curving around low-lying hills with isolated lofty palms and herds of goats. On the way you can't miss the old windmill used to grind cereals for the production of *gofio,* sitting squat across from a distinctive white-domed observatory.

The road continues to wind its way over the crest of the hill before descending dramatically beside a gaping gorge to tiny **Los Molinos**. Expect just a few simple houses overlooking a small grey-stone beach with cliff trails to the east and plenty of goats, geese and stray cats. If you do stop here, make a point of having a seafood meal at beachside **Restaurante Casa Pon** (mains €8-14; ⊙1-4pm & 7pm-late Tue-Sun) while gazing over Atlantic breakers.

A couple of kilometres north of Los Molinos, along a rough track, lies the **Playa de la Mujer**, an enticing stretch of sand particularly popular with surfers.

If you're following the FV-10 rather than the coastal route, look out for the impressively located statue of Miguel de Unamuno part way up **Montaña Quemado** – a place the writer once said he would like to be buried.

Bus 7 from Puerto del Rosario to El Cotillo passes through Tetir, La Matilla and Tindaya three times daily. Bus 2 (€1.70, 20 minutes, twice daily), between Puerto del Rosario and Vega de Río Palmas, passes by Tefía. There are no buses to Los Molinos, but it is a well-surfaced, scenic road if you are driving.

La Oliva

POP 1370

One-time capital of the island, in fact if not in name, La Oliva still bears a trace or two of grander days. The weighty bell tower of the 18th-century **Iglesia de Nuestra Señora de la Candelaria** is the town's focal point of sorts, with its black volcanic bulk contrasting sharply with the bleached-white walls of the church itself.

⊙ Sights

Art and history enthusiasts will have plenty to keep them smiling in La Oliva. Try to visit on Tuesday or Friday, when a food and craft **market** (⊙10am-2pm) is held in town and the **Ruta de los Coroneles** (pass €6; ⊙10am-2pm) pass is available – it allows access to the two museums, the art gallery and the church.

★**Casa de los Coroneles**   MUSEUM
(www.artesaniaymuseosdefuerteventura.org; admission €3; ⊙10am-6pm Tue-Sat; P) This 18th-century building has been beautifully restored, retaining its traditional central patio and wooden galleries. The ground floor now houses temporary exhibitions of world-class modern art, while upstairs you'll find exhibits on the history of the building. Don't miss the simple chapel with its original tiled floor. Adjacent to the *casa,* the perfect cone of the volcano is an example of nature's own art.

The *House of the Colonels* has an interesting history. Beginning in the early 1700s, the officers who presided here virtually controlled the island. Amassing power and wealth, they so exploited the peasant class that, in 1834, Madrid – faced with repeated bloody mutinies on the island – disbanded the militia.

★**Centro de Arte Canario**   ART GALLERY
(Calle Salvador Manrique de Lara; admission €4; ⊙10am-5pm Mon-Fri, 10am-2pm Sat; P) This art museum is an island highlight, with its sculpture garden and galleries containing works by such Canarian artists as César Manrique, Ruben Dario and Alberto Agullo. Two galleries are devoted to the national award-winning watercolourist Alberto Manrique (no relation

FUERTEVENTURA LA OLIVA

POZO NEGRO

About 20km south of Caleta de Fuste is one of Fuerteventura's most pristine fishing hamlets, Pozo Negro. The 5km drive towards the coast from the FV-2 is stunning and you'll probably pass a lot of walkers en route. Palm plantations, green meadows, herds of goats and craggy peaks typify the scenery. Along the way, look out for signs to **Poblado de La Atalayita** (www.artesaniaymuseosdefuerteventura.org; adult/child €2/free; ⊙10am-6pm Tue-Sat), a pre-Hispanic settlement with a small information centre. The centre was closed when we visited, but the volcanic-rock ruins are worth the short dirt road detour to have a look if you're hereabouts.

The tiny fishing community of Pozo Negro is the antithesis of Caleta de Fuste; there are just a cluster of cottages, some brightly painted fishing boats and two popular seafood restaurants, with little to choose between them in the fresh-fish stakes. Both specialise in paella and have terraces overlooking the pebble beach. Pozo Negro is popular with windsurfers, but you'll need your own gear.

A MOUNTAIN OF CONTROVERSY

Its summit reaches just 400m above sea level, but **Mount Tindaya** is the most important – and famous – mountain on the island. The peak, 7km south of La Oliva, has a special place in local history and mythology. More than 200 Guanche rock carvings have been found on the slopes, many of them in the shape of footprints seemingly pointing towards Tenerife's Mount Teide. Locals insist that curious things happen near the mountain: the sick get well, wrongdoers get their comeuppance and so on.

In recent years, the mountain has been in and out of the headlines for a different reason. Way back in 1985, Basque sculptor Eduardo Chillida picked out Mount Tindaya as the site for a gargantuan project and one that was meant to be his masterpiece. The project met with no small amount of protest. It involved removing 64,000 cubic metres of rock to make way for a 40m-high cave. The project, which Chillida called his 'Monument to Tolerance', was meant to allow people to experience the sheer size of the mountain. Chillada died in 2002, but nine years later local authorities finally gave the go ahead. It stalled once more, but in early 2015, Chillada's family gave the rights of the project to the Canarian government and Fuerteventura's *cabildo*. Protests continue to rage but authorities insist that the development, which they hope will attract 'quality tourism', will go ahead.

There is a simple **hiking trail** to the summit, taking in some of the rock etchings en route, but ask at the tourist office in Corralejo – if construction on Chillada's project begins, Fuerteventura's magic mountain will certainly be off limits for some time.

to César), displaying his landscapes and more surreal, mainly interior, scenes. The gallery is located close to Casa de los Coroneles; follow the signs from the centre of town.

Casa Cilla Museo del Grano   MUSEUM
(adult/child €1.50/free; ☺ 10am-3pm & 4-6pm Tue, 10am-3pm Fri, 10am-2pm Sat) Located about 250m north of the church, on the road to El Cotillo, this small museum is devoted to grain – both its production and the harsh life of the farming cycle in general.

❶ Getting There & Away

Bus 7 (€2.40, 35 minutes) between Puerto del Rosario and El Cotillo passes through three times daily.

Corralejo

POP 16,300

Your opinion of this place will depend wholly upon where you are standing. Despite the number of tourists, the former fishing village near the harbour and main beach still has charm, with narrow, uneven streets, good seafood restaurants and even a fisherman's cottage or two. Venture inland a couple of blocks and you find the predictable could-be-anywhere resort with Slow Boat buffets, fish and chips and a grid system of streets. It could be worse: the buildings are low-rise and you can still find a few local Spanish bars.

What makes Corralejo, however, are the miles of sand dunes to the south of town, sweeping back into gentle sugar-loaf rolls from the sea and fabulous broad sandy beaches. Protected as a nature park, no one can build on or near them...for now, that is. Unfortunately, a couple of monolithic concrete eyesores from the Riu hotel chain managed to get here before the regulation was in place.

🏖 Beaches

Parque Natural de Corralejo   BEACH
This nature park stretches along the east coast for about 10km from Corralejo. It can get breezy here, hence its popularity with windsurfers and kiteboarders. The locals have applied their ingenuity to the sand-sticking-to-the-sunscreen problem by erecting little fortresses of loose stones atop shrub-covered sandy knolls to protect sun-worshippers from the wind. The area is also known as **Grandes Playas** and is free to enter; sunloungers and umbrellas are available for hire in front of the two (eyesore) luxury hotels.

Playas Corralejo Viejo & Muelle Chico   BEACH
The small beaches surrounding the town's harbour have fine sand and shallow water – and also serve as a year-round canvas for sand sculptors.

⊙ Sights & Activities

Most of the activities here are centred on the sea, with the main surfing beaches accessible by taxi. For landlubbers there are walking and cycling options, plus a nine-hole golf course just south of the town.

Watersports

Dive Center Corralejo   DIVING
(📞928 53 59 06; www.divecentercorralejo.com; Calle Nuestra Señora del Pino 22; dives from €45) This respected outfit has been operating since 1979. Located just back from the waterfront, you can take the plunge with a beginner's dive (€50) or, if you're already an experienced diver, opt for a more advanced course, such as underwater photography (€240).

Kayak Fuerteventura   KAYAKING
(📞650 899893; www.kayakfuerteventura.com; half-day trip €35) The coastal tour is ideal for beginners, while the more experienced might prefer the longer jaunt out to Isla de Lobos (per person €50), which includes snorkelling gear. You can also rent kayaks (per day €50) and snorkelling equipment (per day €10).

Billabong Surf Camp   SURFING
(📞639 501777; www.billabongsurfcamp.com; Galera Beach; 1-day course €45, advanced 3-day course €120) Corralejo is a justifiably popular base for surfers, with plenty of surf schools dotted around. This long-running company is right on the beach, offering courses, including equipment and insurance, plus transport to the waves. They also run 'surfari' trips to nearby surf spots and have basic beachside accommodation.

Flag Beach Windsurf Center   WINDSURFING
(📞609 029804; www.flagbeach.com; Flag Beach; surfboard hire per day €12; 🚌) Flag Beach has beginner windsurfing courses for €140 for three days and windsurf hire at €35/60 per hour/day. The staff are also excellent kite-surfing instructors, with an introductory two-day course costing €230. They can also arrange accommodation.

Ventura Surf Center   WINDSURFING
(📞928 86 62 95; www.ventura-surf.com; Calle Fragata; 1½hr course from €45, gear hire per day €50) Conditions along much of the coast and in the straits between Corralejo and Lanzarote – the Estrecho de la Bocaina – are ideal for both wind- and kitesurfing. This place is on the beach at the end of Calle Fragata, south of the centre of town. They also offer surfing classes (full day €45) and rent out surfboards (€12 per day).

Boat Trips

Grupo Lobos   BOAT TRIPS
(📞616 986982; www.grupolobos.es; Estacíon Marítimo; adult/child €15/7.50; 🚌) There are regular ferries to Isla de Lobos with seven daily departures from 10am to 5.15pm. The last boat back leaves at 6pm. The company also operates one-hour minicruises (adult/child €18/9) in glass-bottom boats to the islet, leaving at 1pm daily, plus 4.30pm and 5.15pm according to demand. Buy your tickets from the kiosk at the port.

Cycling & Hiking

Easy Riders Bikecenter   CYCLING
(📞928 86 70 05; www.easyriders-bikecenter.com; Calle Nuestra Señora del Carmen 5; 4hr trip €42; ⊙9am-1pm & 6-8pm Mon-Sat) Organises year-round guided excursions with flexible times according to demand, including a tour around Isla de Lobos. Also rents bikes (from €10 per day) and provides information on cycling routes.

Natoural Adventure   HIKING
(📞664 849411; www.natouraladventure.com; treks from €48) Offers several different guided treks with distances ranging from 6km to 12km and varying levels of difficulty.

CATCHING THE WAVES

The sea offers most of the action in Fuerteventura. From Caleta de Fuste, Morro Jable and Corralejo, you can both dive and windsurf, though the best spot for the latter is near Costa Calma. The coast between Corralejo and Los Molinos offers excellent surfing possibilities, as do the waters around La Pared. Kitesurfing has fast gained popularity, too, thanks to regular wind gusts on the coast.

You can also pick up the handy *Surfers' Map* available from most tourist offices; it lists surf schools, surf camps, speciality stores and a couple of surf cafes (for surfing the web and meeting like-minded souls). The map also marks and rates the top surfing beaches on the island.

Water-sports tuition and equipment-rental places are listed throughout this chapter.

✗ Eating

The pedestrian area around Corralejo's small port is home to plenty of restaurants with outside terraces for ultimate people-watching potential.

Antiguo Café del Puerto   SPANISH €
(Calle La Ballena 10; tapas from €3; ⊙1-4pm & 7pm-late) Warm and inviting, with rag-washed walls, good wines and 50-plus tapas to enjoy on the terrace overhanging the ocean.

Citrus Surf Cafe   CAFE €
(www.citrus-surfcafe.com; Calle Anzuelo 1; mains €8; ⊙9am-midnight Mon-Sat; 📶🍴) Recommended by readers, this chilled-out place serves a range of cuisines for those tired of tapas. Inventive salads, Tex-Mex dishes, burgers and wraps are all on the menu (which is etched onto a surfboard). Wash down your lunch with a smoothie or freshly squeezed juice. There's live music some evenings on the covered terrace at the back.

La Factoria   ITALIAN €
(Avenida Marítimo 9; pizzas from €8, pastas from €10; ⊙1-4pm & 7pm-late; 🍴) The owner is from Bologna and knows a thing or two about pasta, which is made here daily. The pizzas are similarly authentic with thin, crispy bases and tasty toppings – mama would definitely approve. It's situated right on the beach in the old harbour.

★ Restaurante Avenida   SPANISH €€
(Calle General Prim 11; mains €8-16; ⊙1-4pm & 7pm-late Tue-Sun; 🍴) Despite the location several blocks back from the beach, this place is always heaving with a cheerful, local Canarian crowd who are here for the no-nonsense food. It's a great rustic atmosphere with wooden beams and chunky dark-wood furniture.

The seafood dishes start at just €8 for grilled squid; roasted meats include lamb, chicken, rabbit and pork.

La Arrocería   SPANISH €€
(☎928 53 52 91; Calle Pejin 10; mains €12-17; ⊙1-4pm & 7pm-late Wed-Sun) You know you've found a local haunt in the Canaries when the menu is solely in Spanish. Tucked away in the backstreets, this friendly place has stylish, nautical decor and a minimal but superb menu focusing on rice dishes. Alongside the usual seafood paellas, there are carnivorous and vegetarian versions plus *fideuà*, which uses vermicelli-like noodles instead of rice.

El Andaluz   SPANISH €€
(Calle La Ballena 5; mains €10-18; ⊙6.30-10pm Mon-Sat) This place gets rave reviews. The characterful interior has just a few tables, so get here early to secure a seat. The four-course *menú degustación* (€19) is a good deal, with meat and fish choices. Dishes use more herbs and vegetables than the Spanish norm and there's a tasty leek quiche for vegetarians.

🍷 Drinking

Finding a drink in Corralejo doesn't pose a problem. Bars, discos and, if you must, karaoke clubs take up much of the **Centro Comercial Atlántico** (Avenida Nuestro Señora del Carmen). For something more laid back, head to Calle La Iglesia, a pedestrian strip with a number of wine bars and cool places for a chilled-out cocktail.

Waikiki   CLUB
(Calle Arístides Hernández Morán 11; ⊙10am-late) Although this place doubles as a restau-

---

FUERTEVENTURA FOR CHILDREN

The main attraction for families has to be the **beaches**, many of which have fine white sand and shallow waters that are safe for paddling tots: **Playa del Castillo** (p83) and **Playa del Matorral** (p94) are both good choices. For a manmade water adventure, the massive **Baku Water Park** (Avenida Nuestra Señora del Carmen 41; adult/child €25/19; ⊙10am-6pm) in Corralejo has ten-pin bowling, crazy golf and a driving range, as well as wave pools and kamikaze-style slides and rides.

There are plenty of **boat trips** throughout the resorts as well. At Caleta de Fuste, Oceanarium Explorer has a daily **dolphin-** and **whale-spotting trip**, while in Corralejo, there are regular boats to the **Isla de Lobos**, where there is a lovely Robinson Crusoe–style beach and the possibility to explore the island via pedal power. The best museum for children is the interactive **Museo del Queso Majorero** (p82) in Antigua. Alternatively, if you don't object to zoos, **Oasis Park** (p92) in La Lajita has mammals, birds and sea life, plus shows and camel rides.

ISLA DE LOBOS

The bare Isla de Lobos (4.7 sq km) takes its name from the *lobos marinos* (sea wolves) that once lived there. They were, in fact, *focas monje* (monk seals), which disappeared in the 15th century thanks to a series of hungry mariners landing on the barren island's shores. The good news is that attempts are being made to re-introduce the seals to the island.

It is well worth taking a trip to the islet from Corralejo. Once you've disembarked you can go for a short walk, order lunch at the quayside restaurant (reserve when you arrive if you intend to lunch there) and head for the pleasant, small beach. Hiking around the island takes around an hour – stick to the marked paths. There is also a small **interpretation centre** (☺10am-5pm) FREE with some interesting exhibits on the island's history and geography.

Take your binoculars as it's a popular birdwatching destination, plus you may spot a shark or two, which are common in the waters around Lobos. The island is also great for surfing, so bring your board and don't worry, the sharks are hammerheads – a distant (harmless) relation to Jaws. The island is also popular with divers and snorkellers. A quirky way to see the island is on a stand-up paddleboard (SUP). **Red Shark** (☑928 86 75 48; www.redsharkfuerteventura.com) offers day trips which include transport on a Zodiac, equipment rental and a brief lesson (per person €65).

The cheapest and fastest way to get here is on the **Grupo Lobos ferry** (p87). Departing Corralejo at 10am, 11am, noon, 1pm, 3.30pm, 4.30pm and 5.15pm, it leaves the island at 10.15am, 11.15am, 12.15pm, 1.45pm, 4pm and 5pm. You can also take a minicruise to the island in a glass-bottom boat.

rant during the day, the best time to come is at night when a mix of surfers, party animals, families and friends gather in a hibiscus-fringed beachside setting to sip cocktails and enjoy the late-night music scene. The piña coladas are sublime.

Zazamira　　　　　　　　　　　CAFE
(Calle La Iglesia 7; ☺10am-11pm Wed-Mon; 🛜) Elbowed down a narrow street near the harbour, this is the healthy option with fresh juices like papaya and orange and ginseng-spiked coffee. If you fancy something stronger, sip on a cocktail while admiring the Bob Marley memorabilia adorning the walls.

Mojito Beach Bar　　　　　　　　BAR
(Avenida Marítimo; ☺11am-late; 🛜) A relaxed, hip place just inches from the ocean with a menu of exotic mojitos.

☆ Entertainment

★Rock Island Bar　　　　　　LIVE MUSIC
(www.rockislandbar.com; Calle Crucero Baleares; ☺7.30pm-late; 🛜) Over the last 21 years, Mandy and musician husband Gary have made this bar one of the most popular in town. There is acoustic music nightly, playing to an enthusiastic, music-loving crowd.

🛍 Shopping

Unless you are looking for souvenir placemats or kiss-me-quick caps, your best option for local shopping, including several of the national chains, is the stretch of Avenida Nuestra Señora del Carmen from west of the tourist office to Calle Crucero Baleares.

No Work Team　　　　　　OUTDOOR GEAR
(Avenida Nuestro Señora del Carmen 46; ☺10am-2pm & 5-9pm Mon-Fri, 10am-2pm Sat) One local surf-wear label to check out is No Work Team. You'll find good-quality, comfy duds for men, women and children, with an unmistakeable surfing feel.

ℹ Information

Tourist Office (www.corralejograndesplayas. com; Avenida Marítimo 2; ☺8am-3pm Mon-Fri, from 9am Sat & Sun) Located on the seafront near the harbour, with shelves full of brochures.

ℹ Getting There & Away

BUS

The bus station is located on Avenida Juan Carlos I. Bus 6 (€3.30, 40 minutes) runs regularly from the bus station to Puerto del Rosario.

Bus 8 (€3.10, 40 minutes, 13 daily) heads west to El Cotillo via La Oliva.

CAR & MOTORCYCLE

Cicar (☑ 928 82 29 00; www.cicar.com) Has an office right at the Centro Comercial Atlántico's entrance and has good prices, with an economy car from around €120 for a week's rental.

Rent A Bike Club (☑ 928 86 62 33; Avenida Juan Carlos I 21; ⊙ 9am-1pm & 5-8pm Mon-Sat, 9am-1pm Sun) For motorcycles, stop by the originally named Rent A Bike Club, opposite the bus station. You can rent scooters and motorcycles from €40 and €65 per day respectively, with full insurance.

ℹ Getting Around

The town is easy to navigate and there is plenty of free on-street parking, especially in the side streets off the main Avenida Nuestro Señora del Carmen.

You can call for a **taxi** (☑ 928 53 74 41, 928 86 61 08) or there's a convenient taxi rank near the Centro Comercial Atlántico. A trip from the town centre to the main beaches will cost about €8.

El Cotillo

POP 2100

This former fishing village has real character, marrying the windswept nature of an offbeat coastal town with the laid-back vibe that comes from being a popular surfing destination. El Cotillo has so far managed to avoid major construction and is an excellent place for foodies, water babes or those simply seeking some relaxation. Calle Muelle Pescadroes, behind the old harbour, doubles as an open air gallery, with paintings and sculptures dotted around. This pedestrian strip is dotted with hippie shopping opportunities and lively tapas bars.

Once the seat of power of the tribal chiefs of Maxorata (the northern kingdom of Guanche Fuerteventura), El Cotillo has been largely ig-nored since the conquest. The exceptions to the rule were the cut-throat pirates who occasionally landed here plus the slowly growing invasion of less violent sun-seekers who prize the area's unaffected peacefulness.

◉ Sights

Museo de la Pesca Tradicional MUSEUM
(Museum of Traditional Fishing; Faro de Tostón; adult/child €3/1.50; ⊙ 10am-2.30pm & 3.15-6pm Tue-Sat; P) This interesting museum is located next to the town's distinctive stripy lighthouse (not open to visitors). Climb to the top of the considerably smaller original lighthouse for panoramic sea views and then visit the various galleries. There is English information available and several insightful mini videos about traditional fishing methods.

Castillo de Tostón CASTLE
(adult/child €1.50/free; ⊙ 10am-3pm Mon-Fri, 9am-2pm Sat & Sun) This tubby *castillo* is not really a castle, more a Martello tower. The art and history displays within are interesting, but the star here is the sweeping view of the surf beach.

🏃 Activities

Watersports are the main activity here. Experienced surfers only should make for a wave known as the Bubble north of the centre, which is not as innocuous as it sounds. To get here, you'll need your own transport. Happily, there are plenty of options for the less experienced as well.

Shock Wave SURFING
(www.shockwavesurfschool.com; Calle Pintor Néstor de la Torre 1; half-day course €50) This surf school comes highly recommended by

---

CYCLE THE COASTAL ROUTE

Although you can drive the rough coastal road from Corralejo to El Cotillo, it is particularly well suited to cycling (or hiking) as it is virtually flat. Take the track north of the Corralejo bus station on Avenida Juan Carlos 1. This graded dirt road winds between volcanic lava fields, shifting to a more desert-like landscape after 5km. At 8km you reach the tiny fishing community of Majanicho, the houses clustered around a small inlet complete with scenic bobbing boats and the smallest chapel you have ever seen. From here you can detour along the FV-101 asphalt road to Lajares (7km) for a spot of light refreshment at one of the fabulous bakeries, or continue on your way to El Cotillo. You will pass white, sandy beaches, interspersed with black rocky coves, and a couple of the most popular kite- and windsurfing beaches in these parts. Coming direct from Corralejo you arrive at El Cotillo's lighthouse, Faro de Tostón, after 20km, where you can check out the Museo de la Pesca Tradicional. Alternatively, pedal (or plod) on to the centre of El Cotillo (4.5km), past the scrubby desert setting of Los Lagos.

A GOOD-TIME TOWN: LAJARES

Located 13km southwest of Corralejo via the FV-101 and the FV-109, the modest main street in Lajares has a laid-back feel. A handful of foreigners have opened up an enticing combination of restaurants, shops, surf bars and outstanding bakeries. Fancy a slice of dense chocolate torte, some creamy cheesecake topped with berries or an alternative Scandinavian-style breakfast with boiled eggs and cheese? Then check out Pastelo. If you prefer an exquisite French tart (no pun intended), nip over the road to tiny El Goloso. For something altogether more substantial, stop in at super-cool Canela Café, with its diverse menu that includes creamy pumpkin curry (€8) and the surf-and-turf choice of steak and prawns with garlic butter (€17). There's live acoustic music here on weekends.

One of the better craft markets is also held here on Saturday mornings. Failing that, try the marvellously-named Cabracadabra for silk-screen-printed fashions or nearby La Vaca Loca for hand-knitted jumpers. If you are travelling on to El Cotillo, consider taking the minor road just east of the centre, direction north to Majanicho, then following the coastal road to El Cotillo.

travellers. Courses range from four hours to five days (€195) or you can rent a board and wetsuit (from €15 per day).

Riders Surf 'n' Bike — SURFING
(www.riders-surfnbike.com; Calle 3 de Abril 1979; surf lessons from €45, board hire per day from €10) A friendly set-up at the entrance to the town. In addition to courses you can rent surfboards, boogie boards, stand-up paddleboards and, if you prefer to stay on land, bikes (€10 per day).

✖ Eating

The town has some of the north coast's finest restaurants, with the catch of the day reigning supreme. Check out the pavement cafes on the pedestrian Calle Muelle Pescadores.

★ El Goloso de Cotillo — CAFE €
(Calle Pedro Cabrera Saavedra 1; sandwiches €3, tarts €2; 7.30am-7.30pm;) Enjoy decadent tarts in a quiet spot at the north end of the town. There are fresh juices and shakes, and the coffee is excellent. For dessert, try the lemon meringue – it's divine.

El Mentidero — CAFE €
(Calle Punta Aguda 1; sandwiches €3-8; 8am-5pm Tue-Sun;) A popular cafe with plenty of personality. Great for breakfast, a glass of freshly squeezed juice, light lunch or a slice of cake with a superb cup of coffee.

Mare Alta — TAPAS €
(Calle 3 Abril 1979 25; tapas €4-9, mains €8-12; 4pm-midnight Sun-Fri) Belgian-owned tapas bar with imaginative choices and lovely courtyard setting.

La Marisma — SEAFOOD €€
(Calle Mariquita Hierro; mains €14-20; 1-4pm & 7pm-late) A suitably nautical interior and a menu that includes superbly prepared seafood. In a town full of magnificent views, this place has one of the best.

Casa Rústica — MEDITERRANEAN €€
(Calle Constitución 1; mains €10-15; 7-11pm) This place has enjoyed long-time popularity with visitors and locals alike. A comfortable rustic dining room with a few street-side tables is the setting for a diverse range of well-prepared dishes. The cuisine is Spanish with an Italian flourish, like gnocchi with mascarpone and *jamón serrano* (cured Spanish ham).

Restaurante La Vaca Azul — SPANISH €€
(Old Harbour; mains €14-20; 12.30pm-late Wed-Mon) La Vaca Azul enjoys prime position overlooking the pebbly beach, although the surreal rooftop cow (floodlit in lurid blue at night) has the best spot. It's mostly about the location, though you can't go far wrong with a plate of fresh fish. There are a few vegetarian options.

Azzurro — MEDITERRANEAN €€
(Carretera Al Faro; mains €10-15; 1-11pm Tue-Sun) Overlooking the beach at Los Lagos, Azzurro offers quality pasta and seafood.

🛍 Shopping

Clean Ocean Project — CLOTHING
(www.cleanoceanproject.org; 11 Calle del Muelle de Pescadores; 10am-2pm & 5-9pm Mon-Fri, 10am-2pm Sat) Stop by this ecologically aware place that stocks cool surf wear in soft greens and blues. The business donates

a percentage of all profits to beach-cleaning days and anti-pollution awareness. There are branches in Lajares and Corralejo; check the website for more information.

🛈 Getting There & Away

Bus 7 (€4.20, 45 minutes) for Puerto del Rosario leaves daily at 6.30am, noon and 5pm. Bus 8 (€3.10, 40 minutes, 13 daily) leaves for Corralejo. There is plenty of car parking on the streets of the town, although the one-way system is a tad confusing. There is also plenty of parking near the *castillo*.

THE SOUTHEAST

Tarajalejo

This quiet fishing hamlet goes about its business largely undisturbed by tourists, despite the four-star Bahía Playa hotel that dominates much of the beachfront. The small grey beach is nothing spectacular, but it's reasonably uncrowded and has a wide promenade that's a pleasure to stretch your legs on. Stop for a drink at the simple beachside **Piscolabis Adeyu**, where paella is available on Sundays. This is a popular spot for windsurfers; ask at the Bahía Playa for courses and rentals.

Bus 1 (€5.70, 80 minutes, hourly) between Puerto del Rosario and Morro Jable stops at Tarajalejo.

La Lajita

This little fishing village presents yet another black sand and pebble cove with colourful fishing boats and an unspoilt waterfront. However, a sprawl of unimaginative apartment blocks stretches all the way to the highway. At its southern exit is the island's largest theme park: **Oasis Park** (www.fuerteventuraoasispark.com; Carretera General de Jandía; adult/child €25/16; ⊙9am-6pm; ♿). Here you can wander around the little zoo, populated by monkeys, exotic birds and other animals, and see various shows, which include sea lions, birds of prey and parrots. You can also join a 35-minute **camel trek** (adult/child €11/8). If plant life is more your thing, visit the park's botanical garden, with more than 2300 types of cacti.

Bus 1 (€6, 1½ hours, hourly) stops at the highway exit to town, from where it's a short walk south to the zoo. Oasis Park also offers daily free buses from all the main tourist resorts.

PENÍNSULA DE JANDÍA

Most of the peninsula is protected by its status as the Parque Natural de Jandía. The southwest is a remarkable canvas of craggy hills and bald plains leading to cliffs west of Morro Jable. Much of the rest of the peninsula is made up of dunes, scrub and beaches.

It is said that German submarine crews used to occasionally hole up along the peninsula during WWII. Just imagine the paradise they found with not a single tourist or apartment block; only them and their mates!

According to other stories, Nazi officials passed through here after the war to pick up false papers before heading on to South America. One version of the story even has hoards of Nazi gold buried hereabouts – bring your bucket and spade.

The roads are a combination of graded, unsealed and surfaced. A 4WD is recommended if you're heading to Cofete, but it's not essential. There is one bus that dips into the depths of the peninsula and a white-knuckle trip on this 4WD bus is a worthy enough reason to venture here.

Costa Calma

Costa Calma, about 25km northeast of Morro Jable, is a confusing muddle of one-way streets interspersed with apartments, shopping centres (at least eight!) and the occasional hotel. The long and sandy beach is magnificent, but the whole place lacks soul or anything historic; its lifeline being the (mostly) German tourists.

🛪 Activities

Davinga Surf School　　　　　SURFING
(☑677 411090; www.davinga-surf.com; Centro Commericial El Palmeral; ½-day course €45, ½-day board rental €15) Offers board rental and trial surfing days as well as three- and five-day courses for beginners.

Acuarios Jandia　　　　　　　DIVING
(☑928 87 60 69; www.acuarios-jandia.com; ♿) This well-established company runs a wide range of courses, from pool dives for tots (€30) to advanced open-water dive courses (€290).

Club Mistral　　　　　　　WINDSURFING
(☑667 796688; www.club-mistral-fuerteventura.com; 6hr course from €160, board rental per day from €75) A professional outfit also offering kitesurfing courses (two hours from €120).

✕ Eating & Drinking

Rapa Nui   CAFE €
(Commercial Centre Bahia Calma; sandwiches €3-6;
☉9am-6pm) A good choice on a sunny day
(and there are plenty), this place has a lovely
terrace with sea views. It runs the adjacent
surf shop and serves sandwiches, snacks,
ice cream (made on the premises), cocktails
and coffee to a primarily young and tanned
surfing crowd. They also offer daily surfing
lessons.

Bar Synergy   BAR
(Calle Playa de las Pilas, Centro Comercial Costa
Calma; ☉7pm-3am Mon-Sat) Head here for a
mojito sundowner; it's about as hip as Costa Calma gets, with decor in sleek, neutral
tones and picture windows just about giving
you a view of the distant ocean.

La Pared

Located on the west coast, this is another hot
spot for surfers. As you approach the town
from the south, look for the *queso artesano*
sign on your right where you can pick up a
wheel of local organic goat's cheese.

🏃 Activities

Adrenalin Surf School   SURFING
(🖉928 94 90 34; www.adrenalin-surfschool.com;
4hr beginner course €45) Offer classes and
board rental (€20 per day).

Waveguru   SURFING
(🖉619 804447; www.waveguru.de; ½-day board
rental from €15) A long-running surf school
offering beginner courses from four hours
(€50) to a week (€220) as well as classes for
more advanced surfers. Stand-up paddleboarding classes are also available (one-day
course €80) and they can arrange accommodation in apartments or campsites.

✕ Eating

Restaurante Bahía La Pared   SEAFOOD €€
(🖉928 54 90 30; mains €12-15; ☉1-4pm & 7pm-
late) Overlooking the mottled black basalt
and sandy beach, the specialities here are
fresh fish and seafood paella. The restaurant
also runs an adjacent swimming-pool complex, complete with **kiddie slides** (☉noon-
5pm), which is free for diners.

ℹ Getting There & Away

Bus 4 connects La Pared with Morro Jable
(€2.80, 45 minutes) once a day.

OFF THE BEATEN TRACK

FARO DE LA ENTALLADA

Clinging to a clifftop near the fishing
village of Las Playitas, the Faro de la
Entallada is a worthy destination if
you're looking for a scenic drive that
takes you away from the beaten track.
You can't actually enter the impressive
lighthouse, but the winding drive to get
here is pleasant and the views out to sea
are camera worthy. Follow up your visit
with a seafood lunch in Las Playitas.

Playa de Sotavento de Jandía

The name is a catch-all for the series of truly
stunning beaches that stretch along the east
coast of the peninsula. For swimming, sunbathing and windsurfing, this is paradise,
with kilometre after kilometre of fine white
sand that creeps its way almost imperceptibly
into the turquoise expanse of the Atlantic.

The beach that most people visualise
when they think of Sotavento is **Playa de
la Barca**, signposted from the FV-2, 2.5km
south of Costa Calma. This is the wind- and
kitesurfers' beach par excellence, with superb facilities for both beginners and pros.
At low tide, the powdery white beach is almost 200m wide; when the tide comes in it
creates a shallow, turquoise lagoon ideal for
children – and newbie windsurfers. The watersports action is all organised by **René Egli**
(🖉928 54 74 83; www.rene-egli.com; board rental
per day/week from €70/350, beginner courses from
€140; ☉10am-5pm), which has a windsurfing
centre at the northern end of the beach and a
kitesurfing centre at the south. The latter has
a small bar-restaurant and emits a Caribbean feel, with its palm grove and sun loungers
at the water's edge. Courses and rental are
cheaper if you pre-book and accommodation
can also be arranged.

For 10 days each July, the drowsy calm
is shattered by daytime action and frantic
nightlife as the beach hosts a leg of the **Windsurfing World Championship** (www.fuerte-
ventura-worldcup.org), which attracts windsurfers and kiteboarders from around the globe.

Bus 5 drops off at the Melia Gorriones Hotel, just above Playa de la Barca, on its run
between Costa Calma (€1.40, 20 minutes)
and Morro Jable (€1.70, 30 minutes) seven
times daily.

Morro Jable

POP 16,700

More staid than its northern counterpart Corralejo, Morro Jable is almost exclusively German. The beach is the main attraction, with pale golden sand stretching for around 4km from the older part of town. It's fronted by low-rise, immaculately landscaped apartments and hotels. Back from the beach, the charm palls somewhat with a dual carriageway lined with commercial centres and hotels. The older town centre, up the hill, provides a glimpse of what the town must have looked like before the charter flights started landing.

Beaches

Playa del Matorral   BEACH
Playa del Matorral is the main beach here and it's magnificent, stretching eastwards for over 4km from Morro Jable. A family-friendly beach, it's great for indulging in a variety of watersports, churning a pedalo or just collapsing on the sand. It rarely gets crowded, but for true solitude head for the beaches 7km further east, which are accessible only with your own transport.

Activities

Most of the activities here are based in, on or near the sea.

Ocean World   DIVING
(☑ 928 54 14 18; www.tauchen-fuerteventura.com; dive with equipment €45, open-water diver course €360) Organises daily dives at 9am and 2pm.

Surfers Island   SURFING
(www.surfers-island.es; Calle Melindraga 2; 4hr course €49, board rental per hr €12) A well-respected surf school also offering kitesurfing, stand-up paddleboarding, windsurfing and sailing courses.

Volcano Bike   BICYCLE RENTAL
(www.volcano-bike.com; Calle Melindraga, Club Hotel Aldiana Jandia; bike rental per day from €12; ⊙ 9am-11am & 5-7pm) Also offers a variety of cycling tours around the island.

✕ Eating

You can get the usual bland international cuisine and fast food at innumerable places among the apartments, condos and shopping centres along Avenida Saladar. Head into the older part of town for seafood and more authentic choices.

Bar La Parada   TAPAS €
(Calle Nuesta Señora del Carmen 6; tapas €3-6; ⊙ 1-4pm & 7pm-late; ☎) Although the small menu here is translated into several languages, the voices around you are almost all Canarian. Local *señores* come for the hearty goat, rabbit or chickpea stews. Sunday is paella day, when you can get a generous portion for just €7.50.

CANARIES CONSERVATION

The Peninsula de Jandía is home to an important turtle conservation project, which sees loggerhead turtles being reintroduced after an absence of some 100 years. The programme dates back to January 2007 when 145 loggerhead turtles were successfully hatched on the west coast beach of Cofete in the Parque Natural de Jandía.

The beaches here are only the second site in the world selected for such a translocation of eggs; the first is in Mexico. The eggs came from a turtle colony in the southern islands of Cape Verde, which has similarities to the beaches and environment here, namely the quality of the water, the sand and, above all, the consistently warm climate. The turtle eggs are hatched in artificial nests and, before they can crawl away to an uncertain future, the baby turtles are transferred to special tanks at the 'turtle nursery' in Morro Jable until they are strong enough to swim without water wings. At this stage they are microchipped and released into the sea.

The hope is that when they are all grown up they will return to their Cofete home to lay eggs themselves so the species will once again spontaneously breed on the island. The project organisers hope to repeat the hatching at least every five years in an attempt to reverse the depletion of this species of marine turtle.

You can visit the **nursery** (⊙ 9am-1pm Mon-Fri) FREE, which also takes in injured turtles found around the island. It's in Morro Jable's harbour.

La Bodega de Jandía TAPAS €

(Calle Diputado Manuel Velazquez Cabrera; tapas €4-9; ⏰1-4pm & 7pm-late Wed-Mon) With legs of ham hanging from the ceiling and vocal locals shouting out their orders, this place has more atmosphere than the tourist restaurants along the seafront. Canarian specialities are *ropa vieja* (meat-based stew) and *mousse de gofio* (mousse with roasted grains) feature or on Sunday you can enjoy a plate of paella at a table in the cobbled, pedestrian street.

La Laja SEAFOOD €€

(Calle Tomas Grau; mains €10-18; ⏰1-4pm & 7pm-late) A good seafood choice located on the corner of the boardwalk, with great views.

Drinking & Nightlife

The main nightlife action is along the beachfront part of the resort. There are also a couple of bars and a nightclub in the Cosmo Centro Comercial, though the centre is looking a little neglected these days.

Olympia BAR

(Centro Comercial Playa Paradiso, Avenida Saladar; ⏰10am-1am) With comfortable wicker furniture, a central bar and picture windows overlooking the seafront, this place is perfect for post-dinner cocktails; the music is pretty chill as well.

Shopping

There's a small market (Avenida Saladar; ⏰9am-2pm Mon & Thu) in a car park due west of the tourist office. With most stalls run by traders from West and North Africa, you'll be lucky to find anything that smacks particularly of the Canaries.

Cosmo Centro Comercial SHOPPING CENTRE

(Avenida Saladar) This large centre has plenty of shops selling tax-free goodies.

❶ Information

Tourist Office (Cosmo Centro Comercial, Avenida Saladar; ⏰8am-3pm Mon-Fri) Lots of brochures and helpful staff.

❶ Getting There & Away

The port, Puerto de Morro Jable, is 3km by road from the centre of town.

Bus 1 runs to Puerto del Rosario (€10, two hours, at least 12 daily) between 5.45am (weekdays) and 10.30pm. Bus 10 (€9.70, 1¾ hours, three daily), via the airport, is faster. Bus 5 (€2.70, 40 minutes) to Costa Calma runs frequently.

AUTHENTIC CRAFTS

Throughout Europe, government-endorsed arts-and-crafts shops equal a hike in prices and are places to avoid for euro economisers. In Fuerteventura, however, they have the equation right: the artisans determine the prices and receive 100% of the profits.

The government's role is solely to verify the authenticity of the craft in question, which is, unfortunately, quite important these days, given the prolific sale of Chinese-imported lacework and other similar goods. Look for the distinctive stamp of guarantee, with its green border for creative handicrafts and brown border for traditional handicrafts. All the labels should be numbered and contain the details of the artisan. Look for the shops in the Molino de Antigua, Betancuria, Puerto del Rosario and, yes, even at the airport.

TO/FROM THE AIRPORT
Bus 10 (€8.20, 1½ hours, three daily) connects the town with the airport; taxis cost around €75.

❶ Getting Around

There is a large, free car park next to the tourist office in the Cosmo Centro Comercial. Finding a spot in the older part of the town can be problematic. Call if you need a taxi (☎928 54 12 57).

Around Morro Jable

Much wilder than their leeward counterparts, the long stretches of beach on the windward side of the Península de Jandía are also harder to get to. A 4WD isn't necessary to reach the lighthouse, though you might want one to navigate the winding dirt road to Cofete.

Punta de Jandía

About 2km south of Morro Jable, the tarred road peters out and the dirt roads begin. The track gets plenty of use, though, so is in pretty good nick. From Morro Jable it winds out along the southern reaches of the peninsula to a lone lighthouse (⏰10am-6pm Tue-Sat) FREE at Punta de Jandía. Within the lighthouse you'll find exhibits detailing the flora, fauna and geology of the Parque Natural de Jandía.

LOCAL KNOWLEDGE

VILLA WINTER: THE MYSTERIOUS MANSION

When you finally arrive in Cofete, you can't fail to notice the elaborate, abandoned mansion perched above the coast. You also can't fail to be intrigued – and you won't be the first. The impressive structure, with its castle-like turret, was built by German engineer Gustav Winter in the 1930s. Rumours linking Winter to the Nazi party have never been confirmed, but conspiracy theories regarding Villa Winter (also known as Casa de los Winter) abound. Winter supposedly wanted to establish agriculture in the area, but little evidence of this has been found and, back then, there were likely no roads leading to the eerie mansion. Some think the house was built as a secret hideout for high-ranking Nazis, including Hitler himself. Others have suggested that Cofete was the location of a secret U-boat base, that there are secret tunnels through the mountain or that it was in fact built as a clinic that would specialise in plastic surgery for German generals needing a new look.

There is a caretaker here and for a small tip he will usually show you around the house. Some have said that they've been allowed into the basement, where they've seen shackles, cells and bullet holes, but like pretty much everything about Villa Winter, you can't be too sure. There's really only one thing that you can be certain of: Villa Winter is a fascinating place that will have you digging deeper for the truth. Or at least for a few more stories…

Just before you reach the lighthouse, you get to **Puerto de la Cruz**, a tiny fishing settlement and beach. There are three restaurants here, all specialising in fresh fish. All have outdoor terraces, but only **El Caletón** (mains €8-12; ⊙ lunch Tue-Sun) has ocean views. Fish stew is the local speciality. The lighthouse is a superb spot for sunset, but you have to hightail it back afterwards, unless you want to be caught driving on dirt tracks after dark.

Cofete

About 10km west from Morro Jable, a turnoff leads northeast over a pass and plunges to Cofete, a tiny peninsula hamlet at the southern extreme of the Playas de Barlovento de Jandía. With narrow corners, steep drops and no barriers, driving the dirt road to get here requires nerves of steel. There is a mirador about halfway – a wind-whipped spot where a lot of people give up and turn back. But if you do persevere, you'll be rewarded with one of the most remote and spectacular beaches in the archipelago. Sandy tracks, negotiable on foot or by 4WD, snake off to this wind-whipped stretch of coast. The main beach here, **Playa de Cofete**, is quite beautiful and completely undeveloped, but think twice about swimming here: the waves and currents are more formidable than the generally calmer waters on the other side of the island. If you know what you're doing and have your own gear, it is a good spot for surfers. **Restaurante Cofete** (☑ 928 17 42 43; mains €8-14; ⊙ 11am-7pm) does drinks and excellent snacks and has a more sophisticated menu than you'd expect from a restaurant that's literally at the end of the road. It serves fresh fish as well as *carne de cabra en salsa* (goat in sauce).

If you dare not tackle the road yourself, you can take the funky little 4WD bus (€2.70, 90 minutes) that makes the trip from Morro Jable at 10am and 2pm daily, returning at 12.30pm and 4.30pm. The bus also stops at Puerto de la Cruz and the lighthouse.

Lanzarote

📞 928 / POP 142,000

Best Places to Eat

➡ El Navarro (p104)
➡ Lilium (p101)
➡ La Cabaña (p117)

Best Places to Stay

➡ Hotelito del Golf (p225)
➡ Finca de Arrieta (p224)
➡ Caserío de Mozaga (p225)

Why Go?

A Unesco biosphere reserve, Lanzarote is an intriguing island with an extraordinary geology of 300 volcanic cones, at the same time ticking all the right good-time boxes. There are great beaches, interesting sights and plenty of restaurants and hotels. The landscape has a stark and otherworldly appearance, with the occasional bucolic, palm-filled valley juxtaposed with surreal, crinkly black lava fields.

Long associated with package tourists and pie-and-chips resorts, times are finally changing and there has been a marked increase in the number of independent travellers to the island. In response, the government has undertaken an island-wide initiative to signpost walking trails, and rural accommodation options have increased.

The island's major sights have been aesthetically developed by the late César Manrique, a Lanzarote native and artist. He still has a considerable impact on the island via a cultural foundation that promotes Lanzarote's conservation, culture and architectural integrity.

When to Go

➡ The island's annual Carnaval in February or March pales slightly compared to Tenerife or Gran Canaria, but is still celebrated with great gusto. Processions, music and general merriment abound.

➡ Peak periods are Easter, July, August and December.

➡ Cheaper airfares from other European destinations are normally most plentiful during the autumn and spring (aside from Easter holidays).

➡ Día de San Ginés takes place on 25 August. The festivities happen across the island.

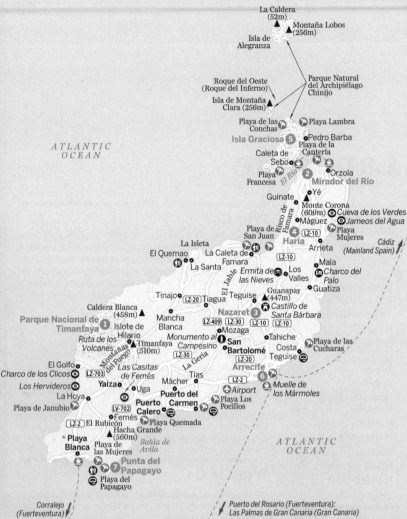

Lanzarote Highlights

1 Get snap-happy in the magnificent **Parque Nacional de Timanfaya** (p114), with its other-worldly lavascapes and lunar-like scenery

2 Enjoy heady sweeping views from mountaintop **Mirador del Río** (p110)

3 Imagine yourself at a 1970s celebrity party at Omar

Sharif's one-time home, **Lagomar** in Nazaret (p106)

4 Experience an oasis of green at lush, palm-filled **Haría** (p110)

5 Spend the night on **Isla Graciosa** (p109), with its empty beaches and gentle hikes

6 Enjoy **Arrecife's** (p99) chilled wining, dining and dancing scene at the Marina Lanzarote

7 Kick back on the golden sandy beaches of **Punta del Papagayo** (p119), on the wild south coast

History

Lanzarote has experienced more than its fair share of misfortune. It was the first island to fall to Jean de Béthencourt in 1402 and was subsequently made the unneighbourly base for conquering the rest of the archipelago. Many locals were sold into slavery and those remaining had to endure waves of marauding pirates from the northwest African coast. Today's popular tourist site, the Cueva de los Verdes, was a refuge for those unable to flee to Gran Canaria, but of course it couldn't protect their homes from large-scale looting. British buccaneers, such as Sir Walter Raleigh, also got in on the plundering act and, by the mid-17th century, the population had dwindled to a mere 300.

Just as the human assault seemed to be abating, nature elbowed in – big time. During the 1730s, massive volcanic eruptions destroyed a dozen towns and some of the island's most fertile land. But the islanders were to discover an ironic fact: the volcanic soil proved a highly fertile bedrock for farming (particularly wine grapes), which brought relative prosperity to the island.

Today, with tourism flourishing alongside the healthy, if small, agricultural sector, the island is home to just over 142,000 people, not counting all the holiday blow-ins who, at any given time, can more than double the population.

Getting There & Away

AIR

The island's **airport** (☑ 902 40 47 04; www.aena.es) is 6km southwest of Arrecife. Both **Binter Canarias** (☑ 902 391 392; www.bintercanarias.com) and newbie airline **Canary Fly** (☑ 902 80 80 65; www.canaryfly.es) operate direct flights to Gran Canaria and Tenerife. Canary Fly also offers direct flights to La Palma.

BOAT

Ferries leaving from Arrecife's Puerto de los Mármoles connect Lanzarote with Gran Canaria and, less frequently, Tenerife and La Palma. From Playa Blanca in the south there are regular ferries taking you just across the water to Corralejo in Fuerteventura.

Trasmediterránea (Map p101; ☑ in Arrecife 902 45 46 45; www.trasmediterranea.es) Runs a weekly ferry on Wednesday at midnight (€33, eight hours) from Arrecife to Las Palmas de Gran Canaria. Buy tickets at the ferry terminal up to one hour before embarkation or via the website. A weekly ferry also runs to Santa Cruz

ROAD DISTANCES (KM)

	Yaiza	Playa Blanca	Puerto del Carmen	Arrecife
Playa Blanca	14			
Puerto del Carmen	13	29		
Arrecife	23	39	38	
La Caleta de Famara	25	40	25	16

Approximate distances only

de la Palma (€35, 32 hours) and Santa Cruz de Tenerife (€35, 17 hours).

Fred Olsen (☑ 902 10 01 07; www.fredolsen.es) Ferries (€30, 25 minutes, six times daily) link Playa Blanca with Corralejo on Fuerteventura.

Naviera Armas (Map p101; ☑ 902 45 65 00; www.navieraarmas.com) Has five ferries per week (€49, 5½ hours, 30 minutes) between Arrecife and Las Palmas de Gran Canaria and six sailings daily (€25, 35 minutes) between Playa Blanca and Corralejo on Fuerteventura. There are also five weekly ferries to Santa Cruz de Tenerife (€72, 10 hours).

Getting Around

BUS

Intercity Bus Lanzarote operates a fairly comprehensive network of buses around the island, though if you're hopping between small towns you'll need to plan carefully as services are infrequent.

CAR

Driving on Lanzarote is the best way to see the island. You'll find plenty of car rental agencies at the airport, in Arrecife and in the main tourist resorts.

ARRECIFE

POP 56,900

Arrecife is a small, manageable city with a pleasant Mediterranean-style promenade, an inviting sandy beach and – it has to be said – a disarming backstreet hotchpotch of sun-bleached, peeling buildings, elegant boutiques, unpretentious bars and good (and bad) restaurants. The sights are scarce, yet interesting, and include a couple of castles, a pretty lagoon and a vibey marina. If anything, Arrecife's most notable quality is that it's a no-nonsense working town that earns its living from something other than tourism.

LANZAROTE ARRECIFE

History

The single biggest factor behind Arrecife's lack of pizzazz is that it only became the island's capital in 1852. Until then, Teguise ruled supreme. In 1574 the Castillo de San Gabriel was first constructed (it was subsequently attacked and rebuilt) to protect the port. Its shorter and squatter younger sibling further up the coast, the Castillo de San José, was built between 1776 and 1779.

By the close of the 18th century, a semblance of a town had taken uncertain shape around the harbour. As commerce grew and the threat of sea raids dropped off in the 19th century, the town thrived and the move of the island's administration to Arrecife became inevitable.

⊙ Sights

Arrecife is easy to navigate. With the notable exceptions of the Castillo de San José and the port, everything of interest is located in a tight area around the centre.

★ Museo Internacional de Arte Contemporáneo
GALLERY

(MIAC; Carretera de Puerto Naos; adult/child €4/2; ⊙10am-8pm) Converted in 1994 by the Fundación César Manrique into a sleek, contemporary art museum and restaurant, the Castillo de San José was built in the 18th century to deal with pirates and provide unemployed locals with a public-works job scheme. Today it houses one of the most important collections of modern art in the Canaries. Aside from a couple of early works by Manrique himself, artists such as Miró, Millares, Rivera, Sempere and Tápies are on show.

Charco de San Ginés
LAGOON

(Avenida César Manrique) This attractive small lake with its colourful boats and resident seagulls could have been as overwrought as picture-perfect Portofino. Instead, the buildings and restaurants here are a beguiling combo of mildly down-at-heel and freshly whitewashed (with blue trim).

Museo de Historia de Arrecife
MUSEUM

(✆928 80 28 84; Calle Aquilino Fernández 26; ⊙10am-5pm Mon-Fri, 10am-2pm Sat) **FREE** Located on a little islet just off the seafront promenade, this small museum is based in the 16th-century Castillo de San Gabriel. Exhibits include information on the island's geology, flora and fauna as well as pre-Hispanic life and the conquest, but all information is in

Spanish only. Head to the roof for an amusingly shot video of the island and good views of the city.

Iglesia de San Ginés
CHURCH

(Plaza de San Ginés; ⊙before & after Mass) Dating from 1665 and featuring a statue of the island's patron saint, who originated in Cuba.

Centro Insular de Cultura El Almacén
CULTURAL CENTRE

(✆928 81 01 21; Calle José Betancourt 33) At the time of research this gallery and cinema had been closed for refurbishment for some time. Check with the tourist office for updates.

🏖 Beaches

Playa del Reducto
BEACH

If you fancy a dip, the city's main beach, Playa del Reducto, is lovely: an arc of pristine pale golden sand fringed with lofty palm trees and a promenade. It's safe for children, reasonably clean and, generally, surprisingly empty. You can also stride south from here on a coastal walk to Puerto del Carmen (12km, about three hours).

🎉 Festivals & Events

Carnaval
CARNIVAL

(⊙Feb or Mar) Celebrated with gusto throughout the island, but particularly in Arrecife, Carnaval festivities kick off the week before Ash Wednesday.

Día de San Ginés
RELIGIOUS

(⊙25 Aug) The day of the island's patron saint is celebrated with a major fiesta in even the smallest *pueblo* (village). In Arrecife, the streets surrounding the Iglesia de San Ginés are home to the most revelry.

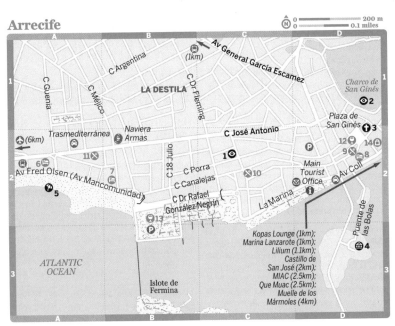

✖ Eating

Fish lovers should head for the Charco de San Ginés, which is surrounded by breezy seafood restaurants. Elsewhere, there's a smattering of outdoor cafes and restaurants on Calle Ruperto González Negrín and Avenida La Marina and some super drinking and dining options at the stylish Marina Lanzarote.

Bar Andalucía   TAPAS €

(Calle Luis Martín 5; tapas €3-8; ⊘1-4pm & 7pm-late Mon-Sat) Open since 1960, this side-street bar oozes charm with its Andalucian tiles, paintings for sale and straight-from-Seville tapas, such as stuffed peppers and sirloin cooked in sherry. There's a good wine list too.

El Barrilito   TAPAS €

(Calle José Antonio; tapas €4-8; ⊘1-4pm & 7pm-late Tue-Sun; 🕾) The terrace overlooking a busy road isn't as inviting as those of the ocean-facing restaurants, but this place is great for a little local flavour. There's a wide range of tapas – try the dates wrapped in bacon – as well as a menu of *montaditos* (like a mini open sandwich).

Arrecife

★ **Lilium**   MODERN CANARIAN €€

(🗾928 52 49 78; www.restaurantelilium.com; Avenida Olof Palme, Marina Lanzarote; mains €12-18; ⊘1-4pm & 7pm-late Wed-Mon; ℗) In a suitably stylish new home in the revamped Marina, Lilium continues to wow with decadent

> **ⓘ APPY TRAVELS**
>
> If you travel with a smartphone in hand, you might want to check out **Lanzarote App** (www.applelanzarote.es), which offers discounts on activities and allows you to book accommodation and restaurants, among other things.

dishes like confit duck leg with fig sauce or grilled scallops with banana, coconut, caviar and lime. Traditional Canarian ingredients get a revamp: *gofio* (corn meal), palm syrup and *almogrote* (a delicious blend of goat's cheese, garlic and chilli) all grace the menu. Bookings recommended.

Domus Pompeii   ITALIAN €€

(Calle José Betancourt 19; mains €7-12; ⊘1-4pm & 7pm-late Mon-Sat; 🖋) The owner of this trattoria is from Pompeii, so expect faux-Roman surroundings and delicious thin-crust Neapolitan pizzas, plus homemade pasta with simple, fresh sauces. The complimentary *limoncello* liqueur is a nice touch.

Que Muac   MEDITERRANEAN €€€

(🖋928 81 23 21; Castillo de San José, MIAC; mains €15; ⊘10am-4pm daily, 7-11pm Fri & Sat; 🅿) Situated in the Castillo de San José, this is one of Arrecife's most upscale dining experiences, though the food, which includes dishes like shoulder of lamb stuffed with nuts, is not quite as spectacular as the setting. Opt for lunch over dinner, when you can fully enjoy the Manrique decor and ocean views through vast wraparound windows.

🍷 Drinking

There are a few clubs and bars on a short strip of central Calle José Antonio. They're open from around 10pm until approximately 4am, though names change too often to rec-

ommend a particular place. The new nightlife zone is at the swanky Marina Lanzarote, where you'll find restaurants and cocktail bars with terraces overlooking the harbour.

La Tentacion   BAR

(Plaza de las Palmas; ⊘7pm-midnight Mon-Sat) Across from the Iglesia de San Ginés, with good wines and tapas, including some Cuban-inspired choices like *yucca frita* (fried yucca).

Star City   BAR

(Arrecife Gran Hotel, Avenida Fred Olsen; ⊘10.30am-midnight) You can't miss this looming green skyscraper that, unsurprisingly, was built before Manrique returned to the island and initiated strict building guidelines. Like it or loathe it, there's no avoiding the fact that the 17th-floor bar has unbeatable panoramic views. Open daily for coffee and cocktails.

Kopas Disco   CLUB

(Avenida Olof Palme, Marina Lanzarote; ⊘11pm-6am Fri & Sat; 🕾) Arrecife's most stylish club attracts a well-heeled crowd who come to hear local DJs and occasional live bands. Adjoining the club is **Kopas Lounge** (Avenida Olof Palme, Marina Lanzarote; ⊘10am-2am Mon-Sat), with sleek white furniture and an expansive selection of gin.

🛍 Shopping

For the highest concentration of shops head for pedestrianised Avenida León y Castillo.

La Recova Market   MARKET

(Calle Manuel Miranda; ⊘9am-2pm Mon-Sat) Located between Avenida León y Castillo and Charco de San Ginés, the historical town market has a few stalls selling handicrafts. It's also a nice place for a cup of coffee under the trees.

WALKS ON THE WILD SIDE

The surreal volcanic landscape on Lanzarote is best appreciated on foot. There are well-signposted hiking trails criss-crossing the island, though figuring out where the hikes begin sometimes takes a little effort. Start at the tourist information office, but if you draw a blank, head to the **cabildo** (www.cabildodelanzarote.com; Avenida Fred Olsen) in Arrecife. The island government is in charge of clearing, signposting and renovating the walking trails and also produces detailed maps showing the routes and essential details such as length of walk, type of terrain and level of difficulty, plus the flora, fauna and points of interest to be found along the way.

There is some basic information on the tourist board's website (www.turismolanzarote.com) to get you started.

NATIVE SON

César Manrique is the island's most famous native son and his influence is everywhere, ranging from the obvious, like his giant mobile sculptures adorning roundabouts, to the (thankfully) unseen: the lack of high-rise buildings and advertising billboards.

Born on 24 April 1919, Manrique was initially best known as a contemporary artist. Influenced by Picasso and Matisse, he held his first major exhibition of abstract works in 1954 and, 10 years later, his art career reached its pinnacle with an exhibition at New York's Guggenheim Museum. But Manrique never forgot his birthplace and returned home in 1966, after his successful US tour, brimming with ideas for enhancing what he felt to be the incomparable beauty of Lanzarote.

He began with a campaign to preserve traditional building methods and a ban on roadside hoardings. A multifaceted artist, Manrique subsequently turned his flair and vision to a broad range of projects, with the whole of Lanzarote becoming his canvas. In all, he carried out seven major projects on the island and numerous others elsewhere in the archipelago and beyond. At the time of his death, he had several more in the works.

On a grander scale, it was primarily thanks to Manrique's persistent lobbying for maintaining traditional architecture and protecting the natural environment that prompted the *cabildo* (island government) to pass laws restricting urban development. The growing wave of tourism, beginning in the early 1980s, has threatened to sweep away all before it. But Manrique's ceaseless opposition to such unchecked urban sprawl touched a nerve with many locals and led to the creation of an environmental group known as El Guincho, which has had some success in revealing – and at times even reversing – abuses by developers. Manrique was posthumously made its honorary president.

As you pass through villages across the island, you'll see how traditional stylistic features remain the norm. The standard whitewashed houses are adorned with green-painted doors, window shutters and strange onion-shaped chimney pots. In such ways, Manrique's influence and spirit endure.

ℹ Information

Main Tourist Office (☏ 928 81 31 74; www.turismolanzarote.com; La Marina; ⊘ 9.30am-5pm Mon-Fri, 10am-1pm Sat) Located in a fabulous bandstand rotunda building on the promenade.

Tourist Office (Marina Lanzarote; ⊘ 8am-7pm Mon-Sat) Situated at the northern end of the marina. There's also a car rental office here.

ℹ Getting There & Away

BUS

Intercity Bus Lanzarote (☏ 928 81 15 22; www.intercitybuslanzarote.es) operates buses to all the major towns and resorts. The main bus station is north of the city centre on Vía Medular though some routes also leave from a more convenient **stop** (Map p101) next to the *cabildo* (island government) on Avenida Fred Olsen. Popular routes include the following:

Bus 1 Costa Teguise (€1.40, 20 minutes, every 20 minutes)

Bus 2 Puerto del Carmen (€1.70, 40 minutes, every 20 minutes)

Bus 6 Playa Blanca (€3.60, one hour, hourly)

Bus 7 Teguise (€1.40, 30 minutes, six daily)

Bus 9 Órzola (€3.60, one hour, five daily)

CAR & MOTORCYCLE

You will find plenty of rental companies, especially around Avenida Mancomunidad and Calle Dr Rafael González Negrín.

ℹ Getting Around

A couple of *guaguas municipales* (local buses) follow circuits around town, but you're unlikely to need them. Street parking is limited. There is free parking besides El Charco de San Ginés. Alternatively, head for the waterfront Gran Hotel, with its underground paying car park. You can call for a **taxi** (☏ 928 80 08 06); otherwise there's a **taxi rank** beside the tourist office on La Marina and another **rank** on Calle José Antonio.

TO/FROM THE AIRPORT

Lanzarote's airport is 6km south of Arrecife. Buses 22 and 23 (€1.40, 10 minutes) run between the airport and Arrecife half-hourly from 7.30am to 10.30pm Monday to Friday and 8am to 9pm on weekends. A taxi will cost about €12.

TO/FROM THE PORT

Puerto de los Mármoles is about 4km northeast of central Arrecife. Bus 1 calls in at the port. A taxi costs about €10.

ℹ BONO BUS

If you are planning on making a few trips, invest in a Bono Bus card, which can save you up to 30% off the fare. The cards cost €10, €20 or €30 (depending on how many trips you plan on taking) and are purchased at bus stations.
Tell the driver your destination and the amount will be deducted from your card via a stamping machine.

NORTH OF ARRECIFE

Costa Teguise

Northeast of Arrecife is Costa Teguise, which is perfectly pleasant provided you are not expecting cobbled streets and crumbling buildings. This is a purpose-built holiday resort with bustling shopping centres, family-geared beaches and water sports, plenty of mediocre (and better) bars and restaurants but, inevitably, no real soul. There's not even an original fishing village at its heart.

The most appealing beach is Playa de las Cucharas. Those further south suffer unfortunate views of the port and industry near Arrecife. The Centro Comercial Las Cucharas shopping centre is the resort's focal point.

◉ Sights & Activities

Lanzarote Aquarium   AQUARIUM
(www.aquariumlanzarote.com; Centro Comercial El Trébol; adult/child €12.50/8; ☺10am-6pm; 🚼) If you're at a loose end with kids, this is an OK wet weather option, though some baulk at the relatively high entrance fees and the dark interior. There are touch pools and a shark tank, plus plenty of colourful fish and sea critters viewed from an underwater tunnel.

★Olita Treks   HIKING
(📞619 169989; www.olita-treks.com; Centro Comercial Las Maretas; walks €40) Conducts excellent walks across the island, which cover turf such as the Isla Graciosa, the island's volcanoes and the wine region. Most walks are around four hours; the price includes transport.

Calipso Diving   DIVING
(📞928 59 08 79; www.calipso-diving.com; Avenida Islas Canarias, Centro Comercial Calipso; dive with equipment rental €44) Long-established and a reliable choice for courses and dives; there is equipment hire for experienced divers.

Aquatis Diving Center   DIVING
(📞928 59 04 07; www.diving-lanzarote.net; Playa de las Cucharas; dive with equipment rental €40, aquarium dive €200) As well as the usual diving packages, there is the more unusual opportunity to dive surrounded by sharks at Lanzarote Aquarium – it's an extra €50 if you're not a qualified diver.

Bike Station   CYCLING
(📞628 102177; www.bikelanzarote.com; Avenida Islas Canarias, Centro Comercial Las Maretas; bike rental per day/week from €14/70; ☺10am-noon & 6-7pm) Rents bikes and arranges tours (from €45) around the island.

✕ Eating & Drinking

There's no shortage of restaurants, although you sometimes have to dig a little to find the Spanish fare hidden away amid all the English pub grub.

★El Navarro   MODERN CANARIAN €€
(📞928 59 21 45; Avenida del Mar 13; mains €12-18; ☺7-11pm Mon-Sat) Advance bookings are absolutely essential if you hope to try out this small restaurant, considered one of the island's best. The menu features just half a dozen main course options, all of them intricately prepared with fresh, local ingredients.

La Bohemia   STEAK €€
(📞928 59 17 72; Avenida Islas Canarias 22; mains €12-18, tapas €4-9; ☺1.30-11pm Thu-Tue) Frequented by locals just as much as tourists, this stylish spot is carnivore heaven, with great steaks and mixed grills. There's also a decent range of tapas – the *papas bravas* are particularly good.

Los Aljibes   MICROBREWERY
(📞610 454294; Calle Bravo Murillo 6; ☺7pm-midnight; 🅟) About halfway between Costa Teguise and Tahiche, near the golf course, you'll find Lanzarote's first microbrewery. Los Aljibes is a bright and funky bar, serving good, honest food and two different beers brewed on site. Sit in the palm- and cactus-dotted garden and enjoy mountain views with your pint.

☆ Entertainment

Jazz...Mi Madre!   LIVE MUSIC
(Avenida Islas Canarias, Centro Comercial Calipso, Local 1; ☺9.30pm-3.30am Wed-Sun) At last! A tourist resort option that doesn't play head-banging techno or cheesy pop for the masses. Expect live jazz and blues played

FUNDACIÓN CÉSAR MANRIQUE

Only 6km north of Arrecife, Fundación César Manrique (César Manrique Foundation; ☑928 84 31 38; www.fcmanrique.org; adult/child €8/free; ⊙10am-6pm) was home to Manrique, who enjoys a posthumous status on the island akin to that of a mystical hero. He built his house, Taro de Tahiche, into the lava fields just outside the town. The subterranean rooms are actually huge air bubbles left behind by flowing lava. It's a real James Bond hideaway, with white-leather seats slotted into cavelike dens, and a sunken swimming pool.

There's a whole gallery devoted to Manrique, plus minor works by some of his contemporaries, including Picasso, Chillida, Miró, Sempere and Tàpies. Tragically, in September 1992, only six months after the foundation opened its doors, Manrique was killed a few metres away in a car accident.

From Sala 10, have a look out the large picture window at the striking modern building semisubmerged into the lava field and topped by a series of cupolas. Formerly owned by a wealthy architect from Tenerife, it was bought by the foundation in early 2011, though it is not open to the public.

Make sure you keep hold of your ticket; if you present it at the Casa Museo César Manrique in Haría (p110), you get you a discount on the entrance fee.

At least seven buses a day stop here on their way from Arrecife to Teguise. Look for the huge mobile sculpture by Manrique dominating the roundabout south of Tahiche, and walk 200m down the San Bartolomé road.

by accomplished musicians and a more mature, albeit enthusiastic, foot-tapping crowd.

ℹ Information

Tourist Office (☑928 59 25 42; Avenida Islas Canarias; ⊙9am-5pm Mon-Fri, 9am-2.30pm Sat & Sun) Ask for the brochure detailing three walks around town and beyond, ranging from 4.6km to 10km.

ℹ Getting There & Away

Bus 1 (€1.40, 20 minutes, every 20 minutes) connects with Arrecife (via Puerto de los Mármoles) from 7am to midnight.

Teguise

POP 1800

Teguise, 12km north of Arrecife, has a North Africa–meets–Spanish *pueblo* feel. It is an intriguing mini oasis of low-rise buildings set around a central plaza and surrounded by the bare plains of central Lanzarote. Firmly on the tourist trail, there are decent restaurants, a couple of bars and a handful of monuments testifying to the fact that the town was the island's capital until Arrecife took the baton in 1852.

Maciot, the son of Jean de Béthencourt, moved here when it was a Guanche settlement and married Teguise, daughter of the one-time local chieftain. Various convents were founded and the town prospered. But with prosperity came other problems, including pirates who plundered the town several times, reaching a violent crescendo in 1618 when an armada of 5000 Algerian buccaneers overran the town, hence the ominously named Callejón de la Sangre (Blood Alley).

Teguise is completely taken over by a mammoth and very touristy Sunday-morning market, complete with burger stalls and human statues. Unless this is your thing, visit another day. There is a dearth of places to stay in town, but Teguise makes for an easy and delightful day trip, thanks to its central location.

◉ Sights

Wandering Teguise's pedestrianised lanes is a pleasure in itself. Pick up a brochure detailing the town's historical buildings from the tourist information office.

★Museo de la Piratería   MUSEUM
(Castillo de Santa Bárbara; www.teguise.es; adult/child €3/free; ⊙9am-4pm Mon-Sat, 10am-4pm Sun; ℙ 🚻) This modest yet fascinating museum is located in the imposing 16th-century Castillo de Santa Bárbara. This is the oldest castle in the Canaries and really looks the part, perched up on Guanapay peak with sweeping views across the plains. The exhibits detail the numerous attacks Lanzarote suffered at the hands of pirates from across Europe and Africa during the 16th century, when Teguise was the island's capital. It's great for kids.

CELEBRITY CAVE COMPLEX

En route from Tahiche to Teguise, you pass through the sleepy small town of Nazaret. In the centre, look for a sign to Lagomar (www.lag-o-mar.com; Calle Los Loros; adult/child €5/2; ⊙10am-6pm; P). Carved into the rock face, with fanciful chimneys, cupolas, miradors and winding staircases, this gallery, museum, restaurant and bar has a New Mexico–meets-Morocco look. Regular exhibitions are held, while a small museum recounts the interesting history of the house. There is a lot of myth and legend surrounding the house, but what is sure is that it was designed by César Manrique and Jesús Soto, a prominent Lanzarote architect. It's billed as the house of Omar Sharif, though the late actor lived here only very briefly, after losing it to a local property developer in a spectacularly unsuccessful game of bridge. It's a hugely underrated and blissfully uncrowded attraction. Best of all is to come in the evening for dinner at the restaurant (☑928 84 56 65; mains €14-20; ⊙noon-11.30pm Tue-Sun) or a cocktail at the bar (⊙6.30pm-1am Tue-Sun) – you can really get a feel for the wild celebrity parties that must once have taken place here and what's more, you don't have to pay the entrance fee if you're drinking or dining!

Nearby is Barstro (☑689 451108; Calle Las Perdices; tapas €4-8, mains €12-20; ⊙1-11pm Thu-Sun, 6-11pm Wed; P), a super-funky tapas bar and bistro serving inventive cuisine of an ilk that you wouldn't expect to find in a town of 900 people.

Convento de Santo Domingo
GALLERY

(Calle Guadalupe; ⊙9am-2pm Mon-Fri, 10am-2pm Sun) FREE The rotating exhibitions of local contemporary art hosted here contrast wonderfully with the stark 17th-century monastery.

Casa Museo del Timple
MUSEUM

(www.casadeltimple.org; Plaza de la Constitución; adult/child €3/free; ⊙9am-4pm Mon-Fri, to 3pm Sun) Based in the 18th-century Palacio Spínola, this museum is dedicated to the *timple,* a traditional Canarian stringed instrument similar to a ukulele. There are displays of *timples* through the ages as well as similar instruments from around the world, but information is in Spanish only. The best bit is the chance to poke your nose around the grand old building.

Museo Diocesano de Arte Sacro
GALLERY

(Calle San Francisco, Convento de San Francisco; adult/child €1.50/free; ⊙9.30am-4.30pm Tue-Sat, 10am-2pm Sun) The 17th-century convent houses a modest collection of religious art.

✦ Festivals & Events

Fiesta de Nuestra Señora del Carmen
RELIGIOUS

(⊙16 Jul) A celebration of the town's saint, with plenty of dancing in the street and general merriment.

✗ Eating

As well as the places mentioned here, there are plenty of nice tapas spots around the main square and surrounding alleys.

★ La Cantina
TAPAS €€

(☑928 84 55 36; www.cantinateguise.com; Calle León y Castillo 8; tapas €6, mains €12-20; ⊙10am-11pm; ☎✐) Run by Benn and Zoe, an enthusiastic English couple, this restaurant is in one of the oldest houses on the island, dating back some 500 years. Local products feature heavily on the menu – try a shared platter of local cheese, *papas arrugadas* (wrinkly potatoes), *gofio* and *mojo* (spicy salsa). There is an excellent wine list and a shop selling local goodies.

Restaurante Hespérides Bio
MEDITERRANEAN €€

(Calle León y Castillo, Casa León; mains €15, tapas €5-15; ⊙1-11pm Mon-Fri, 10am-4pm Sun; ✐) This small restaurant shares its locale with a health-food shop and alternative-therapy centre. The cuisine is eclectic Mediterranean with choices like red lentil and tomato soup, risotto with tofu, and squid stuffed with goat's cheese, washed down with local organic wines. The ambience is laid-back and cosy, with Moroccan lamps and provocative artwork.

❶ Information

Tourist Office (☑928 84 53 98; www.turismoteguise.com; Palacio Spínola; ⊙10am-5pm Mon-Fri, to 3.30pm Sat & Sun) This office was due to move to the Casa de la Cultura, next to the church.

ⓘ Getting There & Away

Numerous buses, including 7 and 9 (€1.40, 30 minutes) from Arrecife, stop in Teguise en route to destinations such as Órzola and Haría. There are also buses and organised tours to the town's Sunday market from Costa Teguise, Puerto del Carmen and Playa Blanca.

THE NORTH

Lanzarote's northern towns and villages are typically clusters of whitewashed buildings surrounded by what looks like a felt-covered landscape of lichen and lava fields. The principal attractions are the combined works of nature and César Manrique, including breathtaking lava caves, a cactus garden and a stunning lookout created out of an old gun emplacement. The island's northwest arguably offers visitors the most rewarding look at Lanzarote's natural beauty. It's a place of attractive, unspoiled towns, some great escapes and stunning panoramic views.

Guatiza & Charco del Palo

Just north of tiny Guatiza is the Jardín de Cactus (Cactus Garden; www.centrosturisticos.com; adult/child €5.50/2.75; ⊙10am-6pm), signalled by an 8m-high spiky metal cactus. According to reliable sources, the garden was Manrique's favourite attraction. Built in an old quarry, it comes across as more a giant work of art than a botanical garden. There are nearly 1500 different varieties of cactus, every single one labelled. The garden's location between Guatiza and Mala is no coincidence, for while cacti are spotted throughout the island, here they were once the backbone of the economy. The cochineal beetle is particularly attracted to the prickly pear cactus and up until the late 19th century, the beetles were harvested and dried, then used to produce a vivid red dye. Although cochineal fell out of favour with the advent of synthetic dyes, some hardy farmers still make a living from the bugs and you'll notice an abundance of cacti in this region. There is a restaurant and bar on site if you want some refreshments.

If you fancy bathing (or even shopping!) in the buff, a few kilometres north of Guatiza is the naturist resort of Charco del Palo, with pleasant sandy beaches and rocky coves. To get there, take the narrow road to the beach just south of Mala.

Arrieta

POP 890

The main attraction of the fishing village of Arrieta is the small beach Playa de la Garita, a combination of volcanic rock and sand with a congenial beach bar and restaurant where you can relax with a beer and tapas.

There are also some good seafood restaurants in town which get packed out with locals at weekends. Right on the main road with a sea-view terrace, Almanecer (La Garita 46; mains €8-12; ⊙Fri-Wed) is a favourite. Unpretentious, the menu really does depend on what is freshly caught in the nets that day.

Buses 7 and 9 (€2.65, 45 minutes) from Arrecife pass by Arrieta en route to Haría and Órzola.

Malpaís de la Corona

Lava is the hallmark of Lanzarote and the 'Badlands of the Crown' are evidence of the volcanic upsurges that shook the north of the island thousands of years ago. Plant life is quietly, patiently winning its way back and it is here that you can visit two of the island's better-known volcanic caverns at the site of an ancient lava slide into the ocean.

The cavernous Cueva de los Verdes and the hollows of the Jameos del Agua – adapted by César Manrique into a kind of New Age retreat-meets-bar – are an easy 1km walk from each other. These two sights are about 4km northwest of Arrieta and well signposted.

★Cueva de los Verdes   CAVE
(☑928 84 84 84; www.centrosturisticos.com; adult/child €9/4.50; ⊙10am-6pm; ℗) Cueva de los Verdes is a yawning, 1km-long chasm,

---

ECO YURT

How's this for something different? Stay in a Mongolian yurt in a totally eco-friendly resort (p224) powered by wind and solar. Organic fruit, vegies and wine can be part of your welcome pack and the resident chickens can keep you in eggs. Owners Tila and Michelle also include a battery-cum-petrol hybrid car with most bookings. Other perks include the option of windsurfing and surfing lessons and advice on local hikes. The yurts are wonderfully furnished with just the right ethnic touches.

LANZAROTE FOR CHILDREN

There's plenty going on for children on the island. Several of the Manrique sights should keep them suitably gobsmacked, while the southern resorts have plenty of kiddie-geared activities. Museum-wise, try the **Museo de la Piratería** (p105) in Teguise. The island's most touted attraction is **Guinate Tropical Park** (p110), with its birds, aquarium, botanical garden and various shows. There are plenty of sea-themed activities, in addition to the ubiquitous glass-bottom boats. **Submarine Safaris** (p117) in Puerto Calero submerges to the watery depths, while high riders can contact **Paracraft** (☑619 068680; www.watersports-lanzarote.com; Playa Chica, Puerto del Carmen; ☺10am-6pm), which offers parascending (10 minutes, €50). If the sea starts to pall, Costa Teguise's **Aquapark** (☑928 59 21 28; www.aquaparklanzarote.es; Avenida del Golf; adult/child €22/17; ☺10am-6pm) has the usual assortment of rides and slides.

which is the most spectacular segment of an almost 8km-long lava tube left behind by an eruption that occurred 5000 years ago. As the lava ploughed down towards the sea, the top layers cooled and formed a roof, beneath which the liquid magma continued to slither until the eruption exhausted itself. Guided tours, lasting about 45 minutes and available in English, take place every 30 minutes or so.

On the tour you walk through two chambers, one below the other. The ceiling is largely covered with what look like mini stalactites, but no water penetrates the cave. The odd pointy extrusions are where bubbles of air and lava were thrown up onto the ceiling by gases released while the boiling lava flowed; as they hit the ceiling and air, they hardened in the process of dripping back into the lava stream.

Anyone with severe back problems might think twice about entering the cave – there are a few passages that require you to bend at 90 degrees to get through, although only very briefly.

Concerts of mainly jazz and blues are held here from September to April.

Jameos del Agua CAVE
(☑928 84 80 20; adult/child €9/4.50; ☺10am-6.30pm; ℗) The first cavern you reach at Jameos del Agua resembles the nave of a vast marine basilica. Molten lava seethed through here en route to the sea, but in this case the ocean leaked in a bit, forming the startling azure lake at the heart of the Jameos. Manrique's idea of installing bars and a restaurant (☺8pm-midnight Tue & Sat) around the lake, adding a pool and a concert hall seating 600 (with wonderful acoustics), was a pure brainwave.

Take a closer look into the lake's waters. The tiny white flecks at the bottom are crabs. Small ones, yes, and the only known examples of *Munidopsis polymorpha* (blind crabs) away from the deepest oceans. Do heed the signs and resist the temptation to throw coins into the water – their corrosion could kill off this unique species. Access for the mobility impaired is not really possible as there are a lot of steps.

From July through September concerts are held on Tuesday and Saturday evenings.

Órzola

Most people just pass through this northern fishing town on their way to Isla Graciosa. It's a pity, though, because this region has some stunning strips of sand, as well as several good seafood restaurants flanking the port, where you can be sure that the fish is flapping fresh.

Bus 9 connects Órzola with Arrecife (€3.60, one hour, five daily).

🏖 Beaches

There is a series of rarely crowded sandy coves just east of town known as **Playas Caletones**. They have a natural, untamed beauty, with fine white sand and shallow lagoons.

Just north of Órzola, **Playa de la Cantería** is another beautiful sandy beach, flanked by cliffs and famed for its big breakers (swimming is not recommended).

Chinijo Archipelago

This mini archipelago consists of five islets scattered to the north of Lanzarote. Along with Lanzarote's Famara cliffs, they form a nature reserve, but on the whole the region is pretty much off limits. The exception is Graciosa, the only inhabited islet in the archipelago. The others – Montaña Clara, Alegranza, Roque del Este and Roque del Oeste – are known for their birdlife and are generally only visited by researchers, though you can admire them up-close on boat trips organised by **Lanzarote Active Club** (www.lanzaroteactiveclub.com; day tour €65).

Isla Graciosa

Graciosa is recommended for the ultimate stress-busting break. In a day or two you could see the whole island and recharge your batteries, but if you fancy sticking around you'll find world-class surf, a variety of water sports, modest hiking and sublime beaches – as well as bucketloads of peace and quiet.

About 700 people live on the island, virtually all in the village of Caleta de Sebo, where the Órzola boat docks at the attractive harbour. Behind it stretches 27.5 sq km of largely barren scrubland, interrupted by five minor volcanic peaks stretching from north to south. About a 30-minute walk southwest of Caleta de Sebo is delightful little Playa Francesa. There's also the lovely long sandy beach of Playa de las Conchas, and Playa Lambra, another sandy stretch, on the northern end of the island. The beaches in the south tend to have calmer waters; swimming at Playa de las Conchas is not advisable.

On a windy day Caleta de Sebo can seem like a cross between a bare Moroccan village and a sand-swept Wild West outpost. This place is worlds away from the tourist mainstream. There are no sealed roads and the main form of transport seems to be battered old Land Rovers.

☉ Sights & Activities

Museo Chinijo MUSEUM
(www.museochinijo.com; Calle Margarona 27; ☺9am-5pm Mon-Sat) FREE Claiming to be the smallest museum in the world, there are well laid-out exhibits on the geography and history of the archipelago here, as well as panels on the region's cetaceans and the production of salt and aloe in Lanzarote.

Buceo La Graciosa DIVING
(www.buceolagraciosa.es; dive with equipment rental from €35) The waters around the Chinijo Archipelago are teeming with fascinating sealife. This company offers dives off the coasts of Graciosa and Alegranza.

BEATING THE CROWDS

Lanzarote's art-meets-nature attractions make a fine alternative to the water slides and dubious theme parks that the archipelago tends to be known for. They are very much on the beaten track though, and the bumper-to-bumper tour buses can mean you're sometimes shuffling through Manrique's masterpieces behind a never-ending stream of fellow visitors. But if you arrive early or leave your visit until later in the day, you'll miss the throngs. For the Jameos del Agua, Cueva de los Verdes and Parque Nacional de Timanfaya in particular, try to visit either first thing in the morning or after 3pm.

La Graciosa Water Experience WATER SPORTS
(☑649 375051; www.lagraciosawaterexperience.com) Offers kitesurfing and stand-up paddle boarding trips as well as surfboard hire.

✗ Eating & Drinking

Girasol SEAFOOD €€
(Avenida Virgen del Mar; mains €8-10; ☺1-4pm & 7pm-late) There's not much that distinguishes one La Graciosa restaurant from another, but Girasol is a long-running place with a popular ocean-facing terrace. There's a good selection of fresh fish as well as a few meatier Canarian dishes. Upstairs there are pleasant *pensión* rooms (€30) with sea-facing balconies.

Las Arenas CLUB
(Calle Mar de Barlovento; ☺from 12.30am Fri & Sat) If you feel like accelerating out of first gear, this disco pub at the back of Pensión Enriqueta opens its steamy doors to revellers after midnight.

ℹ Getting There & Away

There are two boat companies operating ferries between Órzola and Caleta de Sebo: **Biosfera Express** (☑928 84 25 85; www.biosferaexpress.com; adult/child return €20/10) and **Líneas Marítimas Romero** (☑928 59 61 07; www.lineasromero.com; adult/child return €20/11). Sailing times are staggered and in total there are 16 return ferries plying the waters daily. It can get very rocky between Órzola and Punta Fariones, so you may want to pop a seasickness pill.

If you don't mind getting stuck in the sand every now and then, pedal power is a fine way to explore the island. There are a couple of well-signposted bike-hire places near the harbour.

Mirador del Río

About 2km north of Yé, the Spanish armed forces set up gun batteries at the end of the 19th century at a strategic site overlooking El Río, the strait separating Lanzarote from Isla Graciosa. Spain had gone to war with the US over control of Cuba, and you couldn't be too careful! In 1973 the ubiquitous César Manrique left his mark, converting the gun emplacement into a spectacular bug-eyed lookout point.

Mirador del Río (☑928 52 65 51; www.centrosturisticos.com; adult/child €4.50/2.25; ⊙10am-6pm) has a good bar and souvenir shop. There are vertiginous views of the sweeping lava flows – frozen in time – that fall to the ocean, and of Isla Graciosa and the surrounding volcanic islets.

Guinate

The main reason for visiting the village of Guinate is the **Guinate Tropical Park** (www.guinatetropicalpark.com; adult/child €15/9; ⊙10am-5pm), home to around 1300 rare and exotic birds, a penguin pool and other animals, including monkeys and meerkats. The parrot show is best avoided, unless you enjoy birds on bicycles and the like.

Guinate is about 5km south of the Mirador del Río. Just beyond the park is another fine (and completely free) **lookout** across El Río and the islets.

Haría

POP 1004

Eminent Canarian author Alberto Vásquez-Figueroa once described Haría as the most beautiful village in the world. Although a tad exaggerated, the village really does have a pretty bucolic setting, in a palm-filled valley punctuated by splashes of brilliant colour from bougainvillea and poinsettia plants. In the 17th and 18th centuries, locals traditionally planted a palm tree to celebrate a birth (two for a boy, one for a girl!). Later, this North African–style oasis became a popular spa for wealthy Canarians.

The central pedestrian avenue, Plaza León y Castillo, is shaded by eucalyptus trees and is the site of a superb Saturday morning craft and produce market. Handicrafts are available throughout the week at the **Taller de Artesanía Reinaldo Dorta Déniz** (Calle Barranco de Tenesía; ⊙10am-1.30pm Mon, 10am-1.30pm & 4-7pm Tue-Sat), a town hall–backed craft workshop where local artisans produce silverware, ceramics, embroidery and some charming pieces made of palm leaves and reeds. You can watch the crafters at work before buying.

◉ Sights

Casa Museo César Manrique   MUSEUM
(☑928 84 31 38; www.fcmanrique.org; Calle Elvira Sanchez; adult/child €10/5; ⊙10.30am-2pm) This palm-fringed property was the final home of the island's favourite son and has been opened as a museum-cum-shrine. The house is frozen in time, complete with Manrique's clothes in the closet and personal art collection adorning the walls. The decor is fairly modest when compared to his former home in Tahiche, though the main bathroom is sublime. The star attraction is his studio, preserved exactly as it was the day he died, with unfinished works still in situ.

COMPETITIVE SPORTING EVENTS

Music Marathon Festival (www.musicmarathon.com) A range of races up to 20km, with live music along the course; March

Ironman Lanzarote (www.ironmanlanzarote.com) Considered one of the world's toughest Ironman (triathlon) events; May

Volcano Triathlon (www.clublasanta.com) Triathlon aimed at all levels; May

Wine Run Lanzarote (www.lanzarotewinerun.com) Half marathon through the wine region, coinciding with a traditional food festival; June

Haria Extreme (www.hariaextreme.com) A gruelling 80km rail run, with shorter options also available; dates vary

Travesia a Nado 'El Rio' (www.lanzarotedeportes.com) Open water swimming race covering the 2.6km of waves and currents between Lanzarote and Isla Graciosa; October

KIRSTY JONES: WORLD-CHAMPION KITESURFER

I've been going to Lanzarote on holiday with my parents since I was 15 and that's where my passion for surfing and windsurfing began. When I was 16 I decided to try windsurfing one very windy day on Puerto del Carmen beach – from then on I was addicted to the energy and power of the wind and waves. About four years ago, after travelling to many places around the world with my job as a professional kitesurfer, I decided to buy a house on Lanzarote.

Top kitesurfing beach Aside from Famara, I love to kitesurf on the Playa del Risco, which most tourists don't know about. It's at the bottom of the gigantic Mirador del Río cliffs in the north, and quite a tough hike down and back (especially carrying your gear!), but the views are incredible and once you finally walk onto the deserted white sandy beach at the bottom, it's worth every step. If you don't fancy a long hike with kitesurf equipment, some of the surf schools in Famara offer a boat trip to this beach.

Secret spot One of my favourite places is actually right in front of my house in Charco del Palo, but underwater! Whenever the wind drops, there is a place off the rocks here where I can spend hours free diving and snorkelling and exploring the amazing underwater world. There are stunning caves and rock formations, all types of fish and the water is crystal clear.

And on land? I love to explore the rocky shoreline of the northeast and northwest coast and look for driftwood and other interesting things that the tide and waves have brought in, which I then use to decorate my back yard.

Keep hold of your ticket; if you present it at the Fundación César Manrique (p105) in Tahiche you get a discount on the entrance fee.

✕ Eating

La Puerta Verde MEDITERRANEAN €€
(☑ 928 83 53 50; Calle Fajardo 24; mains €12-18; ☺ 1-4pm & 7pm-late) Just north of the centre, Haría's most upmarket eatery is off the tourist bus route. It's a great spot for coffee and a slice of decadent cake, but even better for a special dinner. The creative dishes marry Canarian, Spanish and Italian cuisines, with some northern European touches. The slow-roasted lamb is a winner. Dinner bookings recommended.

ℹ Getting There & Away

Bus 7 (€3.15, 45 minutes) connects Haría to Arrecife via Teguise and Tahiche six times daily.

La Caleta de Famara

Years before he hit the big time, César Manrique whiled away many a childhood summer on the wild beach of La Caleta de Famara. It's one of the best sandy spots on Lanzarote and a place where you don't have to fight for towel space on the sand. This low-key seaside hamlet, with its dramatic cliff views, has a youthful, bohemian vibe

and makes few concessions to the average tourist, aside from a few choice restaurants overlooking the surf.

Famara's excellent waves offer some of Europe's finest breaks, along with El Quemao, around 15km due south (but only suitable for very experienced surfers). If you don't fancy taking a board, then come here to watch the surfing, which is some of the best you will see throughout the Canaries.

If you fancy staying over, look no further than the town's numerous surf schools. All of them can arrange affordable accommodation in nearby apartments.

🏃 Activities

Zoo Park Famara SURFING
(☑ 928 52 88 46; www.zooparkfamara.com; Avenida El Marinero 5; board & wetsuit rental per day €10, surf course per day €40) A long-running surf school that also offers lessons in kitesurfing (€90 per day) and stand-up paddle boarding (€45 per day). Self-catering accommodation can be arranged or there are surf camps, including accommodation and classes (from €300 per week).

Famara Surf SURFING
(☑ 653 989550; www.famarasurf.com; Avenida El Marinero 39; surf course per day €39) If you don't fancy lessons you can rent a board (€12 per day, including wetsuit) or even buy one from

FROM SPICY POTATOES TO SUBLIME WINES

Although the Lanzarote cuisine does not vary dramatically from that of its neighbours, there are some culinary stars. The addictive *papas arrugadas* (wrinkly potatoes) are generally accompanied by a choice of three *mojo* (spicy) sauces (not always the Canarian case), including *mojo verde* (with parsley), *mojo de cilantro* (with fresh coriander) and the classic *mojo picón* (with a spicy chilli kick).

Latin American influences are reflected in several dishes and, for red-blooded appetites, the steaks are typically prime-cut Argentinian beef. Other popular meaty choices for *Lanzaroteños* include goat, baby kid and rabbit – exactly the same choices favoured by their Guanche ancestors who, by all accounts, were not the greatest fishermen. If you fancy a heart-warming homey stew, look for the classic *puchero*, traditionally made with various cuts of meat, fresh root vegetables and chickpeas.

Seafood lovers should look for the indigenous *lapa*, which is a species of limpet, traditionally grilled (which releases the flesh from the shell) and accompanied by a green *mojo*. Note that although they do not look as appealing, the black-fleshed *lapas* are tastier than the orange variety.

Do try the local wines while you are here, particularly the prize-worthy dry white *malvasía* (Malmsey wine). The vines flourish in the black volcanic soil and are planted in small craters to protect them from the wind. The grapes are planted and harvested manually, resulting in high labour costs. When you buy a bottle of local wine you actively contribute to the preservation of a traditional method of viniculture in danger of dying out.

the surf shop and just do your own thing. They also offer a range of accommodation around town.

✕ Eating

Surf Bar Clandestino   PIZZA €

(www.clandestino-surf-adventure.com; Avenida El Marinero 25; pizza €4; ⊙8am-late; 🛜✏) With surfboards hanging from the ceiling, extremely well-priced pizzas and breakfasts (€3) plus a range of cocktails, this cool cafe is definitely geared towards the surf crowd. They can also arrange surfing and yoga classes.

★ El Risco   MODERN CANARIAN €€

(Calle Montaña Blanca 30; mains €10-18; ⊙1-4pm & 7pm-late) El Risco has a superb location, with a terrace overlooking the sea and a nautical blue-and-white interior. The menu offers the most upmarket dishes in town – try the kid and rabbit terrine with brandy reduction.

Restaurante Sol   SEAFOOD €€

(Calle Salvavidas 48; mains €12-18; ⊙1-4pm & 7pm-late) Take a seat on the ocean-facing terrace and watch the surfers while munching on grilled fish or fried baby squid. This place gets packed out with noisy local families at weekends – always a good sign.

ℹ Getting There & Away

Bus 20 (€2.20, 50 minutes) connects Arrecife with La Caleta de Famara five times daily (weekdays only).

WINE COUNTRY

Forget any preconceived notions of what wine country should look like. On Lanzarote you won't find neat lines of vines painting the hills with green stripes. That's not to say that the region isn't beautiful, but like everywhere on the island it's a less obvious beauty. Here, dotted throughout the striking abstract landscape of towering black mountains you'll find small crescent-shaped stone walls. Behind each wall, offering a cheery contrast with the monochrome landscape, is a low-growing vine sheltered from the wind.

Local viticulturists have found the deep, black lava soil, enriched by the island's shaky seismic history, is perfect for grapes, though the yield is low and the toil to get a decent harvest is high. Check out www.dolanzarote.com for details on the various wineries across the island, including a map.

If you don't have your own wheels, there are organised tours to the wineries. Try Lanzarote Active Club's **Bodega Hopping Tour** (☑650 819069; www.lanzaroteactiveclub.com; per person €59), which takes in four wineries and includes a tapas lunch. Buses to this part of the island are thin on the ground. The most useful line is bus 32, which connects Arrecife with La Florida and Masdache (€1.40, 30 minutes, 10 daily).

San Bartolomé & Around

Starting life as the Guanche settlement of Ajei, San Bartolomé (population 5800) ended up in the 18th century as the de facto private fiefdom of a militia leader, Francisco Guerra Clavijo y Perdomo, and his descendants. Set in an 18th-century Canarian house, the rambling **Museo del Tanit** (www.museotanit.com; Calle Constitución 1; adult/child €6/free; ◷10am-2pm Mon-Sat) has exhibits covering just about every aspect of island life from the past 200 years. English explanations are available. It's badly signposted – to get close, first follow signs for 'centro urbano'. Perhaps more appealing than the museum is a simple wander around the sleepy town with its palm-dotted square.

A couple of kilometres northwest of town, on the Tinajo road, rises the modernistic, white **Monumento al Campesino** (Peasants' Monument), erected in 1968 by (surprise, surprise) César Manrique to honour the thankless labour that most islanders had endured for generations. Adjacent stands the **Museo del Campesino** (www.centrosturisticos.com; ◷10am-6pm; P) FREE, which is more a scattering of craft workshops, including weaving and ceramics.

Most people come here to eat at the **restaurant** (mains €12-16; ◷12.30-4pm; 🕸) – ironic for a monument dedicated to those who habitually endured hunger. The dining room is vast, circular and sunken, complete with tunnel. There is a good wine and rum list and well-prepared local cuisine, accompanied by Canarian music. There's a varied tapas menu, a selection of Canarian stews and some local sweet treats, such as *bienmesabe* (a gooey, almond-based dessert).

Two kilometres southwest, en route to Yaiza, you'll reach the first of the wineries on this road, **Bodegas La Florida** (🗐 928 59 30 01; www.bodegaslaflorida.com; Calle La Florida 89; tasting €1.50; ◷11am-6pm; P). You can taste up to six wines in this beautifully restored farmhouse, dating back 150 years. Vineyard and winery tours (€7 per person including tasting) are also available but should be booked in advance.

THE BARD'S FAVOURITE TIPPLE

Shakespeare was reputedly quite fond of a regular swig of 'sack' – which is what *malvasía* (Malmsey wine) was often called. There are numerous references in his works and he's not the only author that enjoyed a Canarian tipple – Robert Louis Stevenson and John Keats also made reference to Canary wine in their day.

Another kilometre further south is the **Museo del Vino El Grifo** (www.elgrifo.com; admission incl glass of wine €4; ◷10.30am-6pm; P), the oldest winery in the Canary Islands, founded in 1775. There's an interesting museum showcasing old winemaking equipment. Most is from the 19th and 20th centuries, though there are some older pieces. Probably of greater interest is the tasting room where you can sample a range of wines still produced here. Single tasters are €1.50 or choose six samples with a local cheese platter for €6 per person. Bookings are required for tours (€10, including tastings).

Due south, en route to Tías, is **Bodegas Vega de Yuco** (🗐 928 52 43 16; www.vegadeyuco.es; Camino del Cabezo; tastings €1; ◷8am-3pm Mon-Fri; P). The terrace here is a lovely spot to sip and admire the landscape and there's a botanical garden to explore once you've sampled the wines.

Tiagua

About 8km northwest of San Bartolomé, the open-air **Museo Agricola El Patio** (www.museoelpatio.com; Calle Echedey 18; adult/child €5/free; ◷10am-5pm Mon-Sat; ♿) recreates a 19th-century traditional farmer's house (complete with wine cellar) and provides an insight into traditional aspects of the island's culture. Signage – including some irritatingly edifying texts – is in English. You can taste local goat's cheese and a selection of *malvasía* (Malmsey wines) and muscatel wines. You'll see loads of old equipment and furniture, a windmill and the odd camel or donkey chewing the cud.

Tiagua is on the bus 16 (€1.40, 30 minutes) route from Arrecife to La Santa. Bus 20 (€1.40, 25 minutes) to La Caleta de Famara also calls in here.

❶ LA GERIA APP

In a bid to attract more visitors to the wine region, the *cabildo* (government) and wineries have produced a free smartphone app called 'La Geria'. The app features maps and information on the wineries as well as other attractions and activities in the area.

La Geria

The LZ-30, meandering southwest between Mozaga and Yaiza, is one of the most interesting and enjoyable drives you can take on the island. A well-surfaced road, it winds through the area of La Geria, passing row upon row of the eye-catching, vine-filled dugouts nurtured behind low semicircular walls.

◎ Sights

Bodega Rubicón   WINERY

(☑928 17 37 08; www.vinosrubicon.com; Ctra La Geria, Km 2; tastings €1-3 per half glass; ⊙9am-6pm; ℗) This bodega is housed in part of a former 17th-century *cortijo* (farm), which now also includes a good restaurant (mains €10 to €12). Wines available for tasting in the bodega include the award-winning muscatel. You can also take a look at the museum, complete with historic wine press.

Bodega La Geria   WINERY

(☑928 17 31 78; www.lageria.com; Ctra La Geria, Km 5; tastings €1.50 per half glass; ⊙9.30am-7pm Mon-Sat, 10am-6pm Sun; ℗) The La Geria wine cellar, established at the end of the 19th century, was the first bodega on the island to offer guided visits and sell wines to the public. You can pick up bottles of dry or semi-sweet *malvasía* (among others) for around €12. There's also a good little bar/cafe (tapas €6 to €8).

★☆ Festivals & Events

Harvests take place from late July until September and during this time you'll find plenty of events happening at the various wineries.

Fiesta de la Vendimia   CULTURAL

(⊙mid-Aug) The largest and best-established wine festival is the jolly Fiesta de la Vendimia, held at Bodega La Geria. Newly harvested grapes are poured into a vast vat for everyone to have a good trample upon (fortunately, they don't find their way into a wine bottle!).

✗ Eating

El Chupadero   TAPAS €

(☑659 596178; www.el-chupadero.com; tapas €4.50-10.50; ⊙1-4pm & 7pm-late; ℗) This stylish, German-owned bar and restaurant is 4km north of Uga off the LZ-30 road. Enjoy homemade soups and great tapas, all washed down with local *malvasía* wines on a terrace overlooking the vineyards. There are live concerts here on Sunday evenings.

THE SOUTH & SOUTHWEST

The island's south is home to the most popular resorts and attracts family groups looking for an easygoing, sunny time, punctuated by deep-sea-fishing excursions and boozy nights out. Over on the west coast though, it's a different world: one of wave-lashed cliffs and quiet, whitewashed villages.

Parque Nacional de Timanfaya

The eruption that began on 1 September 1730 and convulsed the southern end of the island was among the greatest volcanic cataclysms in recorded history. A staggering 48 million cubic metres of lava spurted and flowed out daily, while fusillades of molten rock were rocketed out over the countryside and into the ocean. When the eruption finally ceased to rage after six long years, over 200 sq km had been devastated, including 50 villages and hamlets.

The Montañas del Fuego (Mountains of Fire), at the heart of this eerie 51-sq-km **national park** (☑928 84 00 57; www.centrosturisticos.com; adult/child €9/4.50; ⊙9am-5.45pm, last bus tour at 5pm), are appropriately named. When you reach the Manrique-designed lookout at a rise known as the Islote de Hilario, try scrabbling around in the pebbles and see just how long you can hold them in your hands. At a depth of a few centimetres, the temperature is already 100°C; by 10m it's up to 600°C. The cause of this phenomenon is a broiling magma chamber 4km below the surface.

Some robust scraps of vegetation, including 200 species of lichen, have reclaimed the earth in a few stretches of the otherwise moribund landscape of fantastic forms in shades of black, grey, maroon and red. Fine copper-hued soil slithers down volcanic cones, until it's arrested by twisted, swirling and folded mounds of solidified lava – this is one place where you really must remember to bring your camera.

The people running the show at Islote de Hilario, near the restaurant, gift shop and car park, have a series of endearing tricks. In one, they shove a clump of brushwood into a hole in the ground and within seconds it's converted by the subterranean furnace into a burning bush. A pot of water poured down another hole promptly gushes back up in explosive geyser fashion; you have exactly three seconds to take that impressive snap.

There is no public transport to the park so you'll need your own wheels. Two wheels will suffice – the area is popular with cyclists.

◉ Sights & Activities

Mancha Blanca Visitor Centre　　MUSEUM
(📇 928 11 80 42; www.mma.es; Ctra de Yaiza a Tinajo, Km 11.5; ⏱ 9am-5pm; 🅿) **FREE** There are excellent audiovisual and informative displays about the park here, including a simulation of a volcanic eruption. It's just north of the park boundary on the LZ-67.

Ruta de los Volcanes　　BUS TOUR
This at times nail-biting 14km bus ride is included in the admission price of the park, taking you through some of the most spectacular volcanic country you are ever likely to see. Buses leave every 20 to 30 minutes and the trip takes about 30 minutes. By about 10am there can be long queues to get into the park, so be prepared to wait for a tour.

The trilingual taped commentary on board has a fascinating eyewitness account by local priest Don Agustín Cabrera.

Guided Walks　　WALKING TOUR
(www.reservasparquesnacionales.es) It is possible to walk within the Parque Nacional de Timanfaya, but you'll need to plan in advance as only eight people are permitted at a time. The 3.5km, two-hour Tremesana guided walk (in Spanish and English) leaves from the Mancha Blanca Visitor Centre at 10am on Monday, Wednesday and Friday.

The much more demanding Ruta del Litoral (9km, six hours) takes place once a month (no fixed date). Reservations are made via the website and you need to book several weeks in advance. All walks are free.

Echadero de Camellos　　CAMEL RIDING
(2 people €12) An alternative way to experience the park is on a 20-minute camel ride.

The camels hang out at the southern entrance to the park, just off the LZ-67.

✖ Eating

Restaurant del Diablo　　BARBECUE €€
(📇 928 84 00 56; Islote de Hilario; mains €12-16; ⏱ noon-4.30pm; 🅿) The Manrique-designed restaurant is gimicky but fun – whatever meat you order you can watch sizzling on the all-natural, volcano-powered BBQ out back. The food is none too impressive, but, hey, who's here for the cuisine? Vegetarians might feel a bit left out, though, with all that smoking rabbit, T-bone and chicken. There's a good list of local wines.

Puerto del Carmen

With sunshades four lanes deep, this is the island's most popular beach and its oldest purpose-built resort. If you are seeking an iota of Canarian atmosphere, head for the El Varadero harbour, at the far west of the beachfront, which still has a faint fishing-village feel, with its bobbing boats and uninterrupted ocean views. Otherwise the centre remains a primarily Brit-geared resort with restaurants and bars competing for the cheapest bacon-and-eggs breakfast and the largest (and loudest) Sky Sports screen. The main street is Avenida de las Playas, a gaudy ribbon hugging the beach with shops, bars and restaurants.

🏖 Beaches

Playa Grande　　BEACH
Yes, Playa Grande is crowded and neatly striped with sunbeds and parasols, but, beneath all this, it remains a spectacular 1200m-long beach excellent for families, with shallow waters and good amenities, including toilets and ice creams.

Playa Los Pocillos　　BEACH
A couple of kilometres north of Puerto del Carmen, the golden, sandy arc of Playa Los Pocillos is a kilometre long and known for its windy but calm waters, which create perfect conditions for windsurfers.

🏃 Activities

For many, the main activities seem to be kicking back with a beer or flaking out on the beach, but there's no lack of opportunity for something less supine, including walking the length of the 6km of beaches. There is also a designated cycle path here. Diving is deservedly popular, as are jet skiing and banana and paracraft rides.

Water sports

Safari Diving
DIVING
(☑928 51 19 92; www.safaridiving.com; Playa de la Barrilla 4; dive with equipment rental €39) Offers a range of courses including an introductory scuba diving session for novices for €60.

Canary Island Divers
DIVING
(☑928 51 54 67; www.canaryislanddivers.com; Calle Alemania 1; dive with equipment rental €35) Also offers one-hour bubble-maker courses for children (€40).

Manta Dive Centre
DIVING
(☑928 51 68 15; www.manta-diving-lanzarote.com; Calle Juan Carlos I 6; dive with equipment rental €39) One of the longest-established centres, also offers three-day courses (€420) and half-day snorkelling trips (€25).

School 3S
SURFING
(☑928 51 40 34; www.school3s.es; Calle Chalana 2; 1-day stand-up paddle boarding class €45) As well as the stand-up paddle boarding classes held in Puerto del Carmen, there are surf courses available, though they usually take place elsewhere on the island. The third 's' in the company name stands for 'soul', referring to the yoga lessons on offer (€15 per day).

Cycling

Renner Bikes
CYCLING
(☑928 51 06 12; www.mountainbike-lanzarote.com; Avenida de las Playas, Centro Comercial Marítimo; bike rental per day from €15) A good central place for renting or buying a bike.

Horse Riding

Lanzarote a Caballo
HORSE RIDING
(☑928 83 00 38; www.lanzaroteacaballo.com; Carretera Arrecife-Yaiza; 2hr excursion €60; ⊙10am-1pm Fri-Wed; ☝) There are hour-long rides for beginners (€40) or two-hour guided treks for those with riding experience. Other activities on offer include camel rides and off-road buggy trips.

✗ Eating

Among all the sauerkraut, fish and chips and other international delights on offer along the Avenida de las Playas pleasure zone, you'll occasionally stumble across a place offering some local cuisine. For a more traditional Spanish choice, take a walk to the old port.

Vino + Lanzarote
TAPAS €€
(Calle Roque del Este, Centro Comercial Barracuda; tapas €3-12; ⊙1-4pm & 7pm-late; ☎) 'We are against war and tourist menus' reads the sign outside this funky tapas bar tucked away behind the Hotel Los Fariones. The small menu features some interesting tapas, including a few vegetarian dishes. The wine list is excellent.

Casa Roja
SPANISH €€
(Avenida Varadero; mains €10-18; ⊙1-4pm & 7pm-late) Enjoying possibly the best location in town, this low-key place overlooks the pretty harbour. The menu is appropriately seafood-based, with the obligatory tank of potential dinner mates at the entrance.

Blooming Cactus
VEGETARIAN €€
(☑608 293873; www.bloomingcactus.co.uk; Calle Teide 35; tapas €4-10; ⊙6-11pm Tue-Sun; ☝) A rare vegetarian restaurant on Lanzarote. Typical dishes include vegetable satay, moussaka, curries and *stefado* (vegetable stew). Vegan and wheat-free options are also available.

Restaurante La Cañada
CANARIAN €€
(Calle César Manrique 3; mains €12-18; ⊙1-4pm & 7-11pm Mon-Sat) Located just off Avenida de las Playas, this restaurant lovingly prepares Canarian specialities, including oysters (from €3.50 each), roasted goat, salt-coated sea bass and delicious *papas arrugadas*. Finish off your meal with that retro culinary classic: crêpe Suzette.

🍷 Drinking & Nightlife

The bulk of the bars, discos and nightclubs in Puerto del Carmen are lined up along the waterfront Avenida de las Playas and include Irish pubs, karaoke bars and the inevitable smattering of sleazier options. If you're after maximum-density partying, try the Centro Comercial Atlántico – the club names may change but the atmosphere remains the same.

Cervecería San Miguel
BAR
(Avenida Varadero; ⊙10.30am-3am) A good spot near the harbour for a plate of steamed mussels washed down with cold beer on tap, including Guinness, Paulaner and John Smith's Bitter.

☆ Entertainment

Gran Casino de Lanzarote
CASINO
(Avenida de las Playas 12; ⊙7pm-4am) There's a bar and decent restaurant at this ocean-facing casino, as well as the usual array of slots and tables.

ℹ Information

Tourist Office (www.puertodelcarmen.com; Avenida de las Playas; ⊘ 9am-4pm Mon-Fri, to 1pm Sat) Halfway along Playa Grande.

ℹ Getting There & Around

BUS
Buses run the length of Avenida de las Playas, making frequent stops and heading for Arrecife (€1.70) about every 20 minutes, 24 hours a day.

CAR
Parking is a nightmare here, particularly in midsummer. Head for the paying car park on Calle Juan Carlos or the nearby Biosfera Shopping Centre (Calle Juan Carlos), which also has plenty of parking space.

Puerto Calero

A few kilometres west of Puerto del Carmen, Puerto Calero is a pleasant, relatively tranquil yacht harbour lined with cafes and restaurants. It sports a jaunty maritime vibe that sees plenty of locals in deck shoes. There is a waterbus that leaves from Puerto del Carmen seven times daily (one-way/return €6/10, 15 minutes).

🏖 Beaches

Playa Quemada   BEACH
This unspoiled and secluded black volcanic beach with superb seafood restaurants is around a half-hour walk (1.5km) due south from the port. There are beautiful mountain and sea views en route.

🏃 Activities

Squalo Diving Center   DIVING
(☑928 84 95 78; www.squalodiving.com; Hotel Costa Calero) English-run outfit offering PADI courses, including a night dive course (€290) and a digital underwater photography course (€210).

Catlanza   BOAT TOUR
(☑928 51 30 22; www.catlanza.com; adult/child €59/39) The 74ft-long *Catlanza* sails to Papagayo Bay where it drops anchor and lunch is prepared while you enjoy the complimentary bar, jet skiing, snorkelling – or just sunning on the deck.

Fishing Mizu   FISHING
(☑636 474000; www.sportfishinglanzarote.com; angler/spectator €75/50) Skippered by the well-regarded Tino García, the boat will

transport you to the nearby depths as you cast a line for blue marlin and other big fish. You'll be picked up from your hotel and taken to Puerto Calero. All equipment is included in the price.

Karolines Cruceros   BOAT TOUR
(☑928 84 96 22; www.karolinescruceros.com; adult/child €48/29) You can snorkel, swim or just quaff champagne (included in the price) on this day-long cruise that includes lunch.

Submarine Safaris   BOAT TOUR
(☑928 51 28 98; www.submarinesafaris.com; adult/child €55/32; ⊘10am, 11am, noon & 2pm) The yellow sub makes one-hour dives to a depth of 30m. There's a discount if you book online.

🍴 Eating

La Cabaña   MEDITERRANEAN €€
(☑650 685662; www.lacabanamacher.com; Mácher; mains €14-20; ⊘7pm-late Tue-Sat) A speedy 15-minute drive away is the tiny hamlet of Mácher, home to La Cabaña. This restaurant is run by an enthusiastic and experienced English couple with a superb reputation for innovative Med-inspired dishes. The menu changes weekly but expect dishes like roast duck breast with fig jam or bacon-wrapped tiger prawns stuffed with dates.

Amura   MEDITERRANEAN €€€
(☑928 51 31 81; mains €15-22; ⊘1-4pm & 7pm-late) Keep walking with your nose in the air, past all the English-themed bars and restaurants, until you reach this eye-catching vast terrace commanding sweeping sea views. The menu includes gourmet treats like lobster with cava sauce or boneless suckling pig with mandarin and passion fruit.

Yaiza

POP 884
Yaiza is something of a southern crossroads, so you'll probably pass through (several times) on your travels. It's a tidy whitewashed town and the recipient of numerous awards for cleanliness. For sights, try the local church, **Nuestra Señora de los Remedios**, which was built in the 18th century and features a lovely blue, white and gold painted altarpiece and a folkloric painted wooden ceiling.

There's no specific reason for hanging about, but if you arrive at lunchtime and are feeling peckish, you'll be able to find a few pleasant restaurants, plus the excellent La Bodega de Santiago (☎928 83 62 04; Calle García Escámez 23; mains €15-20; ☉Tue-Sun; ℗). Located at the northern entrance to Yaiza and fronted by a magnificent ficus tree, the building dates back a couple of hundred years and is ideal for courting couples, with several intimate dining rooms and a background of classical music. The menu is modern Canarian, with an emphasis on meaty choices like pork and orange, suckling lamb chops, and similar. Reservations are recommended.

El Golfo & Around

The former fishing village of El Golfo has a laid-back, bohemian feel, with its cluster of traditional buildings and lack of tourist-geared tat for sale. It's a fabulous place to come at sunset, with several bars overlooking the thundering surf. There is no shortage of inviting eating options, either. On the waterfront is a string of seafood restaurants, including Restaurante Placido (Avenida Marítima 39; mains €10-18) and Lago Verde (Avenida Marítima 46; mains €12-22), where you can also enquire about renting an apartment. Slightly away from the main cluster of restaurants is El Caletón (Avenida Marítima 5; mains €8-16), where the outdoor tables sit right on the rocks.

Just south of El Golfo is one of the most dramatic and scenic stretches of road on the island: the LZ-703, flanked by the shifting colours of the volcanic peaks on one side

and the sea and a string of small black-sand beaches on the other.

The beach fronting the Charco de los Clicos is worth taking a look at. The Charco itself is a small emerald-green pond, just in from the beach; the colour comes from the algae in the water. This was the famous backdrop for Raquel Welch who slipped into *that* fur bikini in the iconic publicity still for the 1960s *One Million Years BC* movie. Back to the present, the visual paint palette is further enhanced by the wonderfully colourful and textured volcanic rock surroundings. It is not safe to swim here though, as it can get very rough.

Along the coast road, which eventually leads to La Hoya, stop by Los Hervideros, a pair of caves through which the sea glugs and froths. After about 6km you reach the long Playa de Janubio, behind which are Las Salinas de Janubio, salt pans from where sea salt is extracted (up to around 15,000 tonnes a year).

Playa Blanca

A few years ago Playa Blanca was the quieter, smaller cousin of Puerto del Carmen. To be fair, it still is both smaller and quieter, but the resort has become almost unrecognisable in the past decade, with hotels and apartment complexes – albeit largely low-rise ones – stretching almost to the tip of the Papagayo nature reserve. It has a fairly upmarket feel, but there's something undeniably soulless about much of the resort. You will find a little local character around the

SCENIC DRIVE: THE LZ-702

Lanzarote has several stunning drives, particularly around wine country. Lesser known is the LZ-702, which you pick up just before Uga if you are coming from the west (Arrecife, Puerto del Carmen etc). The road climbs and winds between fields of goats and surprisingly verdant valleys against a backdrop of sea to the west and low-lying peaks to the east.

Pass through the hamlet of Las Casitas de Femés (2.3km) and carry on to Femés (8km). Look for the sign to Femés Quesería Rubicón (Plaza San Marcial 3; ☉10am-8pm Mon-Sat, 10am-3pm Sun), one of the best places to buy the local goat's cheese; better still, you can taste it first. Priced at €9 to €12 per kilo, choose between smoked, fresh, semi-cured, or coated with paprika or traditional *gofio* (ground, roasted grain used in place of bread in Canarian cuisine). Afterwards, you can nip across the road to the Balcón de Femés (Plaza de Femés) for coffee, accompanied by a magnificent view stretching all the way to the coast. There is a signposted scenic footpath from the Plaza de Femés to Playa Quemada (11km), which takes around four hours.

Continue the drive winding down to Playa Blanca (8.3km), surrounded by wide valleys and with the seascape opening up ahead of you.

church, where the original fishing village began. The Blue Flag main beach has very pale sand (hence the name Playa Blanca) and good facilities. That said, you're better off crossing the ocean to Corralejo on Fuerteventura, where the beaches and dunes easily outclass Playa Blanca's. There is a good arts and crafts market at the swanky port, Marina Rubicón, on Wednesday and Saturday mornings.

⚡ Activities

Cala Blanca   DIVING
(✐928 51 90 40; www.calablancasub.com; Centro Comercial el Papagayo; dive with equipment rental €40) Offers individual dives, a range of courses and snorkelling trips (adult/child €40/25).

Papagayo Bike   BICYCLE RENTAL
(✐928 34 98 61; www.papagayobike.com; Calle La Tegala 13; bike rental per day from €16) As well as renting bikes, they offer simple excursions, which include refreshments and transfers from your hotel to the cycling route and back.

✗ Eating

Restaurante Casa José   SPANISH €€
(Plaza Nuestra Señora del Carmen 8; mains €10-15; ⊗8am-11pm Mon-Sat, 1-11pm Sun) Opposite the church, this modest restaurant, with its traditional green paintwork, has an informal atmosphere and excellent seafood dishes.

El Horno de la Abuela   SPANISH €€
(Calle La Tegala; mains €8-16; ⊗1-4pm & 7pm-late) A long-standing restaurant in the old town offering hearty portions of Spanish cuisine, with an emphasis on goat, suckling pig and other meaty fare.

Romantica   INTERNATIONAL €€
(Avenida de Papagayo 10; mains €10-15; ⊗1-4pm & 7pm-late) With ocean views and a menu that's a little more imaginative than most

around here, Romantica gets consistently positive reviews from travellers. There's a little of everything on the menu, including pasta, steaks and duck in mango sauce.

Casa Pedro   SPANISH €€
(Paseo Marítimo 77; mains €10-17; ⊗1-4pm & 7pm-late) Fabulous seafront location and reliably good regional and seafood dishes.

❶ Information

Tourist Office (Calle El Varadero; ⊗7am-7pm) A helpful office with plenty of pamphlets detailing local activities.

❶ Getting There & Away

Bus 6 (€3.60, one hour) runs hourly between Playa Blanca and Arrecife.

Punta del Papagayo

This promontory is a *reserva natural protegido* (protected nature reserve). The road beyond the rickety toll barrier (€3 per vehicle) is dirt, but quite manageable even in a small car. Or take the easy way and hop aboard the **Taxi Boat Papagayo Beach** (✐928 51 90 12; return trip adult/child €18/9; ⊗10am-5pm), which sets out four times daily from Playa Blanca with a pick-up stop at Marina Rubicón.

The southeast coast leading up to Punta del Papagayo is peppered with a series of pretty golden-sand coves and beaches, including Playa del Papagayo and the picturesque and secluded 90m-long **Playa Mujeres**, west of the *punta*. It has fine pale golden sand and is particularly popular with snorkellers and surfers.

Papagayo is extremely popular and, sadly, there seems to be no limit on the number of cars allowed into the reserve per day. Arrive early if you hope to have the sand to yourself for a while.

Tenerife

📞 922, 822 / POP 890,000

Best Places to Eat

➡ Guaydil (p133)

➡ La Hierbita (p128)

➡ Tito's Bodeguita (p140)

Best Places to Stay

➡ Hotel Alhambra (p227)

➡ Hotel Adonis Capital (p226)

➡ Hotel Sun Holidays (p227)

Why Go?

Tenerife is the striking (and slightly saucy) grand dame in the archipelago family. Attracting over 10 million visitors a year, the island's most famous southern resorts offer Brit-infused revelry and clubbing, combined with white sandy beaches and all-inclusive resorts. But step beyond the lobster-red tourists and what you'll find is a cultured and civilised island of extraordinary diversity.

This potpourri of experiences includes tropical-forest walks and designer-shop struts; dark forays into volcanic lava; a sexy and sultry Carnaval celebration that's second only to Rio, and a stash of museums, temples to modern art and creaky old colonial towns. But above all else, this is an island of drama, and nothing comes more dramatic than the snow-draped Pico del Teide, Spain's tallest mountain and home to some of the most fabulous hiking in all the country.

When to Go

➡ December to February is pleasantly warm, except on El Teide where deep winter can see snowfall closing the mountain.

➡ Springtime (March to April) is good for hiking and wildflowers. Surfers will find the best waves in March.

➡ In the summer months from May to September, expect around 11 hours of daily sunshine with an average of 28°C in August; a few degrees cooler during the surrounding months.

➡ As autumn turns from October to November, temperatures fall around the ideal 21°C mark and there's fewer tourists; some hotels may drop their prices slightly.

History

The original inhabitants of Tenerife were primitive cave-dwellers called Guanches, who arrived from North Africa around 200 BC. Tenerife was the last island to fall to the Spanish (in 1496) and subsequently became an important trading centre. As such, it was subject to invasions by marauding pirates and, in 1797, from the British in the battle of Santa Cruz, when Admiral Nelson famously lost his arm (served him right, really).

In 1821 Madrid declared Santa Cruz de Tenerife the capital of the Canaries. The good and great of Las Palmas de Gran Canaria remained incensed about this until 1927, when Madrid finally split the archipelago into two provinces, with Santa Cruz as the provincial capital of Tenerife, La Palma, La Gomera and El Hierro. As economic links between the Canaries and the Americas strengthened, a small exodus of islanders crossed the ocean, notably to Venezuela and Cuba. In later years affluent emigrants and Latin Americans reversed the trend, bringing influences that are still evident in the food and Latino beat of the music of today's Tenerife.

ⓘ Getting There & Away

AIR

Two airports serve the island. **Tenerife Sur** (Reina Sofía; ☎ 922 75 95 10; www.aena.es), about 20km east of Playa de las Américas, handles international flights, while almost all inter-island flights (plus a few international and mainland services) use the older and smaller **Tenerife Norte** (Los Rodeos; ☎ 922 63 56 35; www.aena.es). **Binter Canarias** (☎ 092 39 13 92; www.bintercanarias.com) connects the island with the rest of the archipelago.

BOAT
Ferries from Santa Cruz

Buy tickets for all companies from travel agents or from the main **Estación Marítima Muelle Ribera** (Map p124) building in Santa Cruz (from where the Fred Olsen boats leave). Naviera Armas has its base further to the south.

Trasmediterránea Acciona (☎ in Madrid 902 45 46 45; www.trasmediterranea.com; Estación Marítima Muelle Ribera) runs a weekly ferry at 11.30pm every Friday from Santa Cruz de Tenerife that makes the following stops:

➡ Las Palmas de Gran Canaria, Gran Canaria (from €22, 8½ hours)

➡ Puerto del Rosario, Fuerteventura (from €26, 20½ hours)

➡ Arrecife, Lanzarote (from €28, 24 hours)

ROAD DISTANCES (KM)

	Santa Cruz de la Tenerife	Puerto de la Cruz	Los Cristianos	Puerto de Santiago
Puerto de la Cruz	74			
Los Cristianos	158	140		
Puerto de Santiago	73	40	27	
Parador Nacional de Teide	128	90	64	40

Approximate distances only

Naviera Armas (Map p124; ☎ 902 45 65 00; www.navieraarmas.com) runs an extensive ferry service around the islands from Santa Cruz de Tenerife.

➡ Las Palmas de Gran Canaria, Gran Canaria (from €31, 2½ hours, 21 weekly)

➡ Morre Jable, Fuerteventura (from €70, 6½ hours, one daily)

➡ Puerto del Rosario, Fuerteventura (from €62, 11½ hours, one daily)

➡ Arrecife, Lanzarote (from €72.50, 11 hours, one daily, Monday to Friday)

Fred Olsen (☎ 902 10 01 07; www.fredolsen. es) has three to six daily ferries from Santa Cruz to Agaete in the northwest of Gran Canaria (€36, 1¼ hours), from where you can take its free bus onwards to Las Palmas (35 minutes).

Ferries from Los Cristianos

Ferries come in and out of the Los Cristianos port day and night. Naviera Armas and the faster, but more expensive, Fred Olsen operate from here. Tickets are available from travel agents or from the main Estación Marítima building.

Routes operated by **Naviera Armas** from Los Cristianos include the following:

➡ San Sebastián de la Gomera, La Gomera (€30, one hour, three daily Monday to Friday, one Saturday, two Sunday)

➡ Santa Cruz de la Palma, La Palma (€41, 3½ hours, one daily Sunday to Friday)

➡ Valverde, El Hierro (€49.50, 3¾ hours, 5.30pm Sunday to Friday)

Routes operated by **Fred Olsen** from Los Cristianos include the following:

➡ San Sebastián de la Gomera, La Gomera (€32, 50 minutes, three daily Monday to Friday, two daily Saturday and Sunday)

➡ Santa Cruz de la Palma, La Palma (from €42, two hours, one daily Sunday to Friday)

ATLANTIC OCEAN

→ Santa Cruz de la Palma

0 ——— 20 km
0 ——— 10 miles

Playa de los Troches
Roque de las Bodegas
Playa de San Roque
Faro de Anaga

Punta del Hidalgo
Bajamar
Benijo
Almáciga
Taganana

Tejina
El Socorro
Tegueste

Anaga Mountains ❶

Igu.ste
San Andrés
Playa de las Teresitas

El Sauzal
Tacoronte

La Laguna ❺

La Matanza de Acentejo
La Esperanza

Santa Cruz de Tenerife ❹

Tenerife Norte (Los Rodeos) Airport
TF-24

Las Palmas de Gran Canaria →

TF-5

Buenavista del Norte
El Guincho
Garachico
Playa de San Marcos
Puerto de la Cruz ❼

Las Cruces
Genovés
Icod de los Vinos
La Orotava

Valle de la Orotava

Aguamansa

Candelaria

Punta de Teno
TF-445
TF-42
TF-436
TF-82

Parque Rural de Teno ❻ **Masca**

Pico del Teide (3718m)
Montaña Blanca (2750m)
El Portillo Visitor Centre

Güímar
Puertito

Barranco de Masca
Santiago del Teide

Observatorio del Teide

Acantilados de los Gigantes
Los Gigantes
TF-38
Pico Viejo (3070m)

Parque Nacional del Teide ❸

El Escobonal

Puerto de Santiago

Roques de García
Cañada Blanca Visitor Centre
Fasnia
Icor
Roques de Fasnia

Playa de la Arena
Guía de Isora
Llano de Ucanca
Parador Nacional

TF-28

TF-82
TF-21
Barranco del Infierno
Vilaflor

Arico Viejo
Arico Nuevo
Porís de Abona

Santa Cruz de la Palma →

Playa de las Gaviotas
Adeje
Arona
Grandilla de Abona

TF-1

Costa Adeje
Playa de las Américas ❷
Tenerife Sur (Reina Sofía) Airport
Playa de El Cabezo

Los Cristianos
El Médano

San Sebastián de la Gomera;
Puerto de la Estaca (El Hierro) →

Faro de la Rasca
Costa del Silencio
Las Galletas

ATLANTIC OCEAN

Tenerife Highlights

❶ Do a Darwin and check out the magnificent **Anaga mountains** (p134), the oldest geographical region on the island

❷ Roll out your party gear for a night on the town at the neon-framed hot spots in **Playa de las Américas** (p152)

❸ Hike around the fabulous moonscape of **Parque Nacional del Teide** (p146)

❹ Check out the great wave of the **Auditorio de Tenerife** (p126) in Santa Cruz de Tenerife

❺ Visit **La Laguna** (p130), and the best-preserved historical quarter on the island

❻ Be overawed by tiny **Masca** (p150) and its extraordinary setting

❼ Enjoy the salty sea breezes of the charming resort of **Puerto de la Cruz** (p135)

❶ Getting Around

TITSA (Transportes Interurbanos de Tenerife SA; www.titsa.com) runs a spider's web of bus services all over the island, as well as within Santa Cruz and other towns.

Car-rental agencies are plentiful and you shouldn't have a problem, even if you want same-day rental. International chains are present in all major resort areas and the airports.

You can take a taxi anywhere on the island – but it is an expensive way to get around. You are much better off hiring a car.

SANTA CRUZ DE TENERIFE

POP 207,000

Don't bypass the bustling capital, the port of Santa Cruz, in your haste to reach the beaches. This good-looking and wholly Spanish city is home to evocative, brightly painted buildings, sophisticated and quirky shops, excellent museums, a showstopping auditorium, and a tropical oasis of birdsong, fountains and greenery in the city park. It also has a good range of quality accommodation and restaurants, plus an excellent bus system, making it a sensible base for exploring Tenerife's northeast.

History

Alonso Fernández de Lugo landed on Tenerife in 1494 to embark on the conquest of the final and most resistant island in the archipelago. La Laguna, which is a few kilometres inland, initially blossomed as the island's capital. Santa Cruz de Santiago (as Santa Cruz de Tenerife was then known) remained a backwater until its port began to flourish in the 18th and 19th centuries. Only in 1803 was Santa Cruz 'liberated' from the municipal control of La Laguna by Spanish royal decree; in 1859 it was declared a city.

◉ Sights

The majority of Santa Cruz's sights and museums are within easy walking distance of revamped waterfront **Plaza España** with its huge circular wading pool plus fountain that spouts four times a day (indicating high and low tides). The city's primary pedestrian shopping area, pedestrianised Calle Castillo, is just west of here.

★**Museo de la Naturaleza y el Hombre**　　　MUSEUM
(www.museosdetenerife.org; Calle Fuente Morales; adult/child €3/1.50; ☺9am-7pm Tue-Sun) This brain-bending amalgam of natural science and archaeology is the city's number one attraction, and one of the best museums in all the Canary Islands. Set inside the former civil hospital, the exhibit highlights are undoubtedly the Guanche mummies and skulls, all of which are shrivelled masses of skin, hair and bone, with faces dried into contorted and grotesque expressions.

In addition, there are informative displays on the wildlife, flora and geology; the audiovisual presentation about the eruption of El Teide is particularly powerful. Children will enjoy the interactive displays with their flashing buttons and large TV screens. At present, signage is only in Spanish, although most of the exhibition rooms have laminated explanatory sheets in English. There's a cafe and gift shop.

★**Tenerife Espacio de las Artes**　　ART
(TEA; www.teatenerife.es; Avenida de San Sebastián 10; adult/child €7/free, film admission €4; ☺10am-8pm Tue-Sun) The highlight of this dramatic modern building is the excellent art gallery which covers three large and light galleries. Don't miss the permanent exhibition of both the paintings and audiovisual exhibits dedicated to the life and work of the Tenerife-born Óscar Domínguez, considered the third greatest surrealist Spanish painter in Spain (after Joan Miró and Salvador Dalí). Temporary exhibitions often include up-and-coming Spanish artists and reflect edgy contemporary themes.

There is also a cinema, with films screened at weekends; a vast library and multimedia room, with 36 internet terminals available for use, free of charge; a popular cafe and an excellent gift shop.

★**Iglesia de Nuestra Señora de la Concepción**　　CHURCH
(Plaza Iglesia; ☺9am-9pm Sun, mass 9am & 7.30pm) It's difficult to miss the striking bell tower of the city's oldest church, which also has traditional Mudéjar (Islamic-style architecture) ceiling work. The present church was built in the 17th and 18th centuries, but the original building went up in 1498, just after the island was conquered. At the heart of the shimmering silver altar is the Santa Cruz de la Conquista (Holy Cross of

Santa Cruz de Tenerife

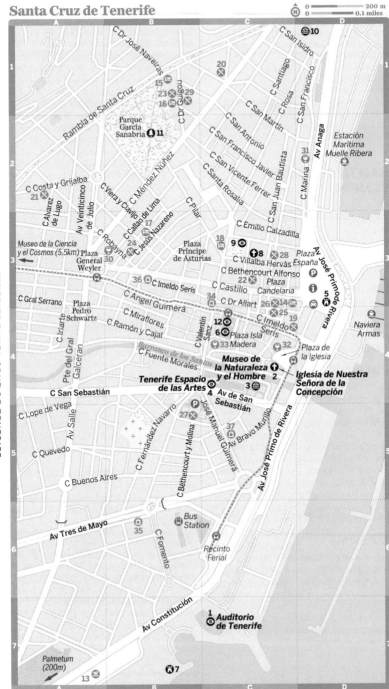

0 — 200 m
0 — 0.1 miles

C San Isidro
C Dr José Naveiras
Rambla de Santa Cruz
C Dr Guigou
C Santiago
C Rosa
C San Francisco
Parque García Sanabria
C San Martín
C San Antonio
Estación Marítima Muelle Ribera
C San Francisco Javier
Av Anaga
C Méndez Núñez
C San Vicente Ferrer
C San Juan Bautista
C Santa Rosalía
C Viera y Clavijo
C Costa y Grijalba
C Álvarez de Lugo
Av Veinticinco de Julio
C Callao de Lima
C Pilar
C Marina
C Emilio Calzadilla
Museo de la Ciencia y el Cosmos (5.5km)
C Robayna
C Jesús Nazareno
Plaza Príncipe de Asturias
C Villalba Hervás
Plaza España
Av José Primo de Rivera
Plaza General Weyler
C Béthencourt Alfonso
Plaza Candelaria
C Gral Serrano
C Imeldo Serís
C Castillo
C Ángel Guimerá
C Dr Allart
Plaza Pedro Schwartz
C Iriarte
C Miraflores
C Valentín Sanz
C Imeldo Serís
C Ramón y Cajal
Plaza Isla Madera
Naviera Armas
Pte del Gral Galcerán
Barranco de los Santos
C Fuente Morales
Museo de la Naturaleza y el Hombre 2
Plaza de la Iglesia
Tenerife Espacio de las Artes
Iglesia de Nuestra Señora de la Concepción
C San Sebastián
Av de San Sebastián
C Lope de Vega
C Fernández Navarro
C Béthencourt y Molina
C José Manuel Guimerá
Av Bravo Murillo
Av Salle
C Quevedo
Av José Primo de Rivera
C Buenos Aires
Av Tres de Mayo
C Fomento
Bus Station
Recinto Ferial
Av Constitución
Auditorio de Tenerife
Palmetum (200m)

Santa Cruz de Tenerife

the Conquest), which dates from 1494 and gives the city its name.

Check out the anteroom to the sacristy. The altarpiece in the chapel beside it was carved from cedar on the orders of Don Matías Carta, a prominent personage who died before it was completed. He lies buried here and the pallid portrait on the wall was done after his death (hence the closed eyes and crossed arms). There's also a fine painting, *La Adoración de los Pastores* (The Adoration of the Shepherds) by Juan de Miranda.

Museo de Bellas Artes   ART

(www.santacruzdetenerife.es; Plaza Príncipe de Asturias; ⊘10am-8pm Mon-Fri, to 3pm Sat & Sun) **FREE** Founded in 1900 and formerly part of the adjacent church (note the fabulous stained glass), this excellent museum has an eclectic collection of paintings by mainly Spanish, Canarian and Flemish artists, including Ribera, Sorolla and Brueghel. There's also sculpture, including a Rodin, and temporary exhibitions. The massive battle scene canvases by Spanish painter Manuel Villegas Brieva are particularly sobering. Note that the galleries are accessed via several flights of stairs and that there is no elevator.

Iglesia de San Francisco   CHURCH

(Calle José Murphy; ⊘variable opening hours) If churches are your religion then don't miss this pretty baroque church from the 17th and 18th centuries with its richly carved ceiling and ornate altarpieces. Check at the tourist office for information about concerts held at the church.

Centro de Arte La Recova   ART

(www.santacruzdetenerife.es; Plaza Isla Madera; ⊘11am-1pm & 6-9pm Tue-Sat) **FREE** Located in a former market, this gallery houses temporary exhibitions of contemporary Canarian and mainland-Spanish artists.

Teatro Guimerá   NOTABLE BUILDING

(www.teatroguimera.es; Plaza Isla Madera; ⊘11am-1pm & 6-8pm Tue-Fri) One of the city's architectural highlights is the 19th-century Teatro Guimerá, fronted by a suitably theatrical giant mask sculpture. The sumptuous interior is reminiscent of Madrid's Teatro Real, with semicircular balconied seating and plenty of gilt.

Castillo de San Cristóbal   CASTLE

(Plaza España; ⊘10am-6pm Mon & Wed-Fri, 11am-7pm Sat & Sun; P) **FREE** Located underneath

Plaza España are the still-standing fragments of the former castle that once sat majestically here. These can be accessed by an entrance on the seaward side of the plaza (which some people apparently mistake as steps down to the public toilets!). There is also a small museum here recounting the history of the castle.

Museo Militar de Almeyda   MUSEUM
(Calle San Isidro 1; ⊙10am-2pm Tue-Sat) FREE
Explains the military history of the islands and the successful defence of the city, brought alive by a superb 30m scale model of the flagship *Theseus*. The most famous item here, however, is *El Tigre* (The Tiger), the cannon that reputedly blew off Admiral Nelson's arm when he attacked Santa Cruz in 1797.

Parque García Sanabria   PARK
(off Calle Méndez Núñez) On the northern fringe of the city centre, the city park is a delightful collection of Mediterranean and subtropical trees and flowers interspersed with sculptures, wide paths and various water features. It's the perfect place for a picnic in the shade of an Indian banyan tree and a lazy afternoon listening to birdsong. There is also a pleasant cafe.

★ Auditorio de Tenerife   NOTABLE BUILDING
(☑922 27 06 11; www.auditoriodetenerife.com; Avenida Constitución; ⊙guided tours 12.30pm Mon-Sat Oct-Jun, 12.30pm & 5.30pm Mon-Sat Jul-Sep; P) FREE This magnificent, soaring white wave of an auditorium was designed by the internationally renowned Spanish architect Santiago Calatrava and possesses a Sydney Opera House presence, as well as superb acoustics. Guided multilingual tours (reserved in advance via the website) will take you behind the scenes of this remarkable building.

If you don't have time for a tour or to attend a performance, at least consider having a drink in the cafe within the sweeping space of the main entrance. You can also walk around the entirety of the building and take plenty of arty shots to impress the folks back home.

Palmetum   GARDENS
(www.palmetumsantacruz.com; Avenida Constitución; adult/child €6/2.80, joint ticket with Parque Marítimo César Manrique adult/child €7.30/3.30; ⊙11am-1pm & 4-8pm Tue-Sun; P) Opened in 2013 on a former landfill area, this 12-hectare botanical garden has the most diverse collection of palm trees in Europe, imported from all over the world. A detailed mapped leaflet helps in identifying the trees, as well as signage. It's a peaceful place for a wander, with strategically placed benches for contemplating the seamless sea views. The central octagon is a shaded walled space with volcanic rock waterfalls designed to accommodate the more delicate species, including climbing palms from Yucatan.

THREE PERFECT DAYS IN TENERIFE

Day One
Start your tour in **Santa Cruz**, fawning over the classical works in the **Museo de Bellas Artes** (p125). Next head up to some natural art in the **Parque García Sanabria** (p126). Get a load of how creative modern Spain can be in the **Tenerife Espacio de las Artes** (p123), a modern art gallery. Then learn about life many yesterdays ago at the **Museo de la Naturaleza y el Hombre** (p123) and finish your day with a stroll to the **Auditorio de Tenerife** (p126) or nearby **Palmetum** (p126).

Day Two
Explore the gracious streets of pretty **Garachico** (p145), on the island's northwest coast, in the morning before driving west towards wild **Punta de Teno** (p150) at the very end of Tenerife. Hold onto the edge of your seat on the drive to spectacular **Masca** (p150) and then drop down to the seaside for some bucket-and-spade fun at **Los Gigantes** and **Puerto de Santiago** (p151).

Day Three
Stick your head high above the clouds in the stunning **Parque Nacional del Teide** (p146). The fit and fearless can make an all-day hiking assault on the summit; the fearless but not so fit can take it easy in the cable car ride to just below the summit. Everyone can enjoy the easy walk around the **Roques de García** (p147).

Fort de San Juan   FORT

(Avenida Constitución) The central waterfront zone has undergone a major facelift and you can now enjoy a pleasant 10-minute walk southwest of Plaza España to reach the squat 17th-century Castillo de San Juan (don't be misled by the name, it's more of a modest fortress than a castle). Stand in the shadow of this protective fort and contemplate its harrowing past when this was the site of an active trade in African slaves.

🏃 Activities

Parque Marítimo César Manrique SWIMMING

(☑657 65 11 27; Avenida Constitución; adult/child €2.50/1.50, joint ticket with Palmetum adult/child €7.30/3.30; ⊙10am-7pm) Located right off the city's main *avenida* is this park, where you can have a dip in one of the wonderful designer pools or collapse on a sunlounger and drink in the beautiful view and something refreshing. It's suitable for all ages, and great for children.

🎉 Festivals & Events

As well as Carnaval, Santa Cruz plays host to a number of other festivals.

Festival de Música de Canarias   MUSIC

(www.festivaldecanarias.com; ⊙ Jan & Feb) This is the biggest event on the serious music calendar, held annually in Santa Cruz de Tenerife and Las Palmas de Gran Canaria (on Gran Canaria).

Día de la Cruz   RELIGIOUS

(⊙3 May) This day is observed throughout the island, but particularly in Santa Cruz (and Puerto de la Cruz), where crosses and chapels are beautifully decorated with flowers in celebration of the founding of the city.

🍴 Eating

Chairs on squares are plentiful here, due to the friendly, gregarious nature of the locals and, still more, to the sunshine. Pleasant cafe *terrazas* (terraces) include those on Plaza Candelaria and the shaded number on the fringe of Parque García Sanabria.

Bodeguita Canaria   CANARIAN €

(www.bodeguitacanaria.es; Calle Imeldo Serís 18; mains €8-10; ⊙1-4pm & 8-11.30pm Mon-Sat; 🚸) This is a local favourite and has an earthy traditional atmosphere with chunky dark furniture and charmingly dated decor. Try local dishes like *ropa vieja* (literally 'old

---

SCULPTURE CITY

In 1974, Santa Cruz hosted an international street sculpture exhibition with leading works by iconic masters of the art such as Henry Moore, Joan Miró and Óscar Domínguez. Today you can enjoy these world-class sculptures while strolling around the city. Check at the tourist office for details on specific sculpture tours departing from the beautiful **Parque García Sanabria** (p126), where several of the works are on permanent display.

---

clothes'), a tasty meat-based stew with chickpeas, vegetables and potatoes. The desserts are similarly heartwarmingly homely and include *torrijas,* the Spanish take on bread-and-butter pudding.

La Llave de Las Nubes   CANARIAN €

(Calle Dr Allart 46; mains €7-10, menú del día €8; ⊙9am-5pm Mon-Fri) The folks behind this delightful small restaurant are passionate about food. Every morning they shop for the freshest produce at the market and create just a few choice dishes with a strong base in home-style traditional cooking. The soups are particularly delectable – try the watercress if available. It's always busy, so you may have to wait for a table (no reservations).

Tasca   CANARIAN €

(Calle Dr Guigou 18; mains €6-10, menú del día €7; ⊙noon-3pm & 7-11pm Mon-Sat) The cultural and culinary opposite to the all-day English breakfasts of the southern resorts, this neighbourhood institution makes no allowances for confused foreigners. The laughably cheap lunch menus (in Spanish) mean there's often a queue of locals waiting for a table and the food, which consists of huge portions of sturdy Canarian classics.

La Casita   CAFE €

(www.lacasitacafe.es; Calle Jesús Nazareno 14; mains €7-8, cakes €2.50; ⊙10am-midnight Tue-Sat; 📶) Managed by a fashionable young team, but themed like grandma's country cottage, this enticing cafe sports antiques, original tile work and several cosy dining rooms. The emphasis is on simple lightweight mains like salads, burgers and croquettes, plus wonderful cakes and pies

CARNAVAL CAPERS

Channelling a true Carnaval spirit of exuberance and mayhem, Santa Cruz's own **Carnaval** (www.carnavaltenerife.com; ☺Feb) is a nonstop, 24-hour party-orgy. Festivities generally kick off in early February and last about three weeks. Many of the gala performances and fancy-dress competitions take place in the Recinto Ferial (fairgrounds) but the streets, especially around Plaza España, become frenzied with good-natured dusk-to-dawn frivolity.

Don't be fooled into thinking this is just a sequin-bedecked excuse to party hearty, though. It may sometimes be hard to see or believe, but there is an underlying political 'message' to the whole shebang. Under the Franco dictatorship, Carnaval ground to a halt and there didn't seem to be too much to celebrate. The Catholic Church's relationship with the fascists was another source of frustration so, when Carnaval was re-launched after the death of General Franco, the citizens of Santa Cruz wasted no time in lampooning the perceived sexual and moral hypocrisy of the church and the fascists. Today, you will still see a lot of people dressed for the event as naughty nuns and perverted priests, and more drag queens than bumblebees in a buttercup field. And all in the name of good, clean fun. Book your accommodation ahead – if you intend to go to bed, that is.

including chocolate, strawberry and the festive-sounding Baileys.

★**La Hierbita** CONTEMPORARY CANARIAN €€
(☐922 24 46 17; www.lahierbita.es; Calle Clavel 19; mains €10-15; ☺noon-4pm & 7-11pm Tue-Sat, noon-4pm Mon) This place oozes atmosphere. And little wonder, given the history. The first restaurant to be licensed in the city, in 1893, Calle Clavel back then was at the heart of the red-light district; part of the current restaurant was actually a brothel. There is nothing seedy about the food, however; dishes are upmarket versions of traditional Canarian recipes.

The building still retains plenty of original features and antique memorabilia. Dining rooms are spread over two creaky wooden floors and faded old photos add to the intrigue. The seafood dishes are particularly memorable, along with the pulse-based soups and stews.

El Lateral 27 CANARIAN €€
(Calle Béthencourt Alfonso 27; mains €10-14; ☺7.30am-midnight Mon-Sat; 🐾) Jovial staff, happy shoppers and a menu of tried and tested local dishes makes this place a perennial Santa Cruz favourite. Dishes like oxtail (or goat) stew, sirloin in garlic sauce and seafood pie will not disappoint any large appetite. Veggie lovers should go elsewhere.

Da Canio III ITALIAN €€
(Map p124; Calle San Martín 76; pizza €8-10, pasta €10-12; ☺1-4pm & 7-11pm Mon-Sat; 🐾) With a dining room tastefully decked out in terracotta and stone, this Italian-owned restaurant serves up a better class of pizza and

pasta. The two-dozen pizza choices are ideal for fussy families, and the pasta and risottos come recommended, as well.

Plaza 18 CONTEMPORARY CANARIAN €€
(☐922 17 30 14; Plaza San Francisco; mains €11-16; ☺noon-11pm Mon-Thu, to 1am Fri & Sat) This fashionable place is located in one of the prettiest corners of the city, overlooking magnificent banyan trees and flower beds with the baroque Iglesia de San Francisco as a backdrop. The decor is colourfully chic and the cuisine hits the mark (most of the time). The menu includes risottos, gourmet burgers, salads and *tostas* with a variety of toppings, plus excellent local wines.

Gom CONTEMPORARY CANARIAN €€
(☐922 27 60 58; Calle Dr Guigou 27; mains €10-15; ☺1-4pm & 7-11pm; P🐾) Part of the adjacent Hotel Taburiente (p226), the modern menu at this sophisticated restaurant offers a creative take on otherwise typical Canarian and mainland fare. One of the more upmarket places in the city centre, it's popular with a slick business crowd at lunchtime.

El Aguarde CONTEMPORARY CANARIAN €€€
(☐922 28 91 42; www.restauranteelaguardetenerife.es; Calle Costa y Grijalba 21; mains €15-25; ☺1-4pm Mon-Sat, 9-11pm Tue-Sat; 🐾) Readers are raving about this special occasion place that exudes a minimalist elegance to accompany the finely crafted dishes. The menu changes according to what is fresh in season, but includes a good selection of meat and fish dishes and at least one vegetarian choice. Desserts are exquisite; try the lemon mousse with cava and mint.

Self-Catering

Mercado de Nuestra Señora de África   MARKET
(Avenida de San Sebastián; ⊘9am-2pm; P)
Dating from 1944, this market has a Latin
American look with its arched entrance,
clock tower and flower sellers. It's not large
by Spanish standards (some 140 stalls) but
is still tantalising, with stalls selling mountains of fresh fruit and vegetables and a variety of fish. You can also buy picnic fare such
as bread, local cheese, wine and cold cuts.

 Drinking & Nightlife

Most of the nightlife is centred around the
northern end of Avenida Anaga although
venues frequently change. For a more sophisticated atmosphere, head to the colourful cafes and bars on Calle Antonio
Domínguez Alfonso (also known as Calle
Noria), one of the oldest streets in the city.

Bar Zumería Doña Papaya   JUICE BAR
(Calle Callao de Lima 3; juices €2-3.50; ⊘9am-
7pm Mon-Fri, to 3pm Sat) Delicious fresh fruit
juices, including strawberry, mango, papaya,
avocado and various delectable-sounding
combinations. Local workers also come here
at lunchtime for a quick and simple meal.

Barbas Bar   BAR
(Calle Marina 9; ⊘6pm-2am Mon-Sat) Yes guys, if
you have a *barba* (beard) you will be made
particularly welcome at this saloon-style bar
across from the port. The emphasis is, fittingly, on imported beer, with a vast choice
ranging from Crabbie's Original to Corona.
Good atmosphere and occasional live music.

JL Murphy   IRISH PUB
(Plaza de la Concepción; ⊘5pm-2.30am Mon-Thu,
to 3.30am Fri & Sat, 6.30pm-2.30am Sun; 🐛) This
Irish pub has a chummy atmosphere and
Guinness on tap, but is classier than many
Irish imports. Live music most weekends.

Mojos y Mojitos   BAR
(Calle Antonio Domínguez Alfonso 38; ⊘noon-mid-
night Sun-Thu, to 4am Fri & Sat; 🐛) A laid-back
place that serves decent food during the day,
but at night morphs into a combination of
cool cocktail bar and pulsating nightclub
with DJs and occasional live music.

☆ Entertainment

Bars and clubs here often double as occasional live music venues, particularly
around Calle Antonio Domínguez Alfonso
(also known as Calle Noria).

★**Auditorio de Tenerife**   LIVE MUSIC
(✒ box office 902 31 73 27; www.auditoriodeten-
erife.com; Avenida Constitución; 🐛) Tenerife's
leading entertainment option has dramatically designed curved-white concrete shells
capped by a cresting, crashing wave of a
roof. It covers and significantly enhances a
2-hectare oceanfront site. The auditorium
hosts fantastic world-class opera, dance
and classical-music performances, among
others.

Teatro Guimerá   THEATRE
(✒ box office 902 33 33 38; www.teatroguimera.
es; Plaza Isla Madera; tickets €12-18; ⊘11am-1pm
& 5-8pm) This fabulous art deco theatre is a
popular venue for highbrow entertainment,
whether music or theatre.

🛍 Shopping

The main shopping area is the pedestrianised Calle Castillo and surrounding
streets. Increasingly home to the same-again
international chains, there is still a handful
of smaller family-run shops and boutiques.

El Corte Inglés   DEPARTMENT STORE
(www.elcorteingles.es; Avenida Tres de Mayo 7;
⊘9.30am-9pm Mon-Sat; 🐛) This monster-sized
department store will keep you stocked in
whatever your heart desires. It also has a restaurant and an excellent, albeit pricey, supermarket with interesting imported goodies.

Rastro   MARKET
(José Manuel Guimerá; ⊘9am-3pm Sun) This
vast rambling flea market is held along two
parallel streets starting from Mercado de
Nuestra Señora de África and running along
José Manuel Guimerá to the coast every
Sunday. It's the usual mix, including pirat-
ed DVD movies, cut-price underwear and
handmade jewellery, but is bustling and fun.

La Isla Bookshop   BOOKS
(www.laislalibros.com; Calle Imeldo Serís 75;
⊘9.30am-8pm Mon-Fri, to 1.30pm Sat) This
old-fashioned bookshop covers four floors
and has titles in English, including novels,
plus Canaries guidebooks and maps.

Carolina Boix SHOES
(www.carolinaboix.com; Calle Valentín Sanz 10; ☺9.30am-8.30pm Mon-Fri, 10am-8.30pm Sat) Carolina Boix is a Tenerife born and based shoe designer with shops throughout the Canary Islands. Made from man-made fabrics, her inexpensive footwear (for men and women) is renowned for its contemporary comfortable style.

❶ Information

Tourist Office (☑922 23 95 92; www.todotenerife.es; Plaza España; ☺9am-6pm Mon-Fri, 9.30am-1.30pm Sat) The main tourist office is located in Plaza España. Staff organise city tours at noon on Tuesday, Thursday and Saturday (€3, 1½ hours).

❶ Getting There & Away

BUS

TITSA buses radiate out from the **bus station** (Map p124; www.titsa.com; Avenida Tres de Mayo) beside Avenida Constitución. Popular routes:

Bus 102 Puerto de la Cruz (€5.25, 55 minutes, every 30 minutes) via La Laguna and Tenerife Norte

Bus 103 Puerto de la Cruz direct (€5.25, 40 minutes, more than 15 daily)

Bus 110 Los Cristianos and Playa de las Américas direct (€9, one hour, every 30 minutes)

Bus 325 Los Gigantes (€7.10, two hours, six daily)

Bus 350 La Orotava (€1.45, 45 minutes, two daily)

Buses 014 & 015 La Laguna (€1.45, 20 minutes, every 10 minutes)

CAR & MOTORCYCLE

Car-rental companies (some also rent out motorcycles) are plentiful. Major operators also have booths at the *estación marítima* (ferry terminal).

---

❶ BONO BUS

If you'll be travelling much by public transport then it's worth investing in a **BonVia** or **Bono Bus** card (www.titsa.com). Valid on all TITSA buses throughout the island, as well as the Santa Cruz tram network, they provide a 30% discount on standard fares. Cards cost from €7.50 (12 trips) to €45 (a monthly ticket for frequent users) and can be bought from any bus or tram station as well as some newspaper kiosks.

TRAM

A tram line (www.metrotenerife.com) links central Santa Cruz with La Laguna. Tickets cost €1.35 and the full journey takes 40 minutes, making it by far the most pleasant way of travelling between the two towns.

❶ Getting Around

TO/FROM THE AIRPORT

From Tenerife Norte, TITSA buses 102, 107 and 108 (€2.65, 20 minutes) go to Santa Cruz. Bus 102 (€4.75, one hour) carries on to Puerto de la Cruz via La Laguna, only 3km from the airport.

A taxi to Tenerife Norte will cost about €20 and to Tenerife Sur, around €70.

BUS

TITSA buses provide the city service in Santa Cruz. Several buses pass regularly by the centre (Plaza General Weyler and Plaza España) from the bus station, including 910 and 914. Other local services include the circular routes 920 and 921. A local trip costs €1.25.

CAR

Paid parking stations can be found underneath Plaza España and within the Mercado de Nuestra Señora de África off Avenida de San Sebastián.

TAXI

The major taxi stands are on Plaza España and at the bus station.

THE NORTHEAST

La Laguna

POP 153,000

La Laguna is widely considered to be the most beautiful town in Tenerife. An easy day trip from Santa Cruz or Puerto de la Cruz, the historic town centre is a gem, with narrow poker-straight streets flanked by pastel-hued historic mansions, inviting bars and idiosyncratic small shops. Its layout provided the model for many colonial towns in the Americas and, in 1999, La Laguna was added to the Unesco list of World Heritage sites. The town has a youthful energy and possibly the island's most determined *marcha* (nightlife).

◉ Sights

The main sights are all located in the historic centre of town. Don't worry too much if you get lost; this whole *barrio* (district) is like an outdoor museum of historical architecture.

LA LAGUNA'S CANARIAN MANSIONS

Bright facades graced with wooden double-doors, carved balconies and grey stone embellishments typify the pristinely preserved 16th- to 18th-century mansions of La Laguna, while elegant, wood-shuttered windows conceal cool, shady patios surrounded by 1st-storey verandas propped up by slender timber columns.

Calle San Agustín and the surrounding streets are lined with fine old houses. Take a look at the beautiful facade of Casa del Montañés (Calle San Agustín 16; ⊙10am-7pm Mon-Fri) with its decorative carved window frames. Destroyed by a fire in 2006, Casa Salazar (Calle San Agustín 28; ⊙10am-7pm Mon-Fri) has a beautiful, if austere, baroque facade and two lovely patios; it is now used for offices. The imposing Casa de los Capitanes (Calle Carrera 7; ⊙9am-8pm Mon-Fri, to 2pm Sat & Sun) is beside the *ayuntamiento* (town hall) and houses the tourist office. The distinctive blue facade of the mansion at Calle Carrera 66 is the former home of surrealist painter Óscar Domínguez.

Both the exterior and interior of the 19th-century Teatro Leal (Leal Theatre; www.teatroleal.com; Calle Obispo Rey Redondo 54) is a pleasingly over-the-top butterfly of a building that is open to the public only during performances.

Whenever you see an open door, peek inside – with luck the inner sanctum will also be open, but do remember that many are private residences or offices.

★Museo de la Historia de Tenerife MUSEUM
(Casa Lercaro; www.museosdetenerife.org; Calle San Agustín 22; adult/child €3/1.50; ⊙10am-8pm Tue-Sun) The documents, maps, artefacts and descriptions are interesting enough at this museum, but the 16th-century mansion itself is noteworthy with its elaborately carved wooden gallery and lovely patio. Don't miss the two magnificent 18th- and 19th-century carriages housed in a separate exhibition space at the rear of the museum.

Iglesia de Nuestra Señora de la Concepción CHURCH
(Plaza Concepción; tower €2; ⊙8.30am-1.30pm & 6-7.30pm Mon-Fri, to 8.30pm Sat, 7.30am-2pm & 4.30-8pm Sun) Constructed in 1502, one of the island's earliest churches has subsequently undergone many changes. Elements of Gothic and plateresque styles can still be distinguished and the finely wrought wooden Mudéjar (Islamic-style architecture) ceilings are a delight. Take a look at the font where apparently (any remaining) Guanches were traditionally baptised, then climb the five-storey tower for stunning views of the town and beyond.

Catedral CATHEDRAL
(www.catedraldelalaguna.blogspot.com.es; Plaza Catedral; ⊙8am-6pm Mon-Sat, to 2pm Sun) This cathedral was completely rebuilt in 1913. A fine baroque retable in the chapel is dedicated to the Virgen de los Remedios and dates from the 16th century. Other highlights include some impressive paintings by Cristóbal Hernández de Quintana, one

of the islands' premier 18th-century artists, and a splendid Carrara marble pulpit that was carved by Genovese sculptor, Pasquale Bocciardo in 1762.

Convento de Santa Clara CONVENT, MUSEUM
(cnr Calles Anchieta & Viana; adult/child €5/free; ⊙10am-5pm Tue, Thu & Sat) Of all the convents in La Laguna, this is the most interesting, renowned for its beautiful lattice-work wooden balcony and cloister. The museum covers nine rooms and contains some of the most precious artworks and artefacts from the convent collection, including a magnificent 18th-century silver altar. A 10-minute audiovisual presentation (in English and Spanish) explains the fascinating history of the convent from its founding in 1547 by 10 Franciscan nuns.

Fundación Cristino de Vera GALLERY
(www.fundacioncristinodevera.com; Calle San Agustín 18; adult/child €3/free; ⊙11am-2pm & 5-8pm Mon-Fri, 10am-2pm Sat) La Laguna's prime arts venue houses a mixture of top-calibre temporary exhibitions as well as a permanent collection of works by acclaimed contemporary artist Cristino de Vera who was born in Santa Cruz de Tenerife in 1931. There is also a thought-provoking audiovisual presentation about the artist and his work which is subtitled in English.

Iglesia de Santo Domingo CHURCH
(Calle Santo Domingo; ⊙10am-7pm) Originally a hermitage and expanded in the 17th century, this church contains paintings by de

Quintana, as well as vivid murals painted in the 20th century by Mariano de Cossío and Antonio González Suárez. There are temporary art exhibitions plus a small ecclesiastical museum.

Santuario del Cristo
CHURCH
(Santuario del Santísimo Cristo de La Laguna; Plaza San Francisco; ⊙ 8am-1pm & 4-8.45pm Mon-Thu & Sat, to 9pm Fri & Sun) At the northern end of the old quarter, this church contains a blackened wooden sculpture of Christ – the most venerated crucifix on the island. Be as respectful as possible inside, as most of the people here are praying, not sightseeing.

Convento de Santa Catalina
CONVENT
(Plaza Adelantado; adult/child €3/free; ⊙ 10am-5pm) The closed order in this convent is still active. On 15 February each year the remarkably well-preserved body of Sister María de Jesús de León Delgado, who died in 1731, is rather ghoulishly put on display. The convent also contains a small religious museum.

Iglesia y Ex-convento de San Agustín
CHURCH
(Calle San Agustín; ⊙ 10am-8pm Tue-Fri, to 3pm Sat & Sun) This ruined church is out of bounds, but you can peer through the gap in the wall at the cactuses and other plants busy reclaiming the building's structure. The cloisters, filled with tropical plants and flowers, which are open to the public, are probably the prettiest in town. The rooms surrounding the cloisters contain an art gallery of frequently changing local works.

Museo de la Ciencia y el Cosmos
MUSEUM
(🗹 922 31 52 65; www.museosdetenerife.org; Calle Vía Láctea; adult/child/student €5/free/3.50, planetarium €1; ⊙ 9am-7pm Tue-Sun; ℗) If you enjoy pushing buttons and musing on the forces of nature, you can have fun at this museum which introduces key scientific concepts in an engaging and thought-provoking way.

Located about 1.5km south of Plaza Adelantado and easily accessible by the tram to Santa Cruz (which stops right outside), it also has a planetarium, so you can stargaze during the day.

✦ Festivals & Events

Corpus Christi
RELIGIOUS
(⊙ Jun) Celebrated with gusto in La Laguna (the date changes annually, but it's always in June) and also La Orotava, where mammoth floral carpets, using tonnes of volcanic dirt, flower petals, leaves and branches, are painstakingly designed into intricate biblical scenes in the streets and plazas.

Romería de San Benito Abad
RELIGIOUS
(⊙ 1st Sun in Jul) This is one of the most important fiestas in La Laguna, held in honour of the patron saint of farmers and crops.

Fiesta del Santísimo Cristo
RELIGIOUS
(⊙ 7-15 Sep) This annual festival includes religious processions, traditional music and an impressive fireworks display.

✗ Eating

For the best choice of restaurants, head for the grid of streets surrounding the cathedral.

Tasca 61
ORGANIC €
(Calle Viana 61; mains €7-9; ⊙ 12.30-3.30pm & 7.30-10.30pm Wed-Fri, 7.30-10.30pm Sat & Sun) ✐ Organic, locally sourced produce and a slow-food philosophy are the hallmarks of this tiny place with its limited but delicious menu of daily specials. Even the beer is locally crafted at the only eco-brewery in Tenerife: Tierra de Perros.

El Tonique
CANARIAN €
(🗹 922 26 15 29; www.tascaeltonique.es; Calle Heraclio Sánchez 23; mains €8.50-12; ⊙ 1-5pm & 8-11pm Tue-Sat, 8-11pm Mon) Head downstairs to this cosy restaurant, its walls lined with dusty bottles of wine. These are but a sample

---

BEHIND-THE-SCENES TOURS

Much of the interest and beauty of La Laguna is hidden away behind heavy doors and walls from prying tourist eyes; if you want to get a more in-depth feel for the town, it's worth joining one of the frequent **guided tours** (⊙ tours at 10.30am, noon & 4pm Mon-Fri, 10.30am & noon Sat & Sun) FREE organised by the tourist office. Tours are free and are in Spanish (though with 48 hours advance notice the tourist office can cobble together a tour in English, German or French). Tours, which leave from the tourist office, take in most of the buildings and churches mentioned here as well as a number of other historic buildings that cannot be visited independently.

of more than 250 different varieties quietly maturing in Tonique's cellars. The food is very good and worth the wait for a table (it's popular for lunch) and a plate of *setas con gambas* (oyster mushrooms with prawns).

★ **Guaydil**   CONTEMPORARY CANARIAN €€
(www.restauranteguaydil.com; Calle Dean Palahí 26; mains €8-14; ⊙1.30-4.40pm & 8-11.30pm Mon-Sat; 🐾) You can't go wrong at this delightful contemporary restaurant with its punchy, playful decor. Dishes are deftly executed, exquisitely presented and sensibly priced. One tip – if ordering a salad, ask for a half portion, they won't object; they are huge (and recommended). Other typical dishes include oriental couscous, prawn-stuffed crêpes and an irresistible Cuban mojito sorbet.

★ **Mercado de San Pablo**   MARKET €€
(www.mercadossanpablo.com; Calle Herradores 59; snacks €2-5, mains €9-15; ⊙10am-11pm Mon-Wed, to midnight Thu, to 2am Fri & Sat, 1-9pm Sun; 🐾) This sophisticated cosmopolitan market would look happily at home in Manhattan. Over 30 foodstands and bars cover a wide range of cuisines all given the gourmet treatment, and including Cuban, Asian, Japanese, Mexican, Lebanese and Italian. Self-caterers can pick up German breads, local cheeses and baked goodies. Live jazz provides the ideal backdrop.

🍷 Drinking

Thirsty students comprise the town's nightlife, and the bulk of the bars are concentrated in a tight rectangle northeast of the university, known as El Cuadrilátero. At its heart, pedestrianised Plaza Zurita is simply two parallel lines of bars and pubs, so there's no shortage of quaffing choice.

Strasse   BAR
(Calle Doctor Antonio González 17; ⊙6pm-3am; 🐾) A moodily lit bar with a great range of cocktails and imported beers, plus giant-screen music videos and an atmosphere that never misses a beat, thanks to the steady crowd of toe-tapping regulars.

Pub Gabbana   CLUB
(☑922 00 00 00; Calle Doctor Antonio González 11; ⊙6pm-2am) A heaving nightclub that is also increasingly popular for its karaoke nights and contests – just in case you feel a Whitney Houston moment coming on. Located in the heart of the clubbing area and generally packed with a lively bunch of students.

FEAST LIKE A LOCAL: GUACHINCHES

A garden shed, family sitting room, empty garage... these are just a few of the typical locations where you can find *guachinches;* no-frills eateries serving home-cooked traditional meals for less than €10. Particularly prevalent in the north, and very popular at weekends, *guachinches* are difficult to find if you're not a local in the know. One way to savvy up is to download the android or Apple app: guachapp. There is also a Guachinches de Tenerife Facebook page with regularly updated information.

ℹ Information

Tourist Office (☑922 63 11 94; www.todotenerife.es; Calle Carrera 7; ⊙9am-8pm Mon-Fri, to 2pm Sat & Sun) In a lovely old house with an inner courtyard; ask for the fascinating *San Cristóbal de La Laguna, World Heritage Site* brochure.

ℹ Getting There & Away

There is a stream of buses going to Santa Cruz. Bus 015 (€1.35, 25 minutes) is best, as it takes you straight to Plaza España. The tram system also links the two towns. A one-way ticket costs €1.35. Buses 101, 102 and 103 also offer a regular service to Puerto de la Cruz (€4.10, one hour). If La Orotava (€3.15, 1½ hours) is your goal, take bus 62.

Finding a parking space on the streets is migraine-inducing. There's an underground pay car park beneath Plaza San Cristóbal, but if possible come on public transport.

San Andrés & Around

The village of San Andrés, all narrow, shady streets lined with fishers' cottages painted in primary colours, is 6km northeast of Santa Cruz. It is distinguished by the now-crumbled round tower that once protected the town, plus some good seafood restaurants.

🏖 Beaches

Playa de las Teresitas   BEACH
The golden sands of Playa de las Teresitas, just beyond San Andrés village, were imported from the Sahara. It's a lovely beach where the sunbathers are almost exclusively Spanish, whether local or from the mainland. Limited parking is available and it's safe for children to swim here.

✖ Eating

Bar El Peton SEAFOOD €

(☑ 922 59 11 29; Calle Aparejo; mains €7-9; ⊙ 7am-7pm) This cute little place is located next to San Andrés' crumbled tower. There are just three or four tables that are normally buried under a mountain of superlative seafood.

❶ Getting There & Away

There are frequent 910 buses (€1.25, 20 minutes) from Santa Cruz to San Andrés, continuing on to Playa de las Teresitas.

Taganana & the Anaga Mountains

The rugged Anaga mountains sprawling across the far northeast corner of the island offer some of the most spectacular scenery and hiking trails in Tenerife. If hiking isn't your idea of fun, then you can still get a feel for the mountains by driving the numerous switchbacks of the TF-12 road, which links La Laguna and San Andrés. It's also worth making the short, and steep, detour to Taganana along the TF-134.

There's little to see in the small town of Taganana, but it's only a few more kilometres north to the coast and **Roque de las Bodegas**, which has a number of small restaurants and bars. Local surfers favour its beach – and, even more so, the rocky strand of **Almáciga**, 1.25km eastwards.

For serious exploration of these mist-shrouded peaks, though, you need to leave the road behind and strike out on foot. The main visitors centre is the **Cruz del Carmen**, which sits a little under halfway between La Laguna and Taganana on the TF-12 road. Filled with tweeting birds you never actually see, the laurel forests surrounding the visitors centre are a jungle of twisted trees coated in moisture-retaining mosses. Through this forest wind several well-marked trails, including a five-minute one suitable for wheelchairs and strollers. Another easy 1.8km, approximately half-hour return walk, is to the **Llano de los Loros** – a stunning viewpoint. The visitors centre can supply details of these and much more taxing walks around here.

Punta del Hidalgo & Around

Once the pebble beaches and swimming pools around Punta del Hidalgo and Baja-mar were a popular resort but today they're slightly down at heel, and the only visitors are Northern Europeans in search of winter sun and locals out for some salt air. Despite this less-than-rosy picture, the area is a pleasant break from Santa Cruz and La Laguna and the surrounding mountain scenery is spectacular. Continuing northwest from El Socorro, you reach the scrappy seaside resort of **Bajamar** (via Tejina). You can swim in large artificial rock pools awash with Atlantic rollers, which are popular with locals.

Three kilometres northeast, **Punta del Hidalgo** is a more interesting place, although don't expect any crumbling cobbles or medieval churches. Like most of the towns in this region, Punta is comparatively modern, its charm being the dramatic ocean location backed by soaring craggy mountains. Stroll along the boardwalk, stopping for a coffee, *cerveza* (beer) or fishy meal at **Cofradia de Pescadores** (☑ 922 15 69 54; Punta del Hidalgo; mains €10-16; ⊙ 1-4pm & 7-10pm Mon-Sat) across from the harbour. The whole coastline here is excellent surfing country, with some of the best-quality spots on the north coast packed into a tight area.

❶ Getting There & Away

Bus 105 runs to Bajamar (€1.45, one hour) and Punta del Hidalgo (€1.45, 1¼ hours) every 30 minutes from Santa Cruz via La Laguna.

Tacoronte & Around

Tacoronte is located in the heart of one of the island's most important wine regions. Downhill from the modern town centre is the signposted **Iglesia de Santa Catalina** – a bright little whitewashed church built in the Canaries' colonial style. You'll also see a handful of traditional old houses, but otherwise there's not too much to see here.

◉ Sights

Casa del Vino La Baranda MUSEUM

(☑ 922 57 25 35; www.casadelvinotenerife.com; Autopista del Norte, El Sauzal; ⊙ 10.30am-6.30pm Tue, 9am-9pm Wed-Sat, 11am-6pm Sun; ℗) **FREE** This museum, located in a traditional Canarian country house in El Sauzal, is devoted to wine and its production and also offers wine tasting for a nominal cost. It's a charming place, with some beautiful views of El Teide on a clear day. There is a well-regarded restaurant and, during July and August, the

TENERIFE TIPPLES

The wine of Tenerife (and the Canaries in general) isn't well known internationally, but it's starting to earn more of a name for itself. The best-known, and first to earn the DO grade (*denominación de origen*), which certifies high standards and regional origin, is the red Tacoronte Acentejo. Also worth a tipple are the wines produced in Icod de los Vinos and Guimar.

The **Casa del Vino La Baranda** (p134) in El Sauzal offers wine tasting. Other local tipples include La Dorada lager-style beer brewed in Santa Cruz de Tenerife and the Canary Islands first ecological craft brewery based in Los Realejos: Tierra de Perros (www.facebook.com/CervezaArtesanalTierraDePerros), producing pale ale and stout varieties of ale.

central courtyard becomes a tasteful venue for classical-music concerts every other Tuesday from 8.30pm.

The adjacent **Casa de la Miel** (House of Honey) adds a sweet note to your trip with its informative displays about local honey production.

The museum is well signposted just beyond the El Sauzal exit from the motorway.

★ Festivals & Events

Cristo de los Dolores   WINE
(☉ Sep) Held on the first Sunday after 15 September, Cristo de los Dolores is Tacoronte's big fiesta, with harvest festivities and wine tasting.

❶ Getting There & Away

Bus 108 links these towns to Santa Cruz (€2.75, 40 minutes) every 30 minutes or hourly (depending on the time of day).

THE NORTH

Puerto de la Cruz

POP 32,665

Puerto de la Cruz is the elder statesman of Tenerife tourism, with a history of welcoming foreign visitors that dates back to the late 19th century, when it was a spa destination popular with genteel Victorian ladies. These days the town is a charming resort with real character. There are stylish boardwalks, beaches with safe swimming, traditional restaurants, a leafy central plaza, lots of pretty parks and gardens and plenty to see and do. There are also plenty of predominately German tourists and foreign residents here, hence the proliferation of bakeries selling delicious German-style breads and cakes.

History

Until it was declared an independent town in the early 20th century, Puerto de la Cruz was merely the port of the wealthier area of La Orotava. Bananas, wine, sugar and cochineal (dye-producing insects) were exported from here and a substantial bourgeois class developed in the 1700s. In the 1800s the English arrived, first as merchants and later as sun-seeking tourists, marking the beginning of the tourist transformation that characterises the town today.

◉ Sights

The **Plaza Europa**, a balcony of sorts built in 1992, may be a modern addition, but it blends well with the historic surroundings and is a good place to start your visit. The tourist office is also conveniently here, located in the **Casa de la Aduana** (Calle Lonjas; ☉9am-8pm Mon-Fri, to 5pm Sat & Sun), the old customs house (built in 1620), where now you can also find quality arts and crafts for sale. Opposite is the **Ayuntamiento** (Town Hall), which was a banana-packaging factory until 1973. Several Canarian mansions, many of them in poor repair, dot the town centre.

Museo de Arte Contemporáneo   ART
(Casa de la Aduana, Calle Lonjas; adult/child €1.50/free; ☉10am-2pm Mon-Sat) The first contemporary art museum to open in Spain, dating from 1953, this well-displayed collection includes such outstanding foreign, Spanish and Canarian artists as Will Faber, Óscar Domínguez and César Manrique. The setting, in the historic former customs house, is almost as inspiring as the artwork.

Museo Arqueológico   MUSEUM
(Archaeological Museum; www.museosdetenerife.org; Calle Lomo 9; adult/child €1/free; ☉10am-1pm & 5-9pm Tue-Sat, 10am-1pm Sun) This small but well laid-out museum provides an insight

Puerto de la Cruz

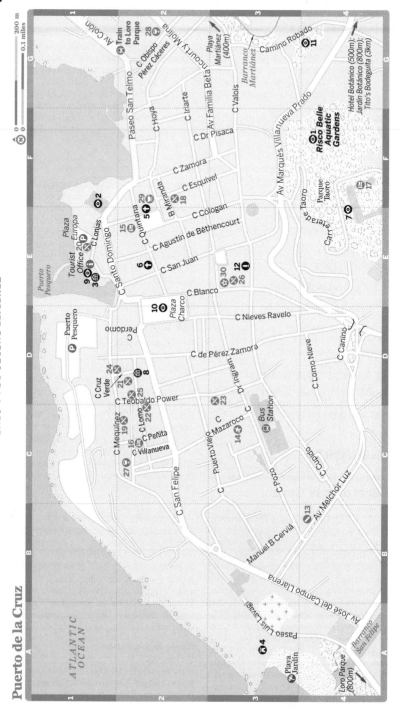

ATLANTIC OCEAN

Loro Parque (800m)

Playa Jardín

Av José del Campo Llarena

Barranco San Felipe

Paseo Luis Lavagi

Manuel B Cerviá

Av Melchor Luz

C Cupido

C Pozo

Bus Station

Dr Ingram

C Puerto Viejo

C Mazaroco

C San Felipe

C Villanueva

C Peñita

C Lomo

C Mequinez

C Teobaldo Power

C Cruz Verde

C de Pérez Zamora

C Nieves Ravelo

C Lomo Nieve

C Camino

Plaza Charco

C Perdomo

Puerto Pesquero

C Blanco

C San Juan

C Agustín de Béthencourt

C Cologan

C Esquivel

B Miranda

C Quintana

C Santo Domingo

C Zamora

C Dr Pisaca

Av Familia Betancourt y Molina

C Iriarte

C Valois

C Hoya

C Obispo Pérez Cáceres

Paseo San Telmo

Av Colón

Train to Loro Parque

Plaza Europa

C Lonjas

Tourist Office

Puerto Pesquero

Puerto Pesquero

Playa Martiánez (400m)

Barranco Martiánez

Camino Robado

Av Marqués Villanueva Prado

Risco Belle Aquatic Gardens

Hotel Botánico (500m); Jardín Botánico (800m); Tito's Bodeguita (3km)

Parque Taoro

Carretera Taoro

N

200 m
0.1 miles

into the Guanche way of life with its replicas of a typical cave dwelling, as well as a burial cave where pots and baked-clay adornments share the same burial area, demonstrating the Guanches' belief in an afterlife. The most interesting exhibit is a tiny clay idol – one of only a few ever found.

Plaza Charco   SQUARE
The translation for this magnificent central square is Puddle Plaza, named because it used to flood from the sea every time there was a storm. Shaded by Indian laurel trees and Canary palms, it's the town's meeting-and-greeting place with kiosks, benches and a children's playground, flanked by bars and restaurants.

Iglesia de Nuestra Señora de la Peña de Francia   CHURCH
(Calle Quintana; ⊙8am-6pm) This pretty 17th-century church boasts three naves, a wooden Mudéjar ceiling and the image of Gran Poder de Dios, one of the town's most revered saints. The church is fronted by lush landscaped gardens.

Iglesia de San Francisco   CHURCH
(Calle Quintana; ⊙variable opening hours) Located just off Puerto's central (and famed) Plaza del Charco is the Iglesia de San Francisco, tacked on to tiny Ermita de San Juan, the oldest structure in town (built in 1599).

Castillo de San Felipe   CASTLE
(🖉922 37 30 39; Paseo Luis Lavaggi 12) This modest castle, located beside Playa Jardín, plays host to a variety of temporary art exhibitions and regular theatre and dance performances. It was closed for refurbishment at research time, however; check at the tourist office for an update.

Torreon de Ventoso   TOWER
(Calle Valois) One of the better-kept historic buildings in Puerto, this tower once formed part of the town's Augustine convent and was used to keep watch over the port.

★ **Jardín Botánico**   GARDENS
(🖉922 92 29 81; Calle Retama 2; adult/child €3/free; ⊙9am-6pm; 🅿) Established in 1788, this magnificent botanical garden has thousands of plant varieties from all over the world and is a delightful place in which to while away an afternoon smelling the roses. As well as the major collections of tropical and subtropical plants, there is a wide variety of palms from all over the world, a fragrant

Puerto de la Cruz

herb garden and a giant 200-year-old Australian gum tree.

The garden is well signposted if you are driving. Alternatively, the majority of interurban buses make a stop near here on their way out of town. A taxi will cost around €8.

★ **Risco Belle Aquatic Gardens**   GARDENS
(Parque Taoro; adult/child €4/free; ⊙9.30am-6pm; 🅿) This is not just any old garden; step through the entrance and you are met by a sweeping lawn punctuated with tables and

chairs, citrus trees and tropical plants, like birds of paradise and poinsettias. In the historic main house, a cafe serves drinks and snacks. For a small admission fee you can also visit the magnificent aquatic gardens with herons, dragonflies, a mock lookout tower and benches for quiet contemplation.

With a backdrop of green and birdsong, these gardens feel a world away from the clamour of the coast. Don't miss them.

Sitio Litre Garden GARDENS
(www.jardindeorquideas.com; Camino Robado; adult/child €4.75/free; ⊙9.30am-5pm) This delightful garden is exquisitely laid out with walkways, fountains, tropical and subtropical plants and flowers, plus the oldest *drago* (dragon) tree in town. The highlight is, naturally enough, the orchid walk through the greenhouse with its well displayed and signed orchids. There is an inviting terrace cafe and a (surprisingly tacky) gift shop. The gardens have an interesting British-based history, which you can read about in the free leaflet.

Take note of the croquet lawn with everything in place ready for a game. Well, aside from the cucumber sandwiches, that is...

Mirador de la Paz SQUARE
(Carreterade Taoro) This square with great views is where Agatha Christie was supposedly inspired to write the novel *The Mysterious Mr Quin*. This is also a good spot to stride out from and discover the town's magnificent parks and gardens.

Loro Parque ZOO
(☑922 37 38 41; www.loroparque.com; Calle Avenida Loro Parque; adult/child €34/23; ⊙8.30am-6.45pm; ℗) Travelling around Tenerife, the Loro Parque flag is so ubiquitous that you could be forgiven for thinking they sponsor Tenerife. But we'll give them their due because where else can you see over 350 species of parrots (the world's largest collection) at once? Today its animal portfolio has grown to include tigers, gorillas and chimpanzees. Note that the park also keeps captive orcas and dolphins, which perform in shows; however, research indicates such captivity is debilitating and stressful for these creatures, and is exacerbated by human interaction.

Other exhibits include a penguin house complete with 'real' snow and a subterranean aquarium with the world's longest submarine tunnel. There is also a variety of other attractions including an HD cinema. You could walk here from town, but it's much easier to hop on the free train that leaves every 20 minutes from outside McDonald's on Plaza Reyes Católicos.

🏖 Beaches

Puerto de la Cruz is home to several beaches, all of them largely sheltered from waves and perfect for young children. In the heart of the town are the rocky and attractive **coves** around the little port just below the Paseo San Telmo.

Playa Martiánez BEACH
(Avenida de Colón) The long sandy Playa Martiánez is located at the eastern end of town. A large jetty filters down the anger of Atlantic swells and turns them into mere gentle rollers, perfect for learning to surf on. The beach itself consists of soft, black sand.

Playa Jardín BEACH
(Paseo Luis Lavagi; ℗) This dark-sand 'garden beach' west of the centre has good facilities, including toilets and showers. Huge boulders and rocks were dumped in the sea here to prevent the sand being swept away.

🏃 Activities

Lago Martiánez SWIMMING
(☑922 37 05 72; Avenida de Colón; adult/child €3.50/1.20; ⊙10am-sunset) Designed by Canario César Manrique, the watery playground of Lago Martiánez has four saltwater pools and a large central 'lake'. It can get just as crowded as the surrounding small volcanic beaches. Swim, sunbathe or grab a bite at one of the many restaurants and bars.

Der Wanderstab HIKING
(☑922 37 60 07; www.derwanderstab.de; tour €25-50) Local guides meet hikers at the bus station, from where they set out on several hikes, including El Teide and the northwest. They aim very much at a German audience; however, the guides generally have an excellent command of English as well. Book via the website.

El Cardumen DIVING, GLIDING
(☑670 38 30 07; www.elcardumen.com; Avenida Melchor Luz 3) Offers a range of diving courses including an introductory 'try dive'. If you prefer to soar like a bird rather than swim like a fish, it also offers paragliding.

GETTING ACTIVE ON TENERIFE

Possibly no other island in the archipelago offers so many opportunities to burn off calories than Tenerife. Windsurfing, kitesurfing, diving, hiking, fishing, golf and cycling are all not just possible here, but almost impossible to avoid. For water sports most facilities are concentrated in and around the southwestern resort areas, although the north coast has a wide variety of surf spots.

Tenerife is marvellous for hiking and climbing, with plenty of scope ranging from easy rambles to mountain assaults. For the most dramatic scenery, choose from the many trails within the Parque Nacional del Teide. Other attractive areas are the Anaga mountains in the northeast and around the Valle de la Orotava. There are numerous companies offering guided walks, as well as the rangers at El Teide. Check the following websites and ask at any tourist office for details:

➡ www.pateatusmontes.com

➡ www.gregorio-teneriffa.de, in German

➡ www.trekking-tenerife.com

➡ www.caminantesdeaguere.com

Mountain Bike Active CYCLING
(☑ 922 37 60 81; www.mtb-active.com; Edificio Daniela 26, Calle Mazaroco; bike rental per day from €30; ⊙ 9.30am-1.30pm & 5-7pm) Located across from the (now derelict) former bus station, this company organises biking trips to El Teide and around.

✦ Festivals & Events

Carnaval CULTURAL
(⊙ Feb) Not to be outdone by Santa Cruz, Puerto de la Cruz holds its own riotous Carnaval celebration each February.

San Juan RELIGIOUS
(⊙ 23 Jun) Held on the eve of the saint's day. Bonfires light the sky and, in a throwback to Guanche times, goats are driven for a dip in the sea off Playa Jardín.

Fiesta de los Cacharros CULTURAL
(⊙ 29 Nov) Held in Puerto de la Cruz (and Taganana), this is a quaint festival where children rush through the streets, dragging behind them a string of old pots, kettles, pans, car spares, tin cans – just about anything that will make a racket.

✗ Eating

Head to the former fishers' quarter of La Ranilla, just a couple of streets northeast of Plaza Charco, for some of the town's most innovative new restaurants.

Selma & Louisa SWEDISH €
(Calle Lomo 18, La Ranilla; breakfast €4.50-5; ⊙ 8.30am-7pm Tue-Sun; ☑) ✔ Follow the enticing smell of freshly baked cinnamon rolls to this Swedish mother-and-daughter-run eco-friendly cafe with its tasty breakfast choice including homemade granola, scrambled eggs and fluffy pancakes. The daily made soups are equally good. Plus there are healthy sandwich combos, quiches and gorgeous cakes.

Meson los Gemelos CANARIAN €
(☑ 922 37 01 33; Calle Peñón 4; mains €8-10; ⊙ noon-11pm Thu-Tue; ℗ ♿) This is a friendly restaurant with a great atmosphere; the house speciality is grilled meats. There's a covered interior barn-size patio decorated with hanging plants and agricultural paraphernalia. Increasingly popular with tourists, you can expect queues at the door. Reserve ahead.

El Limón VEGETARIAN €
(Calle Esquivel 4; mains €7-10; ⊙ noon-11pm Mon-Sun; ☑) A bright vegetarian restaurant with a menu consisting of veggie burgers, seitan kebabs, salads and fresh fruit juices, among others. It also does a good-value set-lunch menu (€10) and the clientele is almost exclusively local.

Tapas Arcón TAPAS €
(Calle Blanco 8; tapas €3-4.50; ⊙ noon-3pm & 5-10pm Mon-Sat) *Papas arrugadas* (wrinkly potatoes) with *mojo* (spicy salsa), or the Arcón special sauces of almond and sweet pepper or parsley and coriander are the must-have tapas here.

TENERIFE PUERTO DE LA CRUZ

★ Tito's Bodeguita

CANARIAN €€

(☑647 93 34 33; www.titosbodeguita.com; Camino de Duraznol; mains €10-16; ⊘12.30-11pm Mon-Sat; ℗) Despite the mildly offputting location right off a busy roundabout, a few kilometres south of the town centre, the patios, flower-filled gardens and atmospheric interior of this 18th-century country mansion are a delight; there is even an attached hermitage. The portions are huge and best for sharing with dishes based on traditional Canarian cuisine with an innovative twist. Hugely popular so book ahead.

To get here take the TF-312 towards Arenas, merging onto the TF-31 towards the Autopista Norte, then onto the TF-5; Tito's is located just beyond exit 35. Alternatively, hop into a taxi (approximately €7 from the town centre).

El Maná

ORGANIC, VEGETARIAN €€

(www.elmana.es; Mequínez 21, La Ranilla; mains €9-16; ⊘1-4pm & 7-10pm Wed-Sun; ☑) ⊘ Choose from innovative, fresh and delicious dishes that obviously (being organic) change depending on what is fresh in the vegetable patch that week. Expect unusual combinations like handmade sour apple ravioli with raisins, and vegetable couscous with an *ajoblanco* (almond-based) sauce. End on a sweet note with the vanilla-and-mango pannacotta.

Restaurante Mil Sabores

MEDITERRANEAN €€

(☑922 36 81 72; Calle Cruz Verde 5, La Ranilla; mains €12-18; ⊘noon-11pm) Styling itself as a temple to modern Mediterranean cooking, this flash restaurant has the looks and the tastes down to a fine art. What sort of things can you expect to find on the menu? How about a prawn lollipop with roasted corn and parmesan or a perfectly combined mix of pork, apple and bacon. It's quite dressy without being formal. Reservations recommended.

La Confradía de Pescadores

SEAFOOD €€

(Calle Lonjas 5; mains €12-20; ⊘noon-3pm; ℗) Come here for the catch of the day; the second best thing to buying it at the fish stall next door and cooking it yourself. Watch the cost though, as some fish dishes are priced per weight. Push the boat out with the lobster soup paella for two (€40). The back terrace has appropriate fishing harbour views.

La Rosa di Bari

ITALIAN €€

(☑922 36 85 23; www.larosadibari.com; Calle Lomo 23, La Ranilla; mains €11-17; ⊘12.30-2.45pm & 7-10.45pm Tue-Sat, 12.30-4pm Sun) Located in a lovely old house with several romantic dining rooms, this unassuming little place is actually one of the classiest restaurants in town. Enjoy innovative dishes like black tagliatelle with courgettes and prawns and fish with a mustard crust.

La Papaya

CANARIAN €€

(☑922 38 28 11; Calle Lomo 10, La Ranilla; mains €10-16; ⊘noon-4pm & 7-11pm Thu-Tue; ⊕) This longtime favourite has a series of small dining rooms with rock-face walls and a pretty patio set around a magnificent tree draped with bougainvillea. There are Canarian touches to the menu, including the succulent salmon in *malvasía* (Malmsey wine) sauce, plus a wide choice for children.

🍷 Drinking & Nightlife

Puerto de la Cruz has a steamy Latino club scene with several bars and nightclubs on Calle Obispo Pérez Cáceres; names change as often as the tide.

Bar Dinámico

BAR

(www.dinamicopuertodelacruz.com; Plaza Charco; ⊘9am-midnight; 📶) Bars and cafes come and go in Puerto but the Dinámico has been around since the '50s in one form or another and has counted the Beatles and Agatha Christie among former patrons. It's a sprawling terraced place in the centre of Plaza Charco with a Latin American vibe and more character than most places encircling the square.

Azucar

CLUB

(Calle Obispo Pérez Cáceres; ⊘10.30pm-6am) This dark and sexy Latino nightclub is located in an atmospheric colonial building.

Agora

BAR

(Plazoleta de Benito Pérez Galdós 6, La Ranilla; ⊘10am-midnight; 📶) Cafe and cocktail bar rolled into one with a chilled-out vibe, art exhibitions, books to borrow, magazines to read and tables overlooking this, one of the prettiest squares in town. Oh, and an owner who is a Mel Gibson lookalike....

Ebano Café

CAFE

(Calle Hoya 2; ⊘10am-midnight; 📶) This is a beautiful building with plenty of original features and which is equally ideal for sipping a cocktail or surfing the web (along with a decent cappuccino). Sit outside in a comfy wicker chair within confessional distance of the church. Tapas also served.

TENERIFE PUERTO DE LA CRUZ

TENERIFE FOR CHILDREN

Tenerife is a favourite destination for families as there are plenty of sights and activities to keep the kiddies amused. Unless your tot is one of that curious breed that objects to sand between the toes (it happens!), the **beaches** in the southern resorts (as well as Puerto de la Cruz) are superb, with sandcastle-friendly sand and shallow waters. Older children can also enjoy water sports ranging from **surfing** to **diving**, or they can take to the high seas on an organised **whale-** or **dolphin-watching excursion**.

If watery pursuits begin to pall, the southern resorts of Los Cristianos and Playa de las Américas equal theme-park heaven. Try **Jungle Park** (p153) or **Siam Park** (p153).

⭐ Entertainment

There is plenty of live music at the terrace restaurants in town, particularly those surrounding Plaza Charco. Aside from these there is a handful of dedicated live music venues.

Blanco Bar   LIVE MUSIC
(🕿 620 95 51 97; www.blancobar.com; Calle Blanco 12; ⊗8pm-3am Sun-Thu, 9pm-5.30am Fri & Sat; 🛜) Check the website beforehand – as well as live music, there are comedy acts, which may not affect your tickle bone unless you speak Spanish. Also hosts art exhibitions and has a great atmosphere with no rip-off drinks prices and free entry to the concerts.

ℹ️ Information

Tourist Office (🕿 922 38 60 00; www.todotenerife.es; Casa de la Aduana, Calle Lonjas; ⊗9am-8pm Mon-Fri, to 5pm Sat & Sun) An excellent tourist office with helpful staff and plenty of brochures and information about the town.

ℹ️ Getting There & Away

Buses leave from Calle Cupido (behind the former bus station which now stands derelict). There are frequent departures for Santa Cruz (€5.25, 55 minutes). Bus 103 is direct while bus 102 calls by Tenerife Norte airport and La Laguna. Other popular routes include bus 348 to El Teide (€6.20, 1½ hours, 9.15am), which returns at 4pm. Bus 343 runs to Costa Adeje (€14.50, two hours, six daily), via Los Cristianos. Bus 345 offers a half-hourly service from 7.15am to 8.40pm to La Orotava (€1.45, 20 minutes).

ℹ️ Getting Around

The long-distance buses starting in or passing through Puerto de la Cruz often double up as local buses.

Taxis are widely available and are a relatively inexpensive way to jet across town (a 15-minute ride should cost around €5).

La Orotava

POP 41,725

This colonial town has the lot, it seems: cobblestone streets, flower-filled plazas and more Castilian mansions than the rest of the island put together. Along with La Laguna, La Orotava is one of the loveliest towns on Tenerife, and one of the most truly 'Canarian' places in the Canary Islands.

The lush valley surrounding the town has been one of the island's most prosperous areas since the 16th century. Most churches and manor houses here were built in the 17th century (with some dating back to the 16th century). The valley is a major cultivator of bananas, chestnuts and grapes (as in vineyards), and is also excellent hiking country, with a maze of footpaths leading you into Canarian pine woods, with 1200m views down over the coastal plain. The tourist office can advise on routes.

👁️ Sights

La Orotava has been able to preserve the beauty of its past. Traditional mansions are flanked with ornate wooden balconies like pirate galleons, surrounded by manicured gardens. You can cover the centre on foot in just half a day. **Plaza de la Constitución**, a large, shady plaza, is a good place to start exploring. On the plaza's northeastern side is the **Iglesia de San Agustín** (Plaza de la Constitución), a simple church with a carved wooden ceiling.

⭐**Casa de los Balcones**   HISTORIC BUILDING
(www.casa-balcones.com; Casa Fonesca, Calle San Francisco 3; ⊗8.30am-6.30pm) **FREE** The setting is sublime – an ornate mansion dating from 1632 with rooms set around a central patio complete with historic photos and memorabilia. One room is devoted to lacework. Bypass the Chinese imports to admire the fine local needlework; there may well be

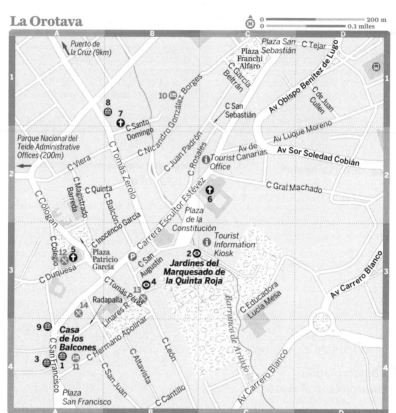

La Orotava

a demonstration taking place. There is also a bodega with an original Lagar wine press. Ask for a taste of the banana liquor but, no, it doesn't count towards your five a day...

★ Jardínes del Marquesado de la Quinta Roja
GARDENS

(Plaza de la Constitución; ⊙9am-6pm Mon-Fri, 10am-3pm Sat & Sun) **FREE** Also known as the Jardín Victoria, these French-influenced 18th-century gardens cascade down the hillside and are crowned by a small marble mausoleum built as a tomb for the Marqués de la Quinta Roja. However, apparently his wife and mother disagreed where to lay his body when he died, so the crypt was not used for its original purpose and no one knows what (or who) lies within.

Iglesia de la Concepción
CHURCH

(www.concepcionorotava.info; Plaza Patricio García; ⊙9am-8pm) Right in the centre of town, the origins of this magnificent church date from

1516, however it was destroyed by the earthquakes of 1704 and 1705 and rebuilt in 1768. Today it is recognised as being one of the finest examples of baroque architecture in the entire archipelago with its three-fronted facade and three 24m-high bell towers.

Hijuela del Botánico
GARDENS

(Calle León; ☉10am-3pm Mon-Fri) **FREE** This small, sweet botanical garden centred around a magnificent *drago* tree was created as a branch of the larger Jardín Botánico in Puerto de la Cruz. It is home to around 3000 plant varieties, as well as plenty of birds, butterflies and strategically located benches.

Casa del Turista
HISTORIC BUILDING

(Calle San Francisco 4; ☉9am-6.30pm) The building was a former 16th-century convent and today houses an art and crafts shop that includes a permanent exhibit of a volcanic-sand carpet that is typical of those produced for the Corpus Christi celebrations.

Museo de Artesanía Iberoamericana
MUSEUM

(Iberoamerican Handicrafts Museum; Calle Tomás Zerolo 34; adult/child €2/free; ☉9am-6pm Mon-Fri, 9.30am-2pm Sat) Housed in the former Convento de Santo Domingo, this museum explores the cultural relationship between the Canaries and the Americas. Exhibits include musical instruments, ceramics and various artefacts. There is also an excellent gift shop.

Museo de las Alfombras
MUSEUM

(Calle San Francisco 5; adult/child €2/free; ☉10am-2pm Mon-Fri) This museum celebrates the town's Corpus Christi festival with its tradition of carpets created from flowers and coloured sands from El Teide. Set in a beautiful galleried mansion dating from 1642, the exhibits explain the history of the tradition, as well as the process. There is also a wonderfully atmospheric and grainy 10-minute black-and-white audiovisual presentation of past festivities.

Iglesia de Santo Domingo
CHURCH

(Calle Santo Domingo; ☉variable opening hours) This church has beautifully carved doors and a rich Mudéjar ceiling.

✨ Festivals & Events

Corpus Christi
RELIGIOUS

(☉Jun) Celebrated with extravagance in La Orotava (the date changes annually, but it's

BEST HISTORIC TOWNS

➡ **La Laguna** (p130) Combines old-fashioned elegance with youthful zeal.

➡ **La Orotava** (p141) The finest colonial architecture in Tenerife.

➡ **Garachico** (p145) Quaint fishing port hemmed in by beautiful scenery.

always in June), an intricately designed, colourful floral carpet is laid on the streets, made from petals, leaves and branches, and in the Plaza de Ayuntamiento, a tapestry of biblical scenes is created using coloured sands from El Teide.

✗ Eating

Popular with tourists on day trips, there is plenty of restaurant choice, mainly centred around Plaza de la Constitución, the heart of the town.

Bar la Duquesa
CANARIAN €

(Plaza Patricio García 6; mains €7.50-10; ☉7am-4pm Mon-Fri, 8am-3pm Sat; ⌖) A family-run bar, the interior is a pleasing clutter of old photos, Virgin posters, decorative gourds and farming utensils. The menu includes sound local choices like lentil soup, paella and grilled pork, plus there are outside tables on the cobbles in the shadow of the church.

Casa Egon
BAKERY €

(Calle León 5; cakes €0.80-1; ☉10am-8.30pm) Founded in 1916, this is the oldest cake shop in the Canaries and has happily maintained its stuck-in-a-time-warp ambience with custard-coloured paintwork, antique weighing scales, original floor tiles and woodwork, and much of the decor. The cakes include all-time local favourites like the *anís*-based *roscos* and apple-filled *cabello de angel*.

Sabor Canario
CANARIAN €€

(www.hotelruralorotava.es; Hotel Rural Orotava, Carrera Escultor 17; mains €10-15; ☉noon-3.30pm & 6-10pm Tue-Sat) Exercise the taste buds with soul-satisfying traditional cuisine at this fabulous restaurant located in the leafy patio of the Hotel Rural Orotava. The building itself is a wonderful old Canarian town house stuffed full of memorabilia.

ℹ Information

Tourist Office (☎922 32 30 41; www. todotenerife.es; Calle Calvario 4; ☉9am-5pm

HIKING WITH GOBLINS

Travel between La Orotava and the Teide massif and around the halfway mark you pass through the little village of **Aguamansa**. Just beyond this village, and a little higher up the mountain slopes, the road passes a number of parking areas away from which radiate an array of brilliantly marked walking trials. The walking here is really easy with only gentle inclines and short distances to cover (although it's simple to join routes up and create much longer walks) and is perfect for gentle family strolling. Most of the routes twist in and out of fantastic laurel forests that are like something out of a children's fantasy story; so dense is the forest that if ever fairies, elves and goblins had a home in Europe then it must surely have been here. In other areas the laurel forests are replaced with magnificent stands of ancient pine trees with girths so thick it would take two or three grown men to encircle them with their arms.

Each parking area has a signboard explaining the different routes leading away from it.

Mon-Fri) A well-marked tourist route of the town's major monuments starts here. There is a small kiosk for tourist information (Plaza de la Constitución; ⊗10am-1.30pm & 5-7pm Mon-Fri, 10am-2pm Sat & Sun) in Plaza de la Constitución.

Parque Nacional del Teide Administrative Offices (Visitors Centre; ☑922 92 23 71; www.reservasparquesnacionales.es; Calle Sixto Perera González 25; ⊗9am-2pm & 3.30-6pm Tue-Sun) You can register here for climbing the El Teide summit. There is also an informative photographic display and a short film about the national park. The centre is located just north of the bus station in La Orotava.

🛈 Getting There & Away

Parking in La Orotava is a nightmare. If you're not staying here then it's far better to come by bus from Puerto de la Cruz, which is just 9km away. Bus 345 (€1.45, 20 minutes) leaves roughly every half-hour from 5.40am to 9.55pm. Bus 350 (€1.45, 45 minutes, two daily), among others, comes from Santa Cruz. If you have to drive, there is street parking here, but you should plan on arriving early to secure a spot.

Icod de los Vinos

POP 23,725

An umbrella-shaped *drago* tree is the cause of a lot of fuss in this town. Indeed, it's worth a look, and the shady main square, Plaza San Marcos, is a lovely, leafy spot to rest and enjoy the town's white-walled church, Iglesia de San Marcos, with its ornate silver high altar. Other than this plaza and the tiny kernel of old streets leading off it, the town is not the most inspiring of places. For restaurants and places to stay, head on to neighbouring Garachico, which is many notches up on the postcard-pretty stakes. The **tourist office**

(☑922 81 21 23; www.todotenerife.es; Calle San Sebastián 6; ⊗9am-7pm Mon-Fri) is just off the main plaza.

⊙ Sights

Drago Park PARK
(adult/child €4/2.50; ⊗9.30am-6.30pm; 🅿) Located past Plaza Constitución (aka Plaza Pila), a square with historic Canary homes, is Drago Park, where you can pay to get up close to the pride of the town – a tree said to be the world's largest and oldest dragon tree, that has allegedly been here for more than 1000 years. On closer inspection, this claim is a little optimistic and it would be better described as the world's largest and oldest Canary Islands dragon tree (there are around 40 different species and sub-species of drago trees).

The park is also home to a pretty botanical garden and a so-called Guanche trail with life-sized Guanche figures placed in natural-looking settings around the park, plus a cave with disarmingly lifelike skulls and bones (great for scaring the tots!).

Artlandya Doll Museum MUSEUM
(www.artlandya.com; Camino el Moleiro 21; adult/child €10/free; ⊗10am-6pm Tue-Sat; 🅿) A collection of dolls and teddy bears may not sound that captivating to anyone over the age of three, but Austrian owner Georg is an enthralling character who brings the doll-making process to life as he shows you around his superb 300-plus collection. The museum is set in beautiful gardens and there is a small cafe.

🛈 Getting There & Away

If you're driving, follow the signs towards the paid car park. Alternatively, bus 106 comes directly from Santa Cruz (€7.45, 1¼ hours) every two hours from 6.45am to 10.45pm. Bus 354 comes from Puerto de la Cruz (€3.60, 45 minutes) every half-hour from 7.30am to 10.30pm, and bus 460 makes the trip up from Playa de las Américas (€7, 1½ hours, eight daily). The bus station is to the northeast of the town centre.

Garachico

POP 6800

A gracious, tranquil town located in a deep valley flanked by forested slopes and a rocky coastline, Garachico has managed to retain its Canarian identity. There are no big hotels, probably because there is no real beach, though swimming in the natural, volcanic coves along the rocky coast is a rare delight.

Named for the rock outcrop off its shore (*gara* is Guanche for island, and *chico* is Spanish for small), Garachico is a peaceful place. You'd never guess the history of calamities that lies behind its whitewashed houses and narrow, cobblestone streets. Garachico was once an important commercial port, but its unlucky inhabitants suffered a series of disasters that all but finished off the hamlet: freak storms, floods, fires, epidemics and, in 1706, a major volcanic eruption that destroyed the port and buried half the town in lava, reducing it to a poor shadow of its former self.

Just outside town, you can hike trails that follow the path of the disastrous lava flow.

◉ Sights

The soul of Garachico is the main **Plaza Libertad**, with its towering palm trees, cafe tables and lively atmosphere. At dusk old men in flat caps play cards surrounded by sauntering couples, children kicking balls, and families. Nearby is the evocative **Iglesia de Santa Ana**, with a dominating white bell tower and original 16th-century doors.

Another rare remnant of the volcano is in the cute **Parque de la Puerta de Tierra**, just off Plaza Juan González (aka Plaza Pila), where the **Puerta de Tierra** (Land Gate) is all that's left of Garachico's once-thriving port. It was once right on the water but thanks to the eruption is now in the centre of town.

Convento de San Francisco — MUSEUM
(Plaza Libertad; adult/child €2/free; ☉ 11am-2pm & 3-6pm Mon-Fri, 10am-4pm Sat) There is plenty to see at this eclectic museum located in a 16th-century convent with a beautiful cloistered interior. Exhibits range from geology and the island's volcanic history (with multimedia installations) to contemporary sculptures and fascinating 19th-century photos of the town complete with resident camels.

Castillo de San Miguel — CASTLE
(Avenida Tome Cano; adult/child €2/free; ☉ 10am-4pm) A squat stone fortress built in the 16th century, with photos and explanations of the area's flora and fauna, as well as a chronological history of the town. Climb the tower for good views of the town and coast.

TASTY TENERIFE

Don't confuse the traditional culinary fare of Tenerife with that of the Spanish mainland; there are distinctive differences, although the ubiquitous tapas of Spain are common here also. The cuisine reflects a Latin American and Arabic influence, with more spices, including cumin, paprika and dried chillies, than the Spanish norm.

As on the other islands, the staple product par excellence is *gofio*, toasted grain that takes the place of bread and can be mixed with almonds and figs to make sweets. The traditional *cabra* (goat) and *cabrito* (kid) remain the staple animal protein. The rich, gamey *conejo en salmorejo* (rabbit in a marinade based on bay leaves, garlic and wine) is common, as well as stews (*potaje, rancho canario* or *puchero*) of meat and vegetables simmered to savoury perfection. Fish is also a winner, with the renowned horse mackerel (*chicharros*) of Santa Cruz de Tenerife even lending their name to the city's residents: the Chicharreros.

Also recommended is the *sancocho canario*, a salted-fish dish with *mojo* (a spicy salsa based on garlic and red chilli peppers). This sauce is the most obvious contribution to the Tenerife table, and is typically served with *papas arrugadas* (wrinkly potatoes; small new potatoes boiled and salted in their skins). The most typical dessert is *bienmesabe* (literally 'tastes good to me'), a mixture of honey, almond, egg yolks and rum.

If you are into self-catering, then hit the local markets. They are the best places to buy the freshest vegetables and fruit.

TENERIFE GARACHICO

✵ Festivals & Events

Romería de San Roque RELIGIOUS
(⊙16 Aug) This is Garachico's most important annual festival when the town fills with pilgrims (and partygoers) from throughout the island. San Roque (St Roch), the town's patron, was credited with saving the town from the Black Death, which arrived in 1601.

✗ Eating

For the best choice of bars and restaurants, head for the tangle of streets surrounding the central main square.

Casa Ramón CANARIAN €
(Calle Esteban de Ponte 4; mains €6-8; ⊙1-8pm Mon-Sat) The wood-panelled dining room of this little restaurant, run by an elderly lady who refuses to make any concessions to the modern age, is a throwback to a bygone era. The music comes courtesy of an old cassette player, the bills are written on scraps of paper and coffee is unheard of. The heart-warming specials are chalked up daily.

★**Mirador de Garachico** CONTEMPORARY CANARIAN €€
(☑922 83 11 98; Calle Esteban de Ponte 28; mains €11-18; ⊙8am-11pm Mon-Sat; ☎) This pleasing combo of contemporary bar and restaurant, plus tasteful art-and-crafts store, serves up creative dishes including a rabbit timbale that came local top in a local foodie contest. Expect combinations like venison in a chocolate-and-pepper sauce and banana, spinach and smoked fish croquettes. Top off your meal with the passionfruit shot; it'll surely make you blush with delight.

❶ Information

The **tourist office** (☑922 13 34 61; www.todotenerife.es; Calle Esteban de Ponte 5; ⊙10am-3pm Mon-Fri) sells a map of town (€1).

❶ Getting There & Away

Bus 107 connects the town with Santa Cruz (€8.15, two hours), La Laguna, La Orotava and Icod de los Vinos, while bus 363 comes and goes from Puerto de la Cruz (€3.75, one hour, up to 20 daily).

THE CENTRE

Parque Nacional del Teide

Standing sentry over Tenerife, formidable El Teide (Pico del Teide) is not just the highest mountain in the Canary Islands but, at a whopping 3718m, the highest in all of Spain and is, in every sense of the word, the highlight of a trip to Tenerife. The Parque Nacional del Teide, which covers 189.9 sq km and encompasses the volcano and the surrounding hinterland, is both a Unesco World Heritage site and Spain's most popular national park, attracting some four million visitors a year. Most serious hikers have heard of Teide, but few realise beforehand just how spectacular the mountain and surrounding national park is. It would be easy to pass a week in and around the park tramping the various hiking trails and not get bored. Most casual visitors arrive by bus or car and don't wander far off the highway that snakes through the centre of the park, but that just means that the rest of us have more elbow room to explore. There are numerous walking tracks marking the way through volcanic terrain, beside unique rock formations and up to the peak of El Teide.

This area was declared a national park in 1954, with the goal of protecting the landscape, which includes 14 plants found nowhere else on earth. Geologically the park is fascinating: of the many different types of volcanic formations found in the world, examples of more than 80% can be found here. These include rough badlands (deeply eroded barren areas), smooth *pahoehoe* or *lajial* lava (rock that looks like twisted taffy) and pebble-like lapilli. There are also complex formations such as volcanic pipes and cones. The park protects nearly 1000 Guanche archaeological sites, many of which are still unexplored and all of which are unmarked, preventing curious visitors from removing 'souvenirs'. Surrounding the peak are the *cañadas*, flat depressions likely caused by a massive landslide 180,000 years ago.

The park is spectacular at any time of the year. Most people attempt to climb to the summit in the summer – and with the weather being at its most stable then this makes perfect sense – but to really see the park at its pinnacle of beauty, early spring, when the lower slopes start to bloom in flowers and, if you're lucky, the summit area still has a hat of snow, is best. Many visitors, having driven up from the hot coastal plains, are surprised at just how cold it can be in the national park. Deep winter in particular can see heavy snow shutting the main roads through the park and access to the summit can be closed for weeks on end.

El Teide dominates the northern end of the park. If you don't want to make the very tough five-hour (one-way) climb to the top, take the cable car.

◎ Sights

Pico del Teide   MOUNTAIN
(☑922 01 04 40; www.telefericoteide.com; cable car adult/child €26/13; ⊙9am-4pm; P) The ca-ble car provides the easiest way to get up to the peak of El Teide. If you don't mind paying up, the views are great – unless a big cloud is covering the peak, in which case you won't see a thing. On clear days, the volcanic valley spreads out majestically below, and you can see the islands of La Gomera, La Palma and El Hierro peeking up from the Atlantic. It takes just eight minutes to zip up 1200m.

A few words of warning: those with heart or lung problems should stay on the ground, as oxygen is short up here in the clouds. It's chilly, too, so no matter what the weather's like below, bring a jacket. The cable cars, which each hold around 35 passengers, leave every 10 minutes, but get here early (before noon) because at peak times you could be queuing for two hours! The last ride down is at 5pm. Be aware also that weather conditions often force the early closure of the cable car – strong winds can whip up suddenly and the cable car can stop running with very little notice. This is normally not a huge problem for casual visitors who've caught the cable car up the mountain as a park warden based at the top cable car station will inform everyone that it's about to stop running, but for hikers climbing all the way up the mountain and intending to take the cable car back down it can be a very serious issue indeed.

Roques de García   ROCK FORMATIONS
A few kilometres south of the peak, across from the *parador* , lies this geological freak show of twisted lava pinnacles with names

TENERIFE'S BEST HIKES

El Teide (p147) Simply the most spectacular walk in the Canaries.

Barranco de Masca (p151) A thrilling descent through a steep gorge.

Pico Viejo (p147) Teide's forgotten peak.

Llano de los Loros (p134) Beautiful, family-friendly forest stroll.

like the Finger of God and the Cathedral. They are the result of erosion of old volcanic dykes, or vertical streams of magma. The weirdest of the rocks is the **Roque Cincha-do**, while spreading out to the west are the otherworldly bald plains of the Llano de Ucanca.

Note that the Roque Cinchado is wearing away faster at the base than above, and one of these days is destined to topple over (so maybe you shouldn't get too close). It is such an iconic symbol in Spain that it featured for years on the old 1000 peseta note. This is the most popular spot in the park and is viewed by nearly 90% of its visitors. The car park is always crowded, but most people just leave their cars or tour buses for a 15-minute glance. If you plan to hike the relatively easy, 1½-hour trail that circles the rocks, you'll most likely be alone.

Pico Viejo   MOUNTAIN
Calling this mountain 'Old Peak' is something of a misnomer considering it was actually the last of Tenerife's volcanoes to have erupted on a grand scale. In 1798 its southwestern flank tore open, leaving a 700m gash. Today you can clearly see where fragments of magma shot over 1km into the air and fell pell-mell. Torrents of lava gushed from a secondary, lower wound to congeal on the slopes.

TENERIFE PARQUE NACIONAL DEL TEIDE

IT'S ASTRONOMICAL

One of the best places in the northern hemisphere to stargaze is the **Observatorio del Teide** (C-824). Set just off the C-824 highway that runs between La Laguna and the El Portillo visitor centre, scientists from all over the world come to study here and at its sister observatory in La Palma. You can have a free tour and add your name to the list of those who've seen through the mammoth telescopes scattered here from December to March. You'll need to make an appointment first. For more information, see www.iac.es. **Volcano Life Experience** (www.volcanolife.com), a private tour company, also offers a number of stargazing packages starting from €30 per person.

To this day, not a blade of grass or a stain of lichen has returned to the arid slope. The ascent of this peak is often overlooked in the hurry to stand atop Spain, but those in the know often rate it as more impressive than the climb to the summit of Teide itself, and it's certainly much less busy (when we last climbed it we were the only people on the mountain). It also has the advantage of not needing any special permits.

Hiking

For the family-friendly saunter around the Roques de García you won't need anything other than comfortable shoes and some warm clothes. For anything more ambitious, though, you'll need proper walking boots and poles, warm clothes, some food and water and a map and compass. If you're intending to climb Teide or Pico Viejo in the winter, when thick snow is common, you'll need full winter hiking gear including thick fleeces, a waterproof jacket, gloves and a hat, and sunglasses. Poles are an essential item and on some routes crampons wouldn't go amiss either. There are very strict rules about where you can and cannot walk in the park and you must keep to the marked trails at all times (though some of these can be very vague on the less-frequented high-altitude trails). Most importantly don't underestimate Teide: this might not be the Himalayas but it's still a serious mountain (especially in the winter) and its ocean setting means that the weather here can change unbelievably fast, sometimes forcing the sudden closure of the cable car (a serious issue for hikers as-

cending the mountain and expecting a ride back down).

Guided Hikes

Park rangers host free guided walks around the mountain in both Spanish and English. The pace is gentle and there are frequent information pauses. Even though you'll huff and puff rather more than usual because of the high altitude, the walks are suitable for anyone of reasonable fitness (including children aged over 10).

Groups leave at 9.15am and 1.30pm from the visitor centre at El Portillo, and at 9.30am and 1pm from the visitor centre at Cañada Blanca. Walks last about two hours. Groups are small, so it is essential to reserve a place in advance by contacting the Parque Nacional del Teide Administrative Offices (p144).

Self-Guided Hikes

The general park visitor guide lists 21 walks, ranging in length from 600m to 17.6km, some of which are signposted. Each walk is graded according to its level of difficulty (ranging from 'low' – the most common – to 'extreme'). You're not allowed to stray from the marked trails, a sensible restriction in an environment where every tuft of plant life has to fight for survival.

You don't have to be a masochist to enjoy the challenge of walking from road level up to **La Rambleta** at the top of the cable car, followed by a zoom down in the lift, but neither should you take this walk lightly. People unused to serious hiking will find this a very strenuous walk. Get off the bus

> ### ⓘ CLIMBING TO THE SUMMIT – THE PAPERWORK
>
> The key to climbing the summit from the top of the cable car is to plan ahead. There's a permit scheme in force that restricts the number of visitors who can climb to the summit to 150 a day. You can reserve your place online using www.reservasparquesnacionales.es (follow the links through to the Parque Nacional del Teide). You can make a reservation up to 2pm the day before you want to climb (as long as spaces are available!).
>
> Should you really feel the need to make life hard for yourself, it's also possible to make the application in person or by post via the **Parque Nacional del Teide Administrative Offices** (p144) of the national park in La Orotava.
>
> You can choose from several two-hour slots per day in which to make your final ascent to the summit. In addition to the permit, take your passport or ID with you on the walk, as you'll probably be asked to produce it, and don't miss your allotted slot or you won't be allowed beyond the barrier.
>
> Note that bad weather conditions can mean the closure of the summit for weeks at a time. The website has details of any such closures and when they next expect it to be open to hikers.
>
> From the cable car it's about a one-hour walk to the summit.

THE DAY EL TEIDE SWALLOWED THE SUN

These days scientists can explain exactly how a volcano erupts: magma from the earth's core explodes through the crust and spews ash, rock and molten lava over the land. But the Guanches, living in pre-Hispanic Tenerife, had a more romantic version. According to legend, the 13th-century eruption was caused when El Teide swallowed the sun. The people believed that the devil, Guyota, lived inside El Cheide, as El Teide was then known. One day he emerged from his underground lair and saw the sun. Jealous of its light, he stole it and hid it inside his lair, causing death, destruction and darkness all over the island. The Guanches begged Chaman, the sky god, for help, and the god battled Guyota inside the volcano. The Guanches knew Chaman had triumphed when one morning they awoke to see the sun back in the sky and the volcano plugged with rock, trapping the evil Guyota inside forever.

The legend coincides perfectly with what happened following the medieval eruption. An ash cloud covered the sun, and the only light the Guanches saw came from the mouth of the active volcano, leading them to believe the sun was trapped there. The volcano's toxic ash would have killed many plants and animals, and the 'battle' going on inside the volcano was probably the rumblings following the eruption. The 'plug' that safely trapped Guyota in El Cheide was new volcanic rock.

(request the driver to stop) or leave your car at the small road-side parking area (signposted 'Montaña Blanca' and 'Refugio de Altavista') 8km south of the El Portillo visitor centre and set off along the 4WD track that leads uphill. En route, you can make a short (half-hour, at the most), almost-level detour along a clear path to the rounded summit of **Montaña Blanca** (2750m), from where there are splendid views of Las Cañadas and the sierra beyond. For the full ascent to La Rambleta, allow about five hours (one way). If you're intending on taking the cable car back down, it's vital that you allow sufficient time (and have enough food supplies) to walk back down the mountain if the cable car has to close early. Alternatively, make the Montaña Blanca your more modest goal for the day and then head back down again (about 2½ hours for the round trip).

Another long but relatively gentle route is the 16km **Las Siete Cañadas** between the two visitor centres, which, depending on your pace, will take between four and five hours (note that you'll need transport waiting for you at the end of this walk).

Maybe the most spectacular, and certainly the hardest, walk in the park is the climb to the summit of **Pico Viejo**, then along the ridge that connects this mountain to Teide and then up to the summit of Teide. Allow at least nine hours for this hike (one way) and be prepared to walk back down Teide again if the cable car is closed. In fact, for this walk it's actually better to walk to the Refugio de Altavista at 3270m on the first day, overnight there and then continue your ascent to the summit of Teide the following morning as this will allow you most of the second day to descend Teide on foot if required.

ⓘ Information

There are two excellent visitors centres in the park.

El Portillo Visitors Centre (☑922 92 37 71; www.reservasparquesnacionales.es; Carretera La Orotava-Granadilla; ⊙9am-4pm; ☎) A well-stocked visitors centre with a geological exhibition about the park and which can provide hiking maps and advice.

Cañada Blanca Visitors Centre (www.reservasparquesnacionales.es; Cañadas del Teide; ⊙9am-4pm; ☎) An excellent visitors centre with an informative exhibition that includes an audiovisual display about the volcanic history of El Teide; however, it was temporarily closed for renovations at the time of research.

ⓘ Getting There & Away

Surprisingly, only two public buses arrive at the park daily: bus 348 from Puerto de la Cruz (€6.20, one hour), and bus 342 from Los Cristianos (€7, 1½ hours). Bus 348 departs at 9.15am, and bus 342 at 9.30am; both arrive at the *parador*, and leave again at 4pm. That's good news for the countless tour companies that organise bus excursions, though not so encouraging for the independent traveller. The best way to visit is with your own car. There are four well-marked approaches to the park; the two prettiest are the C-824 coming from La Laguna and the C-821 from La Orotava (and Puerto de la Cruz). The C-821 is the only road

ⓘ MAPS & BOOKS

Maps of the island are readily available. Among the best are those by Editorial Everest. There are several good hiking guidebooks to Tenerife although, increasingly, companies are switching to online versions. Some of the best print hiking guides include *Walk! Tenerife* (2nd edition) and the accompanying *Tenerife Hiking Map*, both by David Brawn and published by Discovery Walking Guides; *Tenerife Landscapes*, by Noel Rochford and published by Sunflower (the same people also publish *Southern Tenerife and La Gomera Landscapes*); and Rother Walking Guides' *Tenerife*, by Klaus and Annette Wolfsperger with GPS tracking and last updated in May 2015. *Tenerife & its Six Satellites*, by Olivia M Stone, provides a fascinating glimpse of the island from a late-18th-century viewpoint.

that runs through the park, and the parador, the cable car and the visitor centres are all off this highway, as are several miradors, where you can pull over and take *the* shot to impress the folks back home. To see anything else, you have to walk. The C-821 carries on to Vilaflor, while the C-823 highway links the park with Chío and Los Gigantes.

Vilaflor

The pretty town of Vilaflor, on the sunny southern flanks of Teide, is the highest village in Tenerife and makes a superb base for explorations of the national park. There are a number of places to stay in the village, as well as restaurants, including the excellent **El Rincon de Roberto** (☎922 70 90 35; Avenida Hermano Pedro 27; mains €12-18; ☉noon-5pm Mon, to 10pm Wed-Sat), serving classic Canarian fare.

THE NORTHWEST

Punta de Teno

When Plato mistook the Canary Islands for Atlantis, it must have been because of places like Punta de Teno. It's what daydreams are made of – waves crashing against a black, volcanic beach, solitary mountains rising like giants in the background, the constant whisper of lizards scurrying in the brush... This beautiful spot, the most northwestern on the island, is no secret. But it still has a wild charm that the visitors can't take away. You can fish off the point, splash along the rocky coast or just absorb the view.

Think twice about heading out here if there have been recent heavy rains, as mud and rock slides are common.

ⓘ Getting There & Away

Take the highway towards Buenavista del Norte from Garachico and keep following the signs to the Punta, around 7km further on. Bus 107 comes from Santa Cruz to Buenavista del Norte (€9.35, 1½ hours), but to get out to Punta de Teno, you need your own car.

Santiago del Teide

This small town, sitting just to the northwest of the national park boundary, as well as on the junctions for Los Gigantes and Garachico, makes a superb base for all of these places. In addition Masca and the Teno mountains are just a few minutes to the northwest and the immediate area is littered with fantastic hiking trails, which are at their best in early spring when the cherry blossoms are in bloom. There's a small **tourist office** (☎922 86 03 48; www.todotenerife.es; Avenida Marítima 34; ☉9am-4pm Tue-Sat) on the main square beside the church that can provide information on the many fine walking trails in the area. The town is also home to one of the better places to stay in Tenerife.

Masca

Tiny Masca must be the most spectacular village in Tenerife. It literally teeters on the very brink of a knife-edge ridge and looks as if the merest hint of a puff of wind would blow the entire village off its precipitous perch and send it tumbling hundreds of metres to the valley floor.

🏃 Activities

Parque Rural de Teno   HIKING
The surrounding rugged and beautiful Parque Rural de Teno is popular for hiking – if you don't want to go it alone, **El Cardón** (☎922 12 79 38; www.elcardon.com) provides guides, setting out from Garachico, Los Silos or Buenavista del Norte on Wednesday and Saturday.

SCENIC DRIVE: TO THE END OF TENERIFE

The northwest corner of Tenerife offers some spectacular unspoiled scenery. From Gara-chico, head west on the TF-42 highway past Buenavista del Norte and down the TF-445 to the wild and remote Punta de Teno.

You'll have to return to Buenavista to catch the TF-436 mountain highway to Santiago del Teide. Curve after hairpin curve obligates you to slow down and enjoy the view. Ter-raced valleys appear behind rugged mountains, and Masca makes the perfect pit stop. When the highway reaches Santiago, you can head either north on the TF-82 towards Garachico, or south towards Los Gigantes, where signs point the way down to Playa de la Arena, a sandless beach that's nearly as pretty as Punta de Teno, though more developed.

You'll need at least a full morning to complete this route.

Barranco de Masca　　　　　　HIKING

A popular but demanding trek is down Bar-ranco de Masca to the sea. Allow six hours to hike there and back, or do it the smart way and take bus 355 from Santiago del Teide to Masca at 10.35am, walk down the gorge and then catch the **Excursions Marítimas** (☑922 86 21 20; fare €15) ferry back to Los Gigantes (€15, 1.30pm, 3.30pm and 4.30pm daily) at the end of your walk.

If you need to get from Los Gigantes to Santiago del Teide in order to catch the on-ward bus to Masca, bus 325 leaves Los Gi-gantes at 8.40am (there's another at 5.15pm).

Take note of the warning sign at the start of this hike which advises that the route is not totally safe and that you undertake the hike at your own risk. Do not attempt this hike if there is even the remotest chance of rain or strong winds as the risk of rockfalls and landslides is very high. If you are in-tending to catch the water taxi back to Los Gigantes at the end of the walk then it's ad-visable to take your mobile phone with you and call them if you're going to be late: they will wait for you if they know you're coming. There are sections of this hike that vertigo sufferers will have real problems traversing.

★ Festivals & Events

Fiesta de la Consolación　　　CULTURAL

(☉Dec) The Fiesta de la Consolación takes place in the first week of December. Villag-ers wearing traditional dress bring out their *timples* (similar to a ukulele) and other in-struments for an evening of Canarian music.

✪ Getting There & Away

There are two 355 buses (€1.30, 30 minutes) each day to/from Santiago del Teide. The drive to Masca is so dramatic that vertigo sufferers will want to shut their eyes. However, for your own good we'd suggest you do resist the urge to!

Los Gigantes & Puerto de Santiago

POP 5750

These two towns have merged into one, and a worrying number of cranes can only mean more building is under way, but for the mo-ment at least the low-rise, and low-key, town that sprawls along the rocky, cove-infested coastline is a million miles from Las Améri-cas and is certainly one of the more attrac-tive resort towns in Tenerife. Just to the north of the town rise the awesome **Acanti-lados de los Gigantes** (Cliffs of the Giants), rock walls that soar up to 600m out of the ocean. The submerged base of these cliffs is a haven for marine life, making this one of the island's supreme diving areas.

The best views of the cliffs are from out at sea (there's no shortage of companies offer-ing short cruises) and from **Playa de los Gi-gantes**, a tiny volcanic beach beside Los Gi-gantes' port that offers a breathtaking view. If you are looking for more sunbed space, head to Playa de la Arena, a larger volcanic beach in Puerto de Santiago. Both resorts have a large British expatriate community, which means plenty of restaurants serving beans on toast.

✦ Activities

This is the best place on the island for div-ing, with abundant marine life, as well as being excellent for spotting whales and dol-phins.

Los Gigantes Diving Centre　　DIVING

(☑922 86 04 31; www.divingtenerife.co.uk; Los Gi-gantes Harbour; dive incl equipment rental €49, in-troductory dive €60; ☉9.30am-5pm Mon-Sat) An English-owned diving centre based in Los Gigantes; one of the best places in Tenerife for diving.

BIOCLIMATIC HOUSING

As an environmental counterbalance to Granadilla's controversial new container port, the town is also home of a state-of-the-art bioclimatic housing complex. The 25 houses, which are available to rent, have been built using recycled and recyclable materials, use renewable energy for all their power, water and waste processing and are 100% carbon-dioxide free. Check http://casas.iter.es/en for more information.

Katrin   BOAT TOUR
(☑922 86 03 32; www.dolphinwhalewatch.com; Los Gigantes Harbour; 2hr safari €20; ☉11.30am-1.35pm) A reputable outfit which restricts passengers to just 20 and also takes out groups with special needs.

Nashíra Uno   BOAT TOUR
(☑922 86 19 18; www.maritimaacantilados.com; Los Gigantes Harbour; 2/3hr whale & dolphin cruise €25/35; ☉11am, 2pm & 6pm) Has several daily whale- and dolphin-watching trips and also offers taxi boat services from Masca back to Los Gigantes (€12).

✗ Eating

You won't be hard-pressed to find a restaurant (most are by Los Gigantes Marina or along the Avenida Marítima), but there are slim pickings for truly good ones.

El Mesón   CANARIAN €€
(☑922 86 04 76; Calle La Vigilia, Puerto Santiago; mains €10-14; ☉noon-4pm & 7-10pm Mon-Sat; 🖼) Locals rate this large restaurant as one of the best in town and the owner, who's quite a character, could talk the hind legs off a donkey. It serves an excellent array of seafood and traditional Canarian and mainland meat dishes including a succulent rabbit stew and even a whole suckling pig (with a day's advance notice). Finish off your meal with the complimentary homemade honey rum tipple.

El Baco de Nino   SEAFOOD €€
(☑922 86 83 39; Paseo Marítimo, Puerto Santiago; mains €10-15; ☉1-4pm & 7-11pm Wed-Mon) Seaside-facing restaurant that's a little more expensive than others but its seafood gets votes of confidence from locals. The indoor seating area is fairly formal or you can get casual on the sunny terrace. The baby octopus is well worth slurping down.

El Rincón de Juan Carlos   CONTEMPORARY CANARIAN €€€
(☑922 86 80 40; www.elrincondejuancarlos.es; Pasaje de Jacaranda 2, Los Gigantes; mains €15-25, menús from €29; ☉7-10pm Mon-Sat) If you're all set to splurge, this formal restaurant is just off the main plaza in Los Gigantes. Try one of the sumptuous fit-for-a-King-Juan-Carlos *menús* or, if you're missing a McDonald's, go for the duck burger with mustard and local cheeses. Advance reservations essential.

❶ Information

The **tourist office** (☑922 86 03 48; www.todotenerife.es; Avenida Marítima, local 34; ☉9.30am-4.30pm Mon-Fri, to 12.30pm Sat) is on the 2nd floor of the shopping centre across from Playa de la Arena.

❶ Getting There & Around

Bus 473 comes and goes from Los Cristianos (€4.65, 1¼ hours), and bus 325 (€7.10, 1¾ hours, six daily) travels from Puerto de la Cruz. For those with wheels, it's a well-marked 40km drive from Los Cristianos.

THE SOUTH

Los Cristianos, Playa de las Américas & Costa Adeje

POP AROUND 150,000

Don't forget to wear your shades when you first hit Tenerife's southwestern tip. You'll need them, not just against the blinding sunshine, but also the accompanying dazzle of neon signs, shimmering sand and lobster-pink northern Europeans. Large multipool resorts with all-you-can-eat buffets have turned what was a sleepy fishing coast into a mega-moneymaking resort. The sweeping, sandy beaches are some of the most lively and child-friendly on the island. The nightlife is for those with high energy and high spirits and there is a predictably dizzying array of restaurants.

That said, the old town of Los Cristianos, still retains (just) the feel of a fishing village while just beyond is Playa de las Américas, with its high-rise hotels, glossy shopping centres and Las Vegas–style fake Roman

KNOW YOUR SOUTH-COAST BEACHES

Tenerife's south-coast beaches come complete with mojito-mixing beach bars and chic restaurants; for something more low-key, head to the beaches at the nearby towns of **Las Galletas** (p160) and **El Médano** (p163).

Playa de Los Cristianos (Los Cristianos) This 1km-long taupe-coloured sandy stretch is the main beach in town and very family friendly with a lifeguard, rows of sunbeds, volleyball net, plus bars, restaurants and ice-cream kiosks.

Playa de las Vistas (Map p154; Playa de las Américas) A sublime 1.5km long beach with fine golden sand (imported from the Sahara Desert!), linking Los Cristianos with Playa de las Américas. The beach is backed by bars and restaurants and protected by breakwaters, so it's perfect for swimming.

Playa de Troya (Map p154; Playa de las Américas) One of several beaches that merge seamlessly into each other in central Playa, with soft dark sand and excellent facilities.

Playa del Duque (Costa Adeje) Appropriately named, the 600m-long Duke's beach is an appealing golden sandy stretch backed by jaunty striped changing huts, chic cafes and restaurants.

Playa de la Encaramada (La Caleta, Costa Adeje) A dark volcanic beach with a great beach bar; a popular launch spot for hang-gliding.

statues and pyramids. The Costa Adeje flows seamlessly north of here and is home to luxury hotels, sophisticated clubs and restaurants and superb beaches.

Many independent travellers bound for the western islands end up having to spend at least one night here and most aim straight for Los Cristianos, which has the best facilities for independent travellers.

If you get lost, do what the locals do – orientate yourself by the hotels and large buildings.

☉ Sights

Jungle Park ZOO
(Map p158; www.aguilasjunglepark.com; Los Cristianos-Arona, Km 3; adult/child €24/16; ☺10am-5.30pm; ℗) Jungle Park is by far the most popular attraction in the south. There are close to 500 animals here, including two rare white tigers, surrounded by lush landscaping with lagoons, walkways and subtropical plants and trees.

Siam Park AMUSEMENT PARK
(Map p158; ☑902 06 00 00; www.siampark.net; Autopista Sur exit 28; adult/child €34/23; ☺10am-6pm; ℗) Southern Tenerife's biggest theme park is the impressive Siam Park, which offers a chance to throw yourself down a 28m-high vertical waterslide, surf in a swimming pool, get spat out of the guts of a dragon and buy tat at a floating market in Bangkok.

Aqualand WATER PARK
(Map p158; www.aqualand.es; Avenida de Austria 15, Costa Adeje; adult/child €25/17.50; ☺10am-5pm Sep-Jun, to 6pm Jul & Aug; ℗) This vast water park comes with all the standard slides and pools, but also has captive dolphins in a dolphinarium, which may concern some visitors, as research indicates such captivity is stressful to these complex creatures.

🏃 Activities

The 2800 average hours of yearly sunshine mean that beaches are the star turn here, but if you just can't take another day of lying prone on a sunbed, there are other, more energetic options.

Diving

The volcanic coast here makes for excellent diving, and calm waters mean that even a first-timer can have a thrilling 'try dive' in the ocean. A standard dive runs upwards of €35, though the per-dive rate drops if you're planning several days of diving. There are several outfits to choose from.

Aqua Marina DIVING
(Map p154; ☑922 79 79 44; www.aquamarinadivingtenerife.com; Playa de la Vistas, Playa de las Américas; single dive €39, kids bubblemaker course €35; ☺9am-6pm;) Offers the standard array of boat dives, courses and speciality dives as well as plain old snorkelling for those who don't want to get their hair wet. Also runs bubblemaker courses for children.

Playa de las Américas

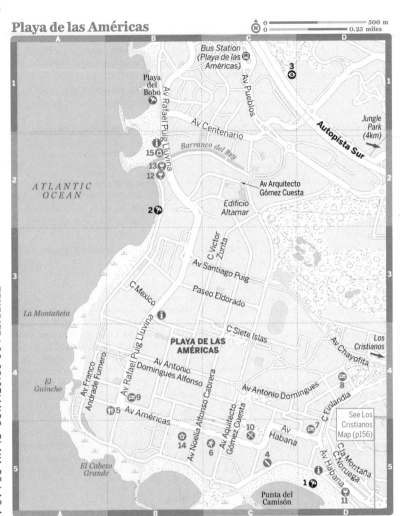

See Los Cristianos Map (p156)

Sailing & Surfing

You won't have to sail far from shore before the hotel jungle of Tenerife's largest resort melts into the gentle slopes of the island. Rent a boat, take an excursion or sign up for a whale-watching trip and cruise the waters between Tenerife and La Gomera with the beautiful outline of El Teide behind you. The tourist office in Los Cristianos has a list of companies that organise all kinds of boat trips, some of which even set sail on the high seas in a pirate ship – who could resist!

The best-known surf spot in town is the creatively named La Izquierda (Spanish Left), which is found just west of Playa de Troyo. A long and easy left with some hollow sections, it's one of the most localised spots in Europe.

K-16 Surf SURFING
(Map p154; ☎922 79 84 80; www.k16surf.com; Calle México 1-2, Playa de las Américas; surf lessons from €35, board rental per day from €12) Rents out surfboards and provides tuition for only slightly more than the price of rental.

Horse Riding

Note that although there are several places that offer horse riding, not all are accredited and safe.

Finca Cabuquero HORSE RIDING
(☑ 646 88 38 23; www.horseridingintenerife.com; Aldea Blanca, San Miguel de Abona; 1/2hr trek €25/45; ⊙ 10am-2pm & 4-7pm Tue-Sun; 🚗) A British-run horse-riding school that offers a pick-up service from your hotel to their centre in San Miguel de Abona. Horse and pony treks range from beginning routes to more challenging trails for experienced riders.

Golf

Constant mild weather means that Tenerife is a place where golfers can play year-round. It's not the most ecologically sound activity on the island (water is a constant problem, and golf courses need plenty of it) but that hasn't stopped sprawling courses from emerging all around Playa de las Américas. Some of the best courses are listed here. Note that the fees are for the winter season; prices can drop considerably in midsummer.

Golf Costa Adeje GOLF
(www.golfcostaadeje.com; Finca Los Olivos, Adeje; adult/child 18 holes €96/30; ⊙ 7.30am-7pm) Has both an 18- and 9-hole course. The eyecatching driving range is set on three levels with a connecting elevator. Also home to a luxury hotel offering villa-style accommodation. Located in Adeje, approximately 6km northwest of Plaza del Duque. Take the exit 79B from the TF-1 Autopista del Sur and follow the signs.

Golf del Sur GOLF
(www.golfdelsur.net; Urbanizacíon Golf del Sur, San Miguel de Abona; adult/child 18 holes €87/43; ⊙ 7.30am-7pm) An attractive mature course with water features, lofty palms and sea views.

Los Palos Centro de Golf GOLF
(www.golflospalos.com; Carretera Guaza-Las Galletas Km 7, Arona; adult/child 9 holes €25/17; ⊙ 7am-7pm) Attractive small course surrounded by banana trees with an emphasis on instruction; ideal for beginners.

Whale Watching

Companies offering two-, three- and five-hour boat cruises to check out whales and dolphins are set up at the end of Playa de Los Cristianos, near the port, and in Puerto Colón in Costa Adeje. Most trips include food, drink and a quick swim. There are several such

companies but all are basically the same, with a two-hour trip costing upwards of €18.

Travelin' Lady BOAT TOUR
(Map p156; ☑ 609 42 98 87; Rincon de Arona, Puerto de Los Cristianos; adult/child €18/free; ⊙ 9.30am-8pm Sun-Fri, noon-3pm Sat) Organises two-hour whale-watching trips and uses an enclosed propeller to prevent any injury to the mammals.

Fishing

Deep-sea-fishing jaunts start at about €49 for a three-hour trip. Get information from the kiosks set up at the western end of Playa de Los Cristianos or from a tourist office.

★ Festivals & Events

Canarian Food Fair FOOD
(⊙ mid-Mar) A week-long event in Los Cristianos showcasing food and produce from all over the islands, with free tastings and an opportunity to purchase.

✗ Eating

You won't go hungry here. The dilemma is more likely to be choosing where to go for the best quality and good value. Avoid restaurants that advertise their international

Los Cristianos

cuisine with sun-bleached posters on the pavement; though, in general, the quality of restaurants has improved over the recent years and you can, increasingly, find more sophisticated places to eat, and traditional Spanish and Canarian food on offer.

On the waterfront in the port area of Los Cristianos is a handful of kiosks, including the ever-popular **Pescaderia Dominga** (Map p156; Puerto de Los Cristianos; fish €5-9; ⊙noon-7pm Mon-Fri, to 3pm Sat), selling fresh-off-the-boat fish. You can either buy it un-cooked to take away and deal with yourself or they'll fry it up for you and then you can dangle your legs over the edge of the nearby jetty and eat the freshest and best fish picnic you'll ever have.

⭐**El Cine**   SEAFOOD €
(Map p156; www.barelcine.es/en; Calle Juan Bariajo 8, Los Cristianos; mains €8-10; ⊙11am-11pm) Yes, it's probably been said before, El Cine

deserves a medal for its inexpensive, simply prepared seafood. Here since the '80s, the menu is reassuringly brief; the fish of the day is always a good bet. Tucked in an elbow off the promenade, its atmosphere of no frills and few tourists adds to the appeal.

Sopa   VEGETARIAN €
(Map p156; Calle Montaña Chica 2, Los Cristianos; salads & soups €4-7; ⊙8am-9pm Mon-Sat, 9am-9pm Sun; 🛜🖉♿) A chilled-out space with sofas, books and magazines provides the backdrop for a menu of healthy soups, salads and burgers (spinach, that is). There are also delicious cakes. Try the cherry and marzipan for a real taste-bud treat.

La Pepa Food Market   MARKET €
(🖉922 79 48 85; www.mercadolapepa.es; Centro Comercial La Pasarela, Los Cristianos; snacks €2.50-5; ⊙10am-11pm Mon-Thu, to midnight Fri-Sun; P🛜♿) This gourmet food market opened in 2015 and is still expanding. At the

time of research there were some 25 stalls including upmarket delis, seafood counter, pancakes and waffles stand, sushi, a wine bar and a vegetarian snack stall. There is plenty of seating on a vast terrace with rooftop views that stretch to the sea, plus a children's playground.

Bar Nuestro   CANARIAN €
(Map p156; Calle San Roque 12, Los Cristianos; mains €5-8; ⊙8am-10pm Thu-Tue) A cloth-cap-authentic local bar, Bar Nuestro has a barnlike interior and an unwaveringly authentic Canarian menu that includes dishes such as chickpeas with pork sausages and grilled sardines.

Bar Gavota   CAFE €
(Map p156; Avenida los Playeros 27, Los Cristianos; breakfast €5; ⊙8am-11pm Mon-Sat) Opposite the church in Los Cristianos, this is one of the few central bars that retains its typical Spanish feel – as well as a local crowd of regulars. It's perfect for a toast-and-coffee breakfast or drinks at any time.

★ **Le Bistrôt d'Alain**   FRENCH €€
(Map p156; ☑922 75 23 36; Calle Valle Menéndez 23, Los Cristianos; mains €10-15; ⊙7.30-11pm Tue-Sun) Hidden away from the masses, this formal but unassuming restaurant serves quality classic French fare such as steak with a Roquefort sauce, frogs' legs, and more unusual dishes such as a fish stew crammed with prawns, salmon and veggies. It's one of the better-regarded places to eat in town and is understandably popular with French visitors.

Cofradia de Pescadores   SEAFOOD €€
(Map p156; Muelle Los Cristianos, Los Cristianos; mains €10-20; ⊙noon-10pm Sun-Fri) Run by the local fishing co-op, this place has access to the freshest fish and seafood on a daily basis. Choose yours from a large tank near the entrance or go by the daily recommendations. The dining room is light and spacious with harbour views; to find it, look for the sign to a small side door, signed 'Bar', then follow the fish frieze upstairs.

Original Bistro   BISTRO €€
(Map p156; ☑922 79 20 31; Callejón Gonzalo, Los Cristianos; mains €10-12; ⊙6-11pm Wed-Mon; 🐾) Run by a Spanish-English couple, this enormously popular bistro offers a three-course menu with several choices. You won't find any foam or drizzle here; dishes are homely and (mainly) traditionally British – but ex-

Los Cristianos

ecuted with finesse with not an overboiled veg in sight.

La Torre del Mirador   CANARIAN €€
(Map p158; ☑922 71 22 09; www.latorredemirador. es; Playa del Duque, Costa Adeje; mains €12-16; ⊙10am-8pm) This elegant bar and restaurant has a lovely terrace with colourful flowers and palms and delightful sea views. The menu has several sound seafood choices, including king prawns in garlic. Or share a platter of *pimientos de padron* (small fried green peppers), the perfect accompaniment to a long cold *cerveza* after your promenade stroll.

HALF-BOARD HEADACHE

Bars and restaurants throughout Tenerife are seriously suffering as hotels here are increasingly offering half-board all-inclusive deals to their guests at cheap-as-chips prices. Hotel buffets are typically based on bland international cuisine aimed at appealing to the masses. Spread the word to support the local restaurants and bars, before still more *se vende* signs appear.

TENERIFE LOS CRISTIANOS, PLAYA DE LAS AMÉRICAS & COSTA ADEJE

Costa Adeje

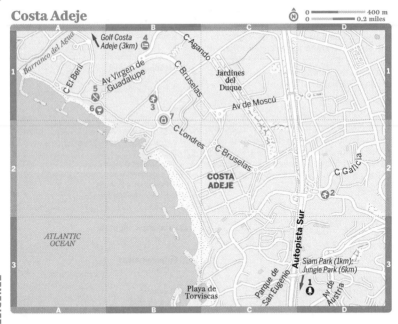

Costa Adeje

Rincón del Marinero　　　　　SEAFOOD €€
(Map p156; Muelle Los Cristianos, Los Cristianos; mains €9-15; ☺noon-11pm) Specialising in local seafood, including a tasty *zarzuela* (fish and seafood stew), this nautical-themed restaurant has all its tables under a covered terrace (proof that there's never bad weather here).

★**Oriental Monkey**　　　　　ASIAN €€€
(Map p158; ☑922 78 92 91; www.theorientalmonkey.com; Avenida de las Américas, Central Comercial Oasis, Playa de las Américas; mains €18-25; ☺7-11pm Mon-Sat; ☏) Voted top Canary Island international restaurant in 2013 and with celebrated chef, Nacho Hernández at the helm, this gourmet restaurant combines exotic decor with an exotic menu of innovatively prepared Asian-inspired dishes, ranging from marinated cod in miso, to tuna tataki with smoked aubergine and couscous.

Expect an entertaining evening with video projections of pink butterflies flying across your table or fish swimming across your plate and muted coloured lights that constantly shift and change.

🍷 Drinking & Nightlife

Post-midnight, Los Cristianos' main action takes place at the Centro Comercial San Telmo, the shopping centre behind Playa de las Vistas, when this daytime-dull little strip is transformed into a string of nightclubs pumping out music late into the night. Look elsewhere if you are seeking somewhere classier; there are alternatives which are increasing all the time.

★ Papagayo
BAR, CLUB

(Map p154; www.papagayobeachclub.com; Playa de Troya, Avenida Rafael Puig Lluvina, Playa de las Américas; ⊙10am-late; 🛜) This restaurant, bar and nightclub oozes sophistication and good taste. The decor is predominantly white, with kick-back seating, shady canopies and water features, while the menu is best for light dishes like sushi. Come night time the place metamorphoses into a fashionable nightclub, complete with a slick professional DJ and dancers.

Chiringuito del Mirador
BAR

(Map p158; Playa del Duque, Costa Adeje; ⊙noon-7pm) This beach bar (and restaurant) has a sparkling summer-in-the-sun feel with its glossy white furniture and decor contrasting with the deep blue of the sea, just a few metres away. It's a lovely place for a midday cocktail or *cerveza,* accompanied by a plate of *gambas a la plancha* (grilled prawns) to share.

Beach House
BAR

(Map p156; Paseo Dulce María Lenaz, Los Cristianos; ⊙5pm-late; 🛜) This Italian-run bar has a classy feel with its chill-out music, pale-grey paintwork, candy-coloured cushions and TV switched to the fashion (rather than football) channel. Good for cocktails.

Las Verónicas
CLUB

(Map p154; Centro Commercial Las Verónicas, Playa de las Américas) Comprising three adjacent buildings, Las Verónicas has a number of loud and boisterous nightlife options primarily aimed at a heavy-drinking British clientele.

Casablanca
CLUB

(Map p154; Centro Comercial San Telmo local 17, Los Cristianos; ⊙11pm-late) The most famous club in this pulsating strip heaves with gyrating bodies post-midnight.

☆ Entertainment

Many of the bars along the main Playa de las Américas strip have live music at weekends. Check at the tourist office for any current live-music events.

Centro Cultural
THEATRE

(Map p156; www.centroculturalcristiano.org; Plaza Pescador 1, Los Cristianos; ticket prices vary) Offers a variety of cultural events, such as Cine de Verano, a summer festival of open-air movies (in Spanish) showing nightly except Wednesday. An auditorium acts as a concert venue.

La Pirámide
LIVE MUSIC

(Map p154; ✆922 75 75 49; www.piramidearona.com; La Pirámide, Avenida de las Américas, Playa de las Américas; tickets from €50; ⊙8pm Wed, 9pm Tue, Thu-Sun) This vast auditorium (one of the largest in Europe) regularly stages world-class shows that typically combine flamenco, opera and dance. There is an option to combine the show with a buffet dinner (from €75) with dining times set at 6.30pm and 7pm. However, by all reports, the food is decidedly less impressive than the show.

🛍 Shopping

Modern shopping centres are mushrooming throughout the resorts. Los Cristianos has the best choice of small family-owned shops selling more unusual products and souvenirs.

Plaza del Duque
COMMERCIAL CENTRE

(Map p158; www.plazadelduque.com; Playa del Duque, Costa Adeje; ⊙10am-7pm Mon-Fri, to 2pm Sat; 🛜🅿) A luxurious small shopping centre with around 60 shops, including designer boutiques and a kids zone.

Artenerife
CRAFTS

(Map p154; www.artenerife.com; Avenida Rafael Puig Lluvina, Playa de las Américas; ⊙9.30am-1.30pm & 5-7pm Mon-Sat) Part of an island-wide chain where quality control is very much in evidence, Artenerife carries a superb range of quality handicrafts originating in the Canary Islands.

La Alpizpa
CRAFTS

(Map p156; Paseo Marítimo, Los Cristianos; ⊙10am-2pm & 5-7pm Mon-Sat) Located right on the seafront, this shop sells high-quality and diverse arts and crafts created by people with disabilities.

Librería Barbara
BOOKS

(Map p156; ✆922 79 23 01; Calle Pablo Abril 6, Los Cristianos; ⊙10am-1pm & 5-7.30pm Mon-Fri, 10am-1pm Sat) Founded in 1984 and selling a wide range of books in several languages including English, French, German and Spanish, plus magazines and children's titles.

ℹ Information

Tourist Office (www.todotenerife.es) Los Cristianos (Map p156; ✆922 75 71 37; www.arona.org; Centro Cultural, Plaza Pescador 1); Playa de las Vistas (Map p154; ✆922 78 70 11; Centro Comercial San Telmo); Playa de las Américas (Map p154; ✆922 79 76 68; Centro Comercial City Center, Avenida Rafael Puig

GETTING AWAY FROM IT ALL – TENERIFE SPAS

Holidaying can be tough, especially when there's so darn much to see and do. Thank goodness for day spas.

Aqua Club Termal (Map p158; ☑ 922 71 65 55; www.aquaclubtermal.com; Calle Galicia, Torviscas Alto, Costa Adeje; ☉8am-10pm) Around Costa Adeje, escape to this sophisticated aqua club which, according to its promotional literature, is the most comprehensive thermal and sports complex in Europe. It has 6000 sq metres of floor space, all dedicated to pampering. Don't miss the Turkish bath.

Vitanova Spa (Map p158; ☑ 922 71 99 10; www.vitanovatenerife.com; Calle Alcalde Walter Paetzman, Playa del Duque, Costa Adeje; ☉9am-9pm) Located on the Costa Adeje, this spa offers massages and facials as well as such scrumptious delights as a chocolate massage and an anticellulite scrub with seaweed and grapes.

Mare Nostrum (Map p154; ☑ 922 75 75 45; www.marenostrumspa.es; Avenida de las Américas, Playa de las Américas; ☉10am-7pm) Part of this major resort in Playa de las Américas and sure to spoil. There are these enticing-sounding fungal wraps and electrotherapy for serious spa-goers, and massages and steam baths for those seeking to de-stress.

Hotel Botánico Spa (☑ 922 38 14 00; www.hotelbotanico.com; Avenida Richard J Yeoward 1, Puerto de la Cruz) This exclusive hotel has an oriental spa centre offering wellness therapies and treatments, plus a Thai pagoda surrounded by lush gardens for traditional Thai massage, and a *hammam* (Turkish-style steam bath).

Lluvina); Costa Adeje (Map p154; ☑ 922 71 65 39; Avenida Litoral) The Costa Adeje office is by the Barranco del Rey.

ℹ Getting There & Away

BUS

Plenty of Tenerife's bright-green TITSA buses come through the area, stopping at stations in Los Cristianos and Playa de las Américas. Buses 110 (direct; €12.40, one hour, every 30 minutes) and 111 (indirect) come and go from Santa Cruz. Bus 343 goes to Tenerife Sur airport (€3.70, 45 minutes). The same bus continues on to Tenerife Norte airport. Plenty of other buses run through the two resorts, en route to destinations such as Arona (bus 480), Los Gigantes (bus 473), Puerto de la Cruz (bus 343), El Médano (bus 470) and Las Galletas (bus 467).

The Playa de las Américas bus station is situated between central Las Américas, San Eugenio and the *autovía*. There's no Los Cristianos bus station, as such; the buses stop on Avenida Juan Carlos I, just beyond the cross road with Avenida Amsterdam, opposite the Valdes Commercial Centre. For 24-hour bus information, call ☑ 922 53 13 00.

ℹ Getting Around

Most of the long-distance bus routes double as local routes, stopping along the major avenues of Los Cristianos and Playa de las Américas before heading out of town.

There are taxi stands outside most shopping centres. Getting a taxi at night usually isn't a problem, as most people choose to walk. A ride across town should cost between €6 and €8.

Las Galletas

Las Galletas is a small resort town a few kilometres south of the Las Américas strip and, in comparison, is as quiet as a Sunday afternoon in a library; for many people it is its attraction. A block back from the boardwalk, the leafy Rambla Dionisio González, with benches and playgrounds, leads to the tourist office and the sea.

🏖 Beaches

Playa Las Galletas   BEACH
Bring your own towel and sunshade to this pleasant volcanic sand-and-pebble stretch in Las Galletas. It is backed by a lovely promenade with bars and some excellent seafood restaurants.

🏃 Activities

Wind and water have carved the dramatic rock formations of **Montaña Amarilla** (Yellow Mountain), a volcanic mound on the coast outside town. To get here, take Avenida José Antonio Tavio (beside the Ten Bel complex) down to Calle Chasna. At the end of the street is a small car park and a path leading you down to the water. You can ramble across the rocks, enjoying a building-free view of the coast, or hike around the *montaña*.

Buceo Tenerife Diving Center DIVING
(☑922 73 10 15; www.buceotenerife.com; Calle María del Carmen García 22; dive with equipment rental €36; ⊙9am-6pm) This well-established diving school offers discounts for multiple dives.

Escuela de Vela las Galletas WINDSURFING
(☑629 87 81 02; Playa Las Galletas; windsurfer/ catamaran rental per hr €17/35; ⊙11am-6pm Tue-Sun) This well-established place rents sailboats and windsurfers and also offers courses.

✖ Eating

For simple tapas bars frequented by locals enjoying a tipple, head for the small streets leading off the central Rambla Dionisio González. Otherwise, the promenade has the best restaurant choice.

Bajío SEAFOOD €€
(☑922 73 10 39; Puerto de Las Galletas; mains €12-15) A friendly young team run this sea-blue-painted fish restaurant overlooking the boat-yard. Prettily presented and tasty, the dishes here include a succulent *tagliolini con mejil-lones* (pasta with mussels) and a *fritura de pescada* (fried fish) platter for two.

La Gaviota SEAFOOD €€
(☑922 78 59 44; Calle La Marina 9; mains €10-16; ⊙noon-10pm Thu-Tue; P) Continue west along the promenade and beyond to reach this atmospheric seafood restaurant right on the beach. There's a live Canarian croon-er at Sunday lunchtime to accompany your *zarzuela* platter (€24 for two people), or similar.

❶ Information

Tourist Office (☑922 73 01 33; www.todoten-erife.es; ⊙8.30am-3.30pm Mon-Fri, 9am-4pm Sat & Sun) At the western end of La Rambla, the tree-lined walkway that runs parallel to the Paseo Marítimo.

❶ Getting There & Away

Las Galletas is a few kilometres off the TF-1, exit 26. Buses 467, 470 and 473 connect the town hourly with Los Cristianos (€1.90, 30 minutes), while buses 112 and 115 (€8.50, 1¼ hours) come and go from Santa Cruz.

THE EAST

The east coast of Tenerife is the forgotten coast of the island and at first glance that's hardly surprising: the landscape of the east is dry, dusty and sterile, but it is speckled with bright and colourful little villages, which bring life to the otherwise stark sur-roundings. If you have the time, then it pays to explore this region a little more. There are some pleasant low-key beach towns and a much more local vibe than can be found in the international resorts of the south coast.

If you're approaching the east coast from the southern resorts, do yourself a favour by taking the winding TF-28 highway, former-ly the principal thoroughfare, which crawls along the scenic mountain ridge above the coast. The alternative is the very busy mo-torway (TF-1), which links the south to San-ta Cruz in an approximately 40-minute easy drive.

Candelaria

POP 16,000

Just 18km south of Santa Cruz is Candelaria, a charming small fishing village where the main claim to fame is the basilica, home to the patron saint of the entire Canary archipelago. It is well worth a visit, par-ticularly on Sundays when the atmosphere takes on an almost pilgrimage feel as locals throng to the church to attend mass and the

TENERIFE CANDELARIA

OFF THE BEATEN TRACK

EXPLORING THE EAST COAST

After visiting the pyramids at Güímar, continue on past El Escobonal to Fasnia and the tiny **Ermita de la Virgen de los Dolores**, a chapel perched on a hill at the edge of town (off the TF-620 high-way). It's usually closed, but is worth the short drive up for the panoramic views of the harsh, dry landscape. Keep on the TF-620 past the *ermita* to reach **Roques de Fasnia**, a little town carved into the volcanic cliff. There's a tranquil black-sand beach that's rarely crowded. A bit further south is **Porís de Abona**, a charming little fishing village albeit surrounded by new housing. There's an attractive small cove here, complete with fishing boats and a dark sandy beach where you can take a dip.

THE VIRGIN OF CANDELARIA

In 1392, a century before Tenerife was conquered, a statue of the Virgin Mary holding a *candela* (candlestick) washed up on the shore near modern-day Candelaria. The Guanche shepherds who found the statue took it to their king and, according to legend, the people worshipped it. When the Spanish conquered the island a century later, they deemed the statue miraculous, and in 1526 Commander Pedro Fernández de Lugo ordered a sanctuary be built.

The logical explanation of the 'miracle' is that the statue was either the figurehead from a wrecked ship, or a Virgin brought by French or Portuguese sailors, who had been on the island before the Spanish conquest. In either case, the statue was swept away by a violent storm in 1826 and never found. The ornate statue that is today swathed in robes in the Basílica de Nuestra Señora de Candelaria was carved soon after by local artist Fernando Estévenez. On 15 August, the day she was supposedly found by the Guanches, the Virgin is honoured by processions, numerous Masses and a kitschy re-enactment of costumed 'Guanches' worshipping her.

surrounding small shops, selling religious artefacts, flowers, souvenirs and similar, stay open all day. Don't bother visiting the drab modern adjacent resort of Las Caletillas, which has little to commend it aside from a decent-size black pebble beach. There are plenty of earthy local bars and restaurants around the shopping street and harbour in Candelaria.

⊙ Sights

Basílica de Nuestra Señora de Candelaria CHURCH
(⊙7.30am-1pm & 3-7.30pm Tue-Sun; P) This large domed church dates from 1959 and sits at the edge of the town centre, overlooking a rocky beach and flanked by a plaza where nine huge statues of Guanche warriors stand guard. During the official festivities for the Virgen de la Candelaria celebration on 15 August, this plaza fills with pilgrims and partygoers from all over the islands. If you visit during a mass, you will probably find it is standing room only.

ⓘ Information

There's a small **tourist office** (📋 922 50 04 25; Avenida Marítimo 176; ⊙9am-2pm & 4.30-7pm) just north of the basilica.

ⓘ Getting There & Away

If you're driving, take exit 9 off the TF-1 motorway. Buses 111, 112, 115, 116, 122, 123 and 131 connect the town with Santa Cruz (€2.35, 30 minutes).

Güímar & Around

POP 16,000

A rural town with views of a gauzy blue ocean in the distance, Güímar's centre is well kept and pleasant for a stroll. Most folk come here to visit the enigmatic pyramids.

⊙ Sights

Pirámides de Güímar RUINS
(📋 922 51 45 10; www.piramidesdeguimar.net; Calle Chacon, Güímar; adult/child €11/free; ⊙9.30am-6pm; P) These much-restored pyramid ruins explore an intriguing question: could the Canarios have had contact with America before Columbus famously sailed the ocean blue? This theory was developed by renowned Norwegian scientist Thor Heyerdahl, who lived on Tenerife until his death in 2002 and based his ideas on the Mayan-like pyramids discovered in Güímar.

Archeological & Ethnographical Museum of Agache MUSEUM
(📋 922 53 04 95; Plaza El Escobonal, El Escobonal; ⊙5-7pm Mon-Fri) FREE This modest museum in El Escobonal displays all kinds of odds and ends related to Guanche and island culture.

✕ Eating

Café al Mar CAFE €
(📋 626 39 00 96; Porís de Abona; sandwiches €2.50; ⊙8am-5pm) This pint-sized German-owned cafe overlooks the small black-sand cove in Porís de Abona and serves simple fare like sandwiches, as well as great coffee and other drinks.

ℹ Getting There & Away

The roughly hourly buses 120 and 121 from Santa Cruz (€3.40, 50 minutes) stop at the Güímar bus station, a few blocks from the pyramids. To explore the surroundings you really need your own wheels.

El Médano

POP 1250

Not yet squashed by steamroller development, El Médano is a world-class spot for kitesurfers. The laid-back atmosphere they bring with them gives the place a dab of bohemian character and it's altogether a much more pleasant place to stay than nearby Las Américas.

🏖 Beaches

Playa El Médano　　　　　　　　BEACH
El Médano boasts the longest beach in Tenerife (2km), lined by a wooden boardwalk – ideal for evening strolls but that same wind that makes it so good for windsurfing makes it less than ideal for sunbathing.

Playa La Tejita　　　　　　　　BEACH
Stretching for around 1km, this delightful unspoiled beach has a simple straw-roofed bar for drinks and snacks. It's just east of the main Playa El Médano; the first section is nudist.

🏃 Activities

The sails of kitesurfers speckle the horizon here. There are several companies that offer classes and equipment rental, but novices note that the winds are very strong and challenge even the pros.

Azul Kite School　　　　　　KITESURFING
(☑ 922 17 83 14; www.azulkiteboarding.com; Paseo Mercedes Roja 26; 3hr course €145; ☉ 11am-8pm Tue-Sat) A well-established school offering a range of courses for beginners, as well as for more advanced kitesurfers.

30 Nudos Kite School　　　　KITESURFING
(☑ 922 17 89 05; www.30nudos.com; Paseo Nuestra Señora Mercedes de Roja 24; 3hr course €145; ☉ 10am-8pm Mon-Sat) A superfriendly and professional kitesurfing school with an excellent reputation.

🍴 Eating

Imperio del Pintxo　　　　　　TAPAS €
(Emilio José Garrido, Playa Chico; raciónes €7-9.50; ☉ 10am-midnight; 🖶) Run by a young energetic team with a view of the beach and the kitesurfers beyond, like so many colourful butterflies. Come here for tasty tapas and *raciónes* platters to share such as vegetable tempura, goat-cheese parcels in light flaky pastry and prawns topped with a spicy *mojo* sauce.

El Astillero de Avencio　　　　SEAFOOD €€
(☑ 922 17 82 20; Paseo Marcial García 2; mains €12-15; ☉ 1-10.30pm Tue-Sun) Just about the best location in town, overlooking the waves, the seafood and fish here is reliably good and the paella has received rave reviews from readers but, as is so often the case in Spanish seafood restaurants, the veg is a tad sparse, along with the choice of desserts.

ℹ Information

Tourist Office (☑ 922 17 60 02; www.todotenerife.es; Plaza del Médano; ☉ 9am-3pm Mon-Fri, to 1pm Sat) A well-stocked tourist office which can also provide maps covering four local walks.

ℹ Getting There & Away

El Médano is just east of the Tenerife Sur airport, off exit 22 of the TF-1. Bus 470 leaves hourly to Los Cristianos (€3.60, one hour 35 minutes), and bus 116 leaves every two hours from Santa Cruz (€7.35, 1¼ hours).

La Gomera

⏱ 922 / POP 21,952

Best Places to Eat

➡ Restaurante Breñusca (p169)

➡ Casa Efigenia (p171)

➡ Bar-Restaurante El Puerto (p179)

➡ Restaurante Junonia (p176)

Best Places to Stay

➡ Parador Nacional Conde de la Gomera (p230)

➡ Apartamentos Los Telares (p230)

➡ Finca Argayall (p231)

➡ Apartamentos Tapahuga (p231)

➡ Apartamentos Quintero (p230)

Why Go?

From a distance La Gomera appears as an impenetrable fortress ringed with soaring rock walls. Noodle-thin roads wiggle their way alongside cliff faces and up ravines, and the tiny white specks that represent houses seem impossibly placed on inaccessible crags. Viewed from up-close, however, that rough landscape translates into lush valleys, awe-inspiring cliffs and stoic rock formations sculpted by ancient volcanic activity and erosion.

La Gomera does not offer the standard tourist resort trappings of golden beaches and an animated nightlife. It is also relatively laborious to reach; the ferry from Los Cristianos is a filter of sorts, and visitors here tend to be walkers heading for the myriad hiking trails that weave across this lush and spectacular island.

La Gomera also has a tangible bohemian air; and you will spy plenty of grey ponytails from foreign residents who arrived here in the 1960s flower power days – and stayed.

When to Go

➡ March and April are the best months for hiking with an ideal temperate temperature coupled with a dazzle of subtropical flowers on the hillsides.

➡ During the summer months August can reach a sizzling 30°C and sees the most day-trippers from nearby Los Cristianos, while June and September are a tad cooler and good fiesta months with El Día de San Juan (23 to 24 June) and the week-long Fiestas Columbinas (from 6 September) street party taking place.

➡ In winter expect some rainfall in December and January with an average temperature of around 17°C. Look for wild mushrooms on local menus in February.

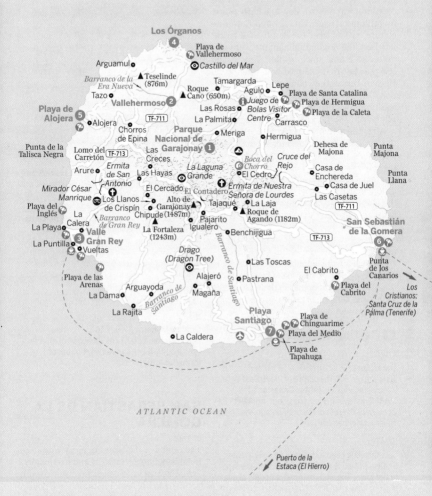

ATLANTIC OCEAN

Los Órganos

Playa de Vallehermoso

Arguamul

Castillo del Mar

Barranco de la Era Nueva

▲ Teselinde (876m)

Tazo

Vallehermoso ②

Tamargarda

Roque Cano (650m) ▲

Agulo

Lepe

Playa de Santa Catalina

Playa de Hermigua

Juego de Bolas Visitor Centre ①

Las Rosas

La Palmita

TF-711

Carrasco

Playa de la Caleta

Playa de Alojera ⑤

Alojera

Chorros de Epina

Meriga

Hermigua

Dehesa de Majona

Punta Majona

Punta de la Talisca Negra

Lomo del Carretón

TF-713

Parque Nacional de Garajonay ①

Las Creces

La Laguna Grande

Boca del Chorro

Cruce del Rejo

Casa de Enchereda

Punta Llana

Arure

Ermita de San Antonio

Las Hayas

El Cedro

Ermita de Nuestra Señora de Lourdes

Casa de Juel

Las Casetas

Mirador César Manrique

El Cercado

Alto de Garajonay

El Contadero

Tajaqué

La Laja

TF-711

Playa del Inglés

Los Llanos de Crispín

Chipude

▲ (1487m)

Pajarito

Roque de Agando (1182m)

San Sebastián de la Gomera ⑥

La Calera

Barranco de Gran Rey

La Fortaleza (1243m)

Igualero

Benchijigua

TF-713

La Playa

Valle Gran Rey ③

La Puntilla

Vueltas

Drago (Dragon Tree)

Las Toscas

El Cabrito

Punta de los Canarios

Los Cristianos; Santa Cruz de la Palma (Tenerife)

Playa de las Arenas

Arguayoda

Alajeró

Magaña

Pastrana

Playa del Cabrito

La Dama

La Rajita

Barranco de Santiago

Barranco de Santiago

Playa Santiago

Playa de Chinguarime

Playa del Medio ⑦

Playa de Tapahuga

La Caldera

ATLANTIC OCEAN

Puerto de la Estaca (El Hierro)

La Gomera Highlights

① Explore the fern-filled trails of the **Parque Nacional de Garajonay** (p171), the *laurisilva* (laurel) forest at the island's heart

② Be amazed by the tropical flowers, plants and fruits of the lush **Vallehermoso** (p175)

③ Soak up the beauty of **Valle Gran Rey** (p178), with its plunging valleys and picture-perfect terraced hillsides

④ Take a cruise to visit **Los Órganos** (p175), a rock formation that resembles a titan's set of pipe organs

⑤ Unwind at the **Playa de Alojera** (p175), the island's remotest beach

⑥ Peer into the well that 'baptised America' and explore the colourful backstreets of the pint-sized capital **San Sebastián de la Gomera** (p166)

⑦ Munch seafood on the seashore in the laid-back beach resort of **Playa Santiago** (p176)

History

Throughout the 15th century the Spaniards tried unsuccessfully to conquer La Gomera. When they finally managed to establish a presence on the island in the middle of the century, it was due to a slow and fairly peaceful infiltration of Christianity and European culture, rather than the result of a battle. Early on, the original inhabitants were permitted to retain much of their culture and self-rule, but that changed when the brutal Hernán Peraza the younger became governor. The *gomeros* rebelled against him, unleashing a bloodbath that killed hundreds of islanders.

After the activity of those first years, and the excitement that accompanied Christopher Columbus' stopovers on the island, there followed a long period of isolation. La Gomera was totally self-sufficient and had little contact with the outside world until the 1950s, when a small pier was built in San Sebastián, opening the way for ferry travel and trade.

Even so, it was difficult to eke out a living by farming on the island's steep slopes, and much of the population emigrated to Tenerife or South America. These days the island is the most popular in the archipelago for hiking, which has resulted in a welcome boost for the economy.

Getting There & Away

AIR

The **airport** (902 87 30 00; www.aena.es) is just 3km outside the centre of Playa Santiago. Inter-island airways **Binter Canarias** (902 391392; www.bintercanarias.com) connects La Gomera to the rest of the archipelago, via Tenerife, several times daily.

BOAT

Several ferries and jetfoils arrive daily at San Sebastián's busy port, which is just at the foot of the town. The vast majority of people arrive here on daily trips from Los Cristianos, Tenerife,

ROAD DISTANCES (KM)

	San Sebastián de la Gomera	Valle Gran Rey	Hermigua	La Laguna Grande
Valle Gran Rey	27			
Hermigua	16	23		
La Laguna Grande	18	11	8	
Vallehermosa	27	16	15	13

Approximate distances only

although there are also less frequent ferries from La Palma and Gran Canaria.

Fred Olsen (902 10 01 07; www.fredolsen.es) The fastest, but most expensive, boats, running to/from Los Cristianos (Tenerife; €32, 40 minutes, three times daily). Also sails to Santa Cruz de la Palma (one way €42, two hours, one daily Monday to Saturday).

Naviera Armas (922 87 13 24; www.navieraarmas.com) Heads to/from Los Cristianos (Tenerife; €30, one hour) three times daily Monday to Friday, one on Saturday and two on Sunday. Also sails to Santa Cruz de la Palma daily except Saturday (one way from €24, 2½ hours).

Getting Around

BUS

Guagua Gomera (922 14 11 01; www.guaguagomera.com) The local bus company runs a comprehensive network of buses throughout the island.

SAN SEBASTIÁN DE LA GOMERA

POP 9055

The capital of the island in every way – economically, bureaucratically and historically – San Sebastián has a delightful historic centre with shaded plazas, sun-bleached colourful buildings and pedestrian-friendly streets. Its main claim to fame is that Christopher Columbus stayed here on his way to the New World, and you'll learn more about the famed explorer here than you ever did at school, as his every footstep (real or imagined) in the town has been well documented for visitors. If you've just hopped off the boat from Los Cristianos in Tenerife, shift down a gear or two; slow-paced San Sebastián feels very different from its neighbour across the water.

History

On 6 September 1492, after loading up with supplies from La Gomera, Christopher Columbus led his three small caravels out of the bay and set sail westwards beyond the limit of the known world. When Columbus was on the island, San Sebastián had barely been founded. Four years earlier, in 1488, there had been a terrible massacre in the wake of the failed uprising against Hernán Peraza, the island's governor. When it was all over, what had been the Villa de las Palmas, on a spot known to the Guanches as Hipalán, was renamed San Sebastián.

The boom in transatlantic trade following Columbus' journeys helped boost the fortunes of the town, which sits on a sheltered harbour and was one of the Canaries' best ports. Nevertheless, its population passed the 1000 mark only at the beginning of the 19th century. The good times also brought dangers, as, like other islands, San Sebastián was regularly subjected to pirate attack from the English, French and Portuguese. In 1739 the English fleet actually landed an invasion force but the assault was repulsed.

The fate of the town was linked intimately with that of the rest of the island. Its fortunes rose with the cochineal (a beetle that produces a red dye) boom in the 19th century, but that industry collapsed with the emergence of synthetic dyes.

◉ Sights

San Sebastián is not a town of theme parks and sandy beaches, but just exploring the relaxed and colourful streets is stimulating enough for most folk over the age of 10. For a panoramic orientation of the town, head up the road to the Parador Nacional Conde de la Gomera hotel, where the **Mirador de la Hila** showcases the coast, the town and the craggy green mountains beyond.

In the town centre, most of the interesting sights are somehow related to Columbus (in either real or contrived ways), and they form a route you can follow around town. Begin at **Plaza Américas**, where you can get a juice in one of the terrace bars, and

---

THREE PERFECT DAYS IN LA GOMERA

Day One

La Gomera is an island seemingly tailor-made for hikers. This perfect day starts from **La Laguna Grande** and weaves in and out of magnificent, mist-drenched laurel forests before emerging, a couple of fairly easy hours later, on the summit of the island, **Alto de Garajonay**. On a clear day Tenerife's El Teide stands snow-bound and proud in the distance and below you the tangled web of La Gomera's forests fall away. Loop back around to your car and head for a well-earned dinner at the rustic **Casa Efigenia** (p171).

Day Two

The northern half of La Gomera is one of the most fertile places in the Canary Islands, and a day spent exploring this area will quickly turn a gardener's fingers green with envy. Start your day among the banana plants of **Hermigua** and learn the secrets of *gofio* (ground, roasted grain used in place of bread in Canarian cuisine) at the **Museo de Gofio** (p173). Next, take the twisting coastal highway to pretty **Agulo** for a stroll around the attractive old quarter. By now you'll be working up a bit of an appetite so stop for lunch at **Restaurante Las Rosas** (p175) and listen to a live performance of **Silbo**, the whistling language of La Gomera. Continue onward to the beautiful-by-name, beautiful-by-nature **Vallehermosa**, where you can finish the day strolling down to the Playa de Vallehermosa.

Day Three

For many people the **Valle Gran Rey** (Valley of the Great King) is quite simply the best reason for coming to La Gomera. This day will show you why. Start your morning taking breakfast overlooking an empty beach in the gardens of the **Finca Argayall**. Stroll to the town port and board a boat for a **whale- and dolphin-watching trip**. Return for a fish lunch at the **Bar-Restaurante El Puerto** (p179), sleep it all off on one of the town's beaches and then, in the evening, head up the valley for a sundowner with a view at the **Mirador César Manrique**.

THE ISLE WHERE COLUMBUS DALLIED

A Genoese sailor of modest means, Cristoforo Colombo (as he is known in his native Italy – Christopher Columbus to the rest of us) was born in 1451. He went to sea early and was something of a dreamer. Fascinated by Marco Polo's travels in the Orient, he decided early on that it must be possible to reach the east by heading west into the sunset. After years of doors being slammed in his face, the Catholic monarchs of Spain, Fernando and Isabel, finally gave him their patronage in 1492.

On 3 August, at the head of three small caravels – the *Santa María*, *Pinta* and *Niña* – Columbus weighed anchor in Palos de la Frontera, Andalucía, on the Spanish mainland. But before heading across the ocean blue, he stopped off at La Gomera for last-minute provisions, unwittingly giving the island its biggest claim to fame and many future tourist attractions. One of the things it's claimed he picked up for the journey was goat's cheese, one of La Gomera's star products to this day.

Columbus set sail on 6 September, a day now celebrated in San Sebastián with the Fiestas Columbinas. His ships didn't see land until 12 October, just as their provisions and the sailors' patience were nearing their ends. The expedition 'discovered' several Caribbean islands on this trip and returned to Spain in March of the following year.

Columbus made three later voyages, but died alone and bitter in Valladolid, Spain, in 1504, still convinced he'd found a new route to the Orient rather than America.

across through **Plaza Constitución**, shaded by enormous Indian laurel trees. There's an arts and crafts market held here on Saturday and Wednesday mornings.

The tourist office runs free tours of the old quarter on Wednesday and Friday at 11am.

★ **Casa de Colón** MUSEUM
(www.museoslagomera.es; Calle Real 56; ⊙10am-1pm & 5-8pm Mon-Fri) FREE This simple house is built on the site where Columbus supposedly stayed while on the island, and today it houses a small museum; the highlight is the gallery of stunning pottery from the Chimú tribes who lived in the region between Ecuador and Lima during the 11th to 15th centuries. The upstairs gallery holds temporary exhibitions, generally of art and photography.

Torre del Conde FORT
(⊙9.30am-1.30pm & 3-6pm Mon-Fri) FREE Set in a lush subtropical park, Torre del Conde is considered the Canary Islands' most important example of military architecture and today is home to a historical exhibition that includes La Gomera maps dating from 1492. It was here where Beatriz de Bobadilla, who was the wife of the cruel and ill-fated Hernán Peraza (p170), had to barricade herself in 1488 until help arrived.

The fort (built in 1447) was the first building of any note to be erected on the island, and is about the only one to have been more or less preserved in its original state.

Iglesia de la Virgen de la Asunción CHURCH
(Calle Real; ⊙8am-6.30pm Mon-Sat, 11am-8pm Sun) This is the site where Columbus and his men supposedly came to pray before setting off for the New World. The original chapel was begun in 1450 but was destroyed by a fire. The 18th-century church here today is constructed in the form of a Latin cross and has three naves and mixes Mudéjar (Islamic-style architecture), Gothic and baroque architectural styles. The carved wooden entrance lobby is stunning.

Museo Arqueológico de la Gomera MUSEUM
(www.museoslagomera.es; Calle Torres Padilla 8; ⊙10am-7pm Tue-Fri, 10am-2pm Sat & Sun) FREE Inside a typical *gomeran* town house, this small museum showcases both the island's Guanche past and its present-day culture. Displays reveal Guanche day-to-day life and their social, political and religious structures; note that all signage is in Spanish only.

Casa de la Aguada MUSEUM
(Calle Real 4; ⊙8.30am-6pm Mon-Sat, 10am-1pm Sun) FREE Just off Plaza Constitución, this place is also referred to as Casa de la Aduana and Casa Condal, since at different times it served as the customs house and the count's residence. Closed for refurbishment at research time, the museum primarily covers the history of the building.

According to folklore, Columbus drew water from the well that sits in the central patio and used it to 'baptise America'.

🏖 Beaches

Playa San Sebastián
BEACH

This is the town's sandy, volcanic beach and is the perfect place to relax and have a swim. It's also the site of some of the town's liveliest festivals. Unlike many beaches in the Canaries, its waters are almost always calm and smooth, making it a great beach for children.

Playa de la Cueva
BEACH

Past the port, and accessible via a small tunnel, is the small and pretty, though often windy, Playa de la Cueva. On a clear day, Tenerife seems like it's within pebble-throwing distance.

🏃 Activities

North of town, at Km 8.4 on the TF-711 highway, is an interesting trail leading into the **Dehesa de Majona**, the largely uninhabited pastureland to the north of the capital. The dirt track begins near a lookout point, venturing towards the goat-herding villages of Casas de Enchereda and Casas de Juel before winding its way towards the coast and eventually joining up with sealed local roads near Hermigua. The lonely route of around 24km can be hiked in about five hours (one way).

Bike Hire Marina La Gomera
BICYCLE RENTAL

(☎922 14 17 69; www.marinalagomera.es; Puerto Deportivo Marina La Gomera, Avenida Fred Olsen; half-/full day €5/7; ⊙10am-6pm; 🚲) A convenient bike-rental place on the waterfront.

🎊 Festivals & Events

For such a small place San Sebastián has a busy festival calendar. The following are just a taster.

Fiesta de San Sebastián
RELIGIOUS

(⊙20 Jan) San Sebastián's festival in honour of the town's patron saint.

El Día de San Juan
RELIGIOUS

(⊙23-24 Jun) St John's Day sees the beach lined with bonfires to celebrate the summer solstice.

Fiestas Columbinas
RELIGIOUS

(⊙from 6 Sep) A week full of street parties, music and cultural events is held in San Sebastián, celebrating Columbus' first voyage.

Bajada de la Virgen de Guadelupe San Sebastián
RELIGIOUS

(⊙5 Oct) Every five years (2018, 2023 etc) the town celebrates its patroness saint with a flotilla of fishing boats escorting the statue of the Virgin Mary from the chapel of Punta Llana southwards to the capital.

🍴 Eating

⭐Restaurante Breñusca
CANARIAN $

(☎922 87 09 20; Calle Real 11; mains €8-12; ⊙9am-10pm Mon-Sat) The daily catch is on display here – go with owner Hipolito's recommendation; he's been here since the 1980s. So has the decor by the look of it: pea green walls, faded pics, dusty ferns... Never mind, the locals rate this place as up there with the best and are usually found crowded around the small corner bar.

Aside from seafood, the menu includes hearty meat dishes and homemade cakes.

La Forastera
BISTRO $

(Calle Real 15; tapas €3.50-7; ⊙12.30-5pm & 5-7.30pm Mon-Sat) This tiny place has a reassuringly brief menu of healthy Med-style tapas like spinach quiche and aubergine and pepper bake, plus imaginative desserts including a feather-light *gofia* mousse topped with local honey. Alfresco seating only with just a few tables that tend to get filled up fast.

LA GOMERA SAN SEBASTIÁN DE LA GOMERA

DON'T MISS

MARKET MUNCHIES

Mercado Municipal (Avenida Colón; ⊙9am-2pm Sat & Wed; 🅿) San Sebastián's market is a good place to pick up some local delicacies such as honey, busily made by *gomeran* bees and considered some of the finest in Spain; *miel de palma* (palm honey), a sweet syrup made from palm-tree sap; and *almogrote*, a spicy cheese pâté made with soft cheese, pepper and tomato, and spread on bread.

The market is also a good place to buy *queso gomero* (fresh *gomeran* goat's cheese), a mild, smooth cheese made with local goat's milk and served with salads, as a dessert, or grilled and smothered in *mojo*, the famed Canarian red or green spicy sauce based on either chillies and paprika or coriander and garlic. The market is located beside the bus station.

THE CRUELTY OF GOVERNOR HERNÁN PERAZA

Governor Hernán Peraza the younger had long been hated for his cruel treatment of the islanders. When, in 1488, he broke a pact of friendship with one of the Gomero tribes and, openly cheating on his wife, began cavorting with Yballa, a local beauty and fiancée of one of the island's most powerful men, the natives rebelled. They surprised Peraza during one of his clandestine meetings with Yballa and killed him with a dart, communicating the news via Silbo (whistle) all over the island. They then proceeded to attack the Spaniards in Villa de las Palmas, the precursor to modern San Sebastián, and Peraza's deceived wife (the famed beauty Beatriz de Bobadilla) barricaded herself in the Torre del Conde, where she waited until help arrived.

Unfortunately, the story didn't end there. 'Help' showed up in the form of Pedro de Vera, governor of Gran Canaria and one of the cruellest figures in Canarian history. His ruthlessness was bloodcurdling. According to one account, de Vera ordered the execution of all *gomeran* males above the age of 15, and in an orgy of wanton violence, islanders were hanged, impaled, decapitated or drowned. Some had their hands and feet lopped off beforehand, just for good measure. The women were parcelled out to the militiamen, and many of the children were sold as slaves. To complete the job, de Vera also ordered the execution of about 300 *gomeros* living on Gran Canaria.

Bar-Restaurante La Hila
CANARIAN **$$**

(☑ 680 58 35 37; Calle Virgen Guadalupe 2; mains €10-15; ☉ noon-4.30pm & 6-10.30pm) If you've just got off the boat from Las Américas and the pies and peas have left you feeling down, head here and choose one of the *a la plancha* fish dishes chalked on the blackboard each day, add a squeeze of lemon and you have a dish that is fit for Neptune himself.

Look for the shutters painted banana-leaf green on the corner of one of the most picturesque lanes in town.

Restaurante El Charcón
SEAFOOD **$$**

(☑ 922 14 18 98; www.restauranteelcharcon.com; Playa de la Cueva; mains €11-18; ☉ 12.15-10.30pm Mon-Sat) A small and fairly upmarket (for San Sebastián) restaurant dug out of the rock near the shore with glorious beach views from the picture windows and small terrace. El Charcón specialises in innovative seafood dishes like sea bream with martini and dill.

Bar-Restaurante La Tasca
INTERNATIONAL **$$**

(☑ 922 14 15 98; Calle Ruiz de Padrón 57; mains €9-12; ☉ noon-4pm & 7-11.30pm Mon-Sat) Spread over two traditional cottages with four homey dining rooms, this intimate tavern serves mainland-style tapas alongside pizzas, lasagne and more elaborate dishes such as grilled rabbit.

Parador Nacional Conde de la Gomera
CONTEMPORARY CANARIAN **$$$**

(☑ 922 87 11 00; www.parador.es; Calle Lomo de la Horca; mains €22-28; ☉ noon-4pm & 6-11pm;

) The elegant restaurant at the Parador Nacional is without doubt the most refined establishment in San Sebastián and serves consistently good creative versions of traditional Canarian favourites. Reservations essential.

Drinking

La Salamandra
CAFE

(Calle Real 16; cocktails €5; ☉ 9am-10pm Mon-Sat; ☎) This dazzling white inner courtyard is hung with contemporary artwork and is a great place to sip a cocktail or a fresh mango or papaya *lassi* (yoghurt drink). There is live music on Tuesdays at 8.30pm. Snacks also available.

ⓘ Information

Tourist Information Kiosk (Plaza Américas; ☉ 9am-12.30pm & 3.30-6.30pm Mon-Fri, 9am-12.30pm & 4-6.30pm Sat) This small kiosk supplies maps but little else.

Tourist Office (☑ 922 14 15 12; www.lagomera. travel; Calle Real 34; ☉ 9am-1.30pm & 3.30-5pm Mon-Sat, 10am-1pm Sun) A helpful tourist office with an adjacent exhibition centre about the mountainous terrain, including the history of the dry stone walls that you see throughout the island. Pick up the free flyer *This Was Columbus's Starting Point*, a self-guided route that covers places of interest relating to Columbus.

 Getting Around

Bus 7 (€4, 30 minutes) runs between the airport and San Sebastián at flight arrival times.

Plan on using your own two feet to get around the town; San Sebastián is very walkable, and is so small that buses merely pass through, not really connecting points of interest within the town centre.

The taxi stand is on Avenida Descubridores. The only reason you might need a car is to move between the town centre and the Parador Nacional Conde de la Gomera, which is a short (though steep) walk or drive away. If you're going further afield, a car is very useful.

There are several car-rental agencies around, and they will arrange to have a car waiting for you at the port or airport when you arrive if you book ahead, which is recommended.

Cicar (✆ 922 14 17 56; www.cicar.com; Estación Marítima, San Sebastián) There is also an office at the airport.

Rent-a-Car La Rueda (✆ 922 87 07 09; www. autoslarueda.es; Calle Real 19, San Sebastián; ⊗ 9am-1.30pm & 4-8pm) A reasonably priced local car-rental agency.

PARQUE NACIONAL DE GARAJONAY

This jungle of nearly impenetrable green was tragically damaged by a massive fire in 2012 that destroyed 750 hectares of the ancestral *laurisilva* (laurel) forests, leaving large areas of stark blackened trees, which, it is estimated, will take around 30 years to recover. There is still plenty of green left, fortunately, and the Parque Nacional de Garajonay remains famous for offering the island's best hiking and cycling trails, and is an essential sight for anyone visiting the island.

A universe of organisms has forged out a life in this damp, dark forest, which covers a full 10% (around 40 sq km) of the island's surface. As many as 400 species of flora, including Canary willows and holly, flourish, and nearly 1000 species of invertebrates make their home in the park; insect lovers will have a field day. Vertebrates here include mainly birds and lizards. Relatively little light penetrates the canopy, providing an ideal landscape for moss and lichen to spread over everything.

Up here, on the roof of the island, cool Atlantic trade winds clash with warmer breezes, creating a constant ebb and flow of mist through the dense forest, something called 'horizontal rain'. The tangle of trees here is absolutely vital to the health of the island. The trees act like sponges, catching this moisture on their leaves and allowing it to drip down into the soil, thus feeding them and the springs of the very island itself.

The frosty fingers of the last Ice Age didn't make it as far as the Canaries, so what you see here was common across much of the Mediterranean millions of years ago. Garajonay was declared a national park in 1981 and a Unesco World Heritage site in 1986.

Lighting fires in the park is forbidden, except in a few designated areas. Free camping is also prohibited. It can get cold here, and the damp goes right to your bones, even when it is not raining. Bring walking boots, warm garments and a rainproof jacket.

✖ Eating

★ **Casa Efigenia** CANARIAN $
(✆ 922 80 40 77; www.efigenianatural.com; Carretera General; menú €10; ⊗ 8am-8pm; P 🌿) On the southern border of Parque Nacional de Garajonay, take a short detour to the town of Las Hayas, where you'll find a local institution serving family-style meals. Efigenia started cooking for the local engineers who were working on the roads in this area in 1960. The long communal tables are still here and the set vegetarian menu remains deliciously unchanged.

Traditional dishes are served, like *puchero gofio* (a chickpea and vegetable-based stew), *almagrote* (spicy cheese spread) and *sopa de berros* (watercress soup), plus fabulous homemade cakes. Doña Efigenia is a charming hostess who makes a point of talking to all her guests. These days her three sons help with the business, which has expanded to encompass a bodega and several *casas rurales* (village or farmstead accommodation; €45) and apartments (€65) in the area. You can buy Efigenia's own label wine, plus a potent orange liquor, marmalade, jams and, naturally enough, the ubiquitous *mojo*.

❶ Information

There are two visitors centres that can provide visitors with hiking route information. Route details are gradually being replaced with barcode optical signage, however, which rangers recommend you upload to your phone, together with the GPS info.

Juego de Bolas Visitor Centre (✆ 922 80 09 93; http://reddeparquesnacionales.mma.es; La Palmita–Agulo Hwy; ⊗ 9.30am-4.30pm; 🖥 ♿) Note that this visitor centre is actually located well outside Parque Nacional de Garajonay and is near Agulo to the north of the island.

STRIDING OUT IN GARAJONAY

Walking is the best way to revel in the natural beauty abounding here, so park the car or get off the bus and set out to explore the national park on foot. Many of the trails that criss-cross Garajonay have been used by the *gomeros* for hundreds of years as a means of getting around the island, and few are strenuous.

Although several guiding companies lead convenient, transport-included hikes in and around the park, it's certainly not necessary to use their services. The park's many and varied access points make it simple to plan a journey on your own and most of the routes are very well waymarked. If you don't have a dedicated walking guide to the island, the national park map and Camino Gomera (hiking map) are available from the **Juego de Bolas** (p171) or **La Laguna Grande visitor centres**. The walks they describe correspond to both the park waymarking and the routes mentioned here. Increasingly, however, barcode optical signage is being used on the trails themselves, which you can 'read' with a smartphone or tablet.

Experienced walkers will find the hiking in the Garajonay area fairly easy (but nonetheless rewarding). Juego de Bolas also offers guided tours here.

Several popular self-guided walks begin in **La Laguna Grande**, a recreation and picnic area just off the TF-713 highway. The *laguna* refers to a barren circle of land in the centre that fills with water when it rains and has always held an air of mystery. Islanders say it's a mystical place and that witches once practised here. For most of the year it's a lovely green spot with playgrounds, barbecue pits and picnic tables.

If you don't have much time to explore, you can take the easy, 20-minute loop (0.75km) that serves as a decent, if too brief, introduction to the park. This route is a good place to view the park's famous laurel trees as well as, sadly, an area that was blackened by the 2012 fire.

A longer walk (around 2½ hours one way, 6.2km) heads to the **Alto de Garajonay** (1487m), the island's tallest peak. The walk begins behind the restaurant at La Laguna Grande and sets off towards **El Cercado** (a town known for its pottery production), then bears left towards Los Llanos de Crispín before winding its way through native vegetation and heading southeast to the Alto. From here, cloud permitting, you can enjoy some jaw-dropping, 360-degree views around the island and even spot Tenerife, La Palma, El Hierro and Gran Canaria in the distance.

From the Alto, you could return to La Laguna Grande (there is an alternative trail so that you don't have to completely backtrack) or continue 45 minutes downhill to **Pajarito**, where there is a bus stop. Bus 1 (€5, around one hour) comes by four times a day weekdays and twice a day on weekends; it will take you towards either San Sebastián or Valle Gran Rey. For those arriving by bus, or looking for an easy parking spot, Pajarito is also a good starting point to begin a short hike up to the Alto.

Around 15 minutes' walk north of Pajarito is **El Contadero**, where another track, signposted **Caserío del Cedro**, leads northeast through a beautiful valley forest. This mostly descending trail (one way 2½ hours, 5.7km) winds its way towards the hamlet of **El Cedro**, famous for its waterfalls. It's possible to continue hiking to Hermigua, two hours away. Or, you could return to the Pajarito bus stop via Tajaqué (around three hours).

Here you'll find information on the park and the island in general, plus have the chance to view a 20-minute video. In the centre's gardens and interior patio flourishes a microcosm of La Gomera's floral riches.

A small museum shows off island handicrafts and explains the park's geology and climate. There is also a small cafe. The centre offers free guided tours of the park on Friday (2½ hours, in Spanish only); call ahead to reserve a spot.

La Laguna Grande (☎ 922 92 26 00; www.lagomera.travel; La Laguna Grande, Parque Nacional de Garajonay; ⊙ 8.30am-3.30pm; 🛜 ♿) This conveniently located visitor centre has hiking-route information, as well as a small exhibition about the bird life in the park, a restaurant and a recreation area.

➊ Getting There & Away

Unlike some other protected parks, Garajonay is extremely accessible. In fact, you won't be able to avoid it if you move much about the island, as the park exists at La Gomera's major crossroads.

The TF-713 highway cuts east to west right through the park until it meets the TF-711 at the park's western extremity. Wheeling through in your own car is certainly the quickest and most comfortable way to move about the park. Bus 1 (€5, around one hour) runs five times daily weekdays and twice on weekends between the capital and Valle Gran Rey. The route runs along a southern secondary road, branching off shortly before Alto de Garajonay and continuing westwards along a decidedly tortuous route, stopping in towns like Igualero, Chipude and El Cercado before branching north again to rejoin the main road at Las Hayas.

A minor sealed road connects the Juego de Bolas visitor centre in the north of the island to La Laguna Grande, about midway along the TF-713, between the park's eastern and western boundaries.

THE NORTH

If you have just one day to spend in La Gomera, you should probably think about spending it in the verdant north, where dense banana plantations and swaying palm trees fill the valleys, cultivated terraces transform the hillsides into geometric works of art and whitewashed houses make the villages seem like something from another era. The resulting landscape is postcard-worthy at every turn, but when admiring the views, spare a moment to remember that these well-manicured terraces represent back-breaking work by the local farmers – the steepness of the slopes means most work here has to be done without machines.

The curvy TF-711, running 42km between San Sebastián and Vallehermoso, is the artery connecting the towns here, and it's pocked with miradors (lookout points) offering gorgeous views. The highway eventually meets up with the TF-713, allowing day-trippers to loop the northern half of the island and end up back in San Sebastián in plenty of time to catch the last ferry off the island. The round trip should take you no more than three hours including plenty of stops to ogle the views.

Hermigua

POP 110

A popular home base for those on walking holidays, the go-slow town of Hermigua, 16km outside San Sebastián, is dripping with that authentic *gomeran* feel. It's also often dripping with water – this is one of the dampest parts of the island. The town itself is strung out along the bottom of a lusciously green ravine full of banana groves and other subtropical flora, its houses like beads on a chain running down the middle. The main road winds down to a captivating blue ocean where the crushing waves are a bit too rough for swimming (although the odd surfer pops by for a wave or two) and the beach itself feels a little forgotten about.

◉ Sights

★**Museo Etnográfico**　　　　MUSEUM

(📞922 88 19 60; www.museoslagomera.es; Carretera General 97; ☉10am-7pm Tue-Fri, to 2pm Sat & Sun) FREE Housed in a handsome historical building, this two-storey museum covers the island's natural resources and ecosystems in exhibits that include fishing, forestry, agriculture and farming. There are also sections on crafts, like pottery and basketry and winemaking. Don't miss the information about the extraction of palm honey, known as *guarapo* (palm tree sap), which is unique to the island and an indispensable ingredient in much of the local cuisine.

Museo de Gofio　　　　MUSEUM

(📞922 88 00 71; www.museslagomera.es; Carretera General; adult/child €3/free; ☉9.30am-5pm Mon-Sat, to 2pm Sun; 🅿) This is a reconstructed windmill where *gofio* (roasted grain used in place of bread in Canarian cuisine) was once ground. The tour takes in the museum, which concentrates on the local rural lifestyle and customs, as well as the mill. There is also a gift shop and an attractive small garden.

Church & Convent of Santo Domingo　　　　CHURCH

(☉9am-6pm) At the heart of Hermigua's original village, to the right as you enter from San Sebastián, lies this 16th-century church and convent, with an intricately carved Mudéjar ceiling.

Iglesia de la Encarnación　　　　CHURCH

(☉8am-6pm) This church dates back to the 17th century but was not completed until the 20th century, partly due to the fact that the original construction crumbled in the early 18th century. Take a look at the adjacent public park, complete with a *lucha canaria* (Canarian wrestling) ring.

🏖 Beaches

Playa de la Caleta   BEACH
(P) The best beach in town is Playa de la Caleta, located 3km southeast down the coast; follow the signs from the waterfront. It's one of the prettier black-sand and pebble beaches in the north of the island.

🍴 Eating

Bar Pedro   TAPAS $
(✆ 922 88 10 23; Carretera General 56; tapas €3-4.50; ⊗ 9am-11pm) With an outdoor terrace overlooking the banana groves, superb tapas and a priceless barman, this is a popular place to snack in town. The house special is the octopus salad, while other dishes include tuna with *mojo* and ratatouille. It also rents out apartments (from €30).

El Faro   SEAFOOD $
(Camino de la Playa Santa Catalina 15; mains €8-12; ⊗ noon-10.30pm; P) Located high above Playa de la Caleta, this is where the locals come for seafood with the *pescado del día* (fish of the day) being the best choice. Pastas are also on the menu if you have had enough of flapping fins. The surroundings are light and modern; take a look at the magnified photographs of rocks, a kaleidoscope of colours and patterns.

Las Chácaras   CANARIAN $$
(www.restauantelaschacaras.blogspot.com; Lomo San Pedro 5, Carretera General; mains €10-15; ⊗ 8.30am-1pm & 12.30-4pm; P) This restaurant is a perennial favourite with visitors who come here to enjoy staunch traditional dishes, like lentil soup, goat stew and fried *calamaris* (squid). The owners take great

---

> ### ℹ MAPS
>
> The 1:40,000 *La Gomera Tour and Trail* (Discovery Walking Guides) is a fairly good walking map with 70 routes described briefly in English. Other good maps include the 1:35,000 *La Gomera – Ile de Gomera*, published by Freytag & Berndt, and the 1:50,000 *La Gomera* by Distrimaps Telestar. These maps are available in bookshops. La Laguna Grande visitor centre also gives out decent free maps of the island.

pride in their homemade desserts, like *quesillo* (a creamy custard) and *chácaras* (cheese based pudding).

ℹ Getting There & Away

Bus 2 (€3) runs four times on weekdays and twice on weekends between San Sebastián and Vallehermoso, stopping in Hermigua along the way.

El Cedro

El Cedro is a rural hamlet set amid farmed terraces and laurel thickets, located southwest of Hermigua, and on the Parque Nacional de Garajonay border. The ravine and waterfall known as **Boca del Chorro** (also called Boca del Cedro) runs in a roughly north–south direction through the village. The waterfalls are just to the northeast of the village. The chapel, **Ermita de Nuestra Señora de Lourdes**, is a 1km wander out from the hamlet.

To walk to El Cedro from Hermigua, ask in town for the way to the *sendero* (trail) to El Cedro and be prepared for a two- to three-hour hike. If you're not up for walking, follow the signs to El Cedro off the main highway south of Hermigua.

You can also reach El Cedro from El Contadero on the Caserío del Cedro trail (p172) in Parque Nacional de Garajonay.

🍴 Eating

Bar La Vista   CANARIAN $
(Carretera General, El Cedro; mains €6-8; ⊗ 9am-7pm Tue-Fri, to 9pm Sat & Sun; P) This popular traditional place offers heart-warming local dishes and tapas, like *papas arrugadas* (wrinkly potatoes) and a tangy red *mojo*. It is also famed for its *sopa de berros* served in a traditional wooden bowl accompanied by *gofio* to stir in and thicken.

Agulo

Agulo is a pretty scrabble of picturesque lanes and tenderly restored buildings. Founded early in the 17th century, it squats on a low platform beneath the steep, rugged hinterland that stretches back towards Parque Nacional de Garajonay.

The town hall has erected a number of information boards throughout Agulo, which trace out a walking tour taking in all the most important buildings. The elegant **Iglesia de San Marcos** dominates the centre; built in

1912, it's a simple temple with a high ceiling and a few interesting pieces of art.

Eating

La Vieja Escuela   CANARIAN $
(www.laviejaescuela.ecoturismogomera.com; Calle Trujillo Armas 2; mains €8-12; ⊙11am-9pm Mon-Sat) Located on a ridge in the Las Casas *barrio* (district) of town (once a hamlet in its own right) and a schoolhouse until 1968, grab a table on the panoramic terrace. Highlights on the menu include the fresh fish of the day and an exceptional *tortilla* (potato omelette). Run by a husband and wife team, service can be slow.

To get here, pass the modern part of Agulo and take the right-hand turn signposted 'Circumcalación'; continue along the cobbled road for 400m where you will see a sign to the restaurant.

Las Rosas

Las Rosas sits at the foot of Parque Nacional de Garajonay. Just before the town centre is the turn-off for the park's Juego de Bolas visitor centre. Las Rosas is located past Agulo on the main highway.

Eating

Restaurante Las Rosas   CANARIAN $
(✏ 922 80 09 16; www.fredolsen.es; Carretera General; set menu €9.50; ⊙ noon-3.30pm; P ⛾) Las Rosas' claim to fame is being the home of the Fred Olsen–owned Restaurante Las Rosas, which is a tourist magnet on the main highway and mainly attracts coach tours here to witness a live and entertaining demonstration of Silbo Gomero (see p177), accompanied by, albeit, fairly bland food. It is essential to reserve in advance.

Vallehermoso

POP 1540
This truly is a 'beautiful valley', as its name translates. Small mountain peaks rise on either side of the deep gorge that runs through town, and the green, terraced hillsides dotted with palm trees complete the picture. Like Hermigua, this makes a good base for exploring the island on foot.

◎ Sights & Activities

The heart of town is **Plaza Constitución**; bars, services and much of the budget accommodation is around here. Take time to search out the stone **Iglesia de San Juan Bautista** behind the town centre.

Just outside town towers the volcanic monolith of **Roque Cano** (650m), a town icon visible from just about everywhere.

Vallehermoso Public Pool   SWIMMING
(admission €2; ⊙noon-6pm Tue-Sun May-Sep) Right on the waterfront near the Roque Cano there is this large public pool. Note that it is open during the summer months only.

🏖 Beaches

Playa de Vallehermoso   BEACH
(Vallehermoso) A beautiful strip of sand pounded by waves and hemmed in by tall cliffs on either side.

Eating

Haute cuisine it ain't, but there are a couple of bars serving tapas and simple meals on the main plaza. Self-caterers can find some fresh produce at the tiny **mercadillo** (⊙9am-1pm Mon-Sat), beside the town hall.

Restaurante Parque Marítimo   SEAFOOD $
(✏ 922 80 15 61; mains €7-9; ⊙ noon-4pm Tue-Sun May-Sep; P) An informal bar and restaurant by the beach, you can order paella, local fish and shellfish here while squinting at the shimmering ocean. It also has a good range of tapas.

Around Vallehermoso

Los Órganos

To contemplate this extraordinary cliffscape (something like a great sculpted church organ in basalt rising from the ocean depths) 4km north of Vallehermoso, you'll need to head out to sea. Boats making the trip set out from Valle Gran Rey in the south of the island. The columned cliff face has been battered into its present shape by the ocean.

Alojera

This sleepy settlement sits in a fertile valley that stands out as an oasis of green amid dry hills. Past the town itself, at the end of a nausea-inducing and seemingly endless series of hairpin curves, you reach pretty **Playa de Alojera**.

This place is no secret, but it's rarely crowded. The sweeping, silty black beach is ideal for swimming – at least when there's no swell; if a big swell is running, keep well away from the water. Cliffs, rock formations and natural pools offshore lend a sense of drama here.

Eating

Bar Prisma SEAFOOD $
(☑922 80 70 30; Playa de Alojera; mains €9-10; ⊙10am-10pm Thu-Tue) Overlooking fishing boats, this simple place serves (what else?) seafood dishes, including a recommended *sopa de pescado* (fish soup). Service can be gruff.

THE SOUTH

The sunniest part of La Gomera, the south is endlessly changing, from dry sunburnt peaks to lush banana-filled valleys, and from stern rocky coasts to silty black-sand beaches. This is where you'll find the island's two resort areas – the modest Playa Santiago and sprawling Valle Gran Rey. Heading here from San Sebastián on the TF-713, look out for the **Mirador Roque de Agando** (just after the turn-off to La Laja). At 1182m, this looming volcanic rock 'needle' is the most impressive in the Canaries.

Playa Santiago

POP 560

Playa Santiago is a small, ocean-side resort with a sleepy village centre and a long dark cobblestone beach with calm waters. The place is so quiet that often the only noise is that of the wind brushing through the banana leaves, the waves slapping the shore and the cock-a-doodle-dooing of cockerels.

Until the 1960s this area was the busiest centre on the island, with factories, a shipyard and a port for exporting local bananas and tomatoes. But the farming crisis hit hard, and by the 1970s the town had all but shut down, its inhabitants having fled to Tenerife or South America. In recent years, tourism has brought new life to the town and a huge luxury-hotel complex owned by Fred Olsen is doing more than its fair share to bring visitors this way.

Beaches

Besides the main beach, Playa Santiago, you can also head to three smaller beaches,

Playas de Tapahuga, del Medio and **de Chinguarime**, which have some sand mixed in with the rocks and are known as hippy hang-outs. Head east, past Hotel Jardín Tecina; the three lie at the end of a bumpy gravel track.

Playa Santiago BEACH
At Playa Santiago, splashing in the waves, rambling along the rocky shore and marvelling over the peaceful ocean view is likely to take up most of your time.

Activities

To get out on the water, you can hop on a cruise boat to go whale-watching.

Tina BOAT TOUR
(☑922 80 58 85; www.excursiones-tina.com; 4hr cruise adult/child €40/23; ⊙10am Mon, 9am Thu) A reputable company that runs whale-watching tours, which include a swim at a secluded beach and lunch.

Tecina Golf Course GOLF
(☑922 14 59 50; www.tecinagolf.com; Lomada del Tecina; 9/18 holes €60/100) A Fred Olsen initiative, this 18-hole golf course is the island's only one; it can be found just outside town.

Eating

Self-caterers will find all the basics at **Supermercado El Paso II** (Calle Anton Gil).

Bar La Chalana SEAFOOD $
(Blvd Colón Laguna; mains €7-9; ⊙10am-7pm) This delightful wooden beach shack, tucked away at the northern end of the beach, is part beach-bar with chilled-out Latin beats, part restaurant with a menu heavy in the fruits of the sea, part craft shop and part art gallery. Whichever bit appeals the most, you'll end up kicking back here for hours longer than anticipated.

★**Restaurante Junonia** INTERNATIONAL $$
(☑922 89 54 50; Avenida Marítima; mains €12-15; ⊙12.30-3.30pm & 6.30-10pm Wed-Mon) A local favourite opposite the harbour with an elegant dining room decorated with edgy contemporary artwork. Dishes include a sophisticated take on Italian dishes like black pasta with salmon in a lobster, vodka and prawn sauce, as well as exquisitely prepared simple fish plates including *dorada a la plancha* (grilled sea bream). Reservations recommended.

SILBO: GOMERO'S WHISTLING LANGUAGE

The first time you hear Silbo Gomero you might think that you're listening to two birds having a conversation. Alternately chirpy and melodic, shrill and deeply resonating, this ancient whistling language really is as lovely as birdsong. Silbo, once a dying art, but now being brought back to life, is steeped in history and boasts a complex vocabulary of more than 4000 whistled words that can be heard from kilometres away.

In pre-Hispanic Gomera, Silbo developed as the perfect tool for sending messages back and forth across the island's rugged terrain. In ideal conditions, it could be heard up to 4km away, saving islanders from struggling up hill and down dale just to deliver a message to a neighbour. At first, Silbo was probably used as an emergency signal, but over time a full language developed. While other forms of whistled communications have existed in pockets of Greece, Turkey, China and Mexico, none is as developed as Silbo Gomero.

Modern conveniences have all but killed the language, but in the past few years Silbo has gone from being La Gomera's near-forgotten heritage to being its prime cultural selling point. Silbo has been a mandatory school subject on the island since 2000, and in 2009 another lifeline was thrown to the language after it was inscribed on the Unesco List of Intangible Cultural Heritage of Humanity. This inclusion will allow more money to be pumped into the promotion of the language and is a big morale boost for *silbadores*.

La Cuevita   SEAFOOD $$

(📞 922 89 55 68; Avenida Marítima; mains €10-14; ⏱ noon-4pm & 7-10.30pm Mon-sat) Tucked into a natural cave beside a small *ermita* (chapel), with leafy plants and low lighting, La Cuevita serves fresh local seafood, such as tuna, *vieja* (parrotfish), *lapas* (limpets) and *chocos* (cuttlefish), along with grilled meats, all served with *papas arrugadas* and a tangy red *mojo*.

ℹ Information

All of Playa Santiago's services, including the post office, petrol station, pharmacy, police station and medical centre, are clustered around Plaza Playa Santiago in the heart of town.

Tourist Office (📞 922 89 56 50; www.lagomera.travel; Edificio Las Vistas, Avenida Marítima; ⏱ 9am-1pm Mon-Sat year-round, plus 4-6pm Mon-Fri winter) This helpful tourist office has plenty of brochures and local information. It is located on your right as you enter the town centre.

ℹ Getting There & Away

Bus 3 (€4, 30 minutes, up to five daily) links Playa Santiago with San Sebastián.

Call a taxi on 📞 922 89 50 22.

Alajeró & Around

POP 325

The palm trees outnumber the residents in this peaceful oasis situated on a ridge high above the ocean. Alajeró is the only sizeable village outside Playa Santiago in the southeast of the island. It boasts the modest 16th-century **Iglesia del Salvador**.

A good time to be in town is during the **Fiesta del Paso** in September when *gomeros* from far and wide converge on Alajeró to celebrate this chirpy procession that dances its way down from the mountains.

Alajeró is a good starting point for several **hikes**. The long-distance GR132 trail passes through town, as do the shorter PR LG 15 and 16. The latter heads downhill to Playa Santiago or, more challengingly, up to **Benchijigua**, a tiny settlement amid steep green slopes. Information plaques outlining the walks are near the church. If you want to stay in Benchijigua, there are a couple of memorable *casas rurales*. Another option is to take an 8km loop trail to Magaña, along the Lomo de la Montaña and past the island's oldest *drago* (dragon tree) before returning to Alajeró. Allow 2½ hours for the journey.

If you're driving, you can see the *drago* by taking an unsigned left turn, 1.25km north of Alajeró, as far as an old farmhouse, from where a trail drops steeply. If you're on the bus, get off at the Imada stop and turn left down a cobbled track to join this side road. Either way, allow a good 1½ hours for the round trip.

Bus 3 (€4, 40 minutes, up to five daily) runs between Alajeró and San Sebastián, stopping at Playa Santiago on the way. The bus stop is on the main highway.

LA GOMERA ALAJERÓ & AROUND

LA GOMERA FOR CHILDREN

La Gomera doesn't have any of the theme parks, zoos or water parks that make the bigger islands such kid magnets. The fun here is of a less flashy variety and depends on nature to provide the thrills.

The first stop for children is usually the beach. The long, calm beaches of Valle Gran Rey and Alojera, where there is a saltwater wading pool for little ones, are ideal, as is San Sebastián's beach. For tots who aren't strong swimmers, pools like the one in Valle-hermoso might be a better bet.

Short boat trips are guaranteed to brighten childrens' days. Trips to Los Órganos sail from Valle Gran Rey, along with half-day whale-watching cruises, which also sail from Playa Santiago.

You could also plan a stop in a recreational area like La Laguna Grande, a picnic spot and playground rolled into one where children can happily spend an entire afternoon running and playing.

Valle Gran Rey

POP 3440

Bet you can't make it all the way down to the shore without stopping at one of the lookout points to sigh at the natural beauty of the 'Valley of the Great King'. A deep, green gorge running down to meet the island's longest beach, this is La Gomera's tourist epicentre. If you speak German you'll feel right at home, as most services here are geared towards the many Germans in search of sunshine and nature. Talking of sunshine, it's worth noting that when the rest of the island is soaking in a light drizzle the Valle Gran Rey can be happily lazing about working on its suntan.

Before you descend into the valley, you could stop at the Ermita del Santo in Arure, where a tiny chapel is built into the rock face and is surrounded by a mirador showing off the southern landscape.

Also worth a stop, the Mirador César Manrique enjoys incredible views of Valle Gran Rey's gorge and the mountains that loom around it. The restaurant (mains €8-14; 12.30-4pm & 7-11pm Mon-Sat, noon-4.30pm Sun) serves average, rather than exceptional, Canarian dishes and is popular with coach tour groups.

A few kilometres further on is another of the area's many road-side chapels: the best feature of the Ermita de San Antonio is the view from the plaza outside.

Beaches

Though the lush valley itself is perhaps the best the Valle Gran Rey has to offer, most people head straight to the shore. The beaches here are among La Gomera's prettiest, with calm waters and lapping waves. It's worth remembering, though, that the Valle Gran Rey is often very windy.

Playa de las Vueltas   BEACH

The Playa de las Vueltas, beside the port, is the most wind-sheltered – and consequently often the busiest – of the town beaches. A gentle, soft black-sand beach, it's ideal for children, and the water is as calm and current-free as a pond. It also has the advantage of having a couple of bars just behind it; very handy in case mummy and daddy start to get a bit thirsty...

La Playa   BEACH

The beach at La Playa is long and sandy, with bars and a waterside boardwalk nearby.

Activities

Boat Trips

There are a few boat operators offering whale- and dolphin-watching tours.

Oceano   BOAT TOUR

(922 80 57 17; www.oceano-gomera.com; Calle Quema 7; adult/child €40/26; 9.30am-1pm & 5-7pm) Regarded as one of the best outfits, Oceano offers three times daily three- to four-hour tours throughout the year and donates a percentage of the cost to environmental and animal-welfare organisations.

Tina   BOAT TOUR

(922 80 58 85; www.excursiones-tina.com; adult €33-40, child €20) Cruises around the south and west of the island, towards Los Órganos. The day-long trip could include some spontaneous whale- or dolphin-watching, as well as a little tuna fishing. Tours run daily except Saturday and Monday.

Cycling & Hiking

Landlubbers will be pleased to know that Valle Gran Rey is the starting point for an endless array of hikes and cycling trips.

Bike Station Gomera CYCLING
(📋922 80 50 82; www.bike-station-gomera.com; La Puntilla 7, Valle Gran Rey; bike rental per day €21; ☺9am-1pm & 5-8pm) Island-wide bike tours.

Ökotours HIKING
(📋922 80 52 34; www.oekotours.com; Calle Vueltas, Vueltas, Valle Gran Rey; day hike per person €28-35; ☺10.30am-1pm & 5.30-7.30pm Mon-Fri, 10.30am-1pm Sat) Island-wide hiking tours for a mainly German clientele.

Timah HIKING
(📋922 80 70 84; www.timah.net; La Puntilla, Valle Gran Rey; day hike per person €31; ☺10am-1pm & 5-8pm Mon-Sat, 6-8pm Sun) Can organise multiday hiking holidays. A percentage of the profits goes to animal welfare charities.

✖ Eating

★**Bar-Restaurante El Puerto** SEAFOOD $
(📋922 80 52 24; Puerto de Vueltas; mains €6-9; 🅿) Specialising in fresh fish, this traditional place by the port is one of the best spots in town to try local delicacies such as grilled *peto* and *medregal* (both local fish). The clientele is mainly Spanish and the *menú del día* (daily set menu) is outstanding value at just €7. The atmosphere is informal and friendly; you may have to wait for a table on weekends.

Casa de Té INTERNATIONAL $
(Baja Secreto 5, Charco del Conde; mains €7-10; ☺9.30am-8pm Tue-Fri, to 10pm Sat, 10am-8pm Sun; 🐾) This laid-back place has books to borrow, homemade cakes and sharply presented dishes served on volcanic-black square plates. Choices range from salads to crêpes and veggie mains with seitan, as well as chicken and fish. There's a vegetarian buffet on Saturday (€10, 5pm to 10pm), which, thanks to the cocktails and the DJ, has a great party atmosphere.

La Namera INTERNATIONAL $
(Paseo Las Palmeras 8, La Playa; snacks €7-9; ☺9am-6.30pm Fri-Wed, from noon Thu; 🐾) In a wooden balconied building along La Playa's energetic stretch of restaurants and bars, this German-run place sells delicious breads and cakes as well as simple dishes, including salads and sandwiches, along with home-made lemonade. It is extremely popular and has an informal arty vibe.

Tuyo ASIAN $$
(www.tuyo-lagomera.com; Puerto de Vueltas; mains €10-15; ☺noon-3pm & 6-10pm Mon-Sat) Offering a touch of exotica amid the shoal of seafood restaurants in the harbour, this restaurant has an extensive menu of mainly Thai dishes including yellow and green curries and wok stir-fries. The decor is suitably soothing: all warm tones of ochre and yellow. Meditators take note: there are also regular vipassana group sits held here.

Restaurante La Islita ITALIAN $$
(📋922 80 61 61; Calle La Playa; mains €10-18; ☺6-10.30pm Mon-Sat) This is a smarter Italian restaurant than the pizza-pasta norm with some delicate and unusual sauces and plenty of vegetarian options. Note that it is a dress-for-dinner evening place only.

🍷 Drinking

Tambara Café BAR
(📋646 51 13 96; Calle Vueltas, Vueltas; ☺noon-4pm & 7-11pm Thu-Tue) By day enjoy Italian pasta and pizza and by night sip cocktails at this friendly bar, where the sound of breaking waves wafts over the breezy terrace.

Gomera Lounge CLUB
(Calle Punta de la Calera 1, La Playa; ☺8.30pm-1am Mon-Sat; 🛜) This smart central nightclub in La Playa has a great line-up of live music ranging from reggae to salsa to ensure that everyone can work on their hip-swinging skills.

ℹ Information

Tourist Kiosk (📋922 80 50 58; Carretera General; ☺8.30am-3.30pm Mon-Fri) This small wooden hut is off the main highway on your right as you head towards Vueltas.

Tourist Office (📋922 80 54 58; www.lagomera.travel; Calle Lepanto, La Playa; ☺9am-2pm Mon-Sat) Pick up a map and local information here.

ℹ Getting There & Away

Bus 1 (€5, 1¾ hours) connects with San Sebastián several times a day and leaves from the bus station located beside the large traffic circle at the entry to La Playa. To get to Vallehermoso, you can get off at the Las Hayas stop and wait for bus 4 (€4.50, one hour, twice daily Monday to Friday).

La Palma

🎵 922 / POP 86,000

Best Places to Eat

➡ Enriclai (p187)

➡ La Casa del Volcán (p192)

➡ Restaurante Chipi-Chipi (p190)

Best Places to Stay

➡ Hotel La Palma Romántica (p233)

➡ Hotel San Telmo (p232)

Why Go?

La Palma, the greenest of the Canarian islands, offers the chance to experience real, unspoiled nature – from the verdant forests of the north, where lush vegetation drips from the rainforest canopy; to the desertscapes of the south, where volcanic craters and twisted rock formations define the views; to the serene pine forests of the Parque Nacional de la Caldera de Taburiente. No wonder the entire island has been declared a Unesco biosphere reserve.

The absence of golden beaches has diverted many travellers' attention, and tourism (aside from walkers and cruise liners) has yet to make a major mark on the island. The capital is also an architectural gem, with its 16th-century centre lined by beautiful balconied mansions and houses.

In fact it is hard to find an unattractive corner on La Isla Bonita (the Pretty Island) and, provided unchecked development stays at bay, it is likely to remain that way.

When to Go

➡ Spring and autumn offer the most pleasant conditions for hiking, with generally clear skies and warm temperatures.

➡ As the most northwesterly island, La Palma catches more Atlantic cloud, and rain, than any other island and winters in the north can be quite wet.

➡ Carnaval (March/April) in Santa Cruz is an unmissable spectacle of costumes, floats and, ahem, talcum powder...

History

Long before Castilla (Spain) conquered the island in the 15th century, this rugged land was known as Benahoare. The first inhabitants are thought to have arrived as early as the 5th century BC. The island officially became part of the Spanish empire in 1493, after Alonso Fernández de Lugo (a conquistador and, later, island governor) used a tribesman-turned-Christian to trick the Benahoaritas into coming down from their mountain stronghold for 'peace talks'. They were ambushed on the way at the spot now known as El Riachuelo. Their leader, Tanausú, was shipped to Spain as a slave, but went on a heroic hunger strike on board the boat and never saw the Spanish mainland.

The next century was an important one for the island. Sugar, honey and sweet *malvasía* (Malmsey wine) became the major exports and abundant Canary pine provided timber for burgeoning shipyards. By the late 16th century, as transatlantic trade flourished, Santa Cruz de la Palma was considered the third most important port in the Spanish empire, after Seville and Antwerp.

The sugar, shipbuilding and cochineal (a beetle used to make red dye) industries kept the island economy afloat for the next several centuries, but the island's fortunes eventually took a downward turn, and the 20th century was one of poverty and mass emigration, mainly to Venezuela, Uruguay and Cuba. These days around 40% of the island's workforce depends on the banana crop, but the tourism industry is gradually gaining ground and Santa Cruz port is becoming increasingly popular as a cruise ship port of call.

❶ Getting There & Away

AIR
La Palma's **airport** (☑ 902 40 47 04, 922 41 15 40; www.aena.es) is located 7km from Santa Cruz. Services here include car-rental agencies, a currency-exchange bureau, restaurant and a small **tourist office** (☑ 922 42 62 12; www.tourlapalma.com; Airport; ☉ 9am-1pm & 3-6pm).

Airline **Binter Canarias** (☑ 902 39 13 92; www.bintercanarias.com) keeps La Palma well connected to the rest of the archipelago, with several flights daily to Tenerife and Gran Canaria, and more occasional direct flights to some of the other islands.

BOAT
The **Fred Olsen** (☑ 902 10 01 07; www.fred-olsen.es) ferry (€42, two hours) leaves Los Cristianos, Tenerife, at 7pm, and the return trip

leaves Santa Cruz at 5.45am. From Tenerife, you can then continue to La Gomera or El Hierro.

Naviera Armas (☑ 922 79 61 78; www.navieraarmas.com) connects La Palma with the following:

➡ San Sebastián de la Gomera, La Gomera (€24, 2¼ hours, one daily Tuesday to Sunday)

➡ Los Cristianos, Tenerife (€41, 3½ hours, one daily Tuesday to Sunday)

➡ Las Palmas de Gran Canaria, Gran Canaria (€72, 14½ hours, one daily Tuesday to Sunday) with stops at La Gomera and Tenerife

Trasmediterránea (☑ 902 45 46 45; www.trasmediterranea.es) sails the ocean blue for Santa Cruz de la Tenerife, Tenerife (€22, 5½ hours, 4pm Friday). The same boat continues on to Las Palmas de Gran Canaria, Gran Canaria, and Cádiz, Andalucía, in one and three days respectively.

❶ Getting Around

BUS
Transportes Insular (☑ 922 41 19 24; www.transporteslapalma.com; Avenida Los Indianos 14) La Palma buses keep Santa Cruz well connected with the rest of the island. The bus stops are near Plaza Constitución and along Avenida Marítima. Routes include bus 1 (€5.50, 45 minutes) to Los Llanos de Aridane every half-hour or so. If you plan to use the bus often, consider buying a Bono Bus discount card. Cards start at €12 and represent a discount of about 20% off normal individual fares. They are on sale at bus stations, newsstands and tobacco shops and are valid on buses across the island.

CAR
Having your own car is the best way to explore the island. La Palma has plenty of car-rental agencies located throughout the island.

Cicar (☑ 922 42 80 48; www.cicar.com; La Palma airport) Also has an office at the port in Santa Cruz.

Oasis (☑ 922 43 44 09; www.oasis-la-palma.com; Centro Cancajos local 301, Los Cancajos) A reliable local car rental company that also operates out of La Gomera.

ROAD DISTANCES (KM)

	Santa Cruz de la Palma	Los Canarios de Fuencaliente	Puerto Naos	Barlovento
Los Canarios de Fuencaliente	25			
Puerto Naos	47	22		
Barlovento	19	42	44	
El Paso	17	22	10	34

Approximate distances only

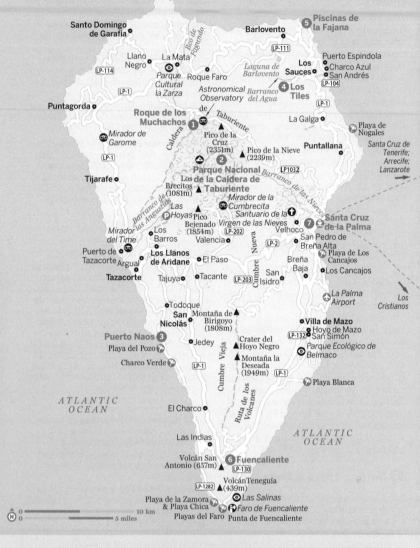

Santo Domingo
de Garafía

Barlovento

5 Piscinas de
la Fajana

Llano
Negro

La Mata

LP-111

*Pico de
la nogemol*

Puerto Espíndola

*Parque
Cultural
la Zarza*

Roque Faro

LP-114

*Laguna de
Barlovento*

Los
Sauces

Charco Azul

San Andrés

LP-104

LP-1

*Astronomical
Observatory*

*Barranco
del Agua*

4 Los
Tiles

Puntagorda

**Roque de los
Muchachos** **1**

de

Taburiente

LP-1

La Galga

Playa de
Nogales

*Mirador de
Garome*

Caldera

Pico de la
Cruz
(2351m)

Pico de la Nieve
(2239m)

Puntallana

Santa Cruz de
Tenerife;
Arrecife;
Lanzarote

LP-1

**Parque Nacional
de la Caldera de
Taburiente** **2**

Los
Brecitos
(1081m)

LP1032

Barranco de las Nieves

Tijarafe

*Mirador de la
Cumbrecita*

*Las
Hoyas*

Pico
Bejenado
(1854m)

*Santuario de la
Virgen de las Nieves*

7 **Sánta Cruz
de la Palma**

Velhoco

LP-202

*Mirador
del Time*

Los
Barros

Valencia

Nueva

San Pedro de
Breña Alta

LP-2

Puerto de
Tazacorte

Arguál

**Los Llanos
de Aridane**

El Paso

Cumbre

Breña
Baja

Playa de Los
Cancajos

Los Cancajos

Tazacorte

Tajuya

Tacante

San
Isidro

LP-203

*La Palma
Airport*

*Los
Cristianos*

Todoque

Montaña de
Birigoyo
(1808m)

Villa de Mazo

Hoyo de Mazo

San Simón

**San
Nicolás**

Puerto Naos **3**

Jedey

Crater del
Hoyo Negro

LP-132

*Parque Ecológico de
Belmaco*

Playa del Pozo

Charco Verde

LP-1

Montaña la
Deseada
(1949m)

Cumbre Vieja

*Ruta de los
Volcanes*

LP-1

Playa Blanca

*ATLANTIC
OCEAN*

El Charco

Las Indias

*ATLANTIC
OCEAN*

Volcán San
Antonio (657m)

6 **Fuencaliente**

LP-130

VolcánTeneguía
(439m)

LP-1282

Las Salinas

Playa de la Zamora
& Playa Chica

Playas del Faro

Faro de Fuencaliente

Punta de Fuencaliente

N

0   10 km
0   5 miles

La Palma Highlights

1 Peer up at the night sky from the **Roque de los Muchachos** (p196), a world-class spot for stargazing

2 Explore the natural wonderland of the **Parque Nacional de la Caldera de Taburiente** (p194)

3 Bask in the sun and the breeze under the swaying

palms of the black-sand beach at **Puerto Naos** (p198)

4 Grab a rain jacket and hiking boots for a trek through the enchanted jungle-like forest of **Los Tiles** (p199)

5 Take a dip in the saltwater pools around **Piscinas de la Fajana** (p201)

6 Visit the lunar landscape and visitor centre at **Fuencaliente** (p191) and gaze into the yawning chasm of a 20th-century volcano

7 Walk with wonder through the historic streets of **Santa Cruz de la Palma** (p183) with its picturesque colourful buildings

SANTA CRUZ DE LA PALMA

POP 17,265

The historic (and bureaucratic) capital of the island, Santa Cruz de la Palma is a compact city strung out along the shore and flanked by fertile green hills. The city centre is breathtakingly picturesque, while the newly overhauled beach and kilometre-long promenade have considerably boosted the city's summer-in-the-sun appeal.

History

In the 16th century the dockyards of Santa Cruz earned a reputation as the best in all the Canary Islands. Ships were made with Canary pine, a sap-filled wood that was nearly impervious to termites, making the ships constructed here some of the most reliable and longest-lasting in the world. The town became so important that King Felipe II had the first Juzgado de Indias (Court of the Indias) installed here in 1558, and every single vessel trading with the Americas from mainland Spain was obliged to register.

The boom brought economic security, but it led to problems as well. Santa Cruz was frequently besieged and occasionally sacked by a succession of pirates, including those under the command of Sir Francis Drake.

◎ Sights

After a stroll along the inviting new beachside promenade, head for Calle O'Daly, the city's main street. Named after an Irish banana merchant who made La Palma his home, the street is full of shops, bars and some of the town's most impressive architecture and sights.

Old Town   HISTORIC SITE
The 17th-century, late-Renaissance **Palacio de Salazar** (☑ 922 41 19 57; Calle O'Daly 22; ⊙ 10am-8pm Mon-Fri, to 2pm Sat) is on your left soon after you enter the street from Plaza Constitución. It's now home to a government-run cultural centre.

Wander north along Calle O'Daly and you'll come to the palm-shaded **Plaza España**, considered the most important example of Renaissance architecture in the Canary Islands. To one side sits the imposing **ayuntamiento** (town hall; ☑ 922 42 65 00; ⊙ 9am-2pm Mon-Fri), built in 1559 after the original was destroyed by French pirates.

Follow the steps heading up out of Plaza España to reach the upper town, where the

shady **Plaza Santo Domingo**, with its terrace cafe, makes an excellent resting point. The **Iglesia de Santo Domingo** (Plaza Santo Domingo; ⊙ opening hours vary) here boasts an important collection of Flemish paintings.

Head southwest on Calle Virgen de la Luz for a look at the simple 17th-century facade of the modest chapel **Ermita de Nuestra Señora de la Luz** (⊙ opening hours vary), one of several small 16th- and 17th-century chapels in town. Another chapel, the **Ermita de San Sebastián** (Calle San Sebastián; ⊙ opening hours vary), is behind the Iglesia de San Salvador. Yet another is **Ermita de San José** (Calle San José; ⊙ opening hours vary), which has given its name to the street on which it stands. From this chapel make your way northeast towards the **Iglesia de San Francisco** (Plaza San Francisco; ⊙ 6-7.30pm), another Renaissance church with a magnificent coffered ceiling.

Wander down to the waterfront to stroll alongside a series of wonderful **old houses** with traditional Canarian balconies overflowing with flowers. Many of the houses date from the 16th century and have been converted into upscale restaurants. The islanders' penchant for balconies came with Andalucian migrants and was modified by Portuguese influences. At the northern end of the seafront, the **Castillo de Santa Catalina** (⊙ 10am-2pm Mon-Fri) was one of several forts built in the 17th century to fend off pirate raids. Across the ravine and higher is a smaller fort, the **Castillo de la Virgen**. Tucked away on the same hill is the 16th-century **Iglesia de la Encarnación** (⊙ opening hours vary), the first church to be built in Santa Cruz after the Spanish conquest.

★**Museo Insular**   MUSEUM
(Plaza San Francisco 3; adult/child €4/free; ⊙ 10am-7.30pm Mon-Sat, to 2pm Sun) This is an excellent museum housed in a former 16th-century monastery. The diverse exhibits range from Guanche skulls to cupboards of sad stuffed birds, pickled reptiles, and an impressive shell and coral collection. There are also galleries dedicated to 20th-century Spanish paintings, as well as some top-quality (and suitably edgy) contemporary art.

★**Iglesia del Salvador**   CHURCH
(Plaza España; ⊙ 9.30am-1pm & 5.30-7.30pm) Though the church's exterior seems more fortress than house of worship, the interior is fabulous so be sure to step inside. It boasts a glittering baroque pulpit dating back to

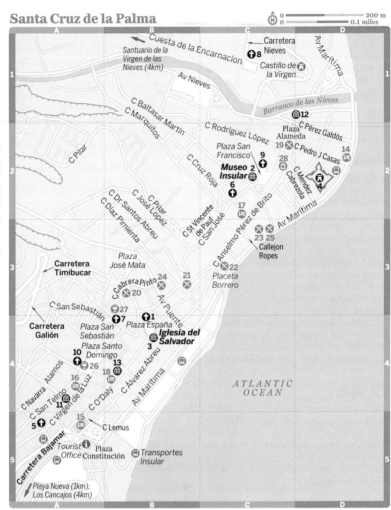

1750 and a stunning ornate and coloured 16th-century wooden ceiling considered to be one of the best Mudéjar (Islamic-style architecture) works in all the Canaries. There are also several fine sculptures and dazzling stained-glass windows.

Museo de Arte Contemporaneo MUSEUM
(☑ 922 41 63 04; 13 Calle Virgen de la Luz; adult/child €3/free; ☺ 10am-3pm Mon-Fri) This contemporary art gallery opened in 2014 and specialises in Canarian artists, with paintings, sculptures and photographs exhibited in several light and spacious galleries. Look for the evocative photographic portrait *Un Aquello Amor* by Jorge Lozano.

Museo Naval MUSEUM
(Calle Pérez Galdós; adult/child €3/1.50; ☺ 10am-2pm Mon-Fri) Gaze north across leafy Plaza Alameda (the *kiosco* here is a good place to sip a *café cortado* – an espresso with a splash of milk) and you'll think Christopher Columbus' ship, the *Santa María,* became stranded here. But no, it's actually the city's naval museum where you can see some magnificent model ships among other marine-related exhibits.

Santa Cruz de la Palma

⭐**Santuario de la Virgen de las Nieves** CHURCH
(Avenida las Nieves; ⏱ 8.30am-8pm; 🅿) For great views over Santa Cruz, take the relatively easy 2km hike north of town to La Palma's main object of pilgrimage, the 17th-century Santuario de la Virgen de las Nieves with its fabulously ornate interior. The wooden Mudéjar-carved ceiling, sculptures galore and sparkling crystal chandeliers are the precursor to the Virgin Mary herself, surrounded by a glittering altar. This 14th-century sculpture is the oldest religious statue in the Canary Islands and is captivatingly original and almost contemporary in its design.

The sculpture was believed to have been brought by merchants before the arrival of the Spaniards; every five years she is carried down to Santa Cruz in a grand procession.

The church sits in a peaceful spot surrounded by trees and greenery, all in typical Canarian colonial style with balconies and simple facades. To walk from Plaza Alameda, follow the road, which becomes a signposted dirt track, westwards up the gorge of the Barranco de las Nieves. It will take nearly 45 minutes to walk up, but coming back is faster. By car, follow signs from Avenida Marítima where it crosses the *barranco* (ravine), then turn right on the Carretera de las Nieves (LP-101) and continue winding up the hillside until you see signs for the sanctuary. The curve-filled 5km trip takes nearly 15 minutes. Bus 10 (€2, approximately 20 minutes) comes up hourly from the town centre from 6.45am

until 8.45pm, less frequently on weekends. There's a restaurant in the church grounds, as well as a children's playground.

🎉 Festivals & Events

Santa Cruz has several memorable knees-up fiestas, as well as more sombre annual events.

Semana Santa RELIGIOUS
(⏱ late Mar-early Apr) Members of lay brotherhoods parade down Calle O'Daly (Santa Cruz) in their blood-red robes and tall, pointy hoods.

Carnaval CARNIVAL
(⏱ 2 weeks in Feb, exact dates vary) This is a riotous two-week celebration with music, dancing and drinking, including that infamous crazy night of talcum-powder throwing, known as **Día de Los Indianos** (p187).

Fiesta de Nuestra Señora de las Nieves RELIGIOUS
(⏱ Jul-Aug) This 'Feast Day of Our Lady of the Snows' is the island's principal fiesta. Don't miss the parade of giants and 'fat heads' (fanciful, rather squat characters with exceptionally large heads), though the high point is the dance of the dwarves, which has been performed here since the early 19th century. The fiesta is celebrated every five years (2020, 2025 etc). It's a religious procession where the islanders take the Virgin around the island throughout July and August, celebrating her arrival in each important town with a big party.

🍴 Eating

Many of Santa Cruz's best restaurants are located along Avenida Marítima, as well as on Calle Anselmo Pérez de Brito in the historic centre.

Mercado Municipal
MARKET **$**

(Avenida Puente; ⊘7am-2pm Mon-Sat) An excellent market for fresh produce as well as deli items, located in a former 16th-century hospital. Try a sugar-cane juice with rum, mint and lemon (€4), sold at a stand here – or possibly without the rum if it's 7am in the morning!

Casa Luís
CANARIAN **$**

(Taburiente; Calle Pedro Poggio 7; mains €7-8.50, menú €10; ⊘10.30am-midnight) Look for the barn-like doors at this locals' place fittingly decorated with faded black-and-white photos of Santa Cruz in yesteryear. Portions are huge, but don't bother asking for a menu; it's whatever struck the owner's fancy that day, but one thing is for sure – the food will be traditional Canarian cuisine through and through.

Bar-Arepera El Encuentro
VENEZUELAN **$**

(Calle Anselmo Pérez de Brito; arepas €1.90, cachapas €2.70; ⊘8.30am-1am; 🕸) Cheap and tasty, Venezuelan *arepas* (hot pockets made of corn or flour and filled with meat or cheese) and *cachapas* (stuffed corn pancakes) are an island staple. The setting is wonderful on a lovely shady square overlooking the historic Cruz de Tercero (1893) monument.

THREE PERFECT DAYS IN LA PALMA

Day One

Wake up in a room with a view in the romantic by name, romantic by nature, **Hotel La Palma Romántica**, a short distance from the northern town of **Barlovento**. From here drive south to the **Los Tiles biosphere reserve**, a fantastic jungle-like forest, and head out on a morning's hike under the shadows of giant trees dripping in moss and water. Tarzan adventures over, drive the short distance to **San Andrés** for the surprise of an Asian-inspired lunch at **La Placita** (p199) and a stroll around the pretty cobbled streets. Next, drive back towards Barlovento but veer off down the steep hillside cloaked in banana plants to the soaring cliffs around the **Piscinas de la Fajana**. The pools themselves are perfect for a bracing swim, and the **La Gaviota** (p201) restaurant that overlooks them is equally perfect for a sunset meal of fresh seafood.

Day Two

Start your day exploring the picturesque streets of **Santa Cruz**, not forgetting to check out the town's famous old waterfront balconies. Drive south for a seafood lunch under the roar of aeroplanes at **Casa Goyo** (p190), which is arguably the best seafood restaurant on an island full of seafood restaurants. Continue on to quaint **Villa de Mazo** for a look at the handicraft museum (and shopping). Wallet lightened, carry on south through an increasingly barren, volcanic terrain to **Fuencaliente**, where you can check for volcanic eruptions in the excellent visitors centre at the **Volcán San Antonio** and then get up close and personal with said volcano on the short and spectacular walk along its crater rim. If time allows, make a diversion to the tip of the island and the **Playas del Faro**. Otherwise push on up the west coast to the attractive resort of **Puerto Naos** and your night stop.

Day Three

It's the central mountains that really bring visitors to La Palma, and this stunning area absolutely lives up to the hype. From Puerto Naos, take the winding road upward to the **Parque Nacional de la Caldera de Taburiente**, where you can lace up your boots and head out on a half-day hike. The walks fanning out from the **Mirador de la Cumbrecita** are the most popular and generally the easiest. If you've got more time, and are feeling fit, then the five-hour clamber to the summit of the **Pico Bejenado** is well worthwhile. Before you start your walk, though, don't forget to call by the excellent visitor centre to learn all about the park's history and wildlife (and if you're doing one of the Mirador de la Cumbrecita walks you have to register here). Afterwards treat your sore and blistered feet to lunch in **Los Llanos de Aridane**. Then, double back and drive the short way to **El Paso**, where you can learn all about the secrets of silk at the **Museo de la Seda** (p193). Return to Puerto Naos for a fish supper under the stars.

DON'T MISS

CARNAVAL: DÍA DE LOS INDIANOS

Tenerife and Gran Canaria are known for their, ahem, lively celebrations of Carnaval, but unassuming Santa Cruz de la Palma also has a wild side. For two weeks in February (exact dates vary) there's music, dancing, drinking and, of course, talcum powder. Known here as Día de Los Indianos, on Carnaval Monday the good citizens of La Palma bring buckets of white, fragrant powder down to the centre of Santa Cruz and prepare to do battle with their neighbours. After loosening up with a few drinks and a little music, the snowy spectacle begins. Anyone is a target in this all-out war and the town ends the night coughing and blinking furiously, covered head to toe with talcum powder. The tradition began to mock *los indios,* Canarian emigrants who became wealthy in the Americas and returned to the island decked out in white suits and Panama hats. Now it's just another excuse for a fiesta.

Habana
CANARIAN **$**

(Calle Anselmo Pérez de Brito 27; mains €7.50-9; ⊙8.30am-11pm) This delightful pink-and-white wedding cake of a building has its terrace on a picturesque plaza overlooking a fountain and surrounded by flower-filled balconies. The coffee is the best in town and the dishes, although limited (and light), won't disappoint with a range that includes risottos, bruschettas and fried cheese with *mojo* (Canarian spicy salsa). Cuban-run, the music should get you foot-tapping, as well.

★ Enriclai
CONTEMPORARY CANARIAN **$$**

(☑687 37 14 53; Calle Dr Santos Abreu 2; mains €12.50-15; ⊙12.30-3.30pm & 7.30-10.30pm Tue-Sat, 7-11pm Sun & Mon; ☑) Just four tables, a 200-year-old building, cool jazz on the soundtrack and a choice of dishes that alters daily according to what is fresh in season. Plus Carmen, an owner-cum-chef who is such a delight you will want to adopt her. The food includes vegetarian options and ecological wines.

Choices can vary from dishes like spinach *pastel* (bake) with a chickpea sauce to simple grilled fish with a slice of lemon. And, nope, you won't hear that dreaded ping of the devil's tumble dryer here – and nothing is fried.

Pizzeria Piccolo
ITALIAN **$$**

(Avenida Marítima 53; pizzas €7-10, pastas €11-13; ⊙noon-4pm & 7pm-midnight Wed-Mon) A slice above the pizza norm, these have crisp thin bases and generous toppings. The homemade pastas are *al dente* delicious, plus there are lighter bites like focaccias and salads. The building is head-spinningly historic with beams, original tiles and loads of creaky atmosphere.

La Lonja
SPANISH **$$**

(☑922 41 52 66; www.lalonjarestaurante.com; Avenida Marítima 55; mains €12-18; ⊙noon-11pm Wed-Mon) Occupying an old Canary house on the seafront with balconies bursting with colourful flowers, La Lonja is perhaps the city's most upscale restaurant, with a mix of Canarian, Castillian and Mediterranean fare, like paella, suckling pig and roasted cheese with *mojo*. It can also prepare more creative and unusual dishes, such as eel and prawns in a cream sauce.

🍷 Drinking

Santa Cruz does not have a wild nightlife; that said, there are plenty of quiet terrace bars where you can nurse a drink or two. Along Avenida Marítima, which is lined with cafes and *zumerías* (juice bars), you'll find a family-friendly atmosphere. In town head to Calle Álvarez Abreu, the closest thing you'll find to a nightlife scene. Plaza José Mata, off Avenida Puente, also has a few late-night bars.

El Portugués Café
BAR

(☑922 41 41 26; Calle San Sebastián 4; ⊙noon-midnight Tue-Sun) A work in progress, but definitely worth dropping by. Owner Ángel is restoring his Portuguese grandmother's fabulous 17th-century house which, to date, contains an atmospheric bar with a central courtyard terrace complete with goldfish pond (the former cistern); live music is being planned – and even a boutique hotel. Check it out.

Cinnamon Bar
BAR

(☑922 41 02 24; Calle San Telmo 2; cocktails €4.50, tablas €7-8; ⊙12.30-4pm & 7.30-11pm; ☎) The interior here is all sharp lines and dazzling white contrasting with red and black, while the tables outside sit beneath the gracious Iglesia de Santo Domingo on one of the most attractive squares in the city. A bar primarily, but also serves *tablas* (platters) to share.

THE SWEET TASTE OF LA PALMA

La Palma's main dishes, like those on other islands, are simple. What the island is really known for is indulgent desserts. Honey is an important food here, and historically La Palma was an important sugar producer. Most of the sugar cane is gone, but the islanders' sweet tooth remains; head to the **mercado municipal** (p186) in Santa Cruz to taste sugar cane juice, which you can have combined with rum, lemon and mint if you're feeling racy. The honey-and-almond desserts *rapaduras* are justifiably popular; also tasty are *almendrados* (almond, sugar and egg cakes baked with cinnamon), *bienmesabe* (a paste of almonds and sugar) and *Príncipe Alberto* (mousse of chocolate and almonds).

Local cheeses, most made with unpasteurised goat's milk and many smoked, are worth trying. Glean more information online at www.quesopalmero.es. For an excellent selection of locally produced cheese, as well as wines and deli items, check out **Vinatería Albillo** (☑ 922 41 08 95; Calle Anselmo Pérez de Brito 59, Santa Cruz de Palma; ⊙ 10am-1.30pm & 5-7pm Mon-Fri, 10am-2pm Sat) in Santa Cruz.

❶ Information

Tourist Office (☑ 922 41 21 06; www.lapalmacit.com; Plaza Constitución; ⊙ 9am-2pm & 4-7.30pm Mon-Fri, 9am-2pm Sat & Sun) This small office stocks lots of information about the town and the island, whether you're interested in hiking, festivals, history or gastronomy.

❶ Getting Around

Bus 8 (€1.50, 35 minutes) makes the journey between Santa Cruz and the airport every 30 minutes from 6.45am to 12.15am, stopping in Los Cancajos on the way. At weekends, the service is provided only hourly. A taxi to the airport costs about €17.

The best way to get around Santa Cruz is on foot. If you come in by car, try to find a parking spot by the waterfront, as the narrow streets are much better enjoyed while walking. If you're in a hurry you can catch one of the buses that run up and down the Avenida Marítima (€1.35) or hop in a **taxi** (☑ 922 18 13 96).

AROUND SANTA CRUZ

Los Cancajos

An appealing waterfront promenade and a small volcanic beach are the main attractions of this cluster of hotels, apartments and restaurants 4km south of Santa Cruz. Los Cancajos has none of the charm of Santa Cruz or other authentic, lived-in towns, but it nevertheless makes a good home base thanks to its abundance of quality lodging options and agreeable beach, which is one of the best on the island. There's a well-stocked **tourist office** (☑ 922 18 13 54; www.lapalmacit.

com; Calle Punta de la Arena, Playa los Cancajos; ⊙ 9am-1pm & 4.30-7pm Mon-Fri, 10am-2pm Sat) on the waterfront.

🏃 Activities

Los Cancajos is a popular spot for diving and is also the base for several tour operators. For something a bit less energetic, don't miss taking a gentle predinner stroll along the seafront promenade. The 20-minute walk takes you past tiny coves and contorted lava flows that have been colonised by hardy plants that seem almost luminous in comparison to the dramatic black rocks on which they live.

Buceo Sub   DIVING
(☑ 922 18 11 13; www.4dive.org; Costa Salinas, Local 3; dive incl equipment from €35; ⊙ 9.30am-6pm Tue-Sat) A reputable diving operator located next to the Spar supermarket with a number of diving packages available, as well as canoeing courses.

La Palma Diving Center   DIVING
(☑ 922 18 13 93; www.la-palma-diving.com; Centro Comercial Los Cancajos, Local 227; dive incl equipment €40; ⊙ 10am-6pm Mon-Sat) Located in the main Los Cancajos shopping centre and aimed mainly at a German clientele, although instructors do speak English.

Natour   HIKING
(☑ 922 43 30 01; www.natour-trekking.com; Apartamentos Valentina 4; guided hikes €35-50; ⊙ 9am-1pm & 5-7pm Mon-Fri) Natour is one of the best-regarded local hiking companies in La Palma and organises a variety of island-wide hiking trips under the guidance of multilingual guides.

Eating

The area around the Centro Comercial Los Cancajos (shopping centre) has several reputable restaurants and bars, many with terraces.

El Pulpo   SEAFOOD **$$**
(☑922 43 49 14; Playa los Cancajos; mains €10-16; ⊗1-3.30pm & 6-10.30pm) This simple beach restaurant started as a rough-and-ready shack back in 1971 and is still renowned by locals as being one of the best places to enjoy fried fish. With chairs sprawled on a terrace on the sand, it's justifiably popular for families with bucket-and-spade aged toddlers.

Restaurante La Fontana   ITALIAN **$$**
(Playa los Cancajos; pizzas €8-10, pastas €9-14; ⊗1-4pm & 6-10.30pm Tue-Sun; P) Overlooking the banana groves and main beach, come here for tasty wood-oven pizzas, various pasta dishes and some delicious desserts (try the almond cake). It'll also package everything up for a picnic on the beach.

Drinking & Entertainment

A handful of bars and terraces scattered behind the Centro Comercial Los Cancajos serves as Los Cancajos' nightlife centre. Offerings vary wildly by season and night, and you may find anything from DJs and dancing, to live music, to a quiet sip-your-drink-and-chat atmosphere.

Getting There & Away

Bus 8 (€1.20, 10 minutes) passes through Los Cancajos every 30 minutes on its way from Santa Cruz to the airport; a second bus does the route in reverse. The main bus stop is at the Centro Comercial Los Cancajos.

Breña Alta

POP 6670
Just outside Santa Cruz, this rural, tranquil area isn't a major destination but it is home to a few notable sights, renowned artisans and the Parador Nacional hotel.

Sights

Maroparque   ZOO
(www.maroparque.com; Calle Cuesta 28; adult/child €11/5.50; ⊗11am-5pm Mon-Fri, to 6pm Sat & Sun; P) Children will love Maroparque, a small zoo where marmosets, toucans and pythons clamber, flap and slide around their (thankfully) spacious cages. Don't miss the latest

residents: a pair of unusual albino wallabies. The zoo is set in pleasantly landscaped gardens and refreshments are available.

THE SOUTH

A truly diverse mix of pine forests, banana plantations, agricultural land and barren volcanic wastelands characterises southern La Palma. The Fuencaliente area, at the southern tip of the island, is home to the most recent volcanic activity in the islands with several eruptions recorded in the 20th century.

Villa de Mazo

POP 4760
A quiet village 13km south of Santa Cruz, Villa de Mazo is surrounded by green, dormant volcanoes. The town is known for its cigars and handicrafts and for being a highlight of La Palma's **winery route** (www.enoturismolapalma.es), an island-wide series of driving routes that take in the best of the island by way of the pleasure of the grape. Leaflets detailing the routes can be picked up at tourist offices or downloaded from the website.

Sights

★ Museo Casa Roja   MUSEUM
(☑922 42 85 87; www.villademazo.es; Calle Maximiliano Pérez Díaz; adult/child €2/free; ⊗10am-2pm Mon-Sat) As soon as you enter town, follow the signs to this lovely ochre-red mansion (built in 1911) with exhibits on embroidery and Corpus Christi – a festival Villa de Mazo celebrates with particular gusto: streets are decorated with elegant 'carpets' made of flower petals, seeds and soil. The house itself has an impressive imperial staircase and ornate tiled floors.

Escuela Insular de Artesanía   MUSEUM
(☑922 44 00 52; Vía de Enlace Doctor Amilcar Morera Bravo 1; adult/child €2/free; ⊗10am-2pm Mon-Fri) This former handicrafts school still has a weaving studio, which you can peek into, but otherwise has been transformed into a museum focusing on crafts and handicrafts on the island. There is a short multilingual film and a shop where you can buy embroidery, ceramics, baskets and other locally produced crafts.

DON'T MISS

HIDDEN DINING GEMS

Some of the island's best restaurants are a short drive from Santa Cruz. For unbeatable local flavour, it doesn't get any better than this.

Restaurante Chipi-Chipi (☑922 41 10 24; Calle Juan Mayor 42, Velhoco; mains €10-15; ◷noon-5pm & 7-11.30pm Mon-Tue & Thu-Sat; P⛟) Despite the name, this is no greasy diner, but a famous local restaurant that specialises in a variety of grilled meats, all served with loads of *papas arrugadas* (wrinkly potatoes) and *mojo* (spicy sauce).

It's located between the Santuario de la Virgen de las Nieves and the village of San Pedro, on the edge of the small hamlet of Velhoco, and has pretty, rambling gardens with individual dining areas, as well as a central terrace.

Casa Goyo (☑922 44 06 03; Carretera General Lodero 120, Los Cancajos; mains €10-15; ◷1-4.30pm Tue-Sun; P) This one-time simple palm-roofed shack has grown to become one of the most famous seafood restaurants on the island. Hear the roar of the planes as you savour *vieja a la plancha* (pan-grilled parrotfish) and *papas* (potatoes). And, yes, the fish here really *is* as fresh as that day's catch.

Templo de San Blas   CHURCH
(◷opening hours vary; P) Down a steep hill from the centre of town is this lovely white-washed church dating from 1512 and over-looking the ocean. Inside, the church boasts a baroque altarpiece and several interesting pieces of baroque art.

Mercado   MARKET
(Vía de Enlace Doctor Amilcar Morera Bravo; ◷3-7pm Sat, 9am-1pm Sun) Produce, handicrafts and textiles are sold at this weekend market.

Cerámica el Molino   MUSEUM
(☑922 44 02 13; Carretera Hoyo de Mazo; ◷9am-1pm & 3-7pm Mon-Sat; P) Well signposted from the town is this meticulously restored mill that houses a ceramics museum (including a short audiovisual presentation) and workshop where artisans make reproductions of Benahoare pottery. There's a vast and popular souvenir shop as well. You can also get here from the LP-132 highway.

✖ Eating

San Blas   CANARIAN $
(Calle Maria del Carmen Martínez Jerez 4; mains €8-10; ◷7am-3pm & 5.30-10.30pm Tue-Thu, to 11pm Fri, 9am-11pm Sat, to 3pm Sun; ⛟) In the centre of town, get simple dishes like pastas, salads, *chocos* (cuttlefish) with *mojo verde* (a coriander-based sauce) or goat with potatoes, served on a pretty outdoor terrace surrounded by stout palms and a dazzle of flowers.

La Cabaña   CANARIAN $
(Carretera a Fuencaliente, Km 6; mains €7-12; ◷11am-11pm Tue-Sun; P) Grab a pew on the terrace of this simple seafood restaurant with its seamless sea views. The menu is no-fuss traditional; fried moray eel is the speciality. Located just off the LP-2 highway south of town.

❶ Getting There & Away

Villa de Mazo is sandwiched between the LP-1 and LP-132 highways. Get here by bus 3 (10 daily), which links Mazo with Los Llanos (€5, one hour), Fuencaliente (€2.20, 30 minutes) and Santa Cruz (€2, 20 minutes).

Parque Ecológico de Belmaco

Parque Ecológico de Belmaco   ARCHAEOLOGICAL SITE
(☑922 44 00 90; www.islabonita.es; Carretera a Fuencaliente, Km 7; adult/child €2/free; ◷10am-3pm Mon-Sat; P) The first ancient petroglyphs (rock carvings) found on the archipelago were discovered at this site in 1752. A 300m trail that winds around various cave dwellings (complete with sound effects!) once inhabited by Benahoare tribespeople is the heart of this 'ecological park', but the real attractions are the whorling, swirling, squiggling rock etchings, which date back to AD 150. There's also a museum with reproductions and information regarding the history of the discovery.

There are four sets of engravings, and experts remain perplexed about their meaning, though they speculate that the etchings could have been religious symbols.

ⓘ Getting There & Away

Bus 3 from Santa Cruz heads down this way four times daily (except weekends; €2, 25 minutes). The nearest bus stop is about 400m south of the Belmaco archaeological site.

Playa Blanca

Playa Blanca ('White Beach', though 'Salt and Pepper Beach' would be a better name) is a perfect picnic spot, where you'll find a tiny hamlet with a few summer homes, a tranquil beach and a rocky coast perfect for fishing or crabbing. An unmarked road leads down to the beach, 1.3km north along the LP-132 highway from the Parque Ecológico de Belmaco.

Fuencaliente

POP 1856

Fuencaliente (Hot Fountain) is the best tourist base in the south of the island and offers a mix of marine and volcanic attractions. The area gets its name from hot springs that were once believed to treat leprosy, but were buried by a fiery volcano in the 17th century. Don't think that the volcanoes have gone all sleepy and tame since then; the last eruption was in 1971, when Volcán Teneguía's lava flow added a few hectares to the island's size.

◉ Sights & Activities

★ Volcanoes   VOLCANO

Creating a stark, at times lunar-like, landscape, the volcanoes in this area are the newest in the archipelago and are the main draw of Fuencaliente. The beauty of their low, ruddy cones belies the violence with which they erupted.

Volcán San Antonio
Visitor Centre   VISITOR CENTRE

(www.lapalmacit.com; Fuencaliente; adult/child €5/free; ⊙9am-6pm; 🅿🚶) The smart new visitor centre is the first stop if you want to explore the volcanoes here. Get explosively clued up by checking out the exhibition hall. You can also take a camel ride (adult/child €8/6, 15 minutes). It takes around 25 minutes to take the short but breathtaking walk along the rim of Volcán San Antonio; a yawning chasm of this great black cone, which last blew in 1949 and is now being repopulated by hardy Canary pines.

WORTH A TRIP

SCENIC DRIVE: TO THE END OF THE ISLAND

If you're in the mood for some scenic driving, and possibly some scenic swimming, take the LP-1282 highway far past the Princess resort complex to the very southern tip of the island and a bird-watchers paradise. Located here are the Playas del Faro (Lighthouse Beach) and Las Salinas (www.salinasdefun-caliente.com), some 35,000 sq metres of salt flats; the salt produced here, under the brand name, Teneguia, is sold throughout the island.

On the coast, the black-lava rock and crystal-blue ocean are perfect contrasts to one another, but if you do choose to swim off one of the beaches here, be wary of heavy undertows and dangerous dumping waves. Return by following the LP-130 highway north to complete the loop.

Volcán Teneguía   VOLCANO

(Fuencaliente) Volcán Teneguía's 1971 eruption was the most recent in the archipelago. A signposted trail from Volcán San Antonio, near the visitors centre, leads you here. The easy to moderate walk there and back takes about two hours. If that's not far enough, you can continue onwards for a further hour (one way) down to the coast at the Faro de Fuencaliente and the end of La Palma.

Bodegas Teneguía   WINERY

(☑922 44 40 78; www.bodegasteneguia.com; Calle Ciudad Real; ⊙9am-6pm Mon-Fri, 10am-1pm Sat & Sun; 🅿) Fuencaliente is famous for the wines made in its volcanic soil. The largest and oldest winery on the island is Bodegas Teneguía, with white, red and the famous Malvía sweet wines that are sold all over the

ⓘ LOS CANARIOS

If you are scratching your head searching, perplexed, on your map for the town Los Canarios (which is often signposted), don't fret. This is just a short version of Los Canarios de Fuencaliente, although the town is rarely referred to by the full name.

SCENIC DRIVE: THE SOUTHWESTERN COAST

The road up the west coast from the bottom tip of the island is full of open curves that swoop past green hills dotted with cacti and low shrubs. The highway runs along a ridge, leaving the glittering ocean a blue haze to the left. Other than the view, there's not much here, unless you count the small bar at the mirador 6km out of Fuencaliente in the tiny town of El Charco, but even so it all makes for a great detour from either Fuencaliente or even Puerto Naos.

Keep heading north and you'll travel through a series of tiny, almost uninhabited villages. Stop in San Nicolás for a while (it's 1km past the village of Jedey) to eat at Bodegon Tamanca (922 49 41 55; Carretera General Las Mancha-Fuencaliente; mains €10-18; 11am-11pm Tue-Sat, to 6pm Sun; P), a very popular and atmospheric restaurant located in a huge natural cave. Its stout lava stone tables and booths seem to be dug into the rock. This is a meat lover's kind of establishment, whether you like it grilled, cured or stewed. Afterwards you can purchase a bottle or two from the attached wine bodega.

island and beyond. Note that the restaurant here is exclusively for tour groups.

There is a wine shop where you can also taste (or rather drink) the wines (you pay per glass from €0.50). If you would like a tour, advance reservations are essential; the price varies according to how many are in your group.

🏖 Beaches

The coast around Fuencaliente is largely inaccessible, with banana plantations, rocky outcrops and steep cliffs lining much of it. Two pleasant exceptions are Playa de la Zamora and Playa Chica, black beaches tucked side by side in coves. They're no secret but are rarely crowded. To get here, take the Carretera de Las Indias (LP-1282) past the San Antonio volcano towards the hamlet of Las Indias. Follow the curves downhill until a small sign indicates a turn-off for the *playas* (beaches) to the right.

🍴 Eating

El Quinto Pino   BISTRO $
(LP-1282, Las Indias; mains €7-9; 1-4pm & 7-11pm Thu-Sun; P) Located in a dizzily high location above the hamlet of Las Indias, northwest of Fuencaliente, this family-run spot has stunning views to the sea, and serves pizzas, *paninis* and grilled meats with daily specials chalked up on a giant blackboard.

⭐ **La Casa del Volcán**   CONTEMPORARY CANARIAN $$
(922 44 44 27; www.lacasadelvolcan.es; Calle Los Volcanes 23; mains €10-15; 12.30-9.30pm Tue-Sun; P) This bodega-cum-sophisticated restaurant is one of the best places on the island to enjoy innovative and exquisitely

prepared Canarian dishes. The atmosphere is rustic yet refined, with an intimate dining room fronted by a wood-clad bar with barrel seating. To find it look for the elegant volcanic stone building just 200m from the Volcán San Antonio Visitor Centre.

The bodega dates from 1919 and produces excellent wines; the owners also organise wine-tasting courses.

Tasca La Era   CANARIAN $$
(Carretera Antonio Paz y Paz 6; mains €11-14; noon-11pm Thu-Tue; P) This farmhouse-style restaurant has a terrace overlooking a pretty garden studded with palms. It's a charming spot for fish and meat dishes; *solomillo* (fillet steak) is the speciality with a choice of eight accompanying sauces.

ℹ Getting There & Away

Bus 3 (€4, one hour, up to five daily) heads between Fuencaliente and Santa Cruz via Villa de Mazo. It then continues onwards to Los Llanos.

THE CENTRE

For most visitors the majority of their time on La Palma is spent in this central region, and for good reason. The bowl-shaped Caldera de Taburiente, and the national park named after it, dominate the centre of La Palma, with rocky peaks, deep ravines and lush pine forests blanketing the slopes. It offers some of the most spectacular hiking in all of the Canary Islands and a visit here is an absolute must.

The LP-2 highway, which links Santa Cruz with Los Llanos, skirts the southern rim of the park, and from the road you can sometimes see the characteristic cloud blanket that fills the interior of the caldera and spills over its sides like a pot boiling over.

Two of the island's important commercial centres, El Paso and Los Llanos (the island's largest town), are in this area, making this region the economic engine of La Palma. It's also a key banana-growing area and, as you near the west coast, banana plantations fill the valleys. To add to the area's prestige the coast here is home to some of the island's longest, prettiest beaches and best 'resorts' (don't worry, it's all fairly low-key).

El Paso

POP 7440

The gateway to the Parque Nacional de la Caldera de Taburiente – the park's visitor centre is just outside town – El Paso is the

island's largest municipality, with sprawling forests and around 8 sq km of cultivated land. The pretty town centre is worth a leisurely amble. If you're driving into town, turn right at the 'Casco Histórico' sign to reach the main attractions. The **tourist office** (☑ 922 48 57 33; www.lapalma-cit.com; Calle Antonio Pino Pérez; ☺ 10am-6pm Mon-Fri, to 2pm Sat & Sun) is inside the town park. If you happen to be here on a Monday morning, you may catch a cigar-making demonstration (11am), given by an elderly local expert.

⦿ Sights & Activities

★**Museo de la Seda**   MUSEUM
(Silk Museum; ☑ 922 48 56 31; Calle Manuel Taño 6; adult/child €2.50/free; ☺ 10am-2.30pm Mon-Fri) Learn the secrets of the caterpillars that spin dresses fit for a marriage. The silk produced here is made according to traditions

---

GETTING ACTIVE IN LA PALMA

La Palma is a paradise for outdoorsy types, with excellent hiking, diving, paragliding and cycling all available. Many outfitting companies operate island-wide, so regardless of where you're based you can enjoy the activities La Palma has to offer.

Hiking

Don't come to La Palma without allowing a generous chunk of time to explore its wondrous landscapes on foot. With 850km of trails, this is the ideal place for a walking holiday. Several companies offer guided hikes; the best is **Natour** (p188), a company operating island-wide. Popular routes include the walk around the Parque Nacional de la Caldera de Taburiente, the Ruta de los Volcanes and the 'Enchanted Forest' walk through forest land in the north. The company will pick you up at your hotel or a central meeting point.

Another reputable guide service is **Ekalis** (☑ 922 44 45 17; www.ekalis.com; Las Indias 51, Fuencaliente; guided hikes, bike trips, caving expeditions & rock climbing per day €38), which also offers hotel pick-ups.

It's not necessary to hike with a guide; La Palma offers safe walking conditions for anyone who's prepared and carries a good map. But the beauty of having a guide, other than the history and anecdotes they can share, is enjoying a long one-way trek with transport arranged at either end.

Adventure Sports

If just plain walking seems too tame, try rock climbing or caving. Ekalis offers a variety of climbing and rappelling experiences as well as a two-hour spelunking expedition. It also offers bike rental and guided mountain-biking trips, another popular activity on the island. If you're in shape, La Palma's endless climbs and dips will be thrilling, but if trudging uphill isn't your thing, guide services like those offered by **Bike'n'Fun** (p197) offer transport to the top of a peak followed by a mostly downhill ride. All operators can pick you up at your hotel or a central meeting point.

In recent years, paragliding has really taken off; the island is considered one of the world's best places to glide. Try it in Puerto Naos with **Palmaclub** (p198).

Diving & Kayaking

For those wanting to get out on the water, diving outfitters in Puerto Naos and Los Cancajos will hook you up with tanks, wetsuits and fins. Sea-kayaking expeditions are also available in Puerto Naos and Los Cancajos; contact Ekalis for more information.

that have barely changed since the industry arrived on the island in the 16th century. There is an upstairs museum with some magnificent silk garments on display from as far afield as China and India, plus a short audiovisual film about silk production. End your visit at the downstairs workshop where you can see the weaving in action.

Ermita de la Virgen de la Concepción de la Bonanza   CHURCH
(☺ opening hours vary) A restored 18th-century, curiously painted little chapel. Renovations mercifully left intact the splendid Mudéjar ceiling above the altar.

Mercado   MARKET
(Calle Antonio Pino Pérez; ☺ 9am-2pm & 3-7pm Fri & Sat) A popular farmers market that also sells arts and crafts.

Ruta de los Volcanes   HIKING
If you prefer to do the hard work yourself, El Paso is a good take-off point for the demanding, but breathtaking (in every sense of the word), Ruta de los Volcanes, a 19km hiking trail that meanders through ever-changing volcanic scenery and gives privileged views of both coasts as it heads south along the mountain ridge, across the heart of volcanic territory and towards Fuencaliente.

This trail is part of the long-distance GR-130. Allow six to seven hours for the trek – it's demanding and is best undertaken on cool, cloudy days, as there is not much shade or fresh water along the way. The trailhead is the Refugio del Pilar, an expansive park with a picnic area, on the LP-203 highway, outside El Paso and off the LP-2. The walk finishes in Fuencaliente, from where you will probably have to arrange homeward-bound transport.

✕ Eating

Tapas Trekking   TAPAS $
(www.tapasytrekking.com; Calle Sagrado Corazón 4; tapas €4-5, tablas €5-7; ☺ 9am-4pm Sun & Mon, to 11pm Wed-Sat; ☎) Location, location, location. Situated in the shadow of the evocative 18th-century *ermita* (chapel), this place keeps it simple with a menu of tapas and *tablas* to share ranging from homemade *croquetas* to local cheese and ham.

Parque Nacional de la Caldera de Taburiente

Declared a national park in 1954, this beautiful park is the heart of La Palma, both geographically and symbolically. Extending across 46.9 sq km, it encompasses thick Canary pine forests, a wealth of freshwater springs and streams, waterfalls, impressive rock formations and many kilometres of hiking trails. Although you can reach a few miradors by car, you'll need to go on foot to really experience the park at its best. The morning, before clouds obscure the views, is the best time to visit (although if you want to see the classic view of clouds spilling over the caldera lips, the afternoon is the best time).

The heart of the park is the Caldera de Taburiente itself (literally, the Taburiente 'Stewpot' or 'Cauldron'). A massive depression 8km wide and surrounded by soaring rock walls (it doesn't take much imagination to see where the name came from), it was first given the moniker in 1825 by German geologist Leopold von Buch, who took it to be a massive volcanic crater. The word 'caldera' stuck, and was used as a standard term for such volcanic craters the world over. This caldera, however, is no crater, although volcanic activity was key in its creation. Scientists now agree that this was a majestically tall volcanic mountain, and that it collapsed on itself. Through the millennia, erosion excavated this tall-walled amphitheatre.

As you explore the quiet park, all may seem impressively stoic and still, but the forces of erosion are hard at work. Landslides and collapsing *roques* (pillars of volcanic rock) are frequent, and some geologists estimate it will finally disappear in just 5000 years. See this fast erosion near the Mirador de la Cumbrecita, where a group of pines stands atop a web of exposed roots, clinging miraculously to the hilltop. These trees were once planted firmly in the ground, but metres of soil have been lost during their lifetime.

Hiking
Many trails traverse the park, but unless you plan to spend several days exploring, you'll probably stick to the better-known paths outlined here. Most are in good shape, though the trail from La Cumbrecita to the campsite is notoriously slippery and should be avoided by novice hikers, and the trail running down the Barranco de las Angustias can be dangerous in rainy weather.

Signposting is improving but may still be confusing. Although you're unlikely to get really lost (and there are usually groups of

FESTIVALS & EVENTS

Like any Spaniards worth their heritage, the *palmeros* love a good party, and the year is packed with festivals and celebrations.

Each town has feast days celebrating its patron saint with several days of parades, parties and other activities. The following are some of the bigger and better events:

➡ Breña Alta (late June)

➡ Breña Baja (25 July)

➡ Barlovento (12–13 August)

➡ San Andrés y Los Sauces (early September)

➡ Tazacorte (late September)

Other festivals worthy of note:

Fiesta of the Almond Blossom (☺ Jan-Feb) A celebration of the beauty of the almond blossom in Puntagorda and of the town's patron saint, San Mauro Abad.

Las Cruces (☺ 3 May) The island's crosses are bedecked in jewellery, flowers and rich clothes. Truly a sight to see.

San Juan (☺ 23 Jun) Marks the summer solstice, and is celebrated in Puntallana with bonfires and firecrackers galore.

El Diablo (☺ 8 Sep) Fireworks, parades of devils and grim music in Tijarife provide a graphic show of the triumph of good over evil. About 30kg of gunpowder is used in the 20-minute show honouring Nuestra Señora de Candelaria.

Castanets (☺ 24 Dec) After Midnight Mass in Breña Alta and throughout the island, *palmero* men perform skits accompanied by the noisy music of castanets.

LA PALMA PARQUE NACIONAL DE LA CALDERA DE TABURIENTE

hikers out on the trail to help you if necessary), you're best off buying a detailed map, like the 1:25,000 *Caldera de Taburiente Parque Nacional,* for sale at the visitor centre. See also the excellent website www.senderosdelapalma.com for further route descriptions.

The Southern End

Most people access the park from either El Paso or Los Llanos. You'll need a car, taxi or guide to cart you up to one of the miradors that serve as trailheads.

To get an overview of the park, there's no better walk than the PR LP 13 trail, which begins at Los Brecitos (1081m). Get there from Los Llanos by following the signs first to Los Barros and then on to Los Brecitos. The path leads through a quiet Canary pine forest, past the park campsite, across a babbling brook, and down the Barranco de las Angustias, crossing countless small streams along the way. Watch out for interesting sights like the brightly coloured mineral water that flows orange and green, the interesting shapes made by pillow lava, and rock formations like the phallic Roque Idafe, an important spiritual site for the Benahoaritas. This six-hour (22km) hike is popular and

is suitable for anyone in average-to-good physical shape. Be careful, however, if it has rained recently or if a storm seems imminent; the 'Gorge of Fear' can quickly become a raging torrent, and people caught in its fast-rising waters have died.

When the trail is fully open the best way to tackle it is to park at Las Hoyas, at the base of the Barranco de las Angustias. From here, 4WD taxi shuttle services (☏ 922 40 35 40; per person €10; ☺ 8am-noon) whisk you up to Los Brecitos and allow you to enjoy the descent back to your car without backtracking.

Another option is to drive up the LP-202 from the visitor centre to the Mirador de la Cumbrecita (1287m), where there is a small information office (☺ 9am-6pm). The 7km drive passes turn-offs for the Pista de Valencia and the Ermita del Pino, leading through a peaceful pine forest to sweeping views of the valley. From the car park, you can make a round-trip hike up to the panoramic views from Pico Bejenado; allow 2½ hours for the trek. Those with less time can take a 3km circuit trail to both the Mirador de los Roques and the Mirador Lomo de las Chozas; the final part of the loop is a flat, wheelchair- and stroller-friendly 1km trail between Lomo de las Chozas and the car park. The very best views can be had at sunrise or sunset. Take note, though, that the trails leading off from the Mirador de la Cumbrecita are by far the most popular in the park and, due to overcrowding and limited space in the car park, park authorities have enforced a strict traffic quota. If you want to drive up to the mirador, you have to put your name down on a list at the visitor centre just past El Paso and wait for your turn to drive up. Sometimes the wait might only be a few minutes but at other times (weekends and in high season) it can be over an hour. If you miss your turn, you must queue again.

Another excellent, moderately hard, walk is the PR LP 13.3 from the Pista de Valencia parking area to the 1845m-high Pico Bejenado. This five-hour (11.4km) return hike climbs up through some wonderful old pine forest before popping out on the caldera ridge for some incredible views. The trail is easy to follow and it's a good choice for any reasonably fit walker who wants something less trodden and more challenging than the routes around the Mirador de la Cumbrecita, but not as demanding as the Los Brecitos trails.

The Northern End

A string of rocky peaks soaring nearly 2500m high surrounds the caldera, and the trail running along these rock walls affords a thrilling vantage point from which to observe the park and the rest of the island. A narrow dirt trail, part of the long-distance GR-131, skims the entire northern border of the park, and shorter trails branch off it and venture down deeper into the park.

One of the most spectacular sections runs between the Roque de los Muchachos and the Pico de la Nieve, which is off the LP-1032, a winding highway that branches off the LP-1 highway 3km north of Santa Cruz and snakes its way across the island, skirting the rim of the park and its northern peaks. Avoid backtracking by taking two cars and leaving one at the *pico* (the parking area is a 20-minute walk from the trail itself). Then drive (or get a ride) up to the Roque de los Muchachos, the highest point on the island at 2426m. The walk back down to the Pico de la Nieve should take four to five hours (approximately 9km).

Numerous miradors dot the LP-1032 highway around the Roque de los Muchachos; even if you don't hike the rim, the views from up here are worth seeking out. At night, this area offers unbeatable stargazing.

❶ Information

Visitor Centre (☑ 922 49 72 77; www.reservasparquesnacionales.es; Carretera General de Padrón 47; ☉ 9am-6.30pm) The visitor centre is 5km outside El Paso on the LP-3 highway and offers free general information (be sure to pick up the English *Caldera de Taburiente Paths* map), detailed maps and guides, an excellent exhibition centre, plus a botanical garden. The centre's 20-minute film (shown occasionally in English) is worth seeing.

If you want to stay in the park, there is a campsite in the centre near Roque Idafe; you will need a permit, available from the visitor centre. You also need a permit to visit the Mirador de la Cumbrecita. Bus 1 (€1.50 from El Paso, 10 minutes) between Santa Cruz de la Palma and Los Llanos stops by hourly.

❶ Getting There & Away

No roads run through the park, and there are only three ways to access it: via the LP-202 near the visitor centre, via the track that goes from Los Llanos to Los Brecitos, or via the LP-1032 highway in the north. There are no buses.

Los Llanos de Aridane

POP 21,045

The economic centre of the island and a true-blue working town, Los Llanos lacks the obvious charm of the capital or some of the smaller villages, but the shady plazas and pedestrian streets of the historic centre are worth exploring. Set in a fertile valley, this

---

LA PALMA FOR CHILDREN

Building sand castles on the black-sand beaches of Puerto Naos and Los Cancajos, or splashing in the saltwater pools in places like Piscinas de la Fajana are givens, but what to do after the beach? Older children may enjoy striding out with suitable hikes including the Mirador de los Roques and the Mirador Lomo de las Chozas, both in the Parque Nacional de la Caldera de Taburiente; at the latter, you can even take a stroller. Throw in some history by taking the 1.5km walk around the Parque Cultural La Zarza. The younger crowd will also get a kick out of the animals at Maroparque (p189).

THE WORLD'S LARGEST TELESCOPE

No, those round, space-age-looking things squatting on the peak of Roque de los Muchachos aren't something from a theme park, and no, they're not alien spaceships come to explore earth. They are the telescopes of the island's astronomical observatory, one of the world's best places to study the night sky. So much so that in 2012 it was deemed the world's first Unesco-certified Starlight Reserve. Tossed out in the Atlantic, far from urban centres and city lights, La Palma is an ideal place to stargaze. More than 75% of the nights on El Roque are clear, a statistic that's hard to beat.

The mammoth Grantecan (Gran Telescopio Canario; GTC), the Observatorio del Roque de los Muchachos boasts one of the world's largest telescopes. The €1 million investment allows scientists to study the formation and evolution of the galaxies throughout the history of the universe as well as investigate the stars and observe the rings of spatial material that give birth to new planets.

The observatory has long been home to Europe's largest telescope and the site of important research. La Palma's observatory is linked with the Observatorio del Teide on Tenerife, and together they form the Instituto de Astrofísica de Canarias (IAC). The observatory can be visited by reserving in advance via the www.iac.es website. Multilingual 90-minute tours take place on Tuesday, Wednesday and Friday and cost €9. There are also a number of private tour companies that organise stargazing tours; look for the flyers at any of the island's tourist offices.

has historically been one of the island's richest areas, with a long tradition of cultivating sugar cane, bananas and, more recently, avocados. These days it's home to many of the island's businesses and services, and many young *palmeros* are moving here to find jobs.

◉ Sights

Colourful murals and modern sculptures are dotted throughout the centre, making the city an open-air museum. A large map in Plaza España gives the artists' names and locations of their works.

Plaza España   PLAZA

Busy Plaza España is the heart of the historic town. Majestic Indian laurel trees provide a much-welcome leafy canopy on even the sunniest days, making this the perfect spot to picnic, people-watch or relax in a cafe. Don't miss the gleaming white Iglesia de Nuestra Señora de los Remedios, built in the Canarian colonial style. Explore the surrounding streets and plazas, which still preserve much of their traditional character.

🏃 Activities

Bike'n'Fun   BICYCLE TOUR

(📞922 40 19 27; www.bikenfun.de; Calle Calvo Sotelo 20, Los Llanos; per person guide service €51, per day bike rental €16; ⊙10am-1pm) This reputable outfit organises a wide range of biking excursions throughout La Palma, including a tour around Los Llanos and bike rental.

✦ Festivals & Events

La Patrona   RELIGIOUS

(⊙2 Jun) The city comes alive for the year's biggest party held in honour of Our Lady of Los Remedios.

✕ Eating

The cafes dotting the Plaza España are ideal for breakfast, a midday coffee break or an informal lunch.

★La Vitamina   VEGETARIAN $

(Calle Real 29; mains €8.50-10; ⊙noon-9.30pm Mon-Sat; 🍴) This is something refreshingly different to the run-of-the-mill meat and fish restaurants that are the standard when dining out in the Canaries. It's laid-back, slightly bohemian and has a range of largely vegetarian meals that put together flavours of Africa, Asia and Spain into some highly unexpected combinations.

The deluxe salad is a particular winner but note that it is easily large enough for two.

Tasco El Patio   TAPAS $

(Calle Rosario 2; tapas €3-4; ⊙9am-11pm; 🛜) Look for this burnt sienna–washed building on the corner of Calle Real and Calle Rosario and head for the pretty interior patio with its tiled tables and leafy plants. The tapas include international dishes, like tuna lasagne, as well as local favourites including seafood salad.

LA PALMA TIPPLES

Since the early 16th century, when Spanish conquerors planted the first vines on the island, La Palma has been known for its sweet *malvasía* (Malmsey wine). Thanks to the merchants and colonists who came in and out of La Palma's ports, the wine acquired fame throughout Europe, and some referred to the tasty stuff as 'the nectar of the gods'. Even Shakespeare wrote about sweet Canary wine, making it Falstaff's favourite in *Henry IV* and calling it a 'marvellous searching wine' that 'perfumes the blood'. You can also find dry *malvasía* as well as a variety of reds, whites and rosé wines, especially in the areas of Fuencaliente and Hoyo de Mazo. For an alcohol-filled journey embark on the **Wine Route** (www.infoisla.org/rutadelvino), which includes 16 visitable wineries.

Although the sugar plantations have all but gone, what remains is put to good use in the production of *ron* (rum) by the last producer on the island, Ron Aldea.

ⓘ Information

Tourist Office (☑ 922 40 25 83; Avenida Dr Fleming; ⊙ 9.30am-2.30pm & 4-6pm Mon-Fri, 9.30am-2pm Sat & Sun)

ⓘ Getting There & Away

Buses from the **bus station** (Calle Luis Felipe Gómez Wanguemert) include bus 1 (€5.50, 45 minutes, up to 17 daily) to Santa Cruz, bus 3 (€4, 40 minutes, up to seven daily) to Fuencaliente and bus 4 (€2.20, 20 minutes, up to 21 daily) to Puerto Naos.

Puerto Naos

One of La Palma's two tourism centres (Los Cancajos, on the east coast, is the other), Puerto Naos is a town that exists almost solely for tourists. Huddled around a rounded bay and protected on either side by tall cliffs, the town makes a good base for sun lovers who want easy access to the north and interior. Unfortunately, the surrounding banana groves are increasingly being cultivated under plastic greenhouses, which are somewhat of an eyesore.

🏖 Beaches

Playa Puerto Naos　　　　　　　　　BEACH
The black-sand beach at Puerto Naos is the longest on the island, measuring around 1km. Backed by towering palm trees, the facilities are excellent and include showers, changing rooms and toilets, plus sunbeds and umbrellas for hire. A bustling promenade of bars, restaurants and shops backs the sweep of sand and includes several places to stay.

🏃 Activities

Lolling on the soft black-sand beach may well take up all your time here. But if you're in the mood for more excitement, try some of the following activities.

Tauchpartner　　　　　　　　　　　DIVING
(☑ 922 40 81 39; www.tauchpartner-lapalma.de; Edificio Playa Delfín 1; dive incl equipment €41; ⊙ 9.30-11am & 5-7pm Mon-Sat) Offers an extensive range of scuba-diving courses as well as single dives.

Bike Station　　　　　　　　　　　CYCLING
(☑ 922 40 83 55; www.bike-station.de; Avenida Cruz Roja, Local 3; per day bike rental €6-24, guided trip €38-44; ⊙ 9am-1pm & 6-8pm Mon-Sat) Offers rentals and a range of challenging guided mountain-bike rides.

Palmaclub　　　　　　　　　　PARAGLIDING
(☑ 610 69 57 50; www.palmaclub.com; Paseo Marítima; tandem glide €100-150; ⊙ noon-6pm) Paragliding is quickly gaining momentum here; aficionados come from throughout Europe to take advantage of the island's ideal conditions and easy take-off and landing sites. Arrange for a tandem glide with Palmaclub, which is based inside the Kiosco Playa Morena. Prices are based on how big a cliff (250m or 950m) you choose to throw yourself off.

You should book as far ahead as possible and be prepared for weather-induced cancellations.

🍴 Eating

Orinoco　　　　　　　　　　SEAFOOD $
(www.islalapalma.com/orinoco; Calle Manuel Rodriguez Quintero 1; mains €7-12; ⊙ noon-11pm) It's not the kind of place that charms by looks alone, but this homey spot up a side street from the main promenade is the locals' favourite for fresh fish and traditional *palmero* desserts like *bienmesabe* and *quesillo* (flan).

Restaurante Playa Chica SEAFOOD $$
(☑922 40 84 52; Playa Chica; mains €15-20; ⊘noon-11pm Wed-Mon) Overlooking the delightful small cove, Playa Chica, this smart seafood restaurant with its jaunty blue decor enjoys one of the best locations in town. Dishes are well executed – even the salads, something of a rarity in a Spanish seafood restaurant.

❶ Getting There & Away

Bus 4 (€2.10, 20 minutes, up to 21 daily) makes the trip to and from Los Llanos.

THE NORTH

The dense tropical forests, fertile hills and towering pines that create a blanket of green over the northern half of the island couldn't be further away from the volcanic, sun-baked south. This is the least-accessible, and many say most beautiful, part of the island, with rocky cliffs plunging into sapphire waters and deserted black beaches surrounded by palm trees.

San Andrés & Los Sauces

POP 5380

San Andrés, 3km off the main LP-1 highway, is like something from a storybook, with hilly, cobblestone streets that lead past low, whitewashed houses. Los Sauces, just north of San Andrés, is a modern town with two pretty, central squares.

More important (and more interesting) than anything in Los Sauces itself is the Los Tiles biosphere reserve just out of town.

◉ Sights

Iglesia de San Andrés CHURCH
(San Andrés) The Iglesia de San Andrés has its origins in 1515 and is one of the first churches the Spanish conquerors built on the island, though most of what you see today was built in the 17th century. Inside, take a look at the lavish baroque altarpieces and the coffered ceiling.

Nuestra Señora de Montserrat CHURCH
(Plaza de la Iglesia, San Andrés) The grand church, Nuestra Señora de Montserrat, is on the town square and has some valuable Flemish artwork inside. Named after the patron of Catalunya, this church is evidence of the many Catalans who participated in the island's conquest.

Charco Azul SALTWATER POOL
Charco Azul is a creatively designed combination of moulded concrete with natural volcanic rocks. The effect is stunning: a series of natural-looking saltwater pools with sunbathing platforms and a walkway between them. Charco Azul is located 6km northwest of San Andrés on the LP-104 highway. Alternatively, bus 104 from Los Sauces passes by here three times daily (€1.50, 10 minutes).

✖ Eating

★Bar Charco Azul SEAFOOD $
(Charco Azul; mains €8-10; ⊘11am-7pm) Owner Willy is a fisherman who is out most mornings at 3am, so you can be guaranteed that your fish is flapping fresh. The bar is right on the water and only closes when it rains; it's a wonderful place with far better (and cheaper) seafood than the smarter places up the road.

★La Placita THAI, CANARIAN $$
(☑922 10 63 34; Calle La Plaza 5, San Andrés; mains €10-14; ⊘11.30am-11pm) Somehow you don't expect to find a Thai restaurant in the middle of a sleepy village like San Andrés. Run by a German-Thai couple, the word is out so there are few empty tables, especially on weekends. Shaded by palms with a terrace overlooking the church, the menu is predominantly Thai but includes some innovatively prepared Canarian dishes.

❶ Getting There & Away

Bus 2 (€4, 35 minutes, up to nine daily) connects Santa Cruz with the centre of Los Sauces; those heading to San Andrés will have to walk or try asking the driver to make a diversion.

Los Tiles

A biosphere reserve since 1983, the nearly 140 sq km of Los Tiles are covered with a lushly beautiful rainforest that's literally oozing with life. This moist, cool, natural wonderland is one of the most magical spots on the island, a must-explore place where you can wander among the diverse flora and fauna and the largest *laurisilva* (laurel) forest on the island.

LA PALMA SAN ANDRÉS & LOS SAUCES

WORTH A TRIP

SCENIC DRIVE: FROM PARQUE CULTURAL LA ZARZA TO TAZACORTE

Ethereal, pristine, stoic, eerie, peaceful...choose your adjective for the lonely landscapes here on the island's northwestern coast. Pine forests, fallow fields, occasional rural settlements and sweeping views of the banana plantations by the Atlantic are the main attractions between La Zarza and Tazacorte. This is a solitary, tranquil area that was largely isolated from the rest of the island until recent times. Countless hiking trails, many of them quite challenging, provide most of the entertainment here.

The small towns of Puntagorda and Tijarafe are worth a brief stop, if only to wander the streets of their historic centres.

Several lookouts offer privileged vantage points of the northwest coast's inspiring scenery. Just south of Puntagorda is Mirador de Garome, overlooking a majestic gorge. Further south, Mirador del Time looks out over Tazacorte.

Eating & Drinking

La Muralla Restaurant (☑ 650 02 16 64; Carretera General Aguatavar, Parque Cultural La Zarza; mains €8-12; ⊙ 1-9pm Tue-Thu, to 10pm Fri & Sat; ℗) Well signposted off the LP-1 highway, from appearances this restaurant appears in the top-end category. Picture windows afford stunning mountain views and the dining room has had the interior designers in: minimalist and contemporary. But the prices are surprisingly reasonable and the quality high.

Restaurant Las Piñas (Carretera General Puntagorda, Parque Cultural La Zarza; mains €8-10; ⊙ 9am-11pm Fri-Wed; ℗) Grab a table on the outside terrace beside the fragrant jasmine bushes and tuck into a bowl of seafood soup or a simple no-fuss plate of grilled fish with potatoes doused with *mojo*. This long-standing family-run restaurant is one of the most popular in La Zarza for locals, particularly on weekends when it packs out with extended families.

Cervecería Isla Verde (☑ 922 49 06 25; www.cervezaislaverde.com; Calle General Plaza el Jesús 41, Tijarafe; ⊙ 1-10pm Wed-Mon) This well-signed place is located right off the LP-1 highway 2km south of Tijarafe. A German-run small craft brewery, you can down a bottle of the local beer here for a euro or so while sitting on a palm-shaded terrace with mountain views. Snacks (€4 to €7.50) also available.

🏃 Activities

Fabulous hiking trails cut through Los Tiles' dense vegetation.

Mirador Topo de las Barandas　　HIKING
The shortest of the hiking trails in Los Tiles is the steep climb up to the Mirador Topo de las Barandas (1.5km; allow one hour for the round trip), which leads to a spectacular view of the gorge running out of the reserve.

Marcos & Cordero Springs　　HIKING
The long, ravine-side trail to the Marcos and Cordero Springs (8.1km) passes through a dozen damp tunnels (bring a flashlight and rain jacket) and winds past waterfalls, through forest and alongside volcanic dikes. It's not incredibly steep (except in short stretches), but it can be slick; be careful.

A popular way to tackle this trail is to get a taxi from Los Tiles car park up to Casa del Monte, from where the hike to the springs and back should take about four hours.

The park office can suggest a number of other walks, including a very simple one-hour return walk that begins from the car park a few hundred metres down the road from the visitor centre. Take the trail on the left-hand side of the road, next to the signpost, and basically follow it through the tunnel and gently uphill for as far as you feel like going.

ℹ Information

Visitor Centre (☑ 922 45 12 46; ⊙ 9am-2pm & 2.30-6.30pm) At the helpful visitor centre you'll find maps, a video about the biosphere reserve and a small exhibition hall.

ℹ Getting There & Away

Coming from Santa Cruz, follow the signs to Los Tiles off the LP-1 highway. The visitor centre is

3km up LP-105, which runs alongside the lush Barranco del Agua. No buses venture up here, so you'll need either your own wheels or strong legs.

Barlovento

POP 2360

Skip the town itself in favour of the natural attractions that lie beyond, like the Piscinas de la Fajana – calm saltwater pools where frothy waves pound just beyond the subtle concrete barriers. About 5km east of Barlovento, on the LP-1 highway, you'll turn off towards this starkly beautiful coastal spot, where dramatic dark rocks and a savage ocean create a memorable panorama.

 Eating

La Gaviota   SEAFOOD $$
(Piscinas de la Fajana; mains €9-16; ⊙ 10am-11pm; P) A suitably marine-themed blue-on-blue restaurant with a vast terrace right on the water; the menu includes all the fishy favourites served with a generous portion of potatoes with *mojo*.

Parque Cultural La Zarza

Parque Cultural La Zarza   ARCHAEOLOGICAL SITE
(La Mata; adult/child €2/1; ⊙ 10am-6pm Mon-Sat, to 3pm Sun; P) Two Benahoare petroglyphs are the main attraction at the Parque Cultural La Zarza. Heading west out along the LP-1 towards La Mata, the park is 1km past the turn-off for La Mata (it's on a curve and easy to miss – keep an eye out for the signpost). To actually see the geometric-shaped etchings, take the 1.5km circuit into the park itself.

Back at the visitor centre, you can watch an informative 20-minute video about the life of the original inhabitants and take a tour around the interactive museum.

LA PALMA BARLOVENTO

El Hierro

📞 922 / POP 10,162

Best Places to Eat

➡ Casa Carlos (p207)

➡ Casa Guayana (p208)

➡ La Taberna de la Villa (p206)

➡ El Refugio (p212)

Best Places to Stay

➡ Hotel Villa El Mocanal (p233)

➡ El Sitio (p234)

➡ Hotel Puntagrande (p234)

Why Go?

Unesco geopark El Hierro is an island where the impenetrable cliff-lined shores and location in the middle of the Atlantic make it both literally and figuratively remote. It was once even considered the end of the world until Columbus famously sailed the ocean blue from here in 1492 (along with his terrified crew!).

El Hierro will always feel remote, which is exactly what is so addictive about this place. It's impossible not to be entranced by the island's slow pace and simple style; by its craggy coast, where waves hurl themselves against lava-sculpted rock; by the pretty farmland and flower meadows; by the eerily beautiful juniper groves; and by the volcanic badland moonscapes in the south.

In short, El Hierro is unique – so much so that it is planning to become the first energy self-sufficient island in the world through a combination of solar, wind and water power.

When to Go

➡ In spring (March) the meadows of the highlands are ablaze with poppies and other wildflowers and hiking is a delight.

➡ For life at lower altitudes, June to early July and September are perfect for lazing around the numerous natural swimming pools or diving into La Restinga's undersea paradise.

➡ For cultural interest, if you're on El Hierro in late April, be sure not to miss the Fiesta de los Pastores (p215), a colourful religious procession in honour of the Virgen de los Reyes (Virgin of the Kings).

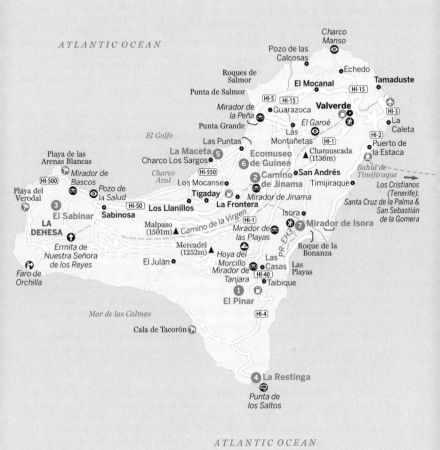

El Hierro Highlights

1 Stroll among the towering pines in the pristine **El Pinar** (p210) forest

2 Tackle the **Camino de Jinama** (p209), one of the island's best downhill walks, for vast views of El Golfo and the Atlantic

3 Walk among juniper trees sculpted by the wind into eerie, gnome-like shapes at **El Sabinar** (p215)

4 Grab your mask and dive into the warm, calm waters near **La Restinga** (p211), the island's best diving spot

5 Splash around in **La Maceta** (p213), an overgrown rock pool battered by Atlantic swells

6 Measure up to the giant lizards of El Hierro and explore village houses of old at the **Ecomuseo de Guinea** (p213)

7 Picnic among the wildflowers at the **Mirador de Isora** (p210), with its breathtaking views to the ocean far, far below

History

Geographically speaking, El Hierro is the youngest island in the archipelago. Through the millennia, volcanic activity built up a steep island with a towering 2000m-high peak at its centre. But, about 50,000 years ago, the area was hit by an earthquake so massive that one-third of the island was ripped off the northern side. The peak and the surrounding land slipped away beneath the waves, creating the amphitheatre-like coast of El Golfo. The event would have been impressive and the ensuing tsunami may have been more than 100m high.

The island's original inhabitants, the Bimbaches, arrived from northern Africa and created a peaceful, cave-dwelling society that depended on agriculture, fishing, hunting and gathering. They may have called the island Hero or Esero, possibly the origin of its modern name. Bimbaches have left interesting petroglyphs (geometrical etchings) on rocks and cave walls throughout the island; the most interesting is at El Julán.

After the Spanish conquest in the 15th century, a form of feudalism was introduced and Spanish farmers gradually assimilated with those locals who had not been sold into slavery or died of disease. In the subsequent quest for farmland, much of El Hierro's forests were destroyed.

In the 20th century many Herreños were forced to emigrate to find work. The island's economy has since recovered and is now based on cheese, fishing, fruit-growing, livestock and, increasingly, tourism. Many

THREE PERFECT DAYS IN EL HIERRO

Day One

Whether arriving by plane or boat it's the eastern half of the island that everyone sees first, but after that initial arrival most people ignore the east until their day of departure. At first glance this does indeed seem to be the least-enticing corner of El Hierro, but first impressions can often be false impressions. Leaving the port or airport, take the road south to **Las Playas**, a long stretch of cobblestone beach. It's battered by the wind, but perfect for an appetite-inducing stroll. Quell that hunger at the nearby Casa Guayana (p208), which dishes up some of the finest seafood on the island. Turn the car around and retrace your steps north to either **Tamaduste**, with its calm cove and crab-filled rock pools, or **La Caleta**, with its stylish saltwater swimming pools ideal for all the family. After a swim, drive up to **Valverde** and check out this pint-sized capital before heading to **El Mocanal** and your overnight stop at the Hotel Villa El Mocanal (p233).

Day Two

From Hotel Villa El Mocanal drive south and up, through a landscape that often starts off shrouded in fog before emerging into blazing sunshine and a thousand flowers around the farming town of **San Andrés**; make the short detour to the incredible **Mirador de Isora** before continuing to the majestic **El Pinar pine forests** for a walk and a picnic lunch. Next zigzag downhill through an increasingly barren, volcanic landscape to coastal **La Restinga** and what is arguably the best scuba diving and snorkelling in the Canaries.

Day Three

El Golfo, the spectacular amphitheatre-shaped depression that so dominates the island, is for many people the most interesting part of El Hierro. Start the day by descending quickly out of the clouds of Valverde on the fast HI-5, stopping on the way at **Mirador de la Peña** for an unforgettable overview of El Golfo. Drop down to the coast and check out the quirky, and former record-breaking, Hotel Puntagrande (p234) and admire the coastal scenery by walking a little way (or the whole way) along the spruced-up walkway between Las Puntas and La Maceta. Return to your car and drive to the nearby **Ecomuseo de Guinea** for a dose of culture and reptiles. Feeling peckish? It's lunchtime so head to Casa Pucho (p213) in workaday Tigady for some excellent Canarian food. After lunch choose between the natural pools at **La Maceta** or quieter **Charco Azul** to sleep it all off and have a splash in the water. If you don't sleep for too long, finish your day by driving to the wild end of Spain and the **La Dehesa** area.

emigrants have returned. The struggle now is balancing the need to conserve the island's unique, Unesco-protected natural beauty with the need for economic growth. More than 60% of the island is classified as protected land, limiting growth options. That's great for conservationists, but as young islanders are forced to move away to study and find jobs, many see it as a problem.

Although El Hierro's last major volcanic eruption was 200 years ago, between October 2011 and March 2012 major underwater volcanic eruptions took place off the coast at La Restinga leading to a precautionary evacuation of the town. Fortunately, there were no casualties. To learn more visit the Centro Vulcanológico (p211) in La Restinga.

ⓘ Getting There & Away

AIR

The island's small **airport** (☏ 922 55 37 00; www.aena.es; ☺ 6am-7pm) is 12km outside Valverde. Inter-island airline **Binter Canarias** (☏ 902 391392; www.bintercanarias.com) connects El Hierro to Tenerife and Gran Canaria and then onward to the rest of the archipelago. At the airport you'll find car-rental offices, a bar and a shop selling maps and local products.

BOAT

El Hierro's Puerto de la Estaca gets little traffic. **Naviera Armas** (☏ 922 55 09 05; www.naviera-armas.com; Muelle de la Estaca) sails once daily from Sunday to Friday to Los Cristianos in Tenerife (€49.50, 2¾ hours). The departure time varies daily; check the website for more details.

ⓘ Getting Around

BUS

Valverde's **bus station** (☏ 922 55 11 75; Calle Molino; ☺ 8am-4pm) is at the southern end of town, and routes do a good job of covering the island. Check schedules online at www.transhierro.com.

CAR

There are a couple of car-rental firms at the airport, and just one in Valverde, which is often unmanned. Reserve in advance as the number of available cars is limited.

Be sure to fill up the petrol tank before leaving Valverde, as there are only three petrol stations on the island! One is in the capital, a second in La Frontera and a third on the highway towards La Restinga.

We recommend the following car-rental company:

Cicar (www.cicar.com; El Hierro airport)

ROAD DISTANCES (KM)

	Valverde	La Restinga	Tigaday	Las Playas
La Restinga	24			
Tigaday	15	41		
Las Playas	11	43	26	
El Pinar	16	11	27	16

Approximate distances only

VALVERDE

POP 1630

The only landlocked Canary capital, Valverde is a rather unremarkable town set atop a windy mountain ridge overlooking the Atlantic. Its low white houses aren't as scenic as those balconied mansions of the other capitals, but when clouds don't interfere, the town offers some pretty valley views. On rare clear days you can see Tenerife's El Teide and La Gomera perfectly from the town centre. Even if you don't stay here, you'll probably have to pass through, as it's the island's centre of commerce and services.

History

Though Jean de Béthencourt conquered the island in 1405, Valverde only really came into being following a devastating hurricane in 1610. Many of the islanders fled to this small inland hamlet seeking shelter, beginning a relative boom that would eventually see the town become the seat of the *municipio* (town council) that covered the whole island. In 1926 the island's first *cabildo insular* (local government) was established here.

⊙ Sights

The lure of the island lies in its natural spaces, not here in town. Still, a short stroll around can be rewarding. Start on pedestrian-friendly Calle Dr Quintero, home to shops and bars, before ducking down to the attractive Plaza Quintero Nuñez (known locally as the Plaza Cabildo), home to a clutch of bars and restaurants, as well as the church.

★ Casa de las Quinteras Centro
Etnográfico   MUSEUM
(☏ 922 55 20 26; Calle Armas Martel; adult/child €3/free; ☺ 9am-2pm Mon-Fri, 10.30am-1.30pm Sat) Exhibits about rural island life are displayed in several small stone houses,

including a blacksmith's forge, traditional clothing, ceramics and some quaint oddities like an ancient gramophone made out of a block of wood. There's an excellent craft shop on-site.

Iglesia de Nuestra Señora de Concepción CHURCH
(⊙8am-6pm) The church is a simple three-nave structure built in 1767 and crowned by a bell tower with a railed-off upper level that serves as a lookout. Inside, it has a magnificent wooden coffered and vaulted ceiling. The polychrome altar *Purísima Concepción* is the town's most prized piece of artwork, although, sadly, it is often partially shrouded with a red cloth (but you can peek behind).

✺ Festivals & Events

A couple of times a year Valverde rouses itself from its stupor and lets its hair down for fiesta time.

Fiesta de San Isidro Valverde SAINT'S FESTIVAL
(⊙15 May) If you're in Valverde on this day, be sure to get a look at the *lucha canaria* (Canarian wrestling) showcase in the afternoon.

Fiesta de la Virgen de la Concepción SAINT'S FESTIVAL
(⊙7 & 8 Dec) The night before Valverde's biggest festival is marked with fireworks and a lively town party, while the day itself (8 December) is devoted to religious celebrations, concerts and various cultural acts.

✗ Eating

El Secreto CANARIAN $
(www.tascaelsecreto.com; Calle Quintero Ramos 2; raciónes €5.50-7; ⊙noon-4pm & 7.30-11pm Mon-Sat) Prepare yourself for head-spinning decor that combines a courtesan's boudoir with 1950s memorabilia and kitsch bric-a-brac; no two tables match and an eclectic combination of chandeliers provide (slightly too much) light. The food is surprisingly conventional with an emphasis on *raciónes* (large/full-plate servings; literally 'rations') to share, like *patatas bravas* (potatoes in a spicy sauce), *quesos fritas* (fried cheese) and croquettes.

★ La Taberna de la Villa CANARIAN $$
(Calle General Rodriguez y Sánchez Espinoza 10; mains €8-14; ⊙9am-11pm Mon-Thu, to 2am Fri, 11am-2am Sat; 🍴) Good, simple food, ranging from *caracoles* (snails) to *mojo queso* (Canarian spicy salsa cheese dip), plus pasta and meat dishes combined with a welcoming atmosphere and a warm ochre-washed interior have made this the most popular spot in town. It morphs into a pub from midnight until 2am on weekends.

La Mirada Profunda BISTRO $$
(☑922 55 17 87; Calle Santiago 25; menú €25; ⊙1-4pm & 8-11.30pm Tue-Sun) At this stylish bistro you don't have much of a say in what you eat, you just get to enjoy whatever the chef has prepared – soups, fresh fish and local fare with an international twist; like roasted duck with a cranberry sauce or cod-stuffed peppers. Reservations recommended.

🍷 Drinking

It doesn't get much more humdrum than Valverde, and during the week everyone heads home early. On weekends the action (if there is any) is centred around the main plaza.

Tasca El Chavelazo BAR
(Calle General Rodriguez y Sánchez Espinoza 8; ⊙8pm-late Thu, from 10pm Fri & Sat) Located across from the town hall, this cavernous bar is the most popular night-time spot in town (possibly the only one...), with moody lighting, thumping music and occasional live acts.

ℹ Information

Tourist Office (☑922 55 03 02; www.elhierro. travel; Calle Dr Quintero 11; ⊙8am-3pm Mon-Fri, 9am-1pm Sat) Get maps and information about a few island attractions.

ℹ Getting There & Away

BUS
From Valverde you can reach destinations including Frontera (€1.20, 30 minutes, up to four daily), Tamaduste (€1.20, 15 minutes, three daily), El Mocanal and La Restinga (€1.20, one hour 10 minutes, up to four daily).

ℹ Getting Around

A **TransHierro** (☑922 55 11 75; www.transhierro.com) bus to Valverde meets the handful of flights that arrive at the airport (€1.20, 20 minutes). **Taxis** (☑922 55 07 29) are a simple but pricey way to move about; it will cost about €15 to reach Valverde from the airport.

The town is small enough to easily explore on foot; if you want to travel further afield, you'll find a **taxi stand** (☑922 55 07 29; Calle San Francisco) just in front of the island transport co-op (Sociedad Cooperativa de Transportes del Hierro).

THE NORTH

The island's north coast is lined with ruggedly beautiful, but for the most part inaccessible, cliffs. The few exceptions are the delightful coves and natural volcanic rock pools in places like Pozo de las Calcosas, Charco Manso, Tamaduste and La Caleta.

Inland, grassy fields and farms extend over much of the landscape. Due to the high altitude, a near-permanent shroud of mist and fog blankets the hilltops, making this quiet, rural area seem almost spooky in its solitude.

El Mocanal

El Mocanal is one of several farming villages northwest of the capital, Valverde. Just outside the town, a well-marked turn leads down to the **Pozo de las Calcosas**, where a summer village of generations-old small houses made of lava rock (called *pajeros*) are huddled around a few natural swimming pools. They are owned by locals from the village who move here in July and August, together with their animals who graze in the precipitous fields above. Walk down the steep, stepped path for 10 minutes to access them. Above the waterfront there's a mirador, a tiny stone chapel and a couple of restaurants.

✖ Eating

★Casa Carlos   SEAFOOD **$**
(Calle el Letime 3; mains €7.50-9; ⊙11am-10pm) The homey old-fashioned dining room seems to drop off the hillside and affords fabulous views of the extraordinary huddle of ancient beach houses below. When she is not catching up on her knitting in the corner, the owner whips up wonderful seafood, including *atún* (tuna), *vieja* (parrot fish), *cabrillas* (comber fish) and *lapas* (limpets).

Meson del Norte   CANARIAN **$$**
(☑922 55 03 73; Calle Barlovento 21; mains €8.50-12; ⊙7am-10.30pm; **P**) This starkly modern place is justifiably popular with locals. The house specials are excellent and include a chickpea and chorizo stew and roast pork with a Roquefort sauce. It's located on the main highway.

❶ Getting There & Away

Bus 5 (€1.20, 20 minutes) links El Mocanal with Valverde several times daily.

Echedo

Echedo is at the heart of El Hierro's wine-growing region with minimalist vineyards planted behind stout dry stone walls that help block the wind that often swirls through. At present wine-tasting and bodega visits are not made available to the general public.

Far more captivating than anything in town are the **Charco Manso**, natural saltwater pools lying at the end of a 4km, meandering, narrow road that winds down among shrubs and volcanic rock. On a fine day the clear turquoise waters are heavenly, but at high tide or when the ocean is stirred there can be strong currents here. Be especially cautious of the caves dug into the shore; peek into them on a calm day, but never swim here.

EL HIERRO EL MOCANAL

THE ECOLOGICAL ISLAND

As your boat pulls into port, dry and rocky El Hierro might not strike you as the most beautiful of the Canary Islands, but clamber up onto the central plateau or head down to the El Golfo area and it quickly becomes apparent that first impressions can be misleading. Not only is the island enveloped in a gentle beauty, it's also home to some of the most unusual plant and animal life in the eastern Atlantic; a distinction that has earned the entire island the label of a Unesco Geopark; the first in the Canary Islands. Environmentalists' attention is mainly focused on protecting the marine reserve in the Mar de las Calmas, the unique juniper trees in El Sabinar and the quiet El Pinar pine forest, but the whole island benefits from its Unesco listing, with funds going to help the island use its unique natural resources in a sustainable way. Read more at www.geoparqueelhierro.es.

In 2014 the island took its conservationist leanings to a whole new level by becoming the world's first island to initiate projects that will allow locals to eventually rely entirely on renewable sources for its energy needs. This ecological mindset is seen in other ways as well, such as the island-wide plan to promote and support organic farming and a scheme to use only electric-powered cars by 2020. Find out more by visiting the **Centro de Interpretación de la Reserva de la Biosfera** (p210) in Isora.

The cave bottoms are pocked with tunnel-like holes called *tragadores* (literally, 'swallowers') that can suck you in as the tide ebbs.

✖ Eating

There's a small kiosk by the *charco* that keeps sporadic hours and, for those who come prepared, there's a fine picnic area with tables and benches.

La Higuera de la Abuela   CANARIAN **$$**
(☑ 922 55 10 26; Calle Tajanis Caba; mains €9-15; ☺ noon-4pm & 7-10pm Wed-Mon) For a delightful dining experience in tranquil surroundings, head to the leafy patio here to enjoy traditional dishes like fried rabbit or goat, grilled shellfish and fresh island fish. The name 'Higuera' is after the enormous fig tree that once stood here.

Tamaduste & La Caleta

These two modest resort villages are Valverde's summer playground. Small, natural coves and beautiful waterfronts make them fantastic spots for swimming, sunbathing, relaxing and fishing, but don't expect much else from these otherwise snoring towns.

Tamaduste is the perfect place to escape from the outside world. At high tide the cove fills with water and kids dive head first into the Atlantic from the various platforms and steps. At low tide, the rough waves disappear, leaving nothing more than still pools. This is the perfect time to fish or collect crabs and ocean snails.

At **La Caleta** the landscaped waterfront boasts a stone-laid promenade, plenty of spots for sunbathing and aqua-blue saltwater pools, which are well maintained and ideal for children (although it can get a little windy here). It used to be possible to see much-weathered Bimbache rock carvings on a rock face by the shore but, sadly, they were accidentally destroyed when the waterfront was reconstructed.

✖ Eating

Harina y Tomate   PIZZA **$**
(☑ 922 10 97 60; Calle Tabaiba, Tamaduste; pizza €8-9; ☺ 1-3.30pm & 7-11.30pm) There are just a couple of places to grab a bite in Tamaduste and this is one of them. Order a pizza to go from a wide choice of standard toppings or grab a table on the small front terrace. Find it next to the minimarket.

❶ Getting There & Away

A bus connecting Valverde with the port stops three times daily in Tamaduste (€1.20, 15 minutes) and La Caleta (€1.20, 20 minutes).

Puerto de la Estaca & Las Playas

The island's only ferry port, Puerto de la Estaca becomes the centre of attention when it greets the odd ferry coming in from Tenerife. Otherwise, this place is so sleepy it borders on comatose. Five buses (€1.20, 50 minutes) daily link the port with Valverde.

Past the port, the highway curves around the coast towards Las Playas, 10km further on, slicing through a no-man's-land of rocky shores and rockier hillsides. You'll pass the little town of **Timijiraque**, where there is a small black pebble beach (watch the undertow here) and the unassuming **Casa Guayana** (☑ 922 55 04 17; Carretera General; mains €8-12; ☺ 7am-10pm Sun-Fri), fronted by a couple of plastic chairs and with no visible sign, but where the food is so good that locals make a special effort to drive out here for lunch. Tasty local fish is served in a cosy dining room with a handful of tables overlooking the ocean. The paella literally tastes of rock

---

EATING LIKE A LOCAL

Food on El Hierro might be simple, but in our opinion it has the best food of any of the western islands. The island is very much self-sufficient and much of what you eat was grown, reared or captured on El Hierro or off its coasts. The lack of tourists also helps to ensure that restaurants are catering mainly to a local audience, which results in a higher standard of food quality (restaurant owners know that they are relying on locals to keep coming back, whereas on touristy islands owners know they're serving a here today, gone tomorrow clientele). Fresh local fish, local meat and local vegetables are often available at restaurants, especially to those who know to ask for it! Specialities on El Hierro include *queso herreño* (local soft cheese); dried figs are another favourite. The fruity white wine from Tigaday is quite good and is sold and served widely on the island.

pools and the sea. Find it on the main road on the left-hand side, around 800m beyond the tunnel coming from Puerto de la Estaca. Look offshore to see the famed Roque de la Bonanza, a rock formation that soars 200m out of the water and has become a symbol of the island. Las Playas itself is a long stretch of black pebble beach with mirror-smooth seas. It is often quite windy, though.

Mirador de la Peña

Designed by famed Lanzarote-born artist César Manrique, the Mirador de la Peña is one of El Hierro's top sites. Make sure you have your camera ready: mist permitting, this mirador affords sweeping views of the valley, the gulf coast and the Roques de Salmor. Wander the pathways surrounded by wild lavender bushes, palms and drago trees, which lead to several vantage points, then dine at the elegant restaurant. Sunset is really the time to see this place at its best. The mirador is just outside the agricultural hamlet of Guarazoca.

Eating

Mirador de la Peña Restaurant   CANARIAN **$$**
(☑922 55 03 00; Mirador de la Peña, Guarazoca; mains €10-15, menu del día €25; ☺12.30-3.30pm & 7-10.30pm; P) This elegant restaurant at the mirador is dominated by a huge picture window looking over El Golfo. The menu is focused on creative ways to use local ingredients, with results like Herreño pineapple stuffed with shellfish, or pork loin with a Herreño cheese sauce and dried figs. There's an informal cafe and bar, as well.

San Andrés & Around

The agricultural centre of this part of the island, San Andrés is made up of a few buildings scattered on either side of the highway. The Fiesta de la Apañada in June sees farmers gather in San Andrés for a noisy livestock sale.

About 3km southwest of San Andrés, turn onto the H-120 towards the Mirador de Jinama for soul-satisfying views over the mammoth amphitheatre that is El Golfo. Of course, depending on the day, you could be looking over a big pot of cloud soup. There's also an excellent (although windy) picnic spot and a small chapel. The H-120 highway continues on its narrow, curvy path towards

the Mirador de la Peña, making it one of the island's most scenic byways.

Heading south on the HI-4 highway, you'll come to a turn-off (the HI-402) for the Mirador de las Playas, where there is a spectacular view of the coast below.

☉ Sights & Activities

El Garoé   LANDMARK
(☑922 55 50 56; La Alberca de Los Lomos, San Andrés; ☺10am-6pm Tue-Sat; P) Gain insight into the Bimbaches culture by visiting the site of their ancient holy tree. According to legend, the tree miraculously spouted water, providing for the islanders and their animals. Today we know that it's really no miracle – mist in the air condenses on the tree's leaves and provides fresh water. The original tree was felled by a hurricane in 1610; the tree here was planted in 1949.

There's a small visitor centre near the tree and pretty walking trails leading to various freshwater pools. Get here along one of the two 2.7km dirt tracks that branch off the highways heading towards San Andrés. Both routes involve rocky, steep drives. Several walking trails set off from here. Take the PR EH 7 3km to El Mocanal or 6km down to the Pozo de las Calcosas, or take the same trail 3.5km in the other direction to San Andrés.

El Garoé is well signposted approximately 7km northeast of San Andrés from the HI-1 highway.

Camino de Jinama   HIKING
You can strike out on the rocky but well-marked Camino de Jinama, an old donkey track that should take about 2½ hours to hike, starting from the Mirador de Jinama down to La Frontera. The reverse route begins near the Plaza de la Candelaria in La Frontera and will take 3½ hours to return.

✖ Eating

Casa Goyo   CANARIAN **$**
(www.elhierro.tv/casagoyo; Carretera General 11, San Andrés; mains €8-10; ☺9am-10pm Tue-Sun) Housed in a typical village house with four small dining rooms and fronted by an earthy local bar, the dishes here are no-fuss traditional like roast lamb, goat and rabbit with *papas arrugadas* (wrinkly potatoes).

❶ Getting There & Away

Four buses (€1, 20 minutes) daily link San Andrés with Valverde.

Isora

The village of Isora is a short drive (or hike, if you're up for it) from San Andrés. The village is most famous for its Herreño cheese produced from a combination of goat, sheep and cows' milk. On the far southern side of town, perched high on El Risco de los Herreños ridge, is the **Mirador de Isora**, where the mountain falls away at your feet to reveal the smooth coast of Las Playas. The 3.5km downhill trek from the mirador to Las Playas is a popular hike with lovely views over the coast; the descent should take two hours and the round-trip about five. The downward part of the hike is extremely jarring on the legs, while coming back up again will really give your heart and lungs a good workout.

◉ Sights

Centro de Interpretación de la Reserva de la Biosfera CULTURAL CENTRE
(www.elhierro.travel; Antiguo Casino de Isora, Calle Ferinto 32; ◎10am-6pm Mon-Sat) FREE Housed in a former casino, this environment and ecology interpretation centre focuses on the island's well-known commitment to a sustainable future with exhibits and photographs of its plans as well as projects already underway, including a hydro wind farm near Valverde.

✖ Eating

Cooperative de Ganaderos Central Quesera CHEESE
(✆922 55 03 27; Poligono el Majano; per kg from €9; ◎8am-2pm Mon-Fri, to 1pm Sat; Ⓟ) Farmers from all over the island bring the milk from their cattle to this cooperative where the Herreño cheese is produced. Choose from several varieties including *queso fresco* (fresh cheese) and *ahumado* (smoked). It also sells local honey.

To get here from San Andrés, take the turn-off signposted 'Poligono el Majano' around 1km before Isora.

❶ Getting There & Away

If you're driving, follow the signs (just northeast of San Andrés) to Isora off the HI-4 highway. If you're walking, the PR EH 4.1km trail to Isora starts in Las Rosas neighbourhood of San Andrés.

Five buses (€1, 30 minutes) daily connect Isora and Valverde.

THE SOUTH

For many people this is the most beautiful part of the island. It's lush and green with an idyllic year-round climate. It's also about the only part of the Canary Islands where you'll see proper livestock farming and fields surrounded by dry stone walls. The landscape undulates gently and in February and March the whole area is nothing less than a carnival of colourful flowers. It really pays to ditch the car and follow some of the easy walking trails that criss-cross this highland region.

El Pinar

The serene El Pinar pine forest covers a long swathe of the southern half of the island, casting cool shade over the volcanic terrain and providing an excellent destination for a day's hiking or a scenic drive. The lonely highway that cuts through El Pinar connects the eastern rim of the forest with the Ermita de Nuestra Señora de los Reyes on the western side of the island; countless trails branch off the main road.

On the HI-4 highway, south of the Mirador de las Playas, you'll pass **Las Casas** and **Taibique**, two small towns built along the steeply descending highway. Although they're technically independent, it's impossible to tell where one town ends and the other begins. While not a destination in its own right, this is a good place for self-caterers to buy supplies. Don't miss the **Mirador de Tanajara**, from where there are lovely views.

◉ Sights

Centro de Interpretación Geológica CULTURAL CENTRE
(✆922 55 84 23; www.elhierro.travel; Travesía del Pino, Tabique; ◎10am-6pm Mon-Sat) FREE This small cultural centre has an interesting exhibition about the landscape and geology of the island, including an extensive exhibit on the various types of volcanic lava rock with their quaint descriptive names like *breadcrust* and *spatter*.

Hoya del Morcillo & Around

Hoya del Morcillo (open 9am to 9pm) is a shady recreational area in the heart of El Pinar. With a football field, a playground and a picnic area, including a large integrated barbecue area, this is the perfect spot to rest among the pines. Don't miss the large-scale map of El Hierro, made with logs. Continuing into the forest you come to the Parque Cultural El Julán. Coming from the HI-4, take the HI-40 highway towards Hoya del Morcillo.

⦿ Sights

Parque Cultural de El Julán   CULTURAL CENTRE
(☑ 922 55 50 56; www.elhierro.travel; Carretera General de El Julán; tour €19; P) Housed in an attractive modern building from where there are stunning coastal views, the exhibits here centre on one of the island's most important cultural sights, **Los Letreros**, where a scattering of indecipherable petroglyphs was scratched into a lava flow by the Bimbaches. The actual site is an 11km round-trip away on the seafront and can only be visited with a guide either by foot (10am daily) or by jeep (3pm daily). Reservations must be made in advance.

If you can't visit the actual site, the centre has excellent reproductions of the petroglyphs, plus other interesting displays about the Bimbaches, including photos of a necropolis discovered in the Cueva de la Lajura cave. There is a cafe and small gift shop.

La Restinga

Quickly becoming El Hierro's tourist hot spot, the once-sleepy fishing village of La Restinga is now turning into something of a resort thanks to the dozens of scuba-diving outfitters that have set up shop here. Hotels and apartment blocks (p234) mainly cater to those exploring the watery depths because, as seasoned divers will know, there is a considerable altitude difference between here and the nearest towns (some 100m) and divers must stay near sea level for at least 12 hours after a dive. The diving schools take advantage of the underwater marvels provided by the **Mar de las Calmas** (Sea of Calm), the warm, still waters that surround the island's southwestern shore. For nondivers, there are two volcanic beaches right on the port, where the ocean is as still as bath water, if none too clean. The town itself still feels like it's being built and is fairly modern and characterless.

The road down to La Restinga rambles through volcanic badlands. Take time to look at the quirky lava shapes, ranging from *pahoehoe* or *lajial,* smooth rock that looks

like twisted taffy, to hard, crumbling rock that looks like wet oatmeal. The gleaming sea stretches out before you as you descend into the town, past a landscape of volcanic ash studded wth bright-green cactus. You can clearly make out the line between the glassy Mar de las Calmas and the windblown open ocean to the west, which is rough and choppy. Part of the sea is a marine reserve, and both fishing and diving are restricted in an effort to provide fish with a safe place to breed.

⦿ Sights

Centro Vulcanológico   CULTURAL CENTRE
(www.elhierro.travel; Carretera HI, La Restinga; adult/child €3/free; ⏰ 10.30am-4.45pm; P) FREE Inaugurated in February 2015, this centre comprises two exhibition halls; the first hall focuses on what exactly causes a volcano via computerised multilingual screens, special effects and a suitably soul-stirring soundtrack. The tour then takes you through actual lava fields to the second hall where the recent eruption in 2011 is brought to life via four giant screens that explain and show the events as they unfolded.

🏃 Activities

There's no shortage of diving companies offering their services to divers, and everyone is offering pretty much the same thing – a €25 to €30 dive around the Mar de las Calmas, where you can expect to encounter colourful

---

WORTH A TRIP

COOLING OFF IN CALA DE TACORÓN

Just before La Restinga, you'll pass the turn-off to Cala de Tacorón, a tranquil series of volcanic rocky coves that bake in a near-ceaseless sun. This is a great area for swimming and diving (many of the La Restinga–based companies come here), and it's popular with kayakers. After enjoying the water, have lunch at the rustic, covered picnic area, made with logs and branches, á la *Swiss Family Robinson.* If DIY lunches just aren't you, there's also a laid-back beach bar, **Kiosco Tacorón** (Cala de Tacorón; ⏰ noon-8pm Tue-Sun), that serves an eclectic mix of dishes from wood-fired pizzas to octopus dragged straight out of the nearby water.

coral, majestic rock formations and a wide variety of marine life. Courses and speciality dives are also available.

El Hierro Taxi Diver   DIVING
(☑ 922 10 40 69; www.elhierrotaxidiver.com; Avenida Marítima 4; ☻ 8am-6pm) Located right on the seafront and one of the longest established operators.

Centro de Buceo el Hierro   DIVING
(www.centrodebuceoelhierro.com; Calle El Rancho 12; ☻ 10am-6pm) A well-established diving school.

★☆ Festivals & Events

Fiesta de la Virgen del Carmen   FIESTA
(☻ Jul) The Fiesta de la Virgen del Carmen, honouring La Restinga's patron saint, is celebrated on the weekend closest to 16 July with a town dance and dinner on Saturday, and a religious procession on Sunday.

✖ Eating

Delicious, fresh seafood is the main attraction at most restaurants here. Self-caterers can shop at the Spar supermarket in town.

Casa Juan   SEAFOOD $
(☑ 922 55 71 02; Calle Juan Gutierrez Monteverde 23; mains €6-9; ☻ 7am-11pm Thu-Tue) Look beyond the peeling paintwork and scuffed interior, the food here is inexpensive and competently cooked. Aside from the seafood, there is the heartwarming *caldo de huevo* (also known as *sopa de queso*) based on pasta, potatoes, cheese and eggs, which sounds strange but tastes delicious!

★ El Refugio   SEAFOOD $$
(☑ 922 55 70 29; Calle la Lapa 1; mains €10-14; ☻ 1-4.30pm & 6-10.15pm) Tucked down a narrow elbow in the town centre, El Refugio's owner has his own fishing boat so seafood here really *is* as fresh as the day's catch – and delicious. Go with the recommendation of the day.

❶ Information

Tourist Office (☑ 922 55 71 37; www.elhierro. travel; Calle Carmen 4; ☻ 8.30am-2.30pm Mon-Fri) Has maps and information about the area, as well as an exhibit focussing on the dramatic 2011 volcano that took place just offshore.

❶ Getting There & Away

The HI-4 highway dead ends in La Restinga; there's no missing it. There are frequent bus services (€1.20, one hour 10 minutes, up to four daily) between Valverde and La Restinga.

EL GOLFO

An amphitheatre-shaped depression dominating El Hierro's northwestern flank, the green Golfo is, like the rest of the island, largely rural, with banana plantations filling the low-lying coastal areas. A string of quiet hamlets, some with tempting swimming holes, are laid out along the coast, while inland, growing commercial centres like La Frontera and Tigaday serve as the economic engines of the western half of the island. To the south, a rugged mountain ridge looms like a wall hiding the rest of the island, while to the north, a desolate volcanic wasteland tempts with its peculiar beauty. More than 90% of the terrain on this part of the island is protected as some sort of reserve.

Thanks to the highway tunnel built a few years back, El Golfo is just a 10-minute drive from Valverde on the HI-5 highway. But for those who love a good scenic drive (and don't get car sick), coming in the old way, on the HI-1, snaking down over the towering mountain ridge flanking El Golfo, is rewarding – just make sure the brakes on your car are in good working order!

Las Puntas

Sitting right on the water, though offering no access to it, the small hamlet Las Puntas exists purely for the tourists who come to relax here. Its main attractions are the view and the sound of the roaring waves.

A pathway runs between Las Puntas and La Maceta. The walk takes about an hour (one way) and is very easy (you could probably just about manage to do it with a baby stroller) and offers sublime ocean views all the way.

From here there is a clear view of Los Roques de Salmor, an important nesting spot for various bird species and one of the last stands of the primeval Lagarto del Salmor (Lizard of Salmor).

✖ Eating

Garoñones   SEAFOOD $$
(☑ 649 50 96 96; Calle Cascadas de Mar 3; mains €10-15; ☻ noon-4pm & 7-10pm Thu-Tue) Look for the jaunty blue window trim; this restaurant is the only spot to eat or drink close to the water and gets lively on weekend nights. At meal times, come to enjoy tapas and seafood meals so fresh the fish on your plate will probably still be flapping their fins in protest. Also rents apartments.

El Hierro is perhaps best known as a scuba-diving destination; La Restinga is the sport's epicentre. Other popular activities include splashing around in the natural volcanic-rock pools, fishing off the shore and hiking.

The island is scored with hiking trails, including the long-distance GR trails (marked with red-and-white signs), the 10km-plus PR trails (marked in yellow and white), and the short and local SL trails (marked in green and white). The island's best-known path is the Camino de la Virgen, stretching from the Ermita de Nuestra Señora de los Reyes to Valverde; this 26km historic trail is walked by thousands during the fiesta Bajada de la Virgen de los Reyes. There are a few very demanding walks on El Hierro, such as the thigh-burning hike from Isora to Las Playas, but most of the walking, whether it be coastal strolling or countryside rambling, is fairly gentle and family friendly – but nonetheless impressive for it.

La Maceta & Charco Los Sargos

For a swim, head down to La Maceta. This series of natural saltwater pools built along the coast is probably the pick of such places on El Hierro, and certainly the most popular with both locals and tourists. At high tide the ocean swallows the pools, making swimming dangerous. At other times, though, taking a cool dip here is a dream. There are several different pools of varying depth and wave shelter including one that is ideal for children. There is a good beach bar here, Kiosco Los Arroyos (La Maceta; mains €6-9; ⊙10am-9pm), that serves excellent seafood and paella on Sundays.

From the main highway, follow the signs to La Maceta, turning down the HI-550 and taking the first sealed road to your right.

Just up the coast is Charco Los Sargos, another swimming spot with calm pools that buffer the crashing waves. It's similar to La Maceta but with less fanfare. There's a small beach shack that keeps erratic hours. From the HI-550, the turn-off is just 300m north of the turn-off for La Maceta.

◎ Sights

Ecomuseo de Guinea   MUSEUM
(☑922 55 50 56; www.elhierro.travel; Carretera General de Las Puntas; adult/child €7.50/free; ⊙10am-5pm, tours 10.30am, 11.30am, 12.30pm, 1.30pm, 3pm, 4pm & 5pm; P⊛) The island's premier cultural site, this outdoor museum is two centres in one. The Casas de Guinea encompasses a fascinating route through a volcanic cave and 20 ancient houses (four of which are visitable). The houses represent islander lifestyles through the centuries.

Next door, the Lagartario is a sanctuary and breeding centre for the giant lizard of El Hierro, where you can see around a dozen lizards lolling about in the sun in vivariums; including the senior member aged 29.

The Ecomuseo is well signposted off Highway 55 around 3km south of Las Puntas. Note that you can only visit with a guide at the times listed above. The tours are in Spanish only, except at 10.30am on Wednesdays when an English- and German-language tour is run.

Tigaday
POP 1231

The nerve centre of the La Frontera municipality, Tigaday is a commercial hub (in El Hierro terms at least) strung out along the highway. There's not much to see in its centre, but as El Hierro's second town, Tigaday is the only place on the island with shops and services to rival the capital, and it has one of the island's three petrol stations. Most shops, bars and services are along Calle Tigaday.

✖ Eating

On Sundays a small artisan and fresh-food market (Plaza Vieja; ⊙8am-1pm) sets up shop on Tigaday's main plaza.

★**Casa Pucho**   CANARIAN $$
(☑922 55 61 48; www.restaurantedondin2.com; Calle La Corredera 5; mains €10-15; ⊙9am-11pm; ⊛) Sit in the shade on the roadside terrace in a small dining room or a bar filled with fruit machines (and locals). The menu includes all the normal Canarian staples, including the speciality, roast lamb, as well as more unexpected dishes and combinations like baby squid wrapped in bacon.

La Frontera

Although La Frontera is the name of the large municipality that extends over the entire gulf coast, it's also the name of a small and very peaceful settlement perched on the hillside behind Tigaday. The most important sight here is the Iglesia de Nuestra Señora de la Candelaria, a 17th-century construction that was redone in 1929. Inside, the three-nave church has two rows of pretty stone columns and an ornate golden altar. It sits on the Plaza de la Candelaria, a charming square with benches and a fountain. Behind the church, you can walk to the empty stone chapel perched on the hill. It's a short but steep climb and, from the top, the gulf valley spreads out before you like a patchwork quilt of fields and banana plantations.

The Camino de Jinama begins (or ends, depending on your route) near the plaza.

✯ Festivals & Events

Fiesta de la Virgen de la Candelaria FIESTA
(☉15 Aug) La Frontera celebrates the Fiesta de la Virgen de la Candelaria with a religious procession and a showcase of *lucha canaria* followed by a lively dance in nearby Tigaday's Plaza Vieja.

✗ Eating

★ Joapira CANARIAN $
(☑922 55 98 03; Plaza Candelaria 8; mains €6-9; ☉7am-11pm Mon-Sat) The chef here takes great pride in her cooking and it shows in such specials as Venezuelan *cachapas* (stuffed corn pancakes; try them filled with cheese) and *carne fiesta* (a huge plate of grilled meats, peppers and potatoes). There are fresh flowers on the tables and you can expect surprising complimentary extras like *tomatoes alinenados* (sliced fresh tomatoes with olive oil and garlic) or a homemade dessert.

The front terrace overlooks the pretty early 19th-century church with a view down to the sea beyond.

Los Llanillos & Sabinosa

The small town of Los Llanillos hugs the HI-50 highway a few kilometres out of Tigaday. Although the town itself won't detain you for long, there is a good restaurant here: Asador Artero (☑922 55 50 37; Calle Artero 2; mains €8-12; ☉1-4.30pm & 7-11.30pm). A cosy yet busy place, it's popular with locals who crowd in for the tasty grilled meats and chicken.

In Los Llanillos, take the turn-off for Charco Azul, a pristine natural cove with calm pools for swimming and hardly another soul in sight.

The highway grows steeper and curvier as it leads to Sabinosa, Spain's westernmost town. This remote little village feels as though it's at the end of the world, which in fact, until Columbus found some place called America, people thought it was. There is not much here to see, but the scenery nearby is breathtaking.

If you take the coastal highway, you'll quickly reach the famed Pozo de la Salud (Well of Health). You can walk down to the small *pozo*, with its waters said to cure a variety of ills, but it's generally closed up. If you fancy taking the waters (including salt baths), check out the adjacent Hotel Balneario Pozo de la Salud (p234).

Just west of the *pozo,* down the HI-500, is Playa de las Arenas Blancas (White Sands Beach). Take a short road down to the coast, where indeed there are a few whitish grains of sand. They quickly melt into volcanic rock at the water's edge, though. Despite this slight abuse of the term white, it is still a fantastic spot – wild and beautiful and almost certain to be deserted. Be careful of dangerous currents if you take to the waters. There's a very simple and well-marked hour-long coastal walk starting from this beach and leading into La Dehesa area.

EL HIERRO FOR CHILDREN

Although it lacks the theme parks, zoos and myriad organised activities of some of the larger islands, there's still plenty of good, clean, healthy outdoors fun for children. The various natural pools that are dotted liberally around the island offer safe swimming for all the family. The best of these are La Maceta and La Caleta. Much less frequented, but undeniably beautiful, is the Charco Azul. Older children will love the snorkelling and diving around La Restinga and everyone likes looking for dragons among the giant lizards housed in the Ecomuseo de Guinea. Up on the inland plateau there are plenty of chances for youngsters to burn off excess energy on the numerous fairly gentle hiking trails.

THE DESCENT OF THE VIRGIN

The fiesta par excellence on El Hierro is the **Bajada de la Virgen de los Reyes** (Descent of the Virgin; ☉early Jul), held every four years (next in 2017). Most of the island's population gathers to witness or join in a procession bearing a statue of the Virgin, seated in a sedan chair, from the Ermita de Nuestra Señora de los Reyes in the west of the island all the way across to Valverde. Her descent is accompanied by musicians and dancers dressed in traditional red-and-white tunics and gaudy caps, and celebrations continue for most of the month in villages and hamlets across the island.

You don't have to wait for the fiesta to make this iconic walk across the island. The ancient 26km Camino de la Virgen trail stretches from Valverde to the *ermita* (chapel), cutting through farms and forest on its journey across the spine of the island. Expect the well-marked walk to take eight hours. It takes in much of the island's most beautiful highland scenery – an area absolutely awash in flowers in the spring.

LA DEHESA

The westernmost point of the island is practically uninhabited and wild volcanic landscapes dominated by fierce-looking rock formations, hardy shrubs and wind-sculpted juniper trees are the main attractions. This part of the island is called La Dehesa (the Pasture), and is only accessible via the arching highway that cuts through volcanic badlands where only a few low shrubs dare to survive.

Stop for a swim at **Playa del Verodal**, a curious red-sand beach that backs up to a majestic rock cliff. The beach itself is 1km off the main highway (follow the signs) and is often deserted, leaving you with your own private paradise.

As the highway nears the southern coast you'll reach the HI-503, the turn-off for the **Faro de Orchilla** (Lighthouse of Orchilla), the most southwesterly point in Spain. Long ago robbed of its status as Meridiano Cero by Greenwich in the UK, the lighthouse is still an island icon. West of the lighthouse is a commemorative monument.

Ermita de Nuestra Señora de los Reyes

This pretty white chapel, made all the more interesting because of the history and tradition behind it, contains the image of the island's patron saint, Nuestra Señora de los Reyes (Our Lady of the Kings), because local shepherds bought her from foreign sailors on Three Kings Day, 6 January (1545). The people attribute several miracles to the Virgin, including ending droughts and epidemics.

Every four years (2017, 2021 etc) in July the Virgin is taken out of the chapel in a lively procession around the island. If you can't be here for this extravaganza, on the feast day of the **Fiesta de los Pastores** (☉25 Apr), the Virgen de los Reyes is taken out of her home in the Ermita de Nuestra Señora de los Reyes and carried to the cave where she was first kept.

El Sabinar & Around

El Sabinar is named after the *sabinas* (junipers) that grow in this area in very weird ways. Along one part of the road here, the way is lined with these trees which, though beautiful, are not as spectacular as the wind-twisted juniper trees further down the road at El Sabinar, which have become the island's symbol. You'll pass a turn-off to the left at a signpost indicating El Sabinar. Park here and wander among some of the most unusual trees you'll ever see. They have been sculpted by nature into wild shapes that look frozen in time.

Wear long trousers if you want to weave your way through the brush and get close to the trees, which are scattered on the hillside. These wonderfully weird *sabinas* are part of the reason that Unesco declared the entire island a biosphere reserve.

Once back at the fork, you could curl north for a further 2km to reach the **Mirador de Bascos**, a spectacular lookout that's unfortunately often cloaked in cloud. If it's a clear day, prepare for a breathtaking view.

Accommodation

Best Places to Sleep

➡ Villa del Conde (p220)

➡ Casa Isaítas (p222)

➡ Hotel Alhambra (p227)

➡ Hotel San Telmo (p232)

Best Budget Options

➡ Downtown House (p218)

➡ Soulsurfer Hotel (p222)

➡ El Sitio (p234)

➡ Hotel Adonis Capital (p226)

Best Self-Catering

➡ Apartamentos Tapahuga (p231)

➡ La Fuente (p232)

Where to Stay

Whitewashed apartments set around bougainvillea-clad gardens, historic farmhouses transformed into charming self-catering cottages, boutique hotels taking advantage of their mountain-top locations and basic *pensiones* located in atmospheric old buildings. Accommodation in the Canary Islands offers far more than the colossal apartment complexes and uber-luxurious five-star hotels typical of tourist resorts – though there are plenty of those as well.

The largest and most popular island is Tenerife, where the high-profile tourist resorts are in the south. Puerto de la Cruz, in the north, has excellent tourist facilities, while historic La Laguna is a charming inland choice.

Fuerteventura has two main resorts: Morro Jable in the south, and Corralejo in the north, which has a pretty harbour at its heart. A quieter coastal option with great budget accommodation is El Cotillo, a short drive from Corralejo. Lanzarote's Puerto del Carmen, Costa Teguise and Playa Blanca are the main tourist areas, while the capital, Arrecife is a good base.

Las Palmas de Gran Canaria combines a great beach with city sophistication, while the southern resorts are unabashedly family orientated. La Palma's Los Cancajos and Puerto Naos beaches are among the best on the island, while the centre hinterland is home to atmospheric *casas rurales*.

On the smallest islands, La Gomera and El Hierro, accommodation is predominantly midrange and includes atmospheric rural offerings.

Pricing

The price indicators in this guide refer to the cost of a double room, including private bathroom and excluding breakfast unless otherwise noted. Where half-board (breakfast and dinner) or full board (breakfast, lunch and dinner) is included, this is mentioned in the price. In the budget category you may have to share a bathroom and facilities will be limited, though wi-fi is becoming more common. Midrange choices often include satellite TV, private balconies and, usually, wi-fi, while top-end rooms offers all this plus more, and are often located in sumptuous historic buildings.

Category	Cost
€ budget	less than €65
€€ midrange	€65–140
€€€ top end	more than €140

Apartments

Apartments for rent are much more common than hotels. Quality can vary greatly, but they can be more comfortable than a simple *pensión* and considerably more economical, especially if there are several of you and you plan to self-cater. The two principal categories are *estudios* (studios), with a living room and bedroom combined, and the more frequent *apartamento,* where you get a double bedroom and separate lounge. Both have separate bathroom and a kitchenette. Also common are *aparthotels* (apartment-hotels), which function exactly like hotels in terms of service, but with large rooms that include a kitchenette – more like a small apartment.

Many apartment complexes are contracted to tour operators and don't rent to independent travellers; even those that do may insist upon a minimum three-night stay.

In the case of privately owned apartments, most of the time the owner doesn't live in the building so there's little point in just turning up – you generally need to call ahead.

Casas Rurales

These rural self-catering houses and hotels are generally converted farmsteads or village houses and are often a highly agreeable option for those seeking to escape the bustle of the resorts. It's essential to call ahead as they usually offer limited places and there may be no-one in attendance. Many *casas rurales* are distant from public transport, so check whether a hire car is necessary or desirable. They usually represent excellent value for the charm of their setting and facilities, and can be a great base for hiking.

Hotels, Hostels & Pensiones

While you will find plenty of four- to five-star *hoteles*, particularly in the resorts, there is a lack of midrange hotel accommodation in the islands. Midrange options are usually of the self-catering ilk. Similarly, budget accommodation can be rather thin on the ground.

In practice, there is little difference between *pensiones* – one- to two-star guesthouses – and *hostales* (small hotels, not youth hostels). At the one-star end of either you may well find cramped, dank rooms and shared bathrooms (with perhaps a simple washbasin in the room), while at a slightly higher price you could find charming gems with private bathrooms and stylish decor. *Hoteles* range from simple places to luxurious, five-star establishments with complimentary bathrobes, spa treatments and superior restaurants.

You will find a few backpacker-style hostels featuring dorms, shared kitchen and the like in Las Palmas de Gran Canaria and some of the surf towns.

Paradores

The *paradores*, a Spanish state-run chain of high-class hotels with six establishments in the Canary Islands, are in a special category. They can be wonderful places to luxuriate. They also offer a range of discounts for senior citizens, under-30s and those staying more than one night. You can find current offers at www.parador.es.

Camping

For a place with so much natural beauty, there are precious few places to camp in the Canary Islands. Most islands have just one token official campsite and free camping is largely prohibited. Occasionally you will happen across a usually amenity-free campsite in some of the smaller towns, but staying there can be a bit of a headache. You have to apply in person for permission from the *ayuntamiento* (town hall) or *cabildo* (island government). If you are travelling with a tent, it's always worth asking the local tourist information office about the availability of campgrounds in the vicinity and how to gain access.

SEASONS

Prices throughout this guide are high-season maximums. That said, virtually any time is tourist time in the Canaries although, strictly speaking, the high season is winter, when the Canaries can offer sunshine, warmth and an escape from the rigours of the northern European winter. July and August are also busy times of year as this is when the majority of mainland Spanish take their holidays.

GRAN CANARIA

Gran Canaria has, arguably, the best range of accommodation in the Canaries, depending on whether you want to wake up to sounds of birdsong, the surf or surrounded by the vigour and excitement of a Spanish mainland–style city.

Las Palmas de Gran Canaria

Vegueta & Triana

⭐ **Downtown House** HOSTEL €
(Map p46; ☎ 639 629335; www.houselaspalmas.com; Calle Domingo J Navarro 10; dm €18, s/d €38/48, without bathroom €28/38; 🛜) Located just off Calle Mayor de Triana, this fabulous 1920s building was designed by the same architect as the elegant Gabinete Literario. Rooms are spotlessly clean and simply decorated, showcasing the original ornate tiled floors. A basic, DIY breakfast is included in the price. There's a minimum two-night stay and advance bookings are required as there is no reception.

Hotel Parque HOTEL €
(Map p46; ☎ 928 36 80 00; www.hotelenlaspalmas.es; Calle Muelle Las Palmas 2; s/d incl breakfast €55/60; 🅿✳🛜) This six-storey hotel is excellently positioned overlooking the Parque San Telmo. The best views are from the rooftop restaurant. The great-value rooms have had a stylish revamp, with simple decor in muted tones. If you're staying a while or plan to spend time in your room, consider upgrading to a considerably more spacious *doble plus* room (€72).

Hotel Madrid HOTEL €
(Map p46; ☎ 928 36 06 64; www.elhotelmadrid.com; Plazoleta Cairasco 4; s/d €35/45, without bathroom €30/40; 🛜) This place abounds in charm and history: General Franco stayed here in 1936 and supposedly launched the coup that started the Spanish Civil War from room No 3 (and reputedly left without paying!). The interior is a beguiling mix of agreeable tat, priceless antiques and hanging plants. Rooms with balconies overlooking the plaza are slightly more expensive.

There's an atmospheric bar and restaurant downstairs.

Ciudad Jardín

Hotel Santa Catalina HOTEL €€
(☎ 928 24 30 40; www.hotelsantacatalina.com; Calle León y Castillo 227; s/d incl breakfast €100/115; 🅿✳@🛜) This historic hotel is truly magnificent, with traditional Canarian balconies, showy turrets and a red-carpet-style arcaded entrance. The rooms won't disappoint: there are king-size beds, antique bedheads, oriental carpets and plush furnishings. It exudes the class of another era, with its piano bar and *hammam* (Turkish bath) and delightful views of either the sea or subtropical gardens.

Santa Catalina & Playa de las Canteras

La Ventana Azul HOSTEL €
(Map p48; ☎ 671 505359; www.ventana-azul.de; Paseo de las Canteras 53; dm €18, s/d without bathroom €32/55; 🛜) A spectacularly located hostel on the beachfront. The six-person dorm has ocean views, but the best place to enjoy the vista is from the rooftop terrace with its chill-out area. Staying here isn't just about relaxing, though – the owner is a surfing fanatic and can advise on which of the city's 12 surf spots will serve your needs. Skateboards and snorkelling gear are free for guests to use and staff can arrange all manner of outdoor pursuits around the island.

Apartamentos Brisamar APARTMENT €
(Map p48; ☎ 928 26 94 00; www.brisamarcanteras.com; Paseo de las Canteras 49; seafacing studio €60; 🛜) The decent-sized studio apartments here aren't going to win any awards for decor, but when it comes to views, Brisamar is unbeatable. The terraces overlook Playa de las Canteras, which is just metres away. The penthouse apartment (two people €80) is huge, with three bedrooms, a large kitchen and two sea-facing balconies. Slightly cheaper rooms without the view are available.

Apartamentos Playa Dorada APARTMENT €€
(Map p48; ☎ 928 26 51 00; www.playadoradaweb.com; Calle Luis Morote 61; studio €65, apt €95; 🛜) These spacious apartments have enough

kitchen cupboards for a family of four and massive ocean-facing terraces. The rooms have a retro '60s feel with their white plastic bar stools, tubular lights and swivel chairs. There are also smaller studio apartments with a more modern look. There are good off-peak discounts and no supplements for ocean-facing rooms.

NH Imperial Playa   HOTEL €€
(Map p48; ☑ 928 46 88 54; www.nh-hoteles.com; Calle Ferreras 1; r with sea views €95; P ❄ 🛜 🛋) The lobby here draws you in with its black tubular lamps, chocolate-brown paintwork, sage-green sofas and a magnificently quirky version of Velázquez' *Las Meninas* executed in colourful tiles. The rooms are pleasant but impersonal, with mostly beige furnishings. Those on the seafront have views of the entire beach stretched out before them.

The East

Agüimes

Hotel Rural Casa de los Camellos   HOTEL €€
(☑ 928 78 50 53; www.hotelruralcasadeloscamellos. com; Calle Progreso 12; r incl breakfast €85; P ❄ 🛜) A lovely place tucked down a narrow pedestrian street in the historic centre. Rooms are elegant yet rustic, with antiques and wooden beams and balconies. Sadly, the excellent restaurant (in a former camel stable) is no longer open to nonguests.

The North

Teror

Casa Rural Doña Margarita   HOTEL €€
(☑ 928 63 19 21; www.margaritacasarural.com; Calle Padre Cueto 4; 2-/4-person apt €85/130; 🛜) A beautifully restored, colonial-style 18th-century house located just off the main square. There are three large and homey apartments with fully equipped kitchens, pleasant bedrooms and large sitting-cum-dining rooms with wooden beams and stone walls. There is a minimum two days' stay.

Arucas

Hacienda del Buen Suceso   HOTEL €€€
(☑ 928 62 29 45; www.haciendabuensuceso. com; Ctra de Arucas a Bañaderos; s/d €128/140;

 P ❄ @ 🛋) Set among lush banana plantations about 1.5km west of town, this aesthetically renovated country estate dates back to 1572. The rooms are rustic yet elegant, with white linen, beamed ceilings and luxuriant carpets. Service can be a little brusque though, and the restaurant receives mixed reviews from readers: consider dining in town. Wi-fi in public areas only.

Agaete & Puerto de las Nieves

Hotel Puerto de las Nieves   HOTEL €€
(☑ 928 88 62 56; www.hotelpuertodelasnieves.es; Avenida Alcalde José de Armas, Puerto de las Nieves; r incl breakfast €80; P ❄ @ 🛜) A bright hotel a few blocks back from the ocean and an easy walk to numerous seafood restaurants. The modern rooms have had funky paint jobs that contrast with the shiny parquet floors. Rooms either have a lounge or – even better – large terraces with sunbed space. The attached spa has thalassotherapy treatments and an array of massages.

Hotel El Cabo   HOTEL €€
(☑ 928 88 75 20; www.hotelelcabo.com; Calle Antón Cerezo 20, Puerto de las Nieves; r incl breakfast €88; ❄ 🛜) Located in the heart of the town, this small hotel has the air of a guesthouse about it, with friendly staff and individually decorated rooms. Rooms are bright and slickly furnished but tight on space. Some overlook an internal courtyard; street-facing rooms are more expensive (€100). Breakfast is the normal continental affair.

Central Mountains

Tejeda

Fonda de la Tea   BOUTIQUE HOTEL €€
(☑ 928 66 64 22; www.hotelfondadelatea.com; Calle Ezequiel Sánchez 22; s/d €60/95; ❄ 🛜) This traditional stone-clad building has been

transformed into a charming small hotel. Rooms are set around a Canarian-style courtyard and are tastefully decorated with plenty of terracotta tiling, pumpkin-coloured paintwork and wood. The solarium has stunning views across the valley and guests have access to the municipal pool in the summer.

Around Tejeda

Parador de Cruz de Tejeda   HOTEL €€

(✆928 01 25 00; www.parador.es; Cruz de Tejeda; r €100; P ✳ 🛜) The interior of this luxurious, state-run hotel matches low-key sophistication with a muted earth-colour palette, accentuated by tasteful artwork and framed by truly outstanding views of the surrounding gorges and cliffs. There is a luxurious spa for enjoying after your daily hikes; the staff can provide detailed maps. There's a good restaurant here serving upmarket Canarian cuisine.

Hotel Rural El Refugio   HOTEL €€

(✆928 66 65 13; www.hotelruralelrefugio.com; Cruz de Tejeda; s/d €65/80; P ✳ 🛤) This hotel has long been a popular choice with walkers. It has an unpretentious rustic charm with a popular and reasonably priced restaurant and bar, and rooms that boast appropriately great views of the surrounding striking landscape.

San Bartolomé de Tirajana

Hotel Rural Las Tirajanas   HOTEL €€€

(✆928 56 69 69; www.hotelrurallastirajanas.com; Calle Oficial Mayor Jose Rubio; s/d €95/150; P✳🛜🛤) This alpine-style lodge has spectacular views of soaring mountains. Rooms are old-school luxurious, with wood furnishings, terracotta tiles and chintzy bedspreads and curtains. There is also a spa, a fitness centre and a chapel if you fancy tying the knot. It's a great base for hikers and bikers.

The South

Playa del Inglés & Maspalomas

Parque Tropical Hotel   HOTEL €€

(✆928 77 40 12; www.hotelparquetropical.com; Avenida Italia 1; s/d €75/105; P🛜🛤) A real gem in this sea of generic high-rise hotels. Dating back to the 1960s, this hotel has a traditional Canarian look with wooden balconies, white

stucco exterior and lush, mature gardens set amid small pools and fountains. The rooms have an Andalucian feel, with terracotta tiles, dark-wood fittings and beams combined with soothing pastel-coloured paintwork.

Sahara Beach Club   HOTEL €€

(✆928 76 07 76; www.sahara-beach-club.com; Avenida Alemania 53; 2-person bungalow €75; 🛜🛤) This low-rise complex overlooks the dunes and has a tranquil, homey atmosphere with basic bungalows and lovely gardens. There are private terraces with small lawns and rose bushes. The minimum stay is four days; most guests stay for several weeks. Book well in advance.

Rainbow Golf Bungalows   BUNGALOW €€

(✆928 58 73 08; www.rainbowgolfbungalows.com; Calle Touroperador Finnmatkat 5; s/d €75/80; ✳🛜🛤) It's not dead central, but this well-regarded complex is worth the walk. The sleek, minimalist bungalows have private terraces and well-equipped kitchenettes – plus a bottle of bubbly on arrival! Facilities include jacuzzi, sauna and outdoor gym. The resort is exclusively for gay men.

★Villa del Conde   HOTEL €€€

(✆928 56 32 00; www.lopesanhr.com; Mar Mediterráneo 7; s/d €145/190; P✳🛜🛤) Luxurious Villa del Conde was designed to showcase typical Canarian architecture. The 'traditional town' approach could feel tacky, but it has been executed so tastefully that it somehow works. Overlooking the mini village is an impressive reception area modelled on the neoclassical church in Agüimes. Facilities include tennis courts, several restaurants, a mini club and a thalassotherapy spa. There's a minimum two-night stay.

Palm Beach   HOTEL €€€

(✆928 72 10 32; www.hotel-palm-beach.co.uk; Avenida Oasis; d from €150; P✳🛜🛤) From outside it looks like just another outsized resort hotel, but step within and the Palm Beach is a riot of colour and exciting modern design. The lobby sports brightly striped sofas, massive abstracts on the walls, white tubular lamps and glass bowls of green apples. The rooms are all different and similarly snazzy.

Puerto De Mogán

Pensión Eva   PENSIÓN €

(✆928 56 52 35; Calle Lomo Quiebre 35; r without bathroom €20) About 750m inland, heading north from town, this excellent-value place has light-filled rooms, a spacious rooftop terrace and – best news of all – a communal kitchen with a couple of fridges that makes self-catering (and socialising) a breeze.

Hotel THE Puerto de Mogán   HOTEL €€
(☑ 928 56 50 66; www.hotelpuertodemogan.com; Playa de Mogán; d incl half-board €140, apt from €70; ❈ 🛜 🏊) Beside the yacht-filled harbour, the accommodation here consists of large airy doubles and apartments (two to four people) with all the trimmings. Bag a room with a terrace overlooking the infinity pool with the beach beyond. Note that half-board is obligatory for the hotel rooms and there is a three-night minimum stay. Facilities include a spa.

La Venecia de Canarias   APARTMENT €€
(☑ 928 56 56 00; www.laveneciadecanarias.net; Local 328, Urbanización Puerto de Mogán; 1-/2-bedroom apt €65/110; 🛜) Right in the thick of the resort's pretty 'Venetian' quarter, with a truly lovely frontage surrounded by terrace bars, this well-managed complex has attractive, if smallish, apartments that sleep between three and five people. You'll pay more for the apartments with roof terraces and harbour views.

Hotel Cordial Mogán Playa   HOTEL €€€
(☑ 928 72 41 00; www.cordialcanarias.com; Avenida de los Marrero 2; s/d incl breakfast €100/145; 🅿 ❈ 🛜 🏊) Despite its size, the Cordial Mogán Playa does not mar the low-rise landscape of the town. Echoing the harbour with waterways and bridges, the public areas are a delight, while the rooms are all earth colours, expensive marble and gold-and-cream striped wallpaper. There's a spa, tennis courts and an excellent restaurant.

Mogán

Casa El Siroco   B&B €€
(☑ 928 56 93 01; www.casa-el-siroco.com; Calle San Antonio 6; r €70-90; 🛜) This charming B&B in an 18th-century former schoolhouse in the centre of Mogán has been creatively transformed by the German artist-owner. There are just two rooms, both boldly colourful with Andrea's evocative landscape photos on the walls. A hearty cooked breakfast is included in the price. It's just behind the church.

FUERTEVENTURA

Corralejo and Morro Jable have the most beds here, although *casas rurales* are increasingly sprouting up in the rural interior.

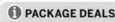

ⓘ PACKAGE DEALS

There are more than 500 hotels, apartment blocks and bungalows in Playa del Inglés and Maspalomas; in peak periods many are full to bursting. Consider booking a package deal before you arrive; this is often the cheapest way to spend a week or two in the Canaries. Use the resort as a base and head out each day to explore, returning for an evening dip at your well-priced apartment complex.

Puerto del Rosario

Hotel Tamasite   HOTEL €
(☑ 928 53 14 94; www.hoteltamasite.com; Calle León y Castillo 9; s/d €25/40; ❈ 🛜) The Tamasite is a well-situated, two-star hotel that has pleasant if mildly scuffed rooms with floral bedspreads, pine furniture and small balconies. The public areas are spacious and comfortable and the service comes with a smile.

Hostal Roquemar   HOSTAL €
(☑ 928 53 15 47; Avenida Ruperto González Negrín 1; s/d €25/30; 🛜) Located on a busy corner across from the promenade, this 10-room hotel has pleasant enough rooms with fridges and fans. Avoid those in the interior, which can be dark. If possible, opt for one of the corner rooms that have two balconies – request room Nos 103, 204 or 304. There is free wi-fi in the lobby.

La Rosa del Taro   CASA RURAL €
(☑ 928 17 51 08; www.fuerterural.com; Atalaya Rosa del Tauro 92; 2-person house €50; 🅿 🛜) 🏃 Situated 13km southwest of the capital, this *casa rural* is ideal for walkers and birdwatchers. The traditional cottage is simply furnished and the price includes fresh eggs and home-grown fruit and veggies from the owners' farm. Solar power, recycled water (for the garden) and a refreshing lack of TV equal a tranquil ecofriendly stay. Minimum three days with discounts for stays of more than a week.

Hotel JM Puerto Rosario   HOTEL €€
(☑ 928 85 94 64; www.jmhoteles.com; Avenida Ruperto González Negrín 9; s/d incl breakfast €78/118; ❈ 🛜) This corporate-style hotel comprises 88 rooms that are more attractive than its looming modern exterior would suggest. Beds are big, bathrooms are decent and facilities are good.

The Centre

Pájara

★ Casa Isaítas CASA RURAL €€
(☑928 16 14 02; www.casaisaitas.com; Calle Guize 7; s/d incl breakfast €66/84; ✺) One of the loveliest *casas rurales* on the island, the lovingly restored 18th-century stone house has two plant-filled central courtyards, traditional wooden balconies and an outside barbecue complete with giant paella pan; evening meals are an optional extra but recommended. There are just four rustic rooms, a couple of which were part of the original house.

Caleta de Fuste & Around

Barceló Castillo Beach Resort RESORT €€
(☑928 16 31 00; www.barcelo.com; Avenida Castillo; bungalows from €85; P✺@ 🛜 🛝) This franchise is so large it deserves its own postcode. The whole place has a sumptuous feel, with bougainvillea-draped bungalows and lush landscaped gardens fronting onto the wide arc of a beach. Facilities are superb and include heated pool, kids club, numerous restaurants and bars plus a beachside spa.

The North

La Oliva

★ Hotel Rural Mahoh HOTEL €€
(☑928 86 80 50; www.mahoh.com; Sitio de Juan Bello, Villaverde; s/d €60/80; P 🛜 🛝) This excellent rural hotel is hard to miss. Set in an early-19th-century stone-and-wood building, it's surrounded by a stunning cactus garden and a small farmyard with goats and a vocal cockerel. There are nine romantic bedrooms decorated with antiques, plus the modern conveniences of TV and wi-fi. The restaurant serves superb Canarian cuisine and comes highly recommended. The hotel is 4km north of La Oliva, just off the FV-101.

Corralejo

Surfing Colors APARTMENT €
(☑670 777189; www.surfingcolors.com; Calle Pejin 2; studio apt €50; 🛜 🛝) These small-but-smart apartments in a quiet street several blocks back from the water offer great value. The emphasis is on surfing and there are packages on offer combining several days of tuition

with accommodation. There's a minimum three-night stay.

THE Corralejo Beach HOTEL €€
(☑928 53 56 51; www.corralejobeach.com; Calle Víctor Grau Bassas 1; studios €75, 2-person apt €100; 🛝) Hard to miss thanks to a somewhat disarming pea-green-and-white exterior. Within you'll find friendly service and decent, if slightly faded, rooms set around a large pool. It's very close to the beach, though only a few rooms have ocean views.

★ Avanti BOUTIQUE HOTEL €€€
(☑928 86 75 23; www.avantihotelboutique.com; Avenida Marítima; r incl breakfast €140; ✺ 🛜) This marvellous boutique hotel exudes chic relaxation with its minimalist design, high-end furnishings and whitewashed everything. Sitting close to the old harbour, it has a definite marine feel, but steers well clear of the tacky. Facilities include a rooftop solarium and jacuzzi. Children must be over 16.

El Cotillo

★ Soulsurfer Hotel HOTEL €
(☑928 53 85 98; www.soulsurfer.es; Calle San Pedro 2; dm €15, s/d €45/49; 🛜 🛝) This funky, long-established hotel is a top spot to stay if you're here to surf. Rooms are bright and there are small (three-bed) dorms if you're trying to keep costs down. The rooftop terrace is an awesome spot to chill, with hammocks, couches and beanbags taking up every nook near the pool. Surf classes and equipment rental are on offer.

Apartamentos Juan Benítez APARTMENT €
(☑629 176348; www.apartamentos-juanbenitez.com; Calle La Caleta 4; 2-person apt €55; 🛜 🛝) These well-equipped apartments are close to both the beach and several good bars and restaurants. The spacious apartments are built around a pool that is well-sheltered from the wind. All have sea views and satellite TV; there is wi-fi in communal areas.

La Gaviota HOTEL €
(☑928 53 85 67; www.la-gaviota.net; Calle Juan de Betancourth 14; studios €38, d €60; 🛜) This laidback, neo-hippy place, which flies the Jolly Roger, has been lovingly created by a German couple. Ralf made most of the furniture and has scavenged ruins for old doors and the like. Every apartment is different, including one built into a cave. The views out to sea are sublime. It sits above the south end of the old harbour.

ONLINE RESOURCES

Casas Rurales (www.ecoturismocanarias.com) Has an extensive selection of rural accommodation throughout the islands, but doesn't cover La Gomera or Lanzarote.

Ecoturismo Gomera (www.casasruralesdelagomera.es) A good network of *casas rurales* across La Gomera.

Rural Accommodation (www.alorustico.com) A Spanish-mainland website that includes some 60 choices for rural accommodation across every island except La Gomera.

Airbnb (www.airbnb.com) There are some spectacularly located properties for rent across all the islands, ranging from city apartments with sea views to enormous houses in the mountains.

Península de Jandía

Costa Calma

H10 Playa Esmeralda   HOTEL €€
(☑928 87 53 53; www.⊙10.es; Punta del Roquito 2; s/d incl breakfast €90/120; [P][✳][⚎][⚓]) This luxurious hotel enjoys prime position above the beach and has extensive facilities, including a state-of-the-art health and fitness club, tennis courts, a children's mini club and a discotheque with regular live acts. The rooms are restrained chic and spacious, decorated in bright yellows and greens. You can walk from here to Playa de Sotavento, the island's windsurfing capital.

Risco del Gato   HOTEL €€€
(☑928 54 71 75; www.vikhotels.com; Calle Sicasumbre 2; s/d €85/150; [P][✳][⚎][⚓]) Accommodation is in spacious and luxurious suites, complete with whirlpool bathrooms, inner patio and small private garden. Located 200m from the white sandy beach of Sotavento, additional facilities include a spa centre, tennis courts, a fitness centre and three restaurants. In other words, the works.

La Pared

Waveguru Surfcamp   CAMPGROUND €
(☑619 804447; www.waveguru.de; Avenida del Istmo 17; camping per week €130) There are precious few places to camp on Fuerteventura so this ocean-side campground is a treat. It's really meant for surfers and special packages are offered to those wanting to take lessons, but nonsurfers are also welcome. There's a shared kitchen, barbecue area and surfing gear is free for guests. In quieter times the week-long minimum might be waived.

Morro Jable

Apartamentos Altavista   APARTMENT €
(☑928 54 01 64; www.altavistafuerteventura.com; Caleta Abubilla 8; 2-person apt €60; [⚓]) Easy to find (but not so easy to park) opposite the modern church in the old town; you can't miss the blue and pink exterior. The apartments are large, have small balconies and are painted a sunny yellow; several have sea views. There is also a rooftop solarium with shaded picnic tables.

Sol Jandia Mar   APARTMENT €€
(☑928 54 13 25; www.solmelia.com; Calle Bentejuí 8; 2-person apt €120; [P][✳][⚎][⚓]) Part of the solidly reliable Melia hotel chain, this centrally located hotel has large modern apartments furnished with dark-blue fabrics and wood fittings. Landscaped gardens surround a pool and facilities include children's entertainment and squash courts.

Apartamentos Palm Garden   APARTMENT €€
(☑928 54 10 00; www.palmgardenfuerteventura.com; Avenida Saladar 26; 2-person apt €90; [P][✳][⚎][⚓]) This huge complex offers studio apartments with small kitchenettes, satellite TV and terraces. It's a no-frills place, and perks like wi-fi come at an extra fee. The building isn't too pretty from the outside, but the vistas of the beach are quite superb from the interior. All rooms have sea views.

LANZAROTE

Although the bulk of Lanzarote's accommodation is in the main tourist resorts, alternative *casas rurales* options are increasing, particularly inland. The capital Arrecife is also home to several sound hotel choices and makes a good central base for exploring the island.

Arrecife

Hotel Lancelot
HOTEL €€
(Map p101; ☑928 80 50 99; www.hotellancelot.com; Avenida Mancomunidad 9; sea-facing s/d incl breakfast €54/69; ❄ 🛜 🏊) The large bright rooms have a luxurious feel with their king-size beds, sexy abstract prints, plush decor and ample balconies with ocean views. There's a rooftop pool with adjacent small gymnasium, plus regular live, smoochy jazz in the bar. Superb value for money.

Hotel Miramar
HOTEL €€
(Map p101; ☑928 80 15 22; www.hmiramar.com; Avenida Coll 2; sea-facing s/d incl breakfast €57/75; ❄ 🛜 🏊) Waterfront Miramar has been subjected to an adventurous paint palette in the public spaces, and each floor sports a different colour scheme in the rooms. It's a friendly place with a low-key cafeteria and rotating art exhibits in the lobby. Breakfast is a high, with its ocean views from the roof terrace.

Hotel Diamar
HOTEL €€
(Map p101; ☑928 07 24 81; www.hoteldiamarlanzarote.com; Avenida Fred Olsen 8; sea-facing s/d incl breakfast €54/65; ❄ 🛜) Privately owned Diamar has a boutique feel and is a welcome addition to Arrecife's hotel scene. Overlooking the beach, the large rooms are painted in cool colours with terraces overlooking the palm-fringed beach across the way. Rooms are set around a central atrium with traditional Canarian balconies. There is wi-fi, a cafeteria and a good restaurant (mains €12).

The North

Arrieta

Apartamentos Arrieta
APARTMENT €
(☑928 84 80 08; Calle Garita 8; 2-person apt €40) You'll find this blue-balconied apartment block on the main street, within walking distance of the beach. A modern low-rise building, it's a well-maintained place with good-sized pine-furnished apartments and a vast rooftop terrace. You'll need to brush up on your Spanish.

Finca de Arrieta
HOTEL €€€
(☑928 82 67 20; www.lanzaroteretreats.com; Arrieta; 2-person yurt/cottage from €130; 🅿 🛜 🏊) 🖋 This curious, eco-friendly place set back from the LZ-10 has a wonderfully random array of accommodation options. Fancy staying in a Mongolian yurt in the Canaries? There are several to choose from, ranging in size and amenities – some even have fitted kitchens, BBQ areas and designer furnishings. Other options include stone cottages, wooden huts and a restored water mill.

Owners Michelle and Tila can also provide fresh eggs from their chickens, organic fruit and veg and invaluable advice about Lanzarote. The whole place is off the grid, using wind turbines and solar panels for power. The daily rate rises for stays of less than a week.

Isla Graciosa

Playa de el Salado
CAMPGROUND €
(☑928 59 29 56; www.reservasparquesnacionales.es; Bahía del Salado) This simple site on the beach is the only place you're allowed to camp on Graciosa. There are ablution blocks and spectacular views. It's free to camp but you need to get advance permission, which you can do online. It's just southwest of Caleta de Sebo.

Pensión Enriqueta
HOSTAL €
(☑928 84 20 51; www.pensionenriqueta.com; Calle Mar de Barlovento 6; d €18-25) This small *pensión* is situated a block back from the waterfront. The rooms are good value, being simply furnished but clean as a whistle, while downstairs there's a lively restaurant and bar.

Evita Beach
APARTMENT €€
(☑928 84 21 85; www.evitabeach.net; Avenida Virgen del Mar 59; 2-person apt €85; 🛜) Graciosa's most upmarket place to stay has simple apartments decked out mostly in white but each with its own splash of colour. The sumptuous suites (from €160) have four-poster beds and a North African feel. There's a communal garden with views across the strait to Lanzarote.

La Caleta de Famara

Bungalows Playa Famara
BUNGALOW €€
(☑928 84 51 32; www.bungalowsplayafamara.com; Urbanización Famara; bungalows from €65; 🏊) This distinctive complex is located 2km north of the main town – you'll pass it on your way into Caleta de Famara. The architecture comprises a modern step-terraced arrangement of semicircular holiday homes, and it looks like suburbia. There's a restaurant and surf school here. Bungalows sleep between two and six, and longer stays equal good discounts.

Wine Country

San Bartolomé & Around

★**Caserío de Mozaga**　　HOTEL €€
(⌨928 52 00 60; www.caseriodemozaga.com;
Calle Mozaga 8; s/d €70/90, restaurant mains
€14; 🖥) Northwest of San Bartolomé in the
village of Mozaga, this 18th-century family
home retains its rustic authenticity with a
central courtyard complete with original
aljibe (water system). The rooms have high
ceilings and are graced with family heir-
looms. The restaurant (dinner only) has an
excellent reputation.

The South

Puerto del Carmen

Pensión Magec　　PENSIÓN €
(⌨928 51 51 20; www.pensionmagec.com; Calle
El Hierro 11; s/d €24/28, s/d without bathroom
€22/26; 🖥) There's just one standard *pensión* in Puerto del Carmen and it's a good
one. Housed in a blue-and-white traditional house, there are sea views from several
rooms. Go for No 21 with its private balcony if you don't mind the shared bathroom.
There's a communal kitchen and a rooftop
terrace for sunset drinks.

Costa Sal　　APARTMENT €€
(⌨928 51 42 42; www.costasal.com; Calle Agonal
16; 1-bedroom apt €70; P🖥🌐) Close to the airport and only a short walk from the beach,
Costa Sal has one- and two-bedroom apartments as well as villas and a few studios.
With tennis courts, a kids' playground and a
range of swimming pools, it's a firm favourite with families and receives great reviews
from travellers.

Hotel Los Fariones　　HOTEL €€
(⌨928 51 01 75; www.farioneshotels.com; Calle
Roque del Este 1; s/d €92/149; P❄@🖥🌐) This
is the *grande dame* of the hotel scene; it
was the first hotel to be built here, over 40
years ago. The rooms are comfortable, if a
tad old-fashioned. Facilities include tennis
courts, mini golf and a large pool overlooking the ocean.

Yaiza

Casa de Hilario　　CASA RURAL €€
(⌨928 83 62 62; www.casadehilario.com; Calle Los
Rostros 5; s/d incl breakfast €55/90; ❄🖥🌐) The
seven individually decorated rooms at this
exceptional *casa rural* have an Asian-art
influence and handmade furniture. The outside area includes a pool, a few lofty palms
and some superb views. Breakfast can be enjoyed on the shady terrace. The owners also
organise activities, including guided bike
treks and boat rides.

Casona de Yaiza　　HOTEL €€
(⌨928 83 62 62; www.casonadeyaiza.com; Calle
El Rincón 11; s/d incl breakfast €55/100; 🖥🌐)
Based in a 19th-century farmhouse on the
edge of town, with views over the region's
rolling volcanic hills. The Renaissance art
theme can get a little too much, but it's a
lovely place to stay, with a small swimming
pool and a decent restaurant.

El Golfo & Around

Hotelito del Golf　　HOTEL €
(⌨928 17 32 72; www.hotelitodelgolfo.com; Avenida Marítima 6; s/d €46/55; 🖥🌐) There is just
one hotel in El Golfo and it's this charming,
friendly, family-run place. The rooms are
bright and simply furnished with fridges
and private terraces. It's worth paying extra
for a sea view. There's a small seawater pool,
plus a sun terrace across from the surf.

Playa Blanca

Apartamentos Gutiérrez　　APARTMENT €
(⌨928 51 70 89; Plaza Nuestra Señora del Carmen
8; s/d apt €40/50) Just by the town church,
and one of the cheapest places to stay in this
area. Seven tidy studio apartments are available, most with small balconies and a few
with sea views. Owner Antonia speaks virtually no English, so brush up on your Spanish
or sign language.

H10 Sentido White Suites　　APARTMENT €€
(⌨928 51 70 37; www.☉10.es; Calle Janubio 1; s/d
ste €80/135; P❄🖥🌐) A huge refurbishment
has transformed this once family-oriented
apartment complex into a super-stylish
adults-only hotel. The sleek suites come
with flat-screen TVs, Nespresso machines
and modern art adorning the walls. There's
a gym, spa and a cool chill-out bar serving
cocktails and *shisha* pipes.

Villas Kamezí BUNGALOW €€
(✐ 928 51 86 24; www.heredadkamezi.com; Calle Mónaco 2; bungalow for up to 8 people from €220; P ✳ @ ☲) A discreet, environmentally friendly complex of 35 stunning villas with two to four bedrooms, all tastefully dec-orated with real *Ideal Home*-style decor. Amenities include a saltwater pool, chil-dren's playground and small supermarket.

TENERIFE

While finding a room is generally not a problem in Santa Cruz and in the north of the island, the same cannot be said for the southern resorts, particularly around Los Cristianos and Playa de las Américas; book in advance when possible.

Santa Cruz de Tenerife

★**Hotel Adonis Capital** HOTEL €
(Map p124; ✐ 922 28 46 01; www.adonisresorts. com; Calle Cruz Verde 24; s/d incl breakfast €47/57; P ✳ @ ☎) This central hotel offers excel-lent value. Rooms have a fairly drab colour scheme (think brown on brown), but are well equipped, a reasonable size and come with large bathrooms. Most have balconies. The top-floor breakfast buffet includes plen-ty of hot and cold choices and fresh fruit. Plus you can enjoy sea views while sipping your cappuccino.

Pensión Casablanca PENSIÓN €
(Map p124; ✐ 922 27 85 99; Calle Viera y Clavijo 15; s/d €15/21) In a great location on a leafy pedestrian street, this building dates from 1902. The rooms are brightly painted with decorative finishes and floral trim. They are small but good value; the only down-side is that there are only three communal bathrooms for 14 rooms, which could mean crossed legs in the corridor.

Hotel Contemporáneo HOTEL €€
(Map p124; ✐ 902 120329; www.hotelcontempora-neo.com; Rambla de Santa Cruz 116; s/d incl break-fast €53/67; P ✳ @ ☎ ☲) As contemporary as the name suggests, this elegant hotel on one of the city's swankiest streets is part of the Spanish Barceló chain. Rooms have mahoga-ny or grey-stained hardwood floors, a plush, yet understated, colour scheme and large bathrooms with walk-in showers. The only downside is that some readers have com-plained about noise from adjoining rooms.

Hotel Taburiente HOTEL €€
(Map p124; ✐ 922 27 60 00; www.hoteltaburiente. com; Calle Dr José Naveiras 24A; s/d incl breakfast €48/78; P ✳ ☎ ☲) The public areas have a fashionable minimalist look – think black glossy pots with a couple of lilies, chunky glass vases filled with green apples, and plenty of soft natural colours. The rooms are pleasant but lack the same wow factor; ask for one with a balcony overlooking Parque Garcia Sanabría. Room 26, a smart cocktail bar and nightclub, opens nightly from 8pm.

Principe de Paz HOTEL €€
(Map p124; ✐ 922 24 99 55; www.hotelprincipepaz. com; Calle Valentin Sanz 33-35; s/d incl breakfast €47/70; ✳ ☎) Wonderfully located across from the leafy Plaza Principe de Asturias, this dusky-pink exterior sets the scene for a marble-clad interior and large pleasant rooms washed in pale cream with light-wood furnishings. Note that the bathrooms have tubs for that restorative post-hiking soak.

The Northeast

La Laguna

Bed & Breakfast La Laguna B&B €
(✐ 824 680066; www.bblalaguna.com; Calle Juan de Vera 21; s/d incl breakfast €18/38; ☎) A cross between a B&B and a hostel with a com-munity kitchen and shared bathrooms. The rooms are a delight; brightly painted and cheerful. There's a pretty patio with citrus trees (you can help yourselves) and the own-er, Chiara, is utterly charming and can help you with any queries you may have about exploring the island.

Hotel Aguere BOUTIQUE HOTEL €€
(✐ 922 31 40 36; www.hotelaguere.es; Calle Car-rera 55; s/d incl breakfast €51/67; ✳ @ ☎) The highlight of this friendly hotel is the central glassed-in patio (housing a popular cafe), which reeks of 1920s high-class society. Up-stairs are a handful of simple old-fashioned rooms with wooden floors so highly pol-ished you could ice skate on them. The only real downside is that, as this is a historic building, the bathrooms are a built-in extra so quite cramped. There are plans to add an-other wing and install an elevator.

Hotel-Apartamentos Nivaria HOTEL €€
(✐ 922 26 42 98; www.hotelnivaria.com; Plaza Ad-elantado 11; s/d incl breakfast €96/120; P ✳ @) The former home of a marquis, the facade is

washed in burnt sienna and has traditional wooden balconies. Rooms are exquisitely done up with elegant furniture, leafy plants and earthy colours. The bathrooms are fashionably mosaic-tiled. Facilities include a spa and gym.

Casa Rural la Asomada del Gato
HISTORIC HOTEL €€

(☑922 26 39 37; www.laasomadadelgato.es; Calle Anchieta 45; d/tr incl breakfast €75/85; ☎) Sitting behind the excellent restaurant of the same name and surrounded by lush subtropical plants, the four rooms at this *casa rural* (village or farmstead accommodation) are colourful and comfortable; on the downside some guests have (seriously!) complained about the noisy cockerel next door.

The North

Puerto De La Cruz

★Hotel Sun Holidays
HOTEL €

(Map p136; ☑922 38 00 87; www.hotelsunholidays.com; Calle La Peñita 6; s/d €25/50; ❋☎) Despite the mildly disquieting name, this hotel is not a tour-company resort, but a small modern hotel in the attractive La Ranilla *barrio* (district). Rooms are plain with ugly marble-chip flooring but are superbly equipped with desks, wardrobes, plenty of plugs and good lighting. There are small tubs, as well as showers, plus most rooms have a balcony.

The rooftop terrace has fabulous views and plenty of lounge chairs for kickback time.

Hotel Monopol
HISTORIC HOTEL €€

(Map p136; ☑922 38 46 11; www.monopoltf.com; Calle Quintana 15; s/d incl breakfast €50/80; ❋@☎❀) This old dame of a hotel, built in 1742, has a covered courtyard so filled with lush green foliage it's like being lost in the Amazon. The service is low-key but efficient, and extras include a heated pool, a sauna and three sun-bronzing terraces.

Original wooden balconies provide plenty of charm, while the rooms are small but well equipped, if starting to look just a shade worn.

Hotel Botánico
HISTORIC HOTEL €€€

(☑922 38 14 00; www.hotelbotanico.com; Avenida Richard J Yeoward 1; s/d incl breakfast €180/265; P❋☎❀) One of the most exclusive hotels in these parts with beautiful gardens and a great pool area. The Botánico's oriental spa centre offers wellness therapies and treatments, plus a Thai pagoda surrounded by lush gardens for traditional Thai massage, and a *hammam* (Turkish-style steam bath).

Hotel Tigaiga
HOTEL €€€

(Map p136; ☑922 38 35 00; www.tigaiga.com; Parque Taoro 28; r/ste from €150/191; P❋@☎❀) Judged on room quality alone, this family-run hotel, mounted like a castle on a hill, is a tad pricey. However, as well as a pleasant, if not extraordinary, room you get superb service, beautiful gardens, an inviting pool and plenty of sporting and relaxation facilities. The suites were renovated in 2014 and are bright and airy with contemporary furnishings.

La Orotava

★Hotel Alhambra
BOUTIQUE HOTEL €€

(Map p142; ☑922 32 04 34; www.alhambra-orotava.com; Calle Nicandro González Borges 19; s/d/ste incl breakfast €85/114/143; ❋☎❀) A simply gorgeous 18th-century manor house filled with period furnishings and wonderful artwork, including a breathtaking 200m-long ceiling fresco. There are only five rooms and all are huge and well furnished in a mix of modern and old. The Andalucian-tiled bathrooms come with tubs and separate showers. There's a small pool and attractive gardens.

Hotel Victoria
BOUTIQUE HOTEL €€

(Map p142; ☑922 33 16 83; www.hotelruralvictoria.com; Calle Hermano Apolinar 8; s/d incl breakfast €73/90; ❋@☎) This is a seductive little number: a 17th-century mansion restored as an exquisite boutique hotel. The rooms are set around a central patio and have plenty of designer detail with textured cream wallpaper, modular light fittings and dark wooden furnishings. There's an excellent restaurant and a rooftop sun terrace.

Garachico

★Hotel La Quinta Roja
BOUTIQUE HOTEL €€

(☑922 13 33 77; www.quintaroja.com; Glorieta de San Francisco; s/d incl breakfast €88/122; ❋@☎) This restored 16th-century manor house with its earthy-toned walls is wonderfully central and a lovely spot in which to while away a few peaceful days. The rooms are centred around a gracious patio complete with fountain and wooden galleries. Rooms have cherry-coloured wooden floors, muted decor and Med-blue mosaic-tiled bathrooms. There is also a good gift shop.

Gara Hotel Rural   BOUTIQUE HOTEL €€

(☑922 83 11 68; www.garahotel.com; Calle Esteban de Ponte 7; r incl breakfast €120; ❄@🖤) A charming hotel with rooms set around a central courtyard. They vary in size but are well equipped with kettles and fridges, plus large walk-in showers. There are two guest terraces with seamless sea views and a small spa with Jacuzzi and sauna.

Hotel Rural El Patio   HOTEL €€

(☑922 13 32 80; www.hotelpatio.com; Finca Malpaís 11; r from €96; P❄@🖤🏊) East of Garachico, in El Guincho, is this tranquil, white-walled place tucked among plantains on a farm. The comfortable and colourful rooms are spread throughout three low-rise buildings set around a stone patio. Sitting out on the patio with a sunset drink listening to classical music is simply perfect. For the more energetic, the facilities include a tennis court and croquet lawn.

It's a little tricky to find so either call ahead for directions or download a map off its website. There's a minimum stay of three nights.

The Centre

Parque Nacional Del Teide

Parador Nacional   PARADOR €€€

(☑922 37 48 41; www.parador.es; d incl breakfast €145; P❄🖤🏊) Located in the heart of Parque Nacional Del Teide, this *parador* was designed with little empathy for the surrounding landscape, but once inside, the rooms are attractively rustic in style, with earthy colours, tasteful original landscapes and king-size beds. Avoid the adjacent cafeteria for anything more than a drink on the terrace; the food is overpriced and pedestrian. Note that you pay slightly more for a Teide view.

Vilaflor

Hotel El Sombrerito   HOTEL €

(☑922 70 90 52; Calle Santa Catalina 15; s/d incl breakfast €35/40) There is real value to be found here, especially if you bag one of the rooms with a terrace. Shiny tiles, canary-yellow walls and tidy (albeit small) bathrooms are all part of the package, while the downstairs bar and restaurant is a favourite with locals and rates high in atmosphere and home-cooked-style cuisine.

The Northwest

Santiago del Teide

Hotel La Casona del Patio   HOTEL €€

(☑922 83 92 93; www.lacasonadelpatio.com; Avenida La Iglesia 72; r incl breakfast €100; P❄🖤) A handsome stone building houses this comfortable hotel with spacious rooms coloured in bright yellows and blues with warm terracotta tiles and lashings of white linen. Ideally located for hiking and biking trails, horse riding can also be arranged, plus there's an excellent restaurant, a spa and a small gym.

Los Gigantes & Puerto De Santiago

Hotel Rural El Navio   HOTEL €€

(☑922 86 56 80; www.elnavio.es; Prolongación Avenida Los Pescadores, Finca El Navío, Alcalá; s/d incl breakfast €70/135; P🖤🏊) Halfway between Los Gigantes and the little town of Alcalá and ferreted away on a banana farm, this peaceful rural hotel, with old-fashioned rooms and a courtyard virtually enveloped in bougainvillea, offers nothing but peace, quiet and total tranquillity. The owners also prepare delicious home-cooked meals. Note that in high season there is a minimum two-night stay.

The South

Los Cristianos, Playa De Las Américas & Costa Adeje

Hotel Andrea's   HOTEL €

(Map p156; ☑922 79 00 12; www.hotel-andreas.com; Calle Valle Menéndez 6, Los Cristianos; s/d €42/55; @🖤) A small but neat hotel with large, if rather bleakly furnished, rooms and small glassed-in terraces (the cheapest singles don't have terraces). There's a comfy communal sitting room with TV and soft drinks, plus a popular pizzeria downstairs.

Hotel Reveron Plaza   HOTEL €

(Map p156; ☑922 75 71 20; www.hotelesreveron.com; Avenida Los Playeros 26, Los Cristianos; s/d €45/62; P❄🖤🏊) This is the oldest hotel in Los Cristianos, dating back to 1949 when it was a simple hostel. Still family run, the rooms are traditionally furnished and comfortable with fridges and balconies. The rooftop pool is a definite plus; there is also a small spa.

BITING THE PACKAGE BULLET

Playa de las Américas is one of those rare hotel jungles where you may have to swallow hard and check out one of the high-profile tour operators, which often have amazing deals. Some of the most reputable agencies are **Thomas Cook** (www.thomascook.com), **Thompson** (www.thomson.co.uk), **First Choice** (www.firstchoice.co.uk) and **Cosmos** (www.cosmos.co.uk). If you decide to stake out your own accommodation and are planning on spending a few nights here, try apartment agencies first. A pleasant apartment for two, with a kitchen, a TV and a living area, starts at around €300 a week (generally the minimum booking period). Contact the tourist office for a full listing of agencies, or start with **Anyka Sur** (Map p154; ☑922 79 13 77; www.anykasur.com; Edificio Azahara, Avenida Habana, Los Cristianos; ☉9.30am-1.30pm & 5-8pm Mon-Fri) or **Marcus Management** (Map p154; ☑922 75 10 64; www.tenerife-apts.com; Apartamentos Portosin, Avenida Penetracíon, Los Cristianos; ☉9am-noon & 1-5pm Mon-Fri).

Baobab Suites　　　DESIGN HOTEL €€€
(Map p158; ☑822 07 00 30; www.baobabsuites. com; Calle Roques del Salmor 5, Costa Adeje; ste €250; P☀☎❄) These elegant minimalist suites range from studios to four-bedroom penthouses with spacious living areas and state-of-the-art kitchens. Other perks include vast terraces with sea views, private swimming pools and Jacuzzis; some suites even have small private beaches. Ideal for families with its access to a kids' club, plus there's a sports club for those post-toddler teens.

Villa Cortés　　　HOTEL €€€
(Map p154; ☑922 75 77 00; www.europe-hotels. org; Avenida Rafael Puig Lluvina, Playa de las Américas; s/d/ste incl breakfast €195/250/455; P☀@☎❄) Designed in the style of an ultra-luxurious Mexican hacienda, this is truly sumptuous, with an exciting and dynamic colour scheme and decor. There are lots of hot yellows, oranges and blues, plus murals, exquisite original artwork and the occasional quirky touch – like the family of giant ceramic frogs just off the lobby and the mini Aztec temple outside.

The gardens have streams with goldfish and a pool with cascading waterfall; the rooms are predictably stunning. Naturally enough, there is also a luxurious spa.

The East

Güímar & Around

Hotel Rural Casona Santo Domingo　　　HOTEL €€
(☑922 51 02 29; www.casonasantodomingo.es; Calle Santo Domingo 32, Güímar; s/d incl breakfast €60/80; P☎) On the edge of Güímar's attractive old quarter and inside a restored

16th-century house, this family-run hotel and restaurant is full of period charm and creaky old furniture. There's a charming whitewashed central courtyard complete with well. The attached restaurant (mains €10 to €15) is one of the town's better places to eat.

El Médano

Hostel Carel　　　HOTEL €
(☑922 17 68 98; Avenida Príncipe de España 22; s/d from €35/45; ☎) There's great value to be found at this clean, friendly and well-run budget hotel. The rooms are large and shiny and come with balconies, some of which have distant sea views. Most have refrigerators – but none have hair dryers! Breakfast is €5 extra. It's located on the northern fringe of town.

Senderos de Abono　　　HOTEL €€
(☑922 77 02 00; Calle Peatonal de la Iglesia 5, Granadilla de Abona; s/d incl breakfast €50/65; ☀☎❄) This rural hotel and restaurant is just across from the lovely stone church in Granadilla de Abona, a genuine working town. A converted post office, its rooms are in a series of old stone buildings with tiny courtyards, foliage-filled gardens and bucketfuls of charm. The inhouse restaurant offers really superb home-cooked, local cuisine (mains €10).

LA GOMERA

The island has, so far, kept grand-scale tourism at bay, and most lodging is in small rural hotels, family-run *pensiones,* refurbished farmhouses and apartments. By far the most appealing and authentically Gomeran places to stay are the *casas rurales* (village or farmstead accommodation), many of which were abandoned by emigrants and have since been refurbished for tourists. For information and to book, contact Eco Turismo La Gomera ([📋] 922 14 41 01; www.casasruralesdelagomera.es; Avenida Pedro García Cabrera 9, Vallehermoso).

San Sebastián de la Gomera

⭐ **Apartamentos Quintero**   APARTMENT €
([📋] 922 14 17 44; www.apartamentosquintero.com; Plaza de las Américas 6; d €50; [P][✳][🛜]) These modern apartments are extremely central. The living rooms are large and cheerily decorated, and have balconies and sea views, and the kitchens are well equipped. Justifiably popular with walkers, the friendly management can advise on bus times and maps. The one downside is that wi-fi is only available in the downstairs lobby.

Pensión Victor   PENSIÓN €
([📋] 607 517565; Calle del Medio 23; s/d without bathroom €25/30) Now owned by a young Cuban couple (try a mojito in the downstairs bar!), this place in a creaky old townhouse has bundles of character. A couple of rooms overlook the bustling street, others span a wooden balcony, sharing a narrow terrace. Rooms are plain but equipped with tables and TV. Note that bathrooms are shared.

Hotel Torre del Conde   HOTEL €€
([📋] 922 87 00 00; www.hoteltorredelconde.com; Calle Ruiz de Padrón 19; s/d €55/69; [🛜]) If you can look beyond the stark modern exterior, the rooms here are solid midrange quality; some with views of the Torre del Conde and surrounding pretty gardens. The hotel has recently expanded and now offers a sauna and Jacuzzi, as well as a solarium for catching the rays.

⭐ **Parador Nacional Conde de la Gomera**   PARADOR €€€
([📋] 922 87 11 00; www.parador.es; Calle Lomo de la Horca; r €195; [P][✳][@][🛜][🏊]) Built to look like an old Canarian mansion, the Parador is arguably the island's top hotel. The rooms are simply but elegantly furnished, with four-poster beds, rich wooden floors and marble bathrooms. Most rooms look out onto the gorgeous gardens, which have many examples of Canarian plants and a small pool area overlooking the ocean.

The reception staff are also worthy of praise and are a credit to the Parador chain.

The North

Hermigua

⭐ **Apartamentos Los Telares**   APARTMENT €
([📋] 922 88 07 81; www.apartamentosgomera.com; El Convento, Carretera General; apt €50-59; [P][🛜][🏊]) Sitting on either side of the main highway coming into Hermigua are these superbly equipped and furnished apartments with stone floors, colourful rustic-style furnishings and windows overlooking the banana groves. The bathrooms are on the small side. There's a choice of studios or larger suites, and over the street is a small pool and solarium (complete with hammocks) for guests' use.

Ibo Alfaro   HOTEL €€
([📋] 922 88 01 68; www.hotel-gomera.com; s/d €52/82; [🛜]) Popular with honeymooning couples, the 20 romantic rooms here have gorgeous mountain views and an aroma of wood polish coming from the floors, ceilings and elegant furniture. The breakfast spread might be the best on the island and the surrounding gardens are a delight. To get here, follow the signs up the unnamed rural road from beside Hermigua Rent-a-Car.

Casa Los Hererra   BOUTIQUE HOTEL €€
([📋] 922 88 07 01; www.casalosherrera.com; Plaza Nuestra Señora de la Encarnación; d incl breakfast €90; [P][🛜][🏊]) This delightful canary-yellow hotel next to the Iglesia de la Encarnación has a sophisticated feel that can seem a rarity in rural-vibe La Gomera. Rooms are traditionally furnished with colourful fabrics. A highlight, literally, is the pool, which is in a lofty position behind the hotel with soul-stirring views of the church and valley beyond.

Vallehermoso

Hotel Añaterve   HOTEL €
([📋] 922 80 03 30; www.anaterve.com; Calle La Rodadera; d incl breakfast €56, apt €69; [✳][🛜]) This building overlooking Vallehermoso and the valley has an interesting history; it was a bodega in the 1900s (the original wine press is still here), as well as the station for the local Guardia Civil. Today this small Dutch-owned hotel has a welcoming informality with just four rooms and an apartment. Breakfast is vegetarian; it's a popular spot for yoga retreats.

Hotel Rural Tamahuche HOTEL €€
(☎ 922 80 11 76; www.hoteltamahuche.com; Calle Hoya 20; s/d incl breakfast €56/83; P @ 🖙) Just outside Vallehermoso, there's superb value to be found at this little B&B-style hotel. Built right into the hillside, it climbs in a series of staircases and terraces, so don't plan to bring much luggage. Rooms, with dark wooden floorboards and a wood-beam ceiling, are decorated in a Canary colonial style.

To find the hotel follow the signs towards Valle Gran Rey and it will be perched atop a hill to your right.

The South

Playa Santiago

★**Apartamentos Tapahuga** APARTMENT €
(☎ 922 89 51 59; www.tapahuga.es; Avenida Marítima; 2-person apt €50-75; 🖙 ⛱) Opposite the harbour, these spacious, light-flooded apartments boast beautiful wooden balconies and marble floors, well-equipped kitchens, and a rooftop sun terrace and pool. Make sure you get an exterior apartment, as a few open onto a cheerless and dark interior patio. All up, it offers exceptional value for money. Note that there is a three-night minimum stay.

Pensión La Gaviota HOTEL €
(☎ 922 89 51 35; Avenida Marítima 35; r €27) Located above a busy local bar, the rooms are small and simple and could do with a lick of paint, but some have wonderful views over a sparkling ocean and the bathrooms are a notch up in quality with marine-blue tile work. No TV.

★**Hotel Jardín Tecina** HOTEL €€
(☎ 902 22 21 40; www.jardin-tecina.com; Playa Santiago; s/d incl breakfast €97/150; P ❄ @ 🖙 ⛱) Sprawled along a cliff above town (a lift goes down to the beach), this is about the closest thing La Gomera has to a proper resort complex. The bungalow-like accommodation is scattered throughout a green, well-kept landscape that's so vast they even manage to conduct nature walks in the gardens! All rooms have balconies and many have ocean views.

Valle Gran Rey

★**Finca Argayall** HOTEL €€
(☎ 922 69 70 08; www.en.argayall.com; Valle Gran Rey waterfront; s/d from €85/125, without bathroom €64/100; P ⛱) This is no ordinary hotel. A rural estate a 15-minute stroll out-

side the tourist bustle of Valle Gran Rey, the *finca* (rural estate) is a tranquil ocean-side centre focused on communal, alternative and ecofriendly living. For lodging, guests can choose options from comfortable beach shacks to luxurious apartments with a private swimming pool.

It's a blissfully chilled out place in which to loll about in hammocks, slip in and out of the swimming pool or laze about on the pebble beach fronting the property. Most staff live on the premises, offering near-daily meditation, yoga, massage and other therapies and activities. The reception is staffed only between 11am and 2pm Wednesday to Monday.

Apartamentos Baja del Secreto APARTMENT €€
(☎ 922 80 57 09; www.bajadelsecreto.es; Avenida Marítima, Charco del Conde; apt €65-95; P 🖙 ⛱) Location, location, location: this place, in front of the Charco del Conde (a natural seawater pool), has the location totally sorted. The rooms, which are clean and comfortable, have less impact than the views but the lush subtropical grounds are a real delight.

Playa Calera APARTMENT €€
(☎ 922 80 57 79; www.hotelplayacalera.com; Calle Punta Calera 2, La Playa; r incl breakfast €120; P ❄ @ 🖙 ⛱) This large four-star hotel fronting the sea has apartments that are more like what you'd expect to find in a swanky New York suburb than a boho-chic beach town in the Spanish sun. The open-plan rooms have beds as big as a small village, plus lounges and small kitchenettes. The inviting infinity pool appears to flow seamlessly into the sea.

The breakfast buffet is excellent; freshly squeezed orange juice no less!

LA PALMA

Live like a local in the *casas rurales* for rent across the island. For information and reservations, contact the **Casa Turismo Rural Isla Bonita** (☎ 922 43 06 25; www.islabonita.es; Calle O'Daly 39, Santa Cruz de La Palma), which rents close to 70 rural houses across the island.

Santa Cruz de la Palma

Santa Cruz has some delightful places to stay in the historic centre and makes a good base for exploring the island.

★ La Fuente
APARTMENT €

([☎] 922 41 56 36; www.la-fuente.com; Calle Anselmo Pérez de Brito 49; apt €42-69; [@]) German owned, the 11 apartments are all different and priced at three levels. The most expensive have large rooms, plus balconies and amazing sea and town views. Room 10 is like a large studio (indeed it was once a dance studio) and has bundles of atmosphere, but all the apartments are well kitted out and decorated with an aesthetic eye for detail. The reception is closed over lunch and all day Sunday.

Pensión la Cubana
PENSIÓN €

([☎] 922 41 13 54; www.la-fuente.com; Calle O'Daly 24; s/d/tr without bathroom €26/32/39; [@]) Pensión la Cubana is the island's only and oldest *pensión*. The quaint whitewashed rooms are all wobbly floorboards and creaky doors, but none of them have private bathrooms. There's a kitchen for guest use, free tea and coffee, and a wonderful large communal lounge with comfy sofas, books to read and a small balcony overlooking the pedestrian street.

Apart-Hotel Castillete
APARTMENT €

([☎] 922 42 08 40; www.hotelcastillete.com; Avenida Maritima 75; 2-person apt €42; [@][✉]) These spacious studio-style apartments have mildly dated decor but are well situated and have balconies from where, on a clear day, you may just spot Teide on Tenerife. There is a cafeteria downstairs that serves a reasonable breakfast for around €3.50, as well as a rooftop pool with mountain views.

★ Hotel San Telmo
BOUTIQUE HOTEL €€

([☎] 922 41 53 85; www.hotel-santelmo.com; Calle San Telmo 5; s/d from €65/75; [@]) This wonderful, German-owned, boutique hotel has just eight rooms: two are located in the original building with beamed ceilings, wooden shutters and balconies overlooking the delightful flower-filled terrace. The other rooms are more contemporarily decorated in tasteful muted earth colours; some have sea views.

Around Santa Cruz

Los Cancajos

Hacienda San Jorge
APARTMENT €€

([☎] 922 18 10 66; www.hsanjorge.com; Playa de Los Cancajos 22; apt from €75; [P][@][@][✉]) The Canary-styled Hacienda offers large and well-thought-out apartments with separate bedrooms, open-plan kitchens, uninspiring

decoration and great views, but what really makes this place special are the verdant gardens with strategically placed hammocks and a fantastic lagoon-style saltwater pool. There is also a handy minimarket on-site.

Breña Alta

Parador Nacional
PARADOR €€

([☎] 922 43 58 28; www.parador.es; Carretera de Zumacal, Breña Baja; r from €98; [P][✻][@][✉]) This *parador* looks like a huge Canary farmhouse overlooking the ocean. There is a pretty pool surrounded by grass and a lovely botanical garden. Rooms are spacious and sun-filled, with a sitting area and panoramic views. The breakfast buffet is superb.

The South

Fuencaliente

Apartamentos & Pensión Los Volcanes
HOTEL €

([☎] 922 44 41 64; Carretera General 86; d/apt €30/32; [P][@]) A homey place with tasteful decor and some rooms with a small balcony. Apartments are studio-style, with a kitchenette, sitting area and bed all in the same room. It's an ideal base for hikers as the owner is a keen walker with lots of route information. There is a communal kitchen, plus a comfortable sitting room for guests' use.

Hotel La Palma Teneguía Princess & Spa
HOTEL €€€

([☎] 922 42 55 00; www.hotellapalmaprincess.com; Carretera La Costa Cerca Vieja 10; r from €100; [P][✻][@][@][✉]) Technically two hotels (La Palma Princess and Teneguía Princess), this sprawling, self-contained resort complex near the waterfront (8km south of Los Canarios) is the most ambitious hotel on the island. With 625 rooms, several pools and marvellous ocean views, the overall effect is pleasing, but it's situated miles from anywhere. There is also a spa. Pack some confetti – this hotel is popular as a wedding venue!

The Centre

El Paso

La Casa Encantada
HOSTEL €

([☎] 661 924972; lacasaencantada.lapalma@gmail. com; Calle Salvador Miralles; r per person €15, d €35; [@]) Opened in 2015, this is a work in progress; a wonderful high-ceilinged, light-filled building with just four rooms, including one double en suite. The communal sitting room is a comfortable clutter, while the rooms are large with up to three beds in each. There is also a kitchen for guests' use.

Los Llanos de Aridane

Hotel Valle Aridane HOTEL €
(☑922 46 26 00; www.hotelvallearidane.com; Glorieta Castillo Olivares 3; r incl breakfast €50; ☎) A comfortable modern hotel, but avoid rooms facing the main road as they can be noisy. The breakfast spread is excellent and the owners are extremely helpful, and can advise on walking routes, bus timetables and transport info in the area. They will even provide a packed lunch if necessary. Wi-fi available in reception only.

Puerto Naos

★Apartamentos Playa Delphin APARTMENT €
(☑922 40 81 94; www.playadelphin.com; Avenida José Guzmán Pérez; 2-/3-person apt €63/68; P☎) This apartment complex is in an imposing semicircular building near the beach; close enough to ensure that you're lulled to sleep by the crack and whip of Atlantic waves. Balconies have sunloungers, and rooms come with the little extras such as toasters and fruit bowls. It's family run and friendly.

Apartamentos Martín APARTMENT €
(☑922 40 80 46; Calle Juana Tabares 1; 2-person apt €35; ☎) Simple apartments with small kitchenettes in a sea-blue block. It's Spanish run and very friendly, but the partition walls are thin indeed.

Sol La Palma HOTEL €€
(☑922 40 80 00; www.solmelia.com; Punta del Pozo, Playa de Puerto Naos; d from €75, apt from €80; P✻☎☒) If you don't want to self-cater, this package-tourism-style hotel is your only bet. With a sprawling, kiddie-filled pool overlooking the Atlantic, beige I-could-be-anywhere-in-the-world rooms and an all-you-can-eat buffet, it's your standard resort hotel but, that said, it is supremely comfortable.

The North

Barlovento

Apartamentos La Fajana APARTMENT €
(☑922 18 61 62; Calle de la Fajana; 2-3-person apt €36-40; P) There's not a massive amount

of self-catering accommodation up on this northern coast, but these apartments, with views over the wild and woolly waves and the Piscinas de la Fajana, have a real away-from-the-world feel and are conveniently located above a good seafood restaurant.

★Hotel La Palma Romántica HOTEL €€
(☑922 18 62 21; www.hotellapalmaromantica.com; Las Llanadas; r incl breakfast €80; P☎☒) The only three-star hotel this side of Santa Cruz, this excellent-value rural hotel has 40 spacious and elegant rooms, with high ceilings, terraces, lounge chairs and a sitting area. If it's sunny (rare up here), take a dip in the outdoor pool and if it's grey, slip into the heated indoor pool. There's a classy restaurant (mains €8 to €12), sweeping views of the valley and great service. There is also a small spa and gym.

EL HIERRO

The most appealing places to stay are the *casas rurales;* contact **Meridiano Cero** (☑922 55 18 24; www.ecoturismocanarias.com; Calle Barlovento 89, El Mocanal) for reservations.

Valverde

Boomerang HOTEL €
(☑922 55 02 00; www.hotel-boomerang.com; Doctor Gost 1; d €60; ✻☎) A convenient central hotel with good-sized rooms if a little too beige on beige (as in colour scheme). A couple of rooms have balconies with distant sea views, and all rooms have tubs, as well as showers. Can be chilly in the winter months.

The North

★Hotel Villa El Mocanal BOUTIQUE HOTEL €€
(☑922 55 03 73; www.villaelmocanal.com; Calle Barlovento 18, El Mocanal; s/d incl breakfast from €62/86; P✻@☎☒) On the main highway through El Mocanal, this is the island's first boutique hotel and although it is starting to look just a shade tired, it is still an excellent place to stay with earthy-toned decor, hardwood furniture, stone construction and fabulous views. It's also one of the few places on the island that has a permanently staffed reception. Note that breakfast is taken at the restaurant across the road.

★ **Parador Nacional** PARADOR €€€
(☑922 55 80 36; www.parador.es; Las Playas; d incl breakfast €150; P ✱ 🛜 ▨) Sitting on the edge of a rocky beach, this is the island's top hotel and rooms are lovely, with hardwood floors, cool blue decor and balconies (ask for one with a view over the electric-blue ocean), though the best thing they offer is the lullaby of the crashing waves. Frequent special offers mean you often pay only €80 for a room. Note that the restaurant is excellent and specialises in local El Hierro dishes (mains €12 to €20).

The South

La Restinga

To be honest, this isn't the island's most charming area to stay, but divers are practically obliged to, since there's an 800m to 1000m altitude difference between sea-level La Restinga and the towns up the highway – it's necessary to remain near sea level for at least 12 hours after a dive.

Apartamentos Bahía APARTMENT €
(☑617 614619; www.apartamentosbahia.info; Avenida Marítima 12; 2-person apt €44; P ✱) These spic-and-span two-bedroom apartments are ideal for families. The open-plan kitchen and living area looks out over the blue waters of the port. The pine furnishings are nothing fancy, but with a view like this, who needs more decoration? Opt for the top floor, if possible.

Apartamentos La Restinga APARTMENT €
(www.apartamentoslarestinga.es; Los Saltos 16; 2-person apt €33; P) These well-equipped apartments are astonishingly reasonable, as well as being located just 100m from the sea. OK, the decor isn't going to win any interior design awards, but the apartments are spotless, and you can even bring along your pet.

El Golfo

Las Puntas

Bungalows Los Roques de Salmor APARTMENT €
(☑922 55 90 16; Carretera Las Puntas; r up to 4 people €55-67; P ✱ 🛜 ▨) This series of small, white-walled bungalows on your left as you enter town is an excellent option. Extremely well kept, they have tiled roofs, stone detailing and tasteful decor. There is also a small summer-only swimming pool. The reception is normally unstaffed.

★ **Hotel Puntagrande** BOUTIQUE HOTEL €€
(☑922 55 90 81; www.hotelpuntagrande.org; Las Puntas; s/d incl breakfast €75/84; P ✱ 🛜) Las Puntas' most famous lodging is something of a tourist attraction and was once listed in the *Guinness World Records* book as being the smallest hotel in the world. An old stone port building, it's perched on a spectacular rock outcrop that makes staying here feel like you're sleeping on a tiny rock in the middle of a vast ocean.

Despite the comfortable rooms it would be hard to imagine that you'd get much sleep here if a big storm were raging all around you. Add to this location a lively common room filled with the flotsam and jetsam of shipwrecks, and you get a truly memorable place to stay. The reception is normally unstaffed.

La Frontera

★ **El Sitio** B&B €
(☑922 55 98 43; www.elsitio-elhierro.es; Calle La Carrera 26; r €41-56; 🛜) Close your eyes and say *ommm*. Tucked away above the Frontera village centre, surrounded by bucolic countryside, this is a unique retreat, accommodation and activity centre in one. The whitewashed rooms are in a cluster of renovated stone farm buildings and have a soothing rustic look. Note that there is no TV.

Various activities such as yoga, massage, hiking or bike excursions are available to guests and nonguests alike. The reception is staffed from 11am to 1pm only from Monday to Saturday.

Hotel Balneario Pozo de La Salud HOTEL €€
(☑922 55 95 61; hotelbalneariopozodelasalud@gmail.com; Pozo de la Salud; d incl breakfast €70; P 🛜 ▨) This modern spa hotel is located next to the famous Pozo de La Salud, which has been recognised for its healing properties since the mid 19th-century when the water was even exported (mainly to New York and Cuba). Rooms are set around a leafy central courtyard; request a sea view.

There is a long list of treatments available ranging from thermal baths (in your room) to reflexology, shiatsu and volcanic hot stones treatment. The Hotel Balneario is famed as being Spain's westernmost hotel.

Understand the Canary Islands

Canary Islands Today

Visitors to this sun-kissed archipelago are generally blissfully unaware of the lingering effects of 'la crisis'. Cripplingly high unemployment and a shaky welfare system suffering from government cuts are realities for many locals. But, thankfully, it's not all doom and gloom: in 2014, tourism and trade was finally showing an upward trend while, concurrently, islanders and environmentalists seem more committed than ever to conserving natural energy resources and curbing unsustainable tourist practices and development.

Best on Film

Broken Embraces (Pedro Almodóvar; 2009) Starring Penelope Cruz. Romantic thriller shot in Lanzarote.

The Dictator (Sacha Baron Cohen, 2012) Satirical political drama extensively filmed in Fuerteventura.

Wild Oats (Andy Tennant; 2015) Action drama with Demi Moore and Billy Connelly shot largely in Gran Canaria.

Fifty Shades of Grey (Sam Taylor-Johnson; 2015) Infamous honeymoon scenes shot at La Tejita in Grandilla de Abona, Tenerife.

Best in Print

More Ketchup than Salsa (Joe Cawley) Rib-tickling account of running a bar in Tenerife.

Canary Island Song (Robin Jones Gunn) Touching tale by the author of the popular Christy Miller series.

Walking in the Canary Islands (Paddy Dillon) Includes mapped-out walks throughout the islands.

The Wind off the Small Isles (Mary Stewart) Romantic thriller set in Lanzarote.

Natural Parks on the Canary Islands (Francisco J Macías Martín) An in-depth look at the national parks, with colourful images.

Tourism & Infrastructure

Tourism continues to represent an essential pillar of the Canarian economy and, in 2014, reached an all-time high with the number of foreign tourists holidaying here peaking at just over four million (some 26% of the total number of visitors to Spain). This is all the more impressive as, during the economic crisis of 2009–10, tourism dropped significantly.

Still representing a small percentage of travellers but predicted to increase is the number of astro tourists to La Palma: the world's first Unesco-recognised starlight reserve. Astro or not, Britons are still starry-eyed when it comes to holidaying here. In 2014, approximately one in three visitors was from the UK, outnumbering even Spanish visitors from the mainland.

Infrastructure is also greasing its cogs with the Gran Canaria train service slated to be running from Santa Catalina in Las Palmas to Meloneras in 2018, impressively powered entirely by a wind farm. Tenerife's train project is similarly back on track with construction of the first phase of the north-to-south track planned for 2016 (from Santa Cruz to Candelaria). A new marina and fishing harbour opened in Tenerife's Garachico in June 2013 providing another boost to the economy. And, after numerous stops and starts, Tenerife's motorway extension between Adeje and Santiago del Teide was completed in 2015.

Environmental Matters

You win some. You lose some. The fact that Repsol has cancelled its plans to drill for oil off the coast of Fuerteventura and Lanzarote has relieved most Canary residents (three out of four were opposed to the plan). At the same time, the huge megaport of Grandilla in Tenerife was finally given the go ahead in June 2013 after the European commission pledged €67 million for construction. This was despite more than 5000 official complaints, mainly from ecological groups concerned about the port's impact on the fauna and flora of the Los Sebadales area, as well as on nearby beaches and the local fishing industry.

No such eco woes in El Hierro which, in September 2014, was designated a Unesco geopark in recognition of the island's noteworthy progress in promoting sustainable development. In 2015, El Hierro upped its green credentials still further with its well publicised plan to become the world's first energy-self-sufficient island via a combination of solar, wind and water power. And, show off or what, El Hierro also plans to run its 6000 vehicles entirely on electricity by 2020. La Gomera was similarly declared a Biosphere Reserve by Unesco in 2012; the same year, ironically, that an arsonist-sparked fire destroyed 750 hectares of laurel trees in the Parque Nacional de Garajonay, which experts say will take some 30 years to recover.

Politics & the Economy
The main force in Canary Islands politics since its first regional election victory in 1993 has been the *Coalición Canaria* (CC). At the 2011 election, Paolino Rivero was re-elected for a second term as president of the CC; however, in 2014, he had stated his decision to withdraw from the 2015 election following a defeat in the first round of party voting. It was under Rivero's watch that unemployment spiraled to a shocking 33.2% in 2013, with roughly the same percentage of residents revealed as being below the poverty level. Ironically, one of the causes of small businesses failing is directly related to tourism as, increasingly, hotels are offering all inclusive deals which is having a knock-on effect, particularly on small independently owned bars and restaurants. More positively, the first quarter of 2014 saw a slight overall improvement in the economy (the first increase since 2007). Migration from Africa has also stabilized with just 288 migrants arriving here in 2014, compared to a staggering 32,000 in 2006 when some days several hundred Africans would reach the islands in their rickety wooden boats.

Wild Weather
El Hierro suffered a 5.1 magnitude earthquake in December 2013 when the island was said to have swelled by 3in with suggestions that a nearby underwater volcano could possibly blow, as it famously did in 2011. The following October (2014) saw flash flooding in Tenerife, which led to landslides, evacuations and the deaths of five people.

POPULATION: **2.1 MILLION**

GDP: **€22 BILLION**

INFLATION: **1.8% (2014)**

UNEMPLOYMENT: **33.2%**

if Canary Islands were 100 people

73 would be Canarian
13 would be European
12 would be Mainland Spanish
2 would be African

belief systems
(% of population)

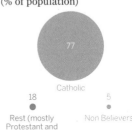

population per sq mile

 ≈ 78 people

History

There is a delightful whiff of mystery concerning both the Canary Islands' origins and the first inhabitants, the indigenous Guanches, who were subsequently banished by waves of marauding invaders. In 1821 the islands were declared a province of Spain, but the economic fallout from the Spanish Civil War and WWII plunged the islands into economic misery. Not until the 1960s did the economy start to pick up with the onset of mass tourism. The rest is history, as they say.

... And in the Beginning

There's a whimsical theory that the Canary Islands are the remains of the legendary sunken continent of Atlantis. More plausible, and similarly intriguing, is the idea that the islands represent the tiniest part of huge volcanoes beneath the sea. Whatever the truth is, according to carbon dating of the sparse archaeological finds, the earliest settlement found here dates to around 2000 BC, although earlier occupation is conceivable – and a goat's bone found in Fuerteventura has been dated back to 3000 years BC.

It is entirely possible that early reconnaissance of the North African Atlantic coast by the Phoenicians and their successors, the Carthaginians, took at least a peek at the easternmost islands of the archipelago. Some historians believe a Phoenician expedition landed on the islands in the 12th century BC, and that the Carthaginian Hanno turned up in 470 BC.

What is definitely known is that the expanding Roman Empire defeated Carthage in the Third Punic War in 146 BC. However, the Romans appear not to have been overly keen to investigate the fabled islands, which they knew as the Insulae Fortunatae (Fortunate Isles). A century and a half later, shortly after the birth of Christ, the Romans received vaguely reliable reports on the isles, penned by Pliny the Elder and based upon accounts of an expedition carried out around 40 BC by Juba II, a client king in Roman North Africa. In AD 150, Egyptian geographer Ptolemy fairly accurately located the islands' position with a little dead reckoning, tracing an imaginary meridian line marking the end of the known world through El Hierro.

Best History Museums

Casa-Museo de Colón, Gran Canaria

Museo de la Piratería (pirates), Lanzarote

Museo Arqueológico de Betancuria, Fuerteventura

Museo Arqueológico, Tenerife

TIMELINE	2000 BC	40 BC	AD 150
	Carbon dating of archaeological discoveries reveal that Cro-Magnon were the first settlers on the Canary Islands, possibly arriving from North Africa.	An expedition lands on the islands, led by King Juba II, Emperor Augustus' protégé, who used Mogador in present-day western Morocco as a base.	The Egyptian geographer Ptolemy fairly accurately locates the islands' position, tracing an imaginary meridian line marking the end of the known world through El Hierro.

Early (Known) Inhabitants

Tall, blond and good looking, how the Guanches actually arrived on the islands has baffled historians for centuries. Could they be a result of Nordic adventurers who left the compass at home? Or Celtic immigrants from mainland Iberia, possibly related to the Basques?

Far more likely is that these first major players on the scene were actually descendents of Libyan-Berber tribes from the Maghreb; the area spanning from present-day Tunisia to Morocco. Similarities in their place names, burial practices and rock carvings suggest a link. Also, the occasional case of blue eyes and blondish hair occurs among the Berbers.

As far as numbers are concerned, before the 15th-century conquest it is believed that the Guanche population numbered approximately 30,000 in Gran Canaria and Tenerife, over 4000 in La Palma, over 1000 in El Hierro and a few hundred in Lanzarote and Fuerteventura.

Early Conquests

After the fall of the Roman Empire, the Canary Islands were off the radar for an incredible 1000-plus years, with virtually no written record of visits here until the early 14th century, when the Genoese captain Lanzarotto (or Lancelotto) Malocello bumped into the island that would later bear his name: Lanzarote.

The conquest of the islands began in earnest in 1402 when Norman noble and adventurer Jean de Béthencourt set out from La Rochelle with a small and ill-equipped party bound for the Canary Islands. So commenced a lengthy and inglorious chapter of invasion, treachery and bungling. Many Guanches would lose their lives or be sold into slavery in the coming century, with the remainder destined to be swallowed up by the invading society.

De Béthencourt's motley crew landed first in Lanzarote, at that stage governed by *mencey* (king) Guardafía. There was no resistance and de Béthencourt went on to establish a fort on Fuerteventura.

That was as far as he got. Having run out of supplies, and with too few men for the enterprise, he headed for Spain to gain the backing of the Castilian crown. Fuerteventura, El Hierro and La Gomera then quickly fell under Spanish control. Appointed lord of the four islands by the Spanish king, Enrique III, de Béthencourt encouraged the settlement of farmers from his Norman homeland and began to pull in the profits. In 1406 he returned for good to Normandy, leaving his nephew Maciot in charge of his Atlantic possessions.

HISTORY EARLY (KNOWN) INHABITANTS

Top Historic Churches

Iglesia de Nuestra Señora de Regla (Pájara, Fuerteventura)

Nuestra Señora de Antigua (Antigua, Fuerteventura)

Catedral de Santa Ana (Las Palmas de Gran Canaria)

Iglesia de Nuestra Señora de la Concepción (Valverde, El Hierro)

Iglesia del Salvador (Santa Cruz de la Palma)

Iglesia de Nuestra Señora de la Concepción (La Laguna, Tenerife)

1312	1402	1464	1479
The Genoese explorer and seafarer Lanzarotto Malocello lands on the furthest northeast island of the archipelago, which is how it subsequently became named Lanzarote.	On 1 May, Jean de Béthencourt, from Normandy (France) and something of an adventurer, sets out from La Rochelle with a small and ill-equipped party bound for the Canary Islands.	On learning of the Portuguese interest in the islands, Spain's Catholic Monarchs grant Diego de Herrera, the appointed lord of La Gomera, the right to attack the remaining islands.	Portugal recognises Spanish control of the Canaries under the treaty of Alcáçovas.

GUANCHE SOCIETY

Guanche society was essentially tribal, with a chieftain or king at its head who enjoyed almost absolute rule. Guanches lived in natural caves or simple low stone houses, while smaller grottoes and caverns were used for storing grain and as places of worship. Today, little remains of the Guanche culture, aside from the *silbo* (whistling language) of La Gomera and a slew of place names and monuments.

Economy

The Guanches relied on farming, herding, hunting and gathering, and their diet was based on protein (goat and fish) and *gofio,* made of toasted and ground barley. These staples are still eaten today.

Clothes & Weapons

Goat-skin leather was the basis of most garments, while jewellery and ornaments were largely restricted to earthenware bead-and-shell necklaces. Implements and weapons were fashioned roughly of wood, stone and bone.

Religion

The Guanches worshipped a god known as Alcorac in Gran Canaria, Achaman in Tenerife and Abora in La Palma. It appears the god was identified strongly with Magec (the sun). Tenerife islanders commonly held that Hades (hell) was in the Teide volcano and was directed by the god of evil, Guayota.

Role of Women

Although living in an essentially patriarchal society, women did have some power. On Gran Canaria, in particular, succession rights were passed through the mother rather than the father. But when times got tough, they got tougher still for women. Infanticide was practised throughout the islands in periods of famine, and it was girls who were sacrificed, never boys.

Power Struggle

The island clans were not averse to squabbling, and by the time the European conquest of the islands got under way in the 15th century, the islands were divided into some 25 fiefdoms (La Palma alone boasted an astonishing 12 cantons).

Squabbles & Stagnation

What followed was scarcely one of the world's grandest colonial undertakings. Characterised by squabbling and occasional revolt among the colonists, the European presence did nothing for the increasingly oppressed islanders in the years following de Béthencourt's departure.

1493	1501–85	1599	1657
Tenerife provides the toughest resistance to Spanish conquest. In May, Alonso Fernández de Lugo lands on the island, with 1000 infantry soldiers and a cavalry of 150.	The islands' wealth leads to attacks by pirates and privateers: Ottoman admiral Kemal Reis ventures into the Canaries, while Murat Reis the Elder captures Lanzarote in 1585.	A major offensive takes place against Las Palma de Gran Canaria during the Dutch War of Independence, with 12,000 men attacking the Castillo de la Luz, which guards the harbour.	Admiral Blake, a general under Oliver Cromwell, captures a Spanish treasure fleet at the cost of only one ship, at Santa Cruz de Tenerife.

The islanders were heavily taxed and Maciot also recruited them for abortive raids on the remaining three independent islands. He then capped it all off by selling to Portugal his rights – inherited from his uncle – to the four islands. Portugal only recognised Spanish control of the Canaries in 1479 under the Treaty of Alcáçovas. (In return, Spain agreed that Portugal could have the Azores, Cape Verde and Madeira.)

Maciot died in self-imposed exile in Madeira in 1452. A string of minor Spanish nobles proceeded to run the show in the Canaries with extraordinarily little success.

The Christian Campaign Continues

In 1478 a new commander arrived with fresh forces and orders from the Spanish Reyes Católicos (Catholic Monarchs), Fernando and Isabel, to finish the Canaries campaign once and for all. Despite being immediately attacked by a force of 2000 men at the site of modern-day Las Palmas de Gran Canaria, they carried the day and went after the *guanarteme* (island chief), Tenesor Semidan, in a naval attack on Galdar. Semidan was sent to Spain, converted to Christianity and returned in 1483 to convince his countrymen to give up the fight. This they did, although 20 years of battles followed which included a failed attempt to deport hundreds of islanders from Las Palmas de Gran Canaria to be sold as slaves in Spain. Fortunately, locals learned of the dastardly scheme and forced the ships transporting the men to dock at Lanzarote instead.

The Final Campaigns

In May 1493, the Spanish commander Alonso Fernández de Lugo landed on Tenerife together with 1000 infantry soldiers and a cavalry of 150, among them Guanches from Gran Canaria and La Gomera. In what was known as the first battle of Acentejo, Lugo suffered defeat by Guanche forces who had the advantage of being familiar with the mountainous terrain.

On 25 December 1494, 5000 Guanches, under the *mencey* Bencomo, were routed in the second battle of Acentejo. The spot, only a few kilometres south of La Matanza, is still called La Victoria (Victory) today. By the following July, when de Lugo marched into the Valle de la Orotava to confront Bencomo's successor, Bentor, the diseased and demoralised Guanches were in no state to resist. Bentor surrendered and the conquest was complete. Pockets of resistance took two years to mop up, and Bentor eventually committed suicide.

Four years after the fall of Granada and the reunification of Christian Spain, the Catholic Monarchs could now celebrate one of the country's first imperial exploits – the subjugation in only 94 years of a small Atlantic archipelago defended by primitive tribes. The contrast between this

Guanches were considered elderly at age 35. They ate lots of sun-dried dates and figs that were concentrated with sugar, and this, combined with the use of mill stones to grind (gritty) grain, meant that people were toothless by their mid-20s, leading to infection and early death.

1666	1730–37	1797	1821
Tenerife's Garachico winemakers revolt against the emergence of a British monopoly of the wine trade, created by recent settlers, by destroying their cellars and wine.	Massive volcanic eruptions of Timanfaya in Lanzarote. The lava flow is devastating in many ways, but creates fertile ground for many crops, in particular grapes.	A British fleet led by Admiral Horatio Nelson attacks Santa Cruz de Tenerife. Sent to intercept a shipment of treasure, he famously loses his right arm in the ensuing battle.	The Canaries are declared a province of Spain, with Santa Cruz de Tenerife as the capital; Las Palmas de Gran Canaria demands that the province be split in two.

conquest and that on the mainland was that the Catholic Monarchs were not dealing with their traditional enemy, Islam, which boasted a culture far richer and more sophisticated than their own, but with a primitive native people whom they proceeded to mercilessly exploit. This could be viewed as the world's first example of true colonialism and a subsequent blueprint for similar conquest in the Americas and elsewhere in the world.

Economic & Foreign Challenges

The island of La Gomera was the last place Christopher Columbus touched dry land before setting sail to the New World.

From the early 16th century, Gran Canaria and Tenerife in particular attracted a steady stream of settlers from Spain, Portugal, France, Italy and even Britain. Each island had its own local authority, and sugar cane became the Canaries' main export.

The 'discovery' of the New World in 1492 by Christopher Columbus, who called in to the archipelago several times en route to the Americas, proved a mixed blessing. It brought much passing transatlantic trade but also led to sugar production being diverted to the cheaper Americas. The local economy was rescued only by the growing export demand for wine, particularly in Britain, which was produced mainly in Tenerife.

Poorer islands, especially Lanzarote and Fuerteventura, remained backwaters, their impoverished inhabitants making a living from smuggling and piracy off the Moroccan coast – the latter activity was part of a tit-for-tat game that had been played out with the Moroccans for centuries.

Spain's control of the islands did not go completely unchallenged. The most spectacular success went to Admiral Robert Blake, one of Oliver Cromwell's three 'generals at sea'. In 1657, Blake annihilated a Spanish treasure fleet (at the cost of only one ship) at Santa Cruz de Tenerife.

British harassment culminated in 1797 with Admiral Horatio Nelson's attack on Santa Cruz. Sent there to intercept yet another treasure shipment, he not only failed to storm the town but lost his right arm in the fighting.

On a more bucolic note, in 1799 the illustrious explorer and botanist Alexander von Humboldt stopped briefly in Tenerife en route to Latin America. Apparently when he spied the Orotava Valley, he famously declared it as 'the most enchanting view that eyes have ever seen'. This comment and his overall praise of the islands certainly contributed to their ensuing popularity and launch as a tourist resort initially reserved for the truly elite only. It was not until around a century later that tourism became a viable part of the local economy.

1850–90	1923	1927	1936
The continuing lack of employment and food leads to emigration figures peaking, with up to 40,000 islanders emigrating to Venezuela and elsewhere in Latin America.	General Miguel Primo de Rivera rises to power in Spain via a military coup and improves the infrastructure in the Canaries, including roads and water supplies.	Madrid finally decides to split the Canaries into two provinces: Tenerife, La Gomera, La Palma and El Hierro to the west; Fuerteventura, Gran Canaria and Lanzarote in the east.	In March the government decides to transfer General Franco, a veteran of Spain's wars in Morocco and sympathetic to the ruthless Spanish Foreign Legion, to the Canary Islands.

Island Divisions

Within the Canary Islands, a bitter feud developed between Gran Canaria and Tenerife over supremacy of the archipelago.

When the Canaries were declared a province of Spain in 1821, Santa Cruz de Tenerife was made the capital. Bickering between the two main islands remained heated and Las Palmas frequently demanded that the province be split in two. The idea was briefly, but unsuccessfully, put into practice in the 1840s.

In 1927 Madrid finally decided to split the Canaries into two provinces: Tenerife, La Gomera, La Palma and El Hierro in the west; Fuerteventura, Gran Canaria and Lanzarote in the east, with land being distributed between the local farmers. The main crops of bananas and tomatoes were cultivated and, even today, remain a major agricultural export. More unusually, cochineal farming was introduced and became one of the most important industries, particularly in Lanzarote. This parasitic beetle feeds on the prickly pear cacti and is cultivated for its crimson dye, although the industry reduced drastically with the subsequent emergence of synthetic dyes.

Capturing the spirit and excitement surrounding Admiral Nelson, *1797: Nelson's Year of Destiny* (Colin White) covers the battle of Cape St Vincent and the fateful attack on Santa Cruz de Tenerife where Nelson lost his arm.

Decades of Emigration

Emigration to the Americas was rife throughout the latter part of the 19th and 20th centuries and it was not uncommon for villages to be left with virtually no young male population. The exodus continued even after the Spanish-American War (1898) when Cuba and Puerto Rico were no longer Spanish territories. Cuba was initially the most popular country, followed by Venezuela, a trend which increased considerably after the Spanish Civil War; a time of considerable economic misery with rationing, food shortages and a thriving black market. In the 1950s the situation was so desperate that 16,000 migrated clandestinely, mainly to Venezuela, even though by then that country had closed its doors to further immigration. One-third of those who attempted to flee perished in the ocean crossings.

Cuba was a particularly welcoming destination for many Canarios fleeing the effects of the Spanish Civil War and there remain strong links between the Canary Islands and Cuba, at both governmental and personal levels.

Franco's Spain

In the 1930s, as the left and the right in mainland Spain became increasingly militant, fears of a coup grew. In March 1936 the government decided to 'transfer' General Franco, a veteran of Spain's wars in Morocco and beloved of the tough Spanish Foreign Legion, to the Canary Islands.

Suspicions that he was involved in a plot to overthrow the government were well founded; when the pro-coup garrisons of Melilla (Spanish North Africa) rose prematurely on 17 July, Franco was ready. Having seized control of the islands virtually without a struggle (the pro-Republican

1940s	1950s	1960s	1983
The damaging effect of the Spanish Civil War on the Canary Islands is considerable, with rationing, food shortages and overall poverty. The black market thrives.	The postwar fallout continues with economic misery throughout Spain and the Canaries. Once again, this is a time of mass emigration, including 16,000 Canarios who head for Venezuela.	Fortunes are reversed as jobs are created in response to the onset of tourism to the islands, particularly from the UK and Germany. Immigration concurrently increases.	The new constitution that was introduced in Madrid in 1978 impacts on the Canary Islands by deeming that they become a *comunidad autónoma* (autonomous region) in August of this year.

commander of the Las Palmas garrison died in mysterious circumstances on 14 July), Franco flew to Morocco on 19 July. Although there was virtually no fighting on the islands, the nationalists wasted no time in rounding up anyone vaguely suspected of harbouring republican sympathies, including writers, artists, teachers and politicians who all mysteriously disappeared.

The postwar economic misery of mainland Spain was shared by the islands, and many Canarios continued to emigrate. During WWII, Winston Churchill developed (but never activated) a plan to invade the Canary Islands to use as a naval base in the event of Gibraltar being invaded by the Spanish mainland. At the same time exports to Europe, aside from Spain, ceased.

Tourism, 'Nationalism' & Current Events

Canary Island Reads

History of the Canary Islands (José M. Castellano Gil)

Notes from the Canary Islands (Camilla Lenning)

The History of the Discovery and Conquest of the Canary Islands (George Glas)

The White Indians of Nivarra (Gordon Kennedy)

When Franco decided to open up Spain's doors to northern European tourists, the Canaries benefited as much as the mainland. Millions of holidaymakers now pour into the islands year-round.

Always a fringe phenomenon, Canaries nationalism started to resurface in opposition to Franco. MPAIC (Movimiento para la Autodeterminación e Independencia del Archipiélago Canario), founded in 1963 by Antonio Cubillo to promote secession from Spain, embarked on a terrorist campaign in the late 1970s, including the bombing of a shopping mall in Las Palmas de Gran Canaria in 1976. There were also bomb threats against the airport and some believed that a chain of events, which included shutting down air traffic control while searching for a bomb, could have contributed to the worst aviation disaster in history when two Boeing 747 airlines collided on the runway killing 583 people in 1977. Dodging Spanish authorities, Cubillo fled to Algeria in the 1960s, but in 1985 he was allowed to return to Spain.

In 1978 a new constitution was passed in Madrid with devolution as one of its central pillars. Thus the Canary Islands became a *comunidad autónoma* (autonomous region) in August 1982, yet the islands remained divided into two provinces.

The main force in Canary Islands politics since its first regional election victory in 1993 has been the Coalición Canaria (CC). Although not bent on independence from Spain (which would be unlikely), the CC nevertheless puts the interests of the islands before national considerations.

Immigration from Africa and other parts of the world has changed the Canaries' population landscape drastically over the past decade and has forced the islands to reassess their relationship with the African continent. Over the past 18 years the islands have made cooperation with Africa a major priority, investing around €17 million in education, health and infrastructure in Africa, especially in transport and communication links with the continent.

1993	2007	2011	2015
The Coalición Canaria (CC) is formed, working in conjunction with the Spanish government.	The world's largest telescope starts monitoring the stars at La Palma's Observatorio del Roque de los Muchachos, one of the top astronomical sites in the northern hemisphere.	El Hierro residents are evacuated after over 8000 minor earthquake tremors are recorded, leading to fears of a volcanic eruption.	Repsol cancels controversial oil drilling some 50km off the shores of Fuerteventura and Lanzarote.

Island Cuisine

Typical Canarian cuisine is all about using simple, fresh ingredients and doing as little as possible to them: grilled fish served with a zesty herb sauce, crinkly boiled potatoes with salted skin, juicy grilled goat, sliced tomatoes drizzled with olive oil and freshly picked fruit for dessert. Through the years, traditional Canarian dishes have rubbed shoulders with mainland Spanish cuisine and even South American specialities, giving way to unique local spins on recipes from elsewhere.

Staples & Specialities

The traditional staple or *pan de los Canarios* (bread of the Canarian people) is *gofio*, a uniquely Canario product and, it must be said, a bit of an acquired taste. A roasted mixture of wheat, barley or, more often, maize, *gofio* has long been an integral part of the traditional Canarian diet, though these days bread is just as common in the home – and far more so in restaurants. *Gofio* is mixed in varying proportions, and used as a breakfast food or combined with almonds and figs to make sweets. If you are really keen, you can seek out *gofio* ice cream or even *gofio* liquor. You can find it at supermarkets or buy directly from the few remaining mills.

The most-often-spotted Canarian dish is *papas arrugadas* (wrinkly potatoes), cooked in an abundance of salt and always served with some variation of *mojo* (spicy sauce made from coriander, basil or red chilli peppers). This sauce has endless variants and is used to flavour everything from chicken legs to cheese. You'll soon find you're addicted to one or another of them.

Of the many soups and stews you'll find, one typically Canarian variant is *potaje de berros* (watercress soup). Also look out for *ropa vieja,* a chickpea stew typically utilising whatever leftovers are lying around, and *rancho canario,* a hearty broth with thick noodles and the odd chunk of meat and potato.

Meat plays an important role in Canarian cooking and while beef and lamb dishes are often sighted on menus, these meats are usually imported. Opt instead for the island specialities: pork, rabbit and, above all, goat.

Like mainland Spain, social eating and drinking is central to the lifestyle here. Locals will think nothing of travelling several kilometres to some new talked-about restaurant or tapas bar, especially at Sunday lunch-time, a traditional time for dining out here.

Market-Fresh Ingredients

Basic foods long common across the islands are bananas and tomatoes, but nowadays the markets are filled with a wide range of fruit and vegetables. You should definitely visit at least one market during your trip. They are a real treat for all the senses with in-season produce such as plump dark figs (cut open to show their scarlet flesh), bundles of fragrant parsley and mint, bunches of brilliant-orange carrots, huge golden-yellow papayas and ropes of plump white garlic bulbs.

Markets are also great places to pack a simple picnic. Pick up freshly baked bread and stuff it with wedges of local cheese, usually made with goat's milk. The cheeses are renowned, particularly in Fuerteventura, where the delicious Majorero is a must for any cheese aficionado.

Latin & Spanish Influences

Canarian cuisine owes a lot to the New World; it was from South America that elementary items such as potatoes, tomatoes and corn were introduced. More exotic delights such as avocados and papayas also originated from there, while sweet mangoes arrived from Asia; look out for all three in the valleys and on supermarket shelves.

Some of the classic mainland Spanish dishes are also widely available, including paella (saffron rice cooked with chicken and rabbit or with seafood – at its best with good seafood), tortilla (omelette), gazpacho (a cold, tomato-based soup usually available in summer only), various *sopas* (soups) and *pinchos morunos* (kebabs).

Traditional Sweet Treats & Desserts

Canarios have a real sweet tooth. Some of the better-known desserts are *bienmesabe* (a kind of thick, sticky goo made of almonds, egg yolks, cinnamon and sugar – deadly sweet!), *frangollo* (a mix of cornmeal, dried fruit, milk and honey), *bizcochos lustrados* (sponge cake) and *truchas de batata* (sweet potato parcels).

Don't miss the *quesadillas* from El Hierro – this cheesy cinnamon pastry (sometimes also made with aniseed) has been baked since the Middle Ages. *Morcillas dulces* (sweet blood sausages), made with grapes, raisins and almonds, are a rather odd concoction; perhaps the closest comparison is a Christmas mince pie.

Papas arrugadas are made by boiling potatoes in heavily salted water, which makes the salt stick to the skin. The variety used is papas antiguas (old potatoes), descended from the first varieties imported from the Americas in the 15th century. Will you ever be able to replicate the recipe back home? Tricky, as the potatoes are only grown here – mainly in Tenerife.

Dining Times & Habits

Breakfast *(desayuno)* is usually a no-nonsense affair, with juice, coffee or tea, cereal or *gofio*, and toast with ham or cheese. *Churrerías* serve deliciously unhealthy deep-fried spiral-shaped *churros* (doughnuts), often accompanied by a cup of thick hot chocolate.

If you are a bacon-and-eggs breakfast person, head for one of the English-owned bars. Most hotels also have a hot and cold breakfast buffet.

The serious eating starts with lunch (*la comida* or, less commonly, *el almuerzo*). While Canarians tend to eat at home with the family, there is plenty of action in the restaurants too, starting at about 1pm and continuing until 4pm. In many restaurants, a set-price *menú del día* is served at lunchtime.

Dinner is served late at home, generally from around 8pm, while restaurants will normally open up at 7pm and serve until 11pm or later, especially in the tourist resorts. At-home dinners tend to be light for locals, but on weekends and special occasions people eat out with gusto.

Snacks are an important part of the Spanish culinary heritage. You can usually pick up a quick bite to eat to tide you over until the main meal times swing around. Standard snacks *(meriendas)* include tapas and *bocadillos*. Typically, this will be a rather dry affair with a slice of *jamón* (ham) and/or *queso* (cheese), or a wedge of *tortilla española* (potato omelette).

MENÚ DEL DÍA

The traveller's friend in the Canary Islands, as in mainland Spain, is the *menú del día*, a set meal available at most restaurants for lunch and occasionally in the evening too. Generally, you get a starter (salad, soup or pasta) followed by a meat, fish or seafood main and a simple dessert, which can include local specialities or Spanish favourites such as *flan* (crème caramel), *helado* (ice cream), a piece of fruit or just a cup of coffee. Water, a glass of wine or a small draught beer may or may not be included.

Drinks

Cafe culture is a part of life here, and the distinction between cafes and bars is negligible; coffee and alcohol are almost always available in both. Bars take several different forms, including *cervecerías* (beer bars, a vague equivalent of the pub), *tabernas* (taverns) and bodegas (old-style wine bars).

Coffee

Coffee is produced on a tiny scale in the islands, mostly in the Agaete Valley in the north of Gran Canaria. Coffee choices include the following:

Café con leche About 50% coffee, 50% hot milk.

Sombra The same, but heavier on the milk.

Café solo A short black coffee (or espresso).

Cortado An espresso with a splash of milk.

Cortado de leche y leche Espresso made with condensed and normal milk.

Barraquito A larger cup of *cortado* coffee.

Café con hielo Glass of ice and hot cup of coffee to be poured over the ice.

Wine

The local winemaking industry is relatively modest, but you can come across some good drops. Wine comes in *blanco* (white), *tinto* (red) or *rosado* (rosé). Prices vary considerably. In general, you get what you pay for and can pick up a decent tipple for about €10.

One of the most common wines across the islands is the *malvasía* (Malmsey wine; also produced in Madeira, Portugal). It is generally sweet *(dulce),* although you can find the odd dry *(seco)* version. It is particularly common on La Palma and Lanzarote.

Tenerife is the principal source of wine, and the red Tacoronte Acentejo was the first Canarian wine to earn the grade of DO (*denominación de origen;* an appellation certifying high standards and regional origin). This term is one of many employed to regulate and judge wine and grape quality. Other productive vineyards are in the Icod de los Vinos, Güímar and Tacoronte areas of Tenerife. In Lanzarote, the vine has come back into vogue since the early 1980s, and in late 1993 the island's *malvasías* were awarded a DO.

Beer

The most common way to order a beer *(cerveza)* is to ask for a *caña,* which is a small draught beer (*cerveza de barril* or *cerveza de presión*). If you prefer a larger version, ask for a *jarra.* Dorada, brewed in Santa Cruz de Tenerife, is a very smooth number. Tropical, which is produced on Gran Canaria and is a little lighter, is a worthy runner-up and the preferred tipple of the eastern isles. There are one or two microbreweries in the islands, though the difficulty in sourcing ingredients is a hurdle for small-scale brewers.

Spirits

Apart from the mainland Spanish imports, which include *coñac* (brandy) and a whole host of *licores* (liqueurs), you could try some local firewater if you come across it. One to seek out is *mistela* from La Gomera, a mixture of wine, sugar, spices and *parra* – a local version of *aguardiente* (similar to schnapps or grappa). Altogether easier to swallow is the rum that is produced across the islands. Dark rum is the favourite tipple while honey rum (*ron miel*) is a sweet concoction sometimes given after meals as a complimentary *chupito* (shot).

The New Spain – Vegetarian & Vegan Restaurants (Jean Claude Juston) should be a bible for vegetarian and vegan visitors.

If you like wine and you like exercise, consider Lanzarote's annual Wine Run, which takes place every June with a choice of 21km (for runners) and 10km (for walkers). Held in the island's wine region, it coincides with a traditional food festival.

Canarian Arts & Culture

Although the Canary Islands are Spanish, their architecture, art and overall culture is subtly distinctive from that of the mainland, with more than a glimmer of Latin American influence. Overall, the Canarians are a warm and friendly people, deeply devoted to tradition, the family and having fun. Fiestas here are wonderfully exuberant affairs: try to attend one if you can.

The Arts

Architecture

Most pre-Hispanic architecture you think you spot on the islands is either a reconstruction, heavily restored – or a theme park. The Guanches lived mainly in caves, and very little of the rudimentary houses they built remains today, though there are a couple of interesting sites in Gran Canaria. Although people often talk about 'typical Canarian architecture', there have been so many different influences over the centuries, it is hard to specify exactly what this is. It is not uncommon, either, for a building to reflect more than one architectural style.

César Manrique Architecture

Jameos del Agua, Malpaís de la Corona, Lanzarote

Parque Marítimo, Santa Cruz de Tenerife

Fundación César Manrique, Tahiche, Lanzarote

Mirador del Río, Lanzarote

Colonial Period

Colonial architecture is a good example of the potpourri of influences, including elements from the Spanish, Portuguese, French, Flemish, Italian and English architectural schools. By the time the conquest of the islands was completed at the end of the 15th century, the Gothic and Mudéjar (a distinctive Islamic-style architecture) influences already belonged more to the past than the present. The interior of the Catedral de Santa Ana in Las Palmas is nevertheless a fine example of what some art historians have denominated Atlantic Gothic. Only a few scraps of the fascinating Mudéjar influence made it to the islands, most in evidence in magnificent wooden ceilings known as *artesonado*.

You can get the merest whiff of plateresque (meaning silversmith-like, so called because it was reminiscent of intricate metalwork) energy at the Catedral de Santa Ana in Las Palmas and the Iglesia de Nuestra Señora de la Concepción in La Laguna – the latter a veritable reference work of styles from Gothic through Mudéjar to plateresque. Baroque, the trademark of the 17th century, left several traces across the archipelago and is best preserved in the parish church of Betancuria, Fuerteventura.

Some of the most distinctive aspects of architecture during this period are the internal courtyards and beautiful carved wooden balconies. Las Palmas de Gran Canaria's historic Vegueta *barrio* (district) has some excellent examples, as does the Avenida Marítima in Santa Cruz de la Palma.

Modern Architecture

Modernism makes an appearance along the Calle Mayor de Triana and in the private houses of the Triana district of Las Palmas de Gran Canaria.

But modern Canary architecture's greatest genius is the late César Manrique. His ecologically sensitive creations, often using volcanic stones and other Canary materials, are found throughout the islands, but especially on Lanzarote, where he was born. His designs are so compelling that some people base an entire trip around visiting them all.

The icon of contemporary Canary architecture is Santiago Calatrava's 'wave', the multifunction Auditorio de Tenerife dominating the waterfront of Santa Cruz de Tenerife with its unmistakable profile of a wave crashing onto shore. Las Palmas de Gran Canaria is another architectural hot spot; interesting architectural spaces include the interior of the Atlantic Modern Art Centre by Sáenz de Oiza, the Auditorio Alfredo Kraus by Óscar Tusquets and the Woermann Tower by Iñaki Ábalos and Juan Herreros.

Painting & Sculpture

For such a relatively small landmass, the Canary Islands have a considerable number of art museums, open-air sculptures and galleries. An appreciation for quality art also seems to have spilt over into the general populace, with restaurants and hotels often preferring to hang original artwork by local painters rather than those same old Picasso prints.

The Guanches

The art tradition dates back to the Guanches and there are some fine examples of their cave drawings at various sites, including the Cueva Pintada in Gáldar, Gran Canaria. Normally geometric in design, the ancient Guanche drawings have served to inspire some of the most famous artists, including Manolo Millares (1926–72), a native of Las Palmas de Gran Canaria, as well as more accessible souvenir T-shirts and ceramic designs. The best-loved sculpture from these times is the *Ídolo de Tara* from Gran Canaria; a curvy feminine figure and Guanche idol which you will see stamped on textiles and in pottery replicas.

17th- to 19th-Century Artists

Gaspar de Quevedo from Tenerife was the first major painter to emerge from the Canary Islands in the 17th century. Quevedo was succeeded in the 18th century by Cristóbal Hernández de Quintana (1659–1725), whose paintings still decorate the Catedral in La Laguna in Tenerife. More important was Juan de Miranda (1723–1805), among whose outstanding works is *La Adoración de los Pastores* (The Adoration of the Shepherds) in the Iglesia de Nuestra Señora de la Concepción in Santa Cruz de Tenerife.

In the 19th century, Valentín Sanz Carta (1849–98) was among the first Canarians to produce landscapes. Others of his ilk included Lorenzo Pastor and Lillier y Thruillé, whose work can be seen in the Museo de Bellas Artes in Santa Cruz de Tenerife.

The Canaries' main exponent of impressionism was Manuel González Méndez (1843–1909), whose *La Verdad Venciendo el Error* (Truth Overcoming Error) hangs in the *ayuntamiento* (town hall) of Santa Cruz de Tenerife.

20th-Century Artists

The Cuban-Canario José Aguiar García (1895–1976), born of Gomero parents, has works spread across the islands. His *Friso Isleño* (Island Frieze) hangs in the casino in Santa Cruz de Tenerife.

All the great currents of European art filtered through to the Canary Islands. Of the so-called Coloristas, names worth mentioning include Francesco Miranda Bonnin (1911–63) and Jesús Arencibia (1911–93), who created the impressive large mural in the Iglesia de San Antonio Abad in Las Palmas de Gran Canaria.

CANARIAN ARTS & CULTURE THE ARTS

Crafted Ceilings

Iglesia de Nuestra Señora de la Concepción, La Laguna, Tenerife
....
Iglesia de Santa Catalina, Tacoronte, Tenerife
....
Iglesia del Salvador, Santa Cruz de la Palma
....
Iglesia de Santa María, Buenaventura, Fuerteventura
....
Iglesia de Nuestra Señora de Rega, Pájara, Fuerteventura

Top Sculptors
....
Eduardo Gregorio
....
Plácido Fleitas
....
Manolo Millares
....
César Manrique
....
Juan Bordes

MARTÍN CHIRINO

Martín Chirino is widely considered to be one of the most significant Spanish sculptors of the 20th century. Born in Las Palmas de Gran Canaria in 1925, he spent time in Africa as a young man, including Morocco and Senegal, and this influence can be seen especially in some of his earlier pieces. Chirino's giant, mainly bronze sculptures are on view throughout the islands. They include *Espiral* (1999) in Santa Cruz de Tenerife; *El Pensador* (2002), gracing the grounds of the University of Las Palmas de Gran Canaria; and perhaps most easily viewed of all, *Lady Harimaguada* (1999), on Avenia Marítima in Las Palmas de Gran Canaria.

The first surrealist exhibition in Spain was held on 11 May 1935 in Santa Cruz de Tenerife. The greatest local exponent of surrealism, Tinerfeño Óscar Domínguez (1906–57), ended up in Paris in 1927 and was much influenced by Picasso. Others of the period include cubist Antonio Padrón (1920–68), who has a superb museum displaying his work in his former Gran Canaria studio.

Leading the field of abstract artists is Manolo Millares (1926–72), while Alberto Manrique (1926–; no relation to César Manrique) from Gran Canaria enjoys altering perspective to dramatic, surreal effect. You can see a permanent exhibition of his work at the Centro de Arte Canario in La Oliva, Fuerteventura.

Traditional Crafts

La Gomera & Tenerife: Guanche-style pottery, basketware

Lanzarote & Gran Canaria: timples (small guitars)

El Hierro, La Palma & La Gomera: woven rugs

Tenerife: Vilaflor lacework

Crafts

There is a deep-rooted tradition of craftwork here with different islands specialising in particular crafts. Fine lacework and embroidered tablecloths, napkins and table linen can be found all over the archipelago, with Ingenio (Gran Canaria), Mazo (La Palma) and La Orotava (Tenerife) particularly famous for their embroidered works of art. Be wary of Chinese imports being passed off as local products, particularly at the street markets. One way to identify the real item (aside from the obvious quality) is cost: original embroidery does not come cheap, reflecting the skill and time taken in the creation. Prices are dropping, however, as there is less demand for these items today.

Simple woven carpets and rugs – usually striped and brightly coloured – have a more timeless quality and are still made painstakingly with a handloom. Other popular items to weigh down your luggage with are woven baskets, Guanche-style pottery, ceramic pots and straw hats of all sizes and shapes.

Music

The symbol of Canarian musical heritage is the *timple,* a ukulele-style instrument of obscure origin, thought to have been introduced to the islands by Berber slaves in the 15th century. It's a small five-stringed instrument with a rounded back (it is said the original Berber version was made of a turtle shell) and a sharp tone.

If you want to catch some traditional Canarian tunes, check out Tenderete, a TV show that's been running for 40 years. Watch it on Sunday evenings on TVE1.

Whenever you see local traditional fiestas, the *timple* will be there accompanying such dances as the *isa* and *folía* or, if you're lucky, the *tajaraste* – about the only dance said to have been passed down from the ancient Guanches and still popular in La Gomera.

Culture

Regional Identity

It's hard to sum up the peoples and traditions of seven islands. Mannerisms, expressions, food, architecture and music vary significantly from island to island and rivalries (especially between heavyweights Tenerife and Gran Canaria) are strong. Yet shared by everyone is a fierce pride

LOS SABANDEÑOS

The Canaries' best-loved folk group, Los Sabandeños, has been singing and strumming since 1966, when these Tinerfeños banded together in an effort to recover and popularise Canary culture across the islands. It's impossible to quantify the effects this group of nearly 25 men (including a few new recruits) has had on the islands. Suffice to say, they have a statue in their honour in Punta de Hidalgo, Tenerife and (at last count) seven streets named after them. Their CDs of light, melodic music are widely available; look for their greatest hits compilation *60 Canciones de Oro* (2012).

in being Canarian, and the belief that their unique history and culture set them apart from the rest of Spain. While most of the Canary Island locals have the classic Mediterranean looks of the Spaniards – dark hair and eyes and an olive complexion – you might find that they don't think of themselves as all that Spanish.

Soon after the socialists' 1982 electoral victory at the national level, the Canary Islands were declared a *comunidad autónoma,* one of 17 autonomous regions across Spain. A few vocal Canarios would like to see their islands become completely autonomous – keep an eye peeled for splashes of graffiti declaring *'Canarias no es España'* (the Canaries are not Spain) or *'Godos fuera'* (Spaniards go home).

The archipelago's division into two provinces, Santa Cruz and Las Palmas, remains intact, as does the rivalry between the two provinces – so much so that the regional government has offices in both provincial capitals, which alternate as lead city of the region every four years.

Lifestyle

The greatest lifestyle change that has come to the Canary Islands has been as a result of the tourism industry. In a matter of decades a primarily agricultural society became a society largely dependent on the service industry. Traditional lifestyles on small *fincas* (farms) or in fishing villages have been supplanted by employment in the tourism sector.

As the islands close the gap between their traditional, rural lifestyles and the fast-paced, modern lifestyle of the rest of Spain, some problems are inevitable. The cost of living has skyrocketed, forcing those who have kept traditional agriculture jobs to supplement their income with positions in the tourism industry. Education is another issue; since the small islands have no universities, young people have to study in Tenerife or Gran Canaria and this can deplete a family's already overstretched budget. After school, many college-educated islanders end up leaving the island of their birth to look for better jobs on Tenerife, Gran Canaria or the mainland. By necessity, many Canarian families are separated.

Nevertheless, family remains at the heart of Canary culture. Big island celebrations are often celebrated with family, and islanders come from as far away as the Americas to reunite with family and friends. Most religious and cultural celebrations are also family-focused. Although families now are smaller than they used to be – one or two children is the norm – they're still an important social unit. As elsewhere in Europe, couples are waiting longer to get married and have children, proving that Canarian society is not as traditional as it once was.

Sport

The Canary Islands are a sport-friendly destination, as they have a balmy, sunny climate, plenty of coastline and a laid-back, outdoor lifestyle that rewards activity. As part of Spain, there are no prizes for guessing the top sport here: football (soccer). Although there is a regional football

Top Spanish actor Javier Bardem (*Eat Pray Love, Skyfall*) was born in Las Palmas de Gran Canaria. He originally set out to be a painter and studied art at the prestigious Escuela de Artes y Oficios in Madrid. Bardem started his acting life as an extra, which led to a full-time acting career (and marriage to Penelope Cruz).

STREET PARTIES, CANARIAN-STYLE

Pretty much every town hosts its own party at some point and it's a rare summer week-end when there isn't a *romería* happening somewhere on the archipelago. The literal translation of *romería* is 'pilgrimage', but while the day-long fiestas usually have their roots in religion, these days the emphasis is more on party than piety. Most people don traditional Canarian costume for the day, which tends to begin with a procession followed by displays of traditional music and dance. Later on, the more modern-day tradition of sipping island-made rum with Coke is the main activity, as town streets and squares become the site of a late-night bash.

team for the Canary Islands, they are not affiliated with FIFA, UEFA or CAF, because the islands are represented internationally by the Spanish national football team. The team only plays friendly matches.

Far more unusual is *lucha canaria* (Canarian wrestling), which is said to date back to the Guanches, a particularly robust and warlike crowd who loved a trial of strength: jumping over ravines, diving into oceans from dizzying heights...and this distinctive style of wrestling. One member of each team faces off against an adversary in the ring and, after a formal greeting and other signs of goodwill, they set about trying to dump each other into the dust. No part of the body except the soles of the feet may touch the ground, and whoever fails first in this department loses. Size and weight are not the determining factors (although these boys tend to be as beefy as rugby front-row forwards), but rather the skill with which the combatants grapple and manoeuvre their opponents into a position from which they can be toppled.

If you want to find out if any matches are due to be held locally, ask at the nearest tourist office or check out www.federacioncanariadelucha-canaria.com (in Spanish only).

Naming Names: People of the Islands

Gran Canaria
Grancanarios or Canariones

....

Tenerife
Tinerfeños

....

Lanzarote
Conejeros

....

Fuerteventura
Majoreros

....

La Gomera
Gomeros

....

La Palma
Palmeros

....

El Hierro
Herreños

Multiculturalism

Nowadays the Canary Islands, for so long a region of net emigration, admit more people than they export. Workers in the hotel, restaurant and construction industries, and migrants from northern Europe seeking a place in the near-perpetual sun, all bolster the islands' population figures. With more than half a million tourist beds in hotels, apartments and houses across the islands, there is a steady influx of tourists from across the world, mainly Europe, some of whom also decide to stay and make a life here.

A newer phenomenon are the immigrants from the Americas, many of them family members of Canarians who emigrated to Venezuela or other South American countries and are now returning to the islands of their ancestors.

In the past, the Canary Islands have faced serious problems with illegal migrants arriving from African shores in droves. In recent years, the number of boats carrying illegal migrants has significantly dropped, though locals are still wary of the situation. Prejudice is hard to gauge, but some tourists of African origin have reported discrimination, mainly in shops and restaurants and particularly in the southern resorts of Tenerife.

Religion

The Catholic church plays an important role in people's lives. Most Canarios are baptised and confirmed, have church weddings and funerals, and many attend church for important feast days – although fewer than half regularly turn up for Sunday Mass. Many of the colourful and often wild fiestas that take place throughout the year have some religious context or origin.

Life on a Volcano

Many people think of the Canary Islands as consisting of little but flat, featureless semi-desert, and while there are areas where this image rings true, anyone who knows the islands well will speak in excited tones about the sheer variety of landscapes, climates and flora and fauna contained within this unique archipelago.

Volcanic Landscape

Formation of the Islands

The seven islands and six islets that make up the Canary Islands archipelago are little more than the tallest tips of a vast volcanic mountain range that lies below the Atlantic Ocean. Just babies in geological terms, the islands were thrown up 30 million years ago when tectonic plates collided, crumpling the land into mammoth mountains both on land, as in the case of Morocco's Atlas range, and on the ocean floor, as in the case of the Cape Verde islands, the Azores and the Canaries. These Atlantic islands are collectively referred to as Macronesia. After the initial creation, a series of volcanic eruptions put the final touches on the islands' forms.

La Palma is the steepest island in the world, relative to its height and overall area.

The Islands Today

The seven main islands have a total area of 7447 sq km. Their size may not be great, but packed into them is just about every imaginable kind of landscape, from the long, sandy beaches of Fuerteventura and dunes of Gran Canaria to the majestic Atlantic cliffs of Tenerife and the mist-enveloped woods of La Gomera. The easternmost islands have an almost Saharan desertscape, while corners of La Palma and La Gomera are downright lush. The highest mountain in Spain is Pico del Teide (3718m), which dominates the entire island of Tenerife.

El Teide & the Others

El Teide, that huge pyramid that stands at the very centre of life on Tenerife, is at 3718m both the highest mountain in Spain and – if measured from its true base on the ocean floor – the third-largest volcano in the world. Teide is what's known as a shield volcano; it's huge and rises in a broad, gently angled cone to a summit that holds a steep-walled, flat-based crater. Although seemingly quiet, Teide is by no means finished.

Wisps of hot air can sometimes be seen around Teide's peak. Where the lava is fairly fluid, steam pressure can build up to the point of ejecting lava and ash or both in an eruption through the narrow vent. The vent can simply be blown off if there is sufficient pressure.

Other volcanoes on the islands have been known to sometimes literally blow their top. Massive explosions can cause an entire summit to cave in, blasting away an enormous crater. The result is known as a caldera, within which it is not unusual for new cones to emerge, creating volcanoes within volcanoes. There are several impressive calderas on Gran Canaria, most notably Caldera de Bandama. Oddly enough, massive Caldera de Taburiente on La Palma does not belong to this group of geological phenomena, although it was long thought to.

Wild Books

Whales and Dolphins of the Canary Islands (Volker Boehlke)

Native Flora of the Canary Islands (Miguel Angel Cabrera Perez)

The Geology of the Canary Islands (Juan Carlos Carracedo & Valentin Troll)

A Field Guide to the Birds of the Atlantic Islands (Tony Clarke)

CUMBRE VIEJA & THE MEGATSUNAMI

On the island of La Palma – yes, that's right, the one very close to the beach you're lying on – is the Cumbre Vieja (Old Ridge). In 1949 a series of volcanic eruptions here caused a fissure about 2.5km long to open up, which sent the western side of the Cumbre Vieja slipping downwards, and westwards, by around 2m.

Experts believe that it's only a matter of time before Cumbre Vieja erupts again. When it does, some people fear that it could send up to 1.5 trillion metric tonnes of rock cascading down into the Atlantic. The resulting tsunami could measure up to 600m in diameter, travelling at a speed of around 1000km an hour, would reach the east coast of the United States within six hours (and the coastlines of Africa and Europe much sooner). By this time the tsunami waves would be around 30m to 60m high, though on reaching shallower water they could grow to a several hundred metres. It's amazing that no Hollywood director has yet to make a film about the theory, which sees the waves travelling around 25km inland, devastating the Caribbean and the eastern shores of the US.

How likely is this to happen? Well, that's where the arguments really start, but some – well, a few – say that it could be imminent. Just time for another cocktail then?

These days in the Canary Islands, you can best get a feel for the rumblings below the surface on Lanzarote, where the Montañas del Fuego still bubble with vigour, although the last eruptions took place way back in 1824. Of the remaining islands, not an eruptive burp has been heard from Fuerteventura, Gran Canaria, La Gomera or El Hierro for centuries; Tenerife's most recent display was a fairly innocuous affair in 1909; and it was La Palma that hosted the most recent spectacle – a fiery outburst by Volcán Teneguía in 1971.

Wild Things
Canaries, Whales & Other Animals

There is wildlife out there, but it tends to be small, shy and largely undetected by the untrained eye. Lizards and birds are the biggest things you'll see – in some cases they are quite big indeed, like the giant lizard of El Hierro, which measures up to around 50cm. There are around 200 species of birds on the islands, though many are imports from Africa and Europe. Five endemics are found in the Canaries: Bolle's pigeon, laurel pigeon, blue chaffinch, Canary Islands chiff-chaff and Canary Islands chat. And yes, before you ask, this is where canaries come from, but the wild cousins are of a much duller colour than the popular cage birds.

If it's big animals you want, you need to turn to the ocean. The stretch of water between Tenerife and La Gomera is a traditional feeding ground

LAND OF GIANTS

The best-known native animals in the Canaries today are the giant lizards, which still hang on in a number of places. Impressive as these are, they're nothing compared to what used to scamper around the hills here. Hailing from Tenerife, *Gallotia goliath* never shared the islands with humans, but fossilised remains show that this colossal lizard measured a good metre in length. Today skeletons and casts of them can be seen in Tenerife's Museo de la Naturaleza y el Hombre.

Living alongside these lizards was a creature straight out of a nightmare. The Tenerife giant rat was around a metre long (including the tail) and weighed around a kilo when fully grown. It was actually still present when the Guanches first arrived on Tenerife, but people, and possibly domestic cats, quickly put an end to this monster. Gran Canaria had its own type of giant rat, but this was a comparative minnow at just 25cm in length.

It's also thought that a type of giant tortoise once lived on the islands.

for as many as 26 species of whales, and others pass through during migration. The most common are pilot whales, sperm whales and bottlenose dolphins.

Whale watching is big business around here, and 800,000 people a year head out on boats to get a look. A law regulates observation of sea mammals, prohibiting boats from getting closer than 60m to an animal and limiting the number of boats following pods at any one time. The law also tries to curb practices such as using sonar and other devices to attract whales' attention. Four small patrol boats attempt to keep a watchful eye on these activities. If you decide to take a whale-watching tour, join up with a reputable company.

Aside from the majestic marine mammals, there are many other life forms busy under the ocean. The waters around the Canary Islands host more than 500 species of fish. You can see them up close either by going scuba diving or eating a fish dinner.

Plants

The islands' rich volcanic soil, varied rainfall and dramatic changes in altitude support a surprising diversity of plant life, both indigenous and introduced. The Canary Islands are home to about 2000 species, about 700 of which are endemic to the islands. The only brake on what might otherwise be a still-more-florid display in this largely subtropical environment is the shortage of water. Even so, botanists will have a field day here, and there are numerous botanical gardens scattered about where you can observe a whole range of local flora.

Possibly the most important floral eco-system in the Canaries is La Gomera's Parque Nacional de Garajonay, host to one of the world's last remaining Tertiary-era forests and a Unesco World Heritage site. Known as *laurisilva,* the beautiful forest here is made up of laurels, holly, linden and giant heather, clad in lichen and moss and often swathed in swirling mist.

Up in the great volcanic basin of the Parque Nacional del Teide on Tenerife, the star botanical attraction is the flamboyant *tajinaste rojo,* or Teide viper's bugloss *(Echium wildpretii),* which can grow to more than 3m high. Every other spring it sprouts an extraordinary conical spike of striking red blooms like a great red poker. After its brief, spectacular moment of glory, all that remains is a thin, desiccated, spear-shaped skeleton, like a well-picked-over fish. Leave well alone; each fishbone has thousands of tiny strands that are as itchy as horsehair.

Environmental Issues

The Problems

As in mainland Spain, the 1960s saw the first waves of mass sea-and-sun tourism crash over the tranquil shores of the Canary Islands. The government of the day anticipated filling up the state coffers with easy tourist dollars, and local entrepreneurs enthusiastically leapt aboard the gravy train. Few, however, gave a thought to what impact the tourists and mushrooming coastal resorts might have on the environment.

The near-unregulated building and expansion of resorts well into the 1980s has created some monumental eyesores, particularly on the southern side of Tenerife and Gran Canaria. Great scabs of holiday villas, hotels and condominiums have spread across much of these two islands' southern coasts. And the problem is not restricted to the resorts – hasty cement extensions to towns and villages mean that parts of the islands' interiors are being increasingly spoiled by property developers and speculators.

The massive influx of visitors to the islands over recent decades has brought or exacerbated other problems. Littering of beaches, dunes and other areas of natural beauty, both by outsiders and locals, remains a

Nature Trek (www.nature trek.co.uk) is a British-based wildlife-watching tour company that runs an eight-day tour in search of the native wildlife and plants of the Canary Islands.

Look out for books by David Bramwell. The curator of Gran Canaria's Jardín Botánico Canario is an authority on the flora of the islands and has penned numerous tomes on the subject.

LIFE ON A VOLCANO ENVIRONMENTAL ISSUES

DRAGON TREES: A LONG, SHADY PAST

Among the more curious trees you will see in the Canary Islands is the *drago* (dragon tree; *Dracaena draco*), which can reach 18m in height and live for centuries.

Having survived the last ice age, it looks different – even a touch prehistoric. Its shape resembles a giant posy of flowers, its trunk and branches being the stems, which break into bunches of long, narrow, silvery-green leaves higher up. As the plant (technically it is not a tree, though it's always referred to as one) grows, it becomes more and more top-heavy. To stabilise itself, the *drago* ingeniously grows roots on the outside of its trunk, eventually creating a second wider trunk. What makes the *drago* stranger still is its red sap or resin – known, of course, as 'dragon's blood' – which was traditionally used in medicine.

The plant once played an important role in Canary Island life, for it was beneath the ancient branches of a *drago* that the Guanche Council of Nobles would gather to administer justice.

The *drago* is one of a family of up to 40 species (*Dracaena*) that survived the ice age in tropical and subtropical zones of the Old World, and is one of the last representatives of Tertiary-era flora.

burning issue. Occasionally, ecological societies organise massive rubbish cleanups along beaches and the like – worthy gestures but also damning evidence of the extent to which the problem persists.

One of the islands' greatest and most persistent problems is water, or rather the lack thereof. Limited rainfall and the lack of natural springs have always restricted agriculture, and water is a commodity still in short supply. Desalination appears to be the only solution for the Canaries; pretty much all potable water on Lanzarote and Fuerteventura is desalinated sea water.

In summer, the corollary of perennial water shortages is the forest fire. With almost clockwork regularity, hundreds of hectares of forest are ravaged every summer on all the islands except the already-bare Lanzarote and Fuerteventura.

The Arguments

For the islands' administrators, it's a conundrum. Tourism has come to represent an essential pillar of the Canaries' economy, which it quite simply cannot do without. They argue that profits from the tourist trade are ploughed back into the community. However, this is still fairly haphazard and there have long been calls for more regional planning – and, every year more insistently, for a total moratorium on further tourism development. Short-term moratoriums are at times established on an island-by-island basis. Some of the damage done over the years, especially to the coastline, is irreversible.

One of the hottest issues of recent years – the proposed port of Granadilla in southeastern Tenerife – is still very much on the minds of locals concerned about the effects such a huge commercial port would have on the environment. Another contentious plan, to drill for gas and oil off the coasts of Fuerteventura and Lanzarote, has happily been laid to rest after exploratory probes deemed the project unworthy. In Fuerteventura though, a controversial art project to hollow out a sacred mountain has also, understandably, been met with concern, though the *cabildo* (island government) insists that the installation will bring in essential coffers with the 'quality tourism' it will attract.

One island that has taken steps towards conservation is El Hierro, where, after years of planning, the government was about to achieve its goal to become the world's first island able to meet all its energy needs with renewable sources (wind, water and solar) alone. Next on the agenda: El Hierro plans to run all its vehicles on electricity by 2020.

If you're interested in getting involved with marine conservation, in particular the protection of whales, get in touch with the Atlantic Whale Foundation (www.awf-volunteering-abroad.org), a group that organises educational trips, volunteer opportunities and conservation campaigns on Tenerife. The website is a mine of information.

Survival Guide

Directory A–Z

Customs Regulations

Although the Canary Islands are part of Spain, for customs purposes they are not considered part of the EU. For this reason, allowances are much less generous than for goods bought within EU countries. You are allowed to bring in or take out duty free a maximum of the following items:

➡ 4L of still wine

➡ 1L of spirits (or 2L of fortified wine)

➡ 16L of beer

➡ 200 cigarettes

➡ €200 worth of other goods and gifts

Discount Cards

To receive any discount, photo ID is essential.

➡ Seniors get reduced prices at various museums and attractions and occasionally on transport. The minimum age varies between 60 and 65 years.

➡ Students receive discounts of usually half the normal fee. Student cards are not accepted everywhere.

➡ Ask at individual tourism offices for discount cards covering local attractions.

Climate

Las Palmas de Gran Canaria

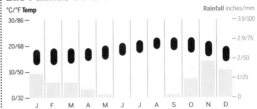

Puerto del Rosario

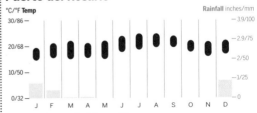

Santa Cruz de Tenerife

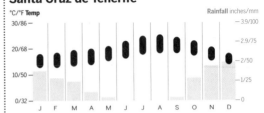

Electricity

220V/50Hz

Embassies & Consulates

Countries have their main diplomatic representation in Madrid but also have consular representation in Las Palmas de Gran Canaria.

German Consulate (☎928 49 18 80; www.spanien.diplo.de; Calle Albareda 3, 2nd fl)

Irish Consulate (☎928 29 77 28; www.embassyofireland.es; Calle León y Castillo 195)

UK Consulate (☎928 26 25 08; www.gov.uk; Calle Luis Morote 6, 3rd fl)

US Consulate (☎928 27 12 59; www.madrid.usembassy.gov; Calle Martínez de Escobar 3)

There are a small number of consulates in Santa Cruz de Tenerife.

French Consulate (☎922 53 35 36; www.ambafrance-es.org; Calle Robayna 25)

Irish Consulate (☎922 24 56 71; www.embassyofireland.es; Calle San Francisco 9)

Netherlands Consulate (☎922 27 17 21; http://espana.

nlembajada.org; Calle Villalba Hervás 5, 3rd fl)

UK Consulate (☎in Gran Canaria 928 26 25 08; www.ukinspain.com; Plaza General Weyler 8, 1st fl)

Gay & Lesbian Travellers

Gay and lesbian marriages are legal in Spain and hence on the Canary Islands. Playa del Inglés and Maspalomas, on the southern end of Gran Canaria, are where the bulk of Europe's gay crowd heads when holidaying in the Canaries, and the nightlife here bumps and grinds year-round. By day, nudist beaches are popular spots to hang out.

Spanish people generally adopt a live-and-let-live attitude to sexuality, so you shouldn't have any hassles in the Canary Islands. That said, some small rural towns may not quite know how to deal with overt displays of affection between same-sex couples.

Canarias Gay (www.canariasgay.com) Search engine for gay-friendly holidays in the islands.

Gamá (www.colectivogama.com) Gay and lesbian association covering the entire archipelago.

Pink Canaries (www.pinkcanaries.com) Gay and lesbian association based in Tenerife, covering clubs, restaurants and gay-friendly accommodation.

Health

Availability of Health Care

Spain has an excellent health-care system that extends to the Canary Islands. If you need an ambulance, call ☎112 (the pan-European emergency telephone number that can be called for urgent medical assistance). An alternative medical emergency number is ☎061. Alternatively, go straight to the *urgencias* (casualty) section of the nearest hospital.

Farmacias (pharmacies) offer valuable advice and sell over-the-counter medication. Throughout the Canaries, a system of *farmacias de guardia* (duty pharmacies) operates so that each district has one open all the time. When a pharmacy is closed, it posts the name of the nearest open one on the door.

The standard of dental care is usually good; however, it is sensible to have a dental check-up before a long trip.

Health Insurance

For EU citizens, the European Health Insurance Card (EHIC), which you apply for online, by phone or by post, entitles you to medical care at the same cost that a local would pay – sometimes for free. It doesn't cover emergency repatriation home and isn't meant as a substitution for travel insurance.

EATING PRICE RANGES

Restaurants are ordered first by price indicator and then by author preference within the price brackets. The following price ranges refer to a standard main course.

€ less than €10

€€ €10–€20

€€€ more than €20

Ask if there is a surcharge to sit on the outdoor terrace – a few places add on an extra 10% to 15%.

PRACTICALITIES

⇒ **Currency** Euro

⇒ **Weights & Measures** Metric

⇒ **Newspapers & Magazines** Local newspapers include *Diario de Avisos, Canarias 7, La Provincia* and the English-language *Island Connections*. You can also get Spanish newspapers *El País* and *El Mundo* and the foreign *International Herald Tribune, Hello!* and – in the resorts – all the British and German tabloids.

⇒ **Radio** Radio Nacional de España has four stations. Local FM stations abound on the islands and the BBC World Service (www.bbc.co.uk/worldservice) can be found mainly on 6195kHz, 9410kHz, 12095kHz and 15485kHz.

⇒ **TV** The Canaries receives the mainland's big TV channels (TVE1, La 2, Antena 3, Cuatro, Tele 5, La Sexta) and has a few local stations that are of very limited interest.

⇒ **Smoking** Laws prohibit smoking in all bars and restaurants, as well as near hospitals, in school playgrounds and even on TV broadcasts.

Citizens from other countries should find out whether there is a reciprocal arrangement for free medical care between their country and Spain. If you need health insurance, strongly consider a policy that covers the worst possible scenario, such as an accident requiring an emergency flight home. Find out in advance if your insurance plan will make direct payments to providers or reimburse you later for overseas health expenditures.

Altitude Sickness

If you are hiking at elevations above 2500m (such as at El Teide in Tenerife), altitude sickness may be a risk. Lack of oxygen at high altitudes affects most people to some extent. Symptoms of acute mountain sickness (AMS) usually develop during the first 24 hours at altitude, but may be delayed up to three weeks. Mild symptoms include headache, lethargy, dizziness, difficulty sleeping and loss of appetite. AMS may become more severe without warning and can

be fatal. Severe symptoms include breathlessness, a dry irritating cough, severe headache and lack of balance.

Treat mild symptoms by resting at the same altitude until you recover, usually for a day or two. Paracetamol or aspirin can be taken for headaches. If symptoms worsen, immediate descent is necessary: even 500m can help.

Heat Exhaustion

Heat exhaustion occurs following excessive fluid loss with inadequate replacement of fluids and salt. Symptoms include headache, dizziness and tiredness. Dehydration is already happening by the time you feel thirsty – aim to drink sufficient water to produce pale, diluted urine. To treat heat exhaustion, replace fluids through water and/or fruit juice and cool the body with cold water and fans.

Required Vaccinations

No jabs are required to travel to Spain. The World Health

Organization (WHO), however, recommends that all travellers should be covered for diphtheria, tetanus, measles, mumps, rubella and polio, regardless of their destination. Since most vaccines don't provide immunity until at least two weeks after they're given, visit a physician at least six weeks before departure.

Water

Much of the tap water found throughout the Canary Islands is desalinated sea water. It is safe to drink, though doesn't taste particularly good and most locals buy bottled water, which is cheap and readily available. If you are in any doubt, ask *¿Es potable el agua (de grifo)?* (Is the (tap) water drinkable?). Do not drink from lakes as they may contain bacteria or viruses that can cause diarrhoea or vomiting.

Insurance

A travel-insurance policy to cover theft, loss and medical problems and cancellation or delays to your travel arrangements is a good idea. Paying for your ticket with a credit card can often provide limited travel-accident insurance and you may be able to reclaim the payment if the operator doesn't deliver. Worldwide travel insurance is available at www.lonelyplanet.com/travel-insurance. You can buy, extend and claim online anytime – even if you're already on the road.

Internet Access

Wi-fi Available at most hotels and many cafes, restaurants and airports; generally, but not always, free. Connection speed often varies from room to room in hotels, so always ask when you check in. Hotels offering wi-fi are indicated throughout this guide with an icon 🛜. If they, instead, have a public-access computer terminal, the icon is @.

Internet cafes You will still find the odd *cibercafe* – ask at the local tourist office. Prices per hour cost €2.50 to €4.

Language Courses

Tenerife is particularly noted for its Spanish-language courses. There are also several schools in Las Palmas de Gran Canaria.

Canarias Cultural (www.canarias-cultural.com; Santa Cruz de Tenerife; 1-week intensive course €145) A range of part- and full-time courses.

Don Quijote (www.donquijote.org; Puerto de la Cruz, Tenerife; ☺1-week intensive course €175) Nationwide organisation offering private or group classes, plus a two-week course for the over 50s (€530).

Galfir (www.galfir.com; La Laguna, Tenerife; 1-week intensive course €140) Also offers cultural activities combining Spanish tuition with Canarian cooking (two weeks €360) or salsa dancing (€376).

Gran Canaria School of Languages (Map p48; ☏928 26 79 71; www.grancanaria-school.com; Calle Dr Grau Bassas 27; 1-week intensive course €170) Has been in business for more than 40 years and has an excellent reputation. Lodging can also be arranged.

Study Abroad International (www.studyabroadinternational.com) A variety of study abroad programs in Gran Canaria and Tenerife.

Legal Matters

Should you be arrested, you will be allotted the free services of an *abogado de oficio* (duty solicitor), who may speak only Spanish. You are also entitled to make a phone call. If you use this call to contact your embassy or consulate, it will probably be able to do no more than refer you to a lawyer who speaks your language. If you end up in court, the authorities are

obliged to provide a translator if you have to testify.

In theory, you are supposed to have your national ID card or passport with you at all times. If asked for it by the police, you are supposed to be able to produce it on the spot. In practice it is rarely an issue and many people choose to leave passports in hotel safes.

There are three main types of *policía:* the Policía Local, the Policía Nacional and the Guardia Civil. Should you need to contact the police, don't agonise over which kind to approach: any of them will do, but you may find that the Policía Local is the most helpful. The Canary Islands government provides a toll-free telephone number (☏112), which ensures that any emergency situation can be attended to by the nearest police available.

Money

The most convenient way to bring your money is in the form of a debit or credit card, with some extra cash for use in case of an emergency.

ATMs

The Canary Islands has a surfeit of banks, and pretty much every one has a multilingual *cajeros automáticos* (ATM). Remember that there is usually a charge of between 2% and 3% on ATM cash withdrawals abroad.

Cash

Even if you're using a credit card you'll still need to carry some cash – bus drivers and some smaller restaurants and shops don't accept cards.

Credit Cards

All major *tarjetas de crédito* (credit cards) and debit cards are widely accepted. They can be used for many purchases (including at petrol stations and larger supermarkets, which sometimes ask to see some form of ID) and in hotels and restaurants (although

smaller establishments tend to accept cash only).

Moneychangers

You'll find exchange facilities at most air and sea ports on the islands. In resorts and cities that attract swarms of foreigners, you'll find them easily – they're usually indicated by the word *cambio* (exchange). Most of the time, they offer longer opening hours and quicker service than banks, and in many cases they offer better rates. Shop around and always ask from the outset about commission, the terms of which differ from place to place, and confirm that exchange rates are as posted. A typical commission is 3%. Places that advertise 'no commission' usually make up the difference by offering poorer exchange rates.

Tipping

Not obligatory but most people at least leave some small change if they're satisfied; 5% is normally fine and 10% considered generous. Porters will generally be happy with €1. Taxi drivers don't have to be tipped but a little rounding up won't go amiss.

Opening Hours

The following standard opening hours are for high season only; hours tend to decrease outside that time.

Banks 8.30am to 2pm Monday to Friday

Bars 7pm to midnight

Post offices 8.30am to 8.30pm Monday to Friday, 9.30am to 1pm Saturday (large cities); 8.30am to 2.30pm Monday to Friday, 9.30am to 1pm Saturday (elsewhere)

Restaurants meals served 1pm to 4pm and 7pm until late

Shops 10am to 2pm and 5pm to 9pm Monday to Friday, 10am to 2pm Saturday

Supermarkets 9am to 9pm Monday to Saturday

Public Holidays

There are at least 14 official holidays a year in the Canary Islands. When a holiday falls close to a weekend, locals like to make a *puente* (bridge) – meaning they also take the intervening day off. On occasion, when a couple of holidays fall close to the same weekend, the *puente* becomes an *acueducto* (aqueduct)!

Following are the major national holidays, observed throughout the islands and the rest of Spain:

Año Nuevo (New Year's Day) 1 January

Día de los Reyes Magos (Three Kings Day) 6 January

Viernes Santo (Good Friday) March/April

Fiesta del Trabajo (Labour Day) 1 May

La Asunción de la Virgen (Feast of the Assumption) 15 August

Día de la Hispanidad (National Day) 12 October

Todos los Santos (All Saints' Day) 1 November. Gets particular attention on Tenerife.

La Inmaculada Concepción (Feast of the Immaculate Conception) 8 December

Navidad (Christmas) 25 December

In addition, the regional government sets a further five holidays, while local councils allocate another two. Common holidays include the following:

Martes de Carnival (Carnival Tuesday) February/March

Jueves Santo (Maundy Thursday) March/April

Día de las Islas Canarias (Canary Islands Day) 30 May

Día de San Juan (St John's Day) 24 June

Día de Santiago Apóstol (Feast of St James the Apostle, Spain's patron saint) 25 July. In Santa Cruz de Tenerife the day also marks the commemoration of the defence of the city against Horatio Nelson.

Día del Pino (Pine Tree Day) 8 September. This is particularly important on Gran Canaria.

Día de la Constitución (Constitution Day) 6 December

Telephone

Mobile Phones

If you have a GSM, dual- or tri-band cellular mobile phone you can buy SIM cards and prepaid time.

All the Spanish phone companies (including Orange, Vodafone and Movistar) offer prepaid accounts for mobiles. You can then top up the cards in their shops or outlets, such as supermarkets and tobacconists.

The Canaries uses GSM 900/1800, which is compatible with the rest of Europe and Australia but not with the North American GSM 1900 or the system used in Japan. From those countries, you will need to travel with a tri-band or quadric-band phone.

Phone Codes

Mobile phone numbers Start with ☏6

International access code ☏00

Canary Islands country code ☏34 (same as Spain)

Island area codes Gran Canaria, Lanzarote and Fuerteventura ☏928; Tenerife, La Gomera, La Palma and El Hierro ☏922

National toll-free number ☏900

Phonecards

You can buy phonecards at tobacco stands, newsstands and *locutorios* (private call centres). In any case, there is an endless variety of phonecards, each with its own pricing scheme. The best card for you will depend on where you plan to call.

Time

The Canary Islands are on Greenwich Mean Time (GMT/ UTC), plus an hour in summer for daylight-saving time. The islands keep the same time as the UK, Ireland and Portugal and are always an hour behind mainland Spain and most of Europe. Daylight-saving (summer) time starts on the last Sunday in March, when clocks are put forward one hour. Clocks are put back an hour on the last Sunday in October.

Australia During the Australian winter (Spanish summer), subtract nine hours from Australian Eastern Standard Time to get Canary Islands' time; during the Australian summer, subtract 10 hours.

US Canary Islands' time is US Eastern Time plus five hours and US Pacific Time plus eight hours.

Although the 24-hour clock is used in writing, you'll find people generally use the 12-hour clock in everyday conversations.

Toilets

Public toilets are not common and rarely inviting. The easiest option is to wander into a bar or cafe and use its facilities. The polite thing to do is to have a coffee or the like before or after, but you're unlikely to raise too many eyebrows if you don't. That said, some curmudgeonly places in popular tourist areas post notices saying that their toilets are for customers only.

The cautious carry some toilet paper with them when out and about as many toilets don't have it. If there's a bin beside the toilet, put paper and so on in it – it's probably there because the local sewage system has trouble coping.

Tourist Information

All major towns in the Canary Islands have a tourist office where you will usually get decent maps and information about the area. Though the Canarian government offers both region-wide and island-specific information on its excellent website www. turismodecanarias.com, the tourist offices themselves are run by the *cabildos* (island governments) or *ayuntamientos* (town halls).

Travellers with Disabilities

Sadly, the Canary Islands are not geared towards smooth travel for disabled people. Most restaurants, shops and tourist sights are not equipped to handle wheelchairs, although the more expensive accommodation options will have rooms with appropriate facilities. Transport is tricky, although you should be able to organise a specially modified hire car from one of the international hire companies (with advance warning). In fact, advance warning is always a good idea; start with your travel agent and see what it can offer in terms of information and assistance. In the archipelago's cities, such as Las Palmas and Santa Cruz, some buildings (eg museums or government offices) provide Braille in the lifts, and some specially textured floors before stairs, but not much else. Few concessions are made in the public infrastructure for deaf people.

Mobility Equipment Hire
Mobility Abroad (www.mobilityabroad.com) A long-standing company with outlets in Gran Canaria, Lanzarote and Tenerife.

Orange Badge (922 79 73 55; www.orangebadge.eu) Wheelchair and mobility-scooter hire in Tenerife.

Organisations
Accessible Travel & Leisure (in the UK 01452-729739; www.accessibletravel.co.uk; Newhaven Rd, Quedge-

ley, Gloucester) Claims to be the biggest UK travel agent dealing with travel for the disabled, and encourages the disabled to travel independently.

Society for Accessible Travel & Hospitality (www.sath.org; 347 Fifth Ave, Ste 605, New York, NY) Although largely concentrated on the USA, this organisation can provide general information.

Visas

Spain is one of the 26 member countries of the Schengen Convention, under which 22 EU countries (all but Bulgaria, Croatia, Cyprus, Ireland, Romania and the UK) plus Iceland, Lichtenstein, Norway and Switzerland have abolished checks at common borders.

The visa situation for entering Spain is as follows:

Citizens or residents of EU & Schengen countries No visa required.

Citizens or residents of Australia, Canada, Israel, Japan, NZ and the US No visa required for tourist visits of up to 90 days.

Other countries Check with a Spanish embassy or consulate.

To work or study in Spain A special visa may be required – contact a Spanish embassy or consulate before travel.

Extensions & Residence
Schengen visas are valid for 90 days and cannot be extended. Nationals of EU countries, Iceland, Norway and Switzerland can enter and leave the archipelago at will and don't need to apply for a *tarjeta de residencia* (residence card), although they are supposed to apply for residence papers if they are staying for longer than 90 days.

People of other nationalities who want to stay in Spain longer than 90 days have to get a residence card, and for

them it can be a drawn-out process, starting with an appropriate visa issued by a Spanish consulate in their country of residence. Start the process well in advance.

Women Travellers

Harassment is much less frequent than the stereotypes of Spain would have you believe, and the country has one of the developed world's lowest incidences of reported rape. Any unpleasantness you might encounter is more likely to come from drunken northern European yobs in the big resorts than from the locals.

In towns you may get the occasional unwelcome stare, catcall or unnecessary comment, to which the best (and most galling) response is indifference. Don't get paranoid about what's being called out; the *piropo* – a harmless, mildly flirty compliment – is deeply ingrained in Spanish society and, if well delivered, even considered gallant.

Topless bathing and skimpy clothes are generally OK at coastal resorts, but otherwise a little more modesty is the norm.

Work

EU, Norway and Iceland nationals are allowed to work anywhere in Spain (including the Canary Islands) without a visa, but if they plan to stay more than three months they are supposed to apply within the first month for a residence card. Virtually everyone else is supposed to obtain (from a Spanish consulate in their country of residence) a work permit and, if they plan to stay more than 90 days, a residence visa. While jobs (especially in tourist resorts) aren't that hard to come by, the procedures necessary to get your paperwork in order can be difficult as well as time-consuming.

Transport

GETTING THERE & AWAY

Getting to the Canary Islands is a cinch. Low-cost carriers are plentiful from all over Europe, particularly from Germany, the UK and, of course, mainland Spain. Flights, tours and rail tickets can be booked online at www.lonelyplanet.com/bookings.

Entering the Canary Islands

Citizens of most EU member states, as well as Switzerland, can travel to the Canary Islands with just their national identity card. UK nationals – and all other nationalities – must have a full valid passport.

Check that your passport's expiry date is at least six months away, or you may not be granted a visa, should you need one.

By law you are supposed to have your identity card or passport with you at all times in the Canaries, in case the police ask to see it. In practice, this is unlikely to cause trouble. You might want to carry a photocopy of your documentation instead of the real thing. You will need to flash one of these documents (the original, not the photocopy) for registration when you take a hotel room.

Air

Airports & Airlines

All of Spain's airports share the user-friendly website and flight information telephone number of **Aena** (☑902 404704; www.aena.es), the Spanish national airport authority.

All seven Canary islands have airports. Tenerife, Gran Canaria, Lanzarote, Fuerteventura and, increasingly, La Palma absorb nearly all the direct international flights and those from mainland Spain, while the others are principally for inter-island hops.

The following main airports handle international flights:

Fuerteventura Located 6km south of the capital, Puerto del Rosario.

Gran Canaria Located 16km south of Las Palmas.

Lanzarote Located 6km southwest of the capital, Arrecife.

Tenerife Norte (Los Rodeos) Handles just about all inter-island flights and most of those to the Spanish mainland.

Tenerife Sur (Reina Sofía) Handles the remaining scheduled flights, and virtually all charter flights to the island.

Dozens of airlines, many of which you'll never have heard of, fly into the Canary Islands; however, there are no nonstop flights from North America to the archipelago. There are direct flights to cities in Morocco, Senegal, Mauritania, Gambia and perhaps most interestingly, the Western Sahara, with **Binter Canarias** (☑902 391392; www.bintercanarias.com).

Sea

Just about everyone flies to the Canaries. The only other alternative (apart from a very long swim) is to take a ferry from mainland Spain.

Trasmediterránea (☑902 454645; www.trasmediterranea.com) Runs a weekly ferry service between Cádiz on the Spanish mainland and Santa Cruz de Tenerife (48 hours), with stops at Lanzarote (31 hours) and Las Palmas de Gran Canaria (39 hours).

Naviera Armas (☑902 456500; www.navieraarmas.com) Runs a weekly service from Huelva on the Spanish mainland stopping at Lanzarote (27 hours), Las Palmas de Gran Canaria (32 hours) and Santa Cruz de Tenerife (36 hours).

GETTING AROUND

Air

All seven islands have airports, making flying the most comprehensive (and quickest) option if you intend to do some island hopping. Binter Canarias is the long-standing airline, with a comprehensive network of flights and on certain routes (particularly in the western islands) some seriously tiny planes! Canary Fly is the newbie on the scene.

Boat travel from mainland Spain isn't cheap and if you opt for a simple seat on the ship, you'll spend a similar amount reaching the Canaries as you would if you flew. If you want a cabin, boat travel will be three to four times the price of a flight – and takes almost 10 times longer!

Binter Canarias (☑902 391392; www.bintercanarias. com) Flights to all islands.

Canary Fly (☑902 808065; www.canaryfly.es) Covers Tenerife, La Palma, Gran Canaria and Lanzarote.

Bicycle

Biking around the islands is an extremely pleasant way to see the sights, but don't necessarily expect drivers to accommodate you (or have much grasp of what it's like to be a cyclist tackling a hairpin bend uphill). Sadly, bicycle lanes in the urban environment are minimal, although Las Palmas now has cycle lanes and beachside boulevards are increasingly incorporating space for bike riding.

If you plan to bring your own bike on a flight, check whether there are any extra costs and whether you'll need to disassemble and pack your bike for the journey.

Taking your bike on ferries is pretty straightforward, and the good news is it's either free or very cheap.

Bicycle Hire

You can rent mountain bikes and city bikes at various resorts and in the more tourist-orientated areas of the islands. Expect to pay a minimum of €12 per day, with a standard deposit of around €50. Rental rates will include a helmet and some basic equipment.

Las Palmas de Gran Canaria offers free bicycle hire with several pick-up and drop-off locations throughout the city. See **By Bike LPA** (www.bybikelpa.com) for more information.

Boat

The islands are connected by ferries, 'fast ferries' and jetfoils.

Do bear in mind that times and prices – and even routes – can and do change. This isn't so important on major routes, where there's plenty of choice, but it can mean a

big delay if you're planning to travel a route that has only a couple of boats per day, or even per week.

Following are the three main companies:

Fred Olsen (☑902 100107; www.fredolsen.es)

Naviera Armas (☑902 456500; www.navieraarmas. com)

Trasmediterránea (☑902 454645; www.trasmediterranea.com)

Bus

A bus in the Canary Islands is called a *guagua*, pronounced 'wa-wa'. If you've bounced around Latin America, you'll be familiar with the term. Still, if you ask about *autobuses*, you'll be understood.

Every island has its own inter-urban service. One way or another, they can get you to most of the main locations but, in many cases, there are few runs each day.

The larger islands of Tenerife and Gran Canaria have an impressive public-transport system covering the whole island. Frequency, however, varies enormously, from a regular service between major towns to a couple of runs per day for transporting workers and school children to/from the capital.

Check the timetable carefully before you travel on weekends. Even on the larger islands' major runs, a frequent weekday service can trickle off to just a few departures on Saturday and one, or none, on Sunday.

In the larger towns and cities, buses leave from an *estación de guaguas* (bus station). In villages and small towns, they usually terminate on a particular street or plaza. You buy your ticket on the bus.

Global (☑928 25 26 30; www.globalsu.net) Provides Gran Canaria with a comprehensive network of routes, although services between rural areas are infrequent.

APPROXIMATE DURATIONS FOR MAIN FERRY ROUTES

From	To	Duration
Agaete (Gran Canaria)	Santa Cruz de Tenerife	1½hr
Arrecife (Lanzarote)	Las Palmas de Gran Canaria	8hr
Las Palmas (Gran Canaria)	Morro Jable (Fuerteventura)	2-3hr
Playa Blanca (Lanzarote)	Corralejo (Fuerteventura)	30min
Las Palmas (Gran Canaria)	Santa Cruz de Tenerife	2½hr
Los Cristianos (Tenerife)	San Sebastián de la Gomera	45min
Los Cristianos (Tenerife)	Valverde (El Hierro)	3hr
Playa Blanca (Lanzarote)	Corralejo (Fuerteventura)	30min
Santa Cruz de la Palma	Los Cristianos (Tenerife)	3½hr

GuaguaGomera (☏922 14 11 01; www.guaguagomera.com) La Gomera's limited service operates seven lines across the island.

Intercity Bus Lanzarote (☏928 81 15 22; www.intercitybuslanzarote.es) A decent network covering Lanzarote's main points of interest.

Tiadhe (☏928 85 57 26; www.tiadhe.com) Provides a reasonable service, with 17 lines operating around Fuerteventura.

TITSA (Transportes Interurbanos de Tenerife SA; ☏922 53 13 00; www.titsa.com) Runs a spider's web of services all over Tenerife.

TransHierro (☏922 55 11 75; www.transhierro.es) El Hierro's bus service has reasonable coverage throughout the island.

Transportes Insular La Palma (☏922 41 19 24; www.transporteslapalma.com) Services La Palma with good overall coverage.

Bus Passes

On some of the islands you can buy a Bono Bus card, which usually comes in denominations of €12, €15 or €30. It's sold at bus stations and shops such as newsagents. Insert the card into the machine on the bus, tell the driver where you are going, and the fare will be deducted from the card. You get about 30% off standard fares with the cards, so they are a good investment if you intend to use the buses a lot. You can share a card with a fellow traveller.

Costs

Fares, especially if you invest in a Bono Bus card, are reasonable. Destinations within each island are calculated pro rata according to distance, so ticket fares vary from €1 for a short city hop to €10 or so for journeys of well over an hour.

Car & Motorcycle

Renting a car in the Canaries is highly recommended. Bus services are great for journeys between major centres, but if you want to hop between smaller towns you might wait all day for the next bus. Exploring in depth is only really possible with your own wheels – unless you can afford to spend a full day and night in every *pueblo* (village) you happen across.

Bringing Your Own Car

Unless you're intending to settle on the islands, there's no advantage whatsoever in bringing your own vehicle. Transport costs on the ferry from Cádiz in mainland Spain are high and car-hire rates on the islands are significantly cheaper than in most EU countries. If you're one of the very rare visitors to bring your own vehicle, you will need registration papers and an International Insurance Certificate (or a Green Card). Your insurance company will issue this.

Driving Licences

Although those with a non-EU licence should also have an International Driving Permit, you will find that national licences from countries like Australia, Canada, New Zealand and the USA are usually accepted.

A driving licence is required for any vehicle over 50cc.

Fuel

Gasolina (petrol) is much cheaper in the Canary Islands than elsewhere in Spain because it's not taxed as heavily. *Sin plomo* (unleaded) and *diesel* petrol are available everywhere with generally two grades on offer for each.

Prices vary slightly between petrol stations and fluctuate according to oil tariffs, Organisation of the Petroleum Exporting Countries (OPEC) arm twisting and tax policy. You can pay with major credit cards at most petrol stations.

Note that some petrol stations have attendants who will pump the gas for you while at others you'll have to get out and do it yourself.

Car Hire

All the big international car-rental companies are represented in the Canary Islands and there are also plenty of local operators. To rent a car you need to have a driving licence, be aged 21 or over, and, for the major companies at least, have a credit card. Smaller firms can sometimes live without this last requirement.

The car-rental companies in the Canaries have an odd system when it comes to refuelling – you're given a car with a full tank of gas and charged for it (plus an administration fee). You're asked to return the car empty and the rental company then returns the money – less anything you've left in the tank and plus another admin fee. It's an infuriating procedure but one that many companies use and not one you can dispute.

If you intend to stay on one island for any length of time, it might be worth booking a car in advance, for example in a fly/drive deal. It's also a good idea to reserve in advance during high season or on the smaller islands where hire cars aren't as abundant.

Generally, you're not supposed to take a hire car from one island to another without the company's explicit permission. An exception for most companies is the Fuerteventura–Lanzarote sea crossing – most have no problem with you taking your car from one to the other and, in some cases, you can hire on one island and drop the car off on the other.

Avis (📞902 180854; www.
avis.es)

Cicar (📞928 82 29 00; www.
cicar.com) Well-regarded local
company that covers all the
islands. Cicar is part of the
Cabrera Medina group and offers
the same conditions and rates.

Europcar (📞902 503010;
www.europcar.es)

Goldcar (📞902 119726; www.
goldcar.es) Spanish company
with competitive prices – just
check the small print for hidden
extras.

Insurance

Third-party motor insurance
is a minimum requirement
in the Canary Islands (and
throughout Europe). Be
careful you understand what
your liabilities and excess
are, and what waivers you are
entitled to in case of accident
or damage to the hired vehicle. Other incidentals (some
optional) include collision
damage waiver, extra pas-
senger cover and 5% General
Indirect Tax to the Canary
Islands (IGIC). A European
breakdown-assistance policy
such as the AA Five Star
Service or RAC Eurocover
Motoring Assistance can be a
good investment. You can ask
your insurer for a European
Accident Statement form,
which can simplify matters
in the event of an accident.
Note that driving on a dirt
road will generally render
your policy null and void.

Road Rules

The blood-alcohol limit
is 0.05% and random
breath-testing is carried out.
If you are found to be over
the limit, you can be fined
and deprived of your licence
within 24 hours. Nonresident
foreigners will be required
to pay up on the spot (with a
30% to 50% discount on the
full fine). Pleading linguistic
ignorance will not help – your
traffic cop will produce a list
of infringements and fines in
as many languages as you
like. If you don't pay, or don't
have a local resident to act as
guarantor for you, your vehicle could be impounded.

Legal driving age for cars
18 years

**Legal driving age for motorcy-
cles & scooters** 16 (80cc and
over) or 15 (50cc and under)
years; a licence is required.

Motorcyclists Must use head-
lights at all times and wear a
helmet if riding a bike of 125cc
or more.

Roundabouts (traffic circles)
Vehicles already in the circle
have the right of way.

Side of the road Drive on the
right.

Speed limits In built-up areas:
50km/h which increases to
100km/h on major roads and
up to 120km/h on *autovias*
(highways).

Hitching

Hitching is never entirely safe
in any country in the world,
and we don't recommend
it. Travellers who decide to
hitch should understand
that they are taking a small,
but potentially dangerous,
risk. People who do choose
to hitch will be safer if they
travel in pairs and let someone know where they are
planning to go.

Hitching is illegal on *autovias*. Choose a spot where
cars can safely stop before
slipways or use minor roads.
The going can be slow on
the latter and traffic is often
light.

Language

The language of the Canary Islands is Spanish (*español*), which many Spanish people refer to as Castilian (*castellano*) to distinguish it from the other tongues spoken in Spain – Catalan (*català*), Galician (*galego*), and Basque (*euskara*).

Spanish pronunciation is straightforward as there's a clear and consistent relationship between what's written and how it's pronounced. In addition, most Spanish sounds are pronounced the same as their English counterparts. The kh in our pronunciation guides is a guttural sound (like the 'ch' in the Scottish *loch*), ny is pronounced as the 'ni' in 'onion', and r is strongly rolled. Those familiar with Spanish might notice the Andalusian or even Latin American lilt of the Canarian accent – 'lli' is pronounced as y and the 'lisp' you might expect with 'z' and 'c' before vowels sounds more like s while the letter 's' itself is hardly pronounced at all – it sounds more like an 'h' – for example, Las Palmas sounds more like Lah Palmah. If you follow our coloured pronunciation guides (with the stressed syllables in italics) you'll be understood just fine.

Spanish nouns and the adjectives that go with them are marked for gender – feminine nouns generally end with -a and masculine ones with -o. Where necessary, both forms are given for the words and phrases in this chapter, separated by a slash and with the masculine form first, eg *perdido/a* (m/f).

When talking to people familiar to you or younger than you, use the informal form of 'you', *tú*, rather than the polite form *Usted*. The polite form is used in the phrases provided in this chapter; where both options are given, they are indicated by the abbreviations 'pol' and 'inf'.

BASICS

Hello.	*Hola.*	o·la
Goodbye.	*Adiós.*	a·dyos
How are you?	*¿Qué tal?*	ke tal
Fine, thanks.	*Bien, gracias.*	byen gra·syas
Excuse me.	*Perdón.*	per·don
Sorry.	*Lo siento.*	lo syen·to
Yes./No.	*Sí./No.*	see/no
Please.	*Por favor.*	por fa·vor
Thank you.	*Gracias.*	gra·syas
You're welcome.	*De nada.*	de na·da

My name is ...
Me llamo ...   me ya·mo ...

What's your name?
¿Cómo se llama Usted? ko·mo se ya·ma oo·ste (pol)
¿Cómo te llamas?   ko·mo te ya·mas (inf)

Do you speak (English)?
¿Habla (inglés)?   a·bla (een·gles) (pol)
¿Hablas (inglés)?   a·blas (een·gles) (inf)

I (don't) understand.
Yo (no) entiendo.   yo (no) en·tyen·do

ACCOMMODATION

I'd like to book a room.
Quisiera reservar una kee·sye·ra re·ser·var oo·na
habitación.   a·bee·ta·syon

How much is it per night/person?
¿Cuánto cuesta por   kwan·to kwes·ta por
noche/persona?   no·che/per·so·na

Does it include breakfast?
¿Incluye el desayuno? een·kloo·ye el de·sa·yoo·no

I'd like a ...	*Quisiera una*	kee·sye·ra oo·na
room.	*habitación ...*	a·bee·ta·syon ...

WANT MORE?

For in-depth language information and handy phrases, check out Lonely Planet's *Spanish Phrasebook*. You'll find it at **shop. lonelyplanet.com**, or you can buy Lonely Planet's iPhone phrasebooks at the Apple App Store.

single	*individual*	een·dee·vee·*dwal*
double	*doble*	*do*·ble
campsite	*terreno de cámping*	te·*re*·no de *kam*·peeng
hotel	*hotel*	o·*tel*
guesthouse	*pensión*	pen·*syon*
youth hostel	*albergue juvenil*	al·*ber*·ge khoo·ve·*neel*
air-con	*aire acondicionado*	*ai*·re a·kon·dee·syo·*na*·do
bathroom	*baño*	*ba*·nyo
bed	*cama*	*ka*·ma
window	*ventana*	ven·*ta*·na

DIRECTIONS

Where's ...?
¿Dónde está ...? — don·de es·*ta* ...

What's the address?
¿Cuál es la dirección? — kwal es la dee·rek·*syon*

Could you please write it down?
¿Puede escribirlo, por favor? — pwe·de es·kree·*beer*·lo por fa·vor

Can you show me (on the map)?
¿Me lo puede indicar (en el mapa)? — me lo pwe·de een·dee·*kar* (en el *ma*·pa)

at the corner	*en la esquina*	en la es·*kee*·na
at the traffic lights	*en el semáforo*	en el se·*ma*·fo·ro
behind ...	*detrás de ...*	de·*tras* de ...
far away	*lejos*	*le*·khos
in front of ...	*enfrente de ...*	en·*fren*·te de ...
left	*izquierda*	ees·*kyer*·da
near	*cerca*	*ser*·ka
next to ...	*al lado de ...*	al *la*·do de ...
opposite ...	*frente a ...*	*fren*·te a ...
right	*derecha*	de·*re*·cha
straight ahead	*todo recto*	*to*·do *rek*·to

EATING & DRINKING

What would you recommend?
¿Qué recomienda? — ke re·ko·*myen*·da

What's in that dish?
¿Que lleva ese plato? — ke *ye*·va e·se *pla*·to

I don't eat ...
No como ... — no *ko*·mo ...

That was delicious!
¡Estaba buenísimo! — es·*ta*·ba bwe·*nee*·see·mo

KEY PATTERNS

To get by in Spanish, mix and match these simple patterns with words of your choice:

When's (the next flight)?
¿Cuándo sale (el próximo vuelo)? — kwan·do sa·le (el prok·see·mo vwe·lo)

Where's (the station)?
¿Dónde está (la estación)? — don·de es·ta (la es·ta·syon)

Where can I (buy a ticket)?
¿Dónde puedo (comprar un billete)? — don·de pwe·do (kom·prar oon bee·ye·te)

Do you have (a map)?
¿Tiene (un mapa)? — tye·ne (oon ma·pa)

Is there (a toilet)?
¿Hay (servicios)? — ai (ser·vee·syos)

I'd like (a coffee).
Quisiera (un café). — kee·sye·ra (oon ka·fe)

I'd like (to hire a car).
Quisiera (alquilar un coche). — kee·sye·ra (al·kee·lar oon ko·che)

Can I (enter)?
¿Se puede (entrar)? — se pwe·de (en·trar)

Could you please (help me)?
¿Puede (ayudarme), por favor? — pwe·de (a·yoo·dar·me) por fa·vor

Do I have to (get a visa)?
¿Necesito (obtener un visado)? — ne·se·see·to (ob·te·ner oon vee·sa·do)

Please bring the bill.
Por favor nos trae la cuenta. — por fa·vor nos tra·e la kwen·ta

Cheers!
¡Salud! — sa·loo

I'd like to book a table for ...	*Quisiera reservar una mesa para ...*	kee·sye·ra re·ser·var oo·na me·sa pa·ra ...
(eight) o'clock	*las (ocho)*	las (o·cho)
(two) people	*(dos) personas*	(dos) per·so·nas

Key Words

appetisers	*aperitivos*	a·pe·ree·tee·vos
bar	*bar*	bar
bottle	*botella*	bo·te·ya
bowl	*bol*	bol
breakfast	*desayuno*	de·sa·yoo·no

cafe	café	ka·fe
children's menu	menú infantil	me·noo een·fan·teel
(too) cold	(muy) frío	(mooy) free·o
dinner	cena	se·na
food	comida	ko·mee·da
fork	tenedor	te·ne·dor
glass	vaso	va·so
highchair	trona	tro·na
hot (warm)	caliente	ka·lyen·te
knife	cuchillo	koo·chee·yo
lunch	comida	ko·mee·da
main course	segundo plato	se·goon·do pla·to
market	mercado	mer·ka·do
menu (in English)	menú (en inglés)	oon me·noo (en een·gles)
plate	plato	pla·to
restaurant	restaurante	res·tow·ran·te
spoon	cuchara	koo·cha·ra
supermarket	supermercado	soo·per·mer·ka·do
with/without	con/sin	kon/seen
vegetarian food	comida vegetariana	ko·mee·da ve·khe·ta·rya·na

Meat & Fish

beef	carne de vaca	kar·ne de va·ka
chicken	pollo	po·yo
duck	pato	pa·to
fish	pescado	pes·ka·do
lamb	cordero	kor·de·ro
pork	cerdo	ser·do
turkey	pavo	pa·vo
veal	ternera	ter·ne·ra

Fruit & Vegetables

apple	manzana	man·sa·na
apricot	albaricoque	al·ba·ree·ko·ke
artichoke	alcachofa	al·ka·cho·fa
asparagus	espárragos	es·pa·ra·gos
banana	plátano	pla·ta·no
beans	judías	khoo·dee·as
beetroot	remolacha	re·mo·la·cha
cabbage	col	kol
carrot	zanahoria	sa·na·o·rya
celery	apio	a·pyo
cherry	cereza	se·re·sa

corn	maíz	ma·ees
cucumber	pepino	pe·pee·no
fruit	fruta	froo·ta
grape	uvas	oo·vas
lemon	limón	lee·mon
lentils	lentejas	len·te·khas
lettuce	lechuga	le·choo·ga
mushroom	champiñón	cham·pee·nyon
nuts	nueces	nwe·ses
onion	cebolla	se·bo·ya
orange	naranja	na·ran·kha
peach	melocotón	me·lo·ko·ton
peas	guisantes	gee·san·tes
(red/green) pepper	pimiento (rojo/verde)	pee·myen·to (ro·kho/ver·de)
pineapple	piña	pee·nya
plum	ciruela	seer·we·la
potato	patata	pa·ta·ta
pumpkin	calabaza	ka·la·ba·sa
spinach	espinacas	es·pee·na·kas
strawberry	fresa	fre·sa
tomato	tomate	to·ma·te
vegetable	verdura	ver·doo·ra
watermelon	sandía	san·dee·a

Other

bread	pan	pan
butter	mantequilla	man·te·kee·ya
cheese	queso	ke·so
egg	huevo	we·vo
honey	miel	myel
jam	mermelada	mer·me·la·da
oil	aceite	a·sey·te
pasta	pasta	pas·ta
pepper	pimienta	pee·myen·ta
rice	arroz	a·ros
salt	sal	sal
sugar	azúcar	a·soo·kar
vinegar	vinagre	vee·na·gre

QUESTION WORDS

How?	¿Cómo?	ko·mo
What?	¿Qué?	ke
When?	¿Cuándo?	kwan·do
Where?	¿Dónde?	don·de
Who?	¿Quién?	kyen
Why?	¿Por qué?	por ke

Drinks

beer	cerveza	ser·ve·sa
coffee	café	ka·fe
(orange) juice	zumo (de naranja)	soo·mo (de na·ran·kha)
milk	leche	le·che
tea	té	te
(mineral) water	agua (mineral)	a·gwa (mee·ne·ral)
(red) wine	vino (tinto)	vee·no (teen·to)
(white) wine	vino (blanco)	vee·no (blan·ko)

EMERGENCIES

Help!	¡Socorro!	so·ko·ro
Go away!	¡Vete!	ve·te
Call ...!	¡Llame a ...!	ya·me a ...
a doctor	un médico	oon me·dee·ko
the police	la policía	la po·lee·see·a

I'm lost.
Estoy perdido/a.   es·toy per·dee·do/a (m/f)

I had an accident.
He tenido un accidente.   e te·nee·do oon ak·see·den·te

I'm ill.
Estoy enfermo/a.   es·toy en·fer·mo/a (m/f)

It hurts here.
Me duele aquí.   me dwe·le a·kee

I'm allergic to (antibiotics).
Soy alérgico/a a (los antibióticos).   soy a·ler·khee·ko/a a (los an·tee·byo·tee·kos) (m/f)

SHOPPING & SERVICES

I'd like to buy ...
Quisiera comprar ...   kee·sye·ra kom·prar ...

I'm just looking.
Sólo estoy mirando.   so·lo es·toy mee·ran·do

May I look at it?
¿Puedo verlo?   pwe·do ver·lo

I don't like it.
No me gusta.   no me goos·ta

How much is it?
¿Cuánto cuesta?   kwan·to kwes·ta

That's too expensive.
Es muy caro.   es mooy ka·ro

Can you lower the price?
¿Podría bajar un poco el precio?   po·dree·a ba·khar oon po·ko el pre·syo

There's a mistake in the bill.
Hay un error en la cuenta.   ai oon e·ror en la kwen·ta

ATM	cajero automático	ka·khe·ro ow·to·ma·tee·ko

NUMBERS

1	uno	oo·no
2	dos	dos
3	tres	tres
4	cuatro	kwa·tro
5	cinco	seen·ko
6	seis	seys
7	siete	sye·te
8	ocho	o·cho
9	nueve	nwe·ve
10	diez	dyes
20	veinte	veyn·te
30	treinta	treyn·ta
40	cuarenta	kwa·ren·ta
50	cincuenta	seen·kwen·ta
60	sesenta	se·sen·ta
70	setenta	se·ten·ta
80	ochenta	o·chen·ta
90	noventa	no·ven·ta
100	cien	syen
1000	mil	meel

credit card	tarjeta de crédito	tar·khe·ta de kre·dee·to
internet cafe	cibercafé	see·ber·ka·fe
post office	correos	ko·re·os
tourist office	oficina de turismo	o·fee·see·na de too·rees·mo

TIME & DATES

What time is it?	¿Qué hora es?	ke o·ra es
It's (10) o'clock.	Son (las diez).	son (las dyes)
Half past (one).	Es (la una) y media.	es (la oo·na) ee me·dya

morning	mañana	ma·nya·na
afternoon	tarde	tar·de
evening	noche	no·che
yesterday	ayer	a·yer
today	hoy	oy
tomorrow	mañana	ma·nya·na

Monday	lunes	loo·nes
Tuesday	martes	mar·tes
Wednesday	miércoles	myer·ko·les
Thursday	jueves	khwe·bes
Friday	viernes	vyer·nes
Saturday	sábado	sa·ba·do
Sunday	domingo	do·meen·go

January	enero	e·ne·ro
February	febrero	fe·bre·ro
March	marzo	mar·so
April	abril	a·breel
May	mayo	ma·yo
June	junio	khoo·nyo
July	julio	khoo·lyo
August	agosto	a·gos·to
September	septiembre	sep·tyem·bre
October	octubre	ok·too·bre
November	noviembre	no·vyem·bre
December	diciembre	dee·syem·bre

TRANSPORT

Public Transport

boat	barco	bar·ko
bus	autobús	ow·to·boos
plane	avión	a·vyon
train	tren	tren
tram	tranvía	tran·vee·a
first	primer	pree·mer
last	último	ool·tee·mo
next	próximo	prok·see·mo

I want to go to ...
Quisiera ir a ... kee·sye·ra eer a ...

Does it stop at (Vilaflor)?
¿Para en (Vilaflor)? pa·ra en (vee·la·flor)

What stop is this?
¿Cuál es esta parada? kwal es es·ta pa·ra·da

What time does it arrive/leave?
¿A qué hora llega/sale? a ke o·ra ye·ga/sa·le

Please tell me when we get to (Arico Nuevo).
¿Puede avisarme pwe·de a·vee·sar·me
cuando lleguemos kwan·do ye·ge·mos
a (Arico Nuevo)? a (a·ree·ko nwe·vo)

I want to get off here.
Quiero bajarme aquí. kye·ro ba·khar·me a·kee

a ... ticket	un billete de ...	oon bee·ye·te de ...
1st-class	primera clase	pree·me·ra kla·se
2nd-class	segunda clase	se·goon·da kla·se
one-way	ida	ee·da
return	ida y vuelta	ee·da ee vwel·ta
aisle seat	asiento de pasillo	a·syen·to de pa·see·yo

cancelled	cancelado	kan·se·la·do
delayed	retrasado	re·tra·sa·do
platform	plataforma	pla·ta·for·ma
ticket office	taquilla	ta·kee·ya
timetable	horario	o·ra·ryo
train station	estación de trenes	es·ta·syon de tre·nes
window seat	asiento junto a la ventana	a·syen·to khoon·to a la ven·ta·na

Driving & Cycling

I'd like to hire a ...	Quisiera alquilar ...	kee·sye·ra al·kee·lar ...
4WD	un todo-terreno	oon to·do·te·re·no
bicycle	una bicicleta	oo·na bee·see·kle·ta
car	un coche	oon ko·che
motorcycle	una moto	oo·na mo·to
child seat	asiento de seguridad para niños	a·syen·to de se·goo·ree·da pa·ra nee·nyos
diesel	gasóleo	ga·so·lyo
helmet	casco	kas·ko
mechanic	mecánico	me·ka·nee·ko
petrol/gas	gasolina	ga·so·lee·na
service station	gasolinera	ga·so·lee·ne·ra

Is this the road to ...?
¿Se va a (La Laguna) se va a (la la·goo·na)
por esta carretera? por es·ta ka·re·te·ra

(How long) Can I park here?
¿(Por cuánto tiempo) (por kwan·to tyem·po)
Puedo aparcar aquí? pwe·do a·par·kar a·kee

The car has broken down (at Masca).
El coche se ha averiado el ko·che se a a·ve·rya·do
(en Masca). (en mas·ka)

I have a flat tyre.
Tengo un pinchazo. ten·go oon peen·cha·so

I've run out of petrol.
Me he quedado sin me e ke·da·do seen
gasolina. ga·so·lee·na

<table>
<tr><td colspan="2">SIGNS</td></tr>
<tr><td>Abierto</td><td>Open</td></tr>
<tr><td>Cerrado</td><td>Closed</td></tr>
<tr><td>Entrada</td><td>Entrance</td></tr>
<tr><td>Hombres</td><td>Men</td></tr>
<tr><td>Mujeres</td><td>Women</td></tr>
<tr><td>Prohibido</td><td>Prohibited</td></tr>
<tr><td>Salida</td><td>Exit</td></tr>
<tr><td>Servicios/Aseos</td><td>Toilets</td></tr>
</table>

GLOSSARY

aljibe – water system
artesonado – coffered ceiling
autovía – motorway
ayuntamiento – town hall

barranco – ravine or gorge
barrio – district, quarter (of a town or city)
Bimbaches – indigenous Herreños
bocadillo – sandwich made with baguette bread
bodega – traditional wine bar, or a wine cellar
bote – local variety of shuttle boat developed to service offshore vessels
buceo – scuba diving

cabildo insular – island government
cabra – goat
cabrito – kid (goat)
caldera – cauldron
calle – street
cambio – exchange
cañadas – flatlands
Carnaval – festival celebrating the beginning of Lent, 40 days before Easter
casa rural – a village or country house or farmstead with rooms to let
caserío – traditional farmhouse or hamlet
catedral – cathedral
centro comercial – shopping centre, usually with restaurants, bars and other facilities for tourists
chiringuito – kiosk
churros – fried dough
comida – lunch
Corpus Christi – festival in honour of the Eucharist, held eight weeks after Easter
cruz – cross
cueva – cave

denominación de origen – appellation certifying a high standard and regional origin of wines and certain foods
desayuno – breakfast
drago – dragon tree

ermita – chapel
estación – terminal, station
estación de guaguas – bus terminal/station
estación marítima – ferry terminal

faro – lighthouse
feria – fair
fiesta – festival, public holiday or party
finca – farm

gofio – ground, roasted grain used in place of bread in Canarian cuisine
Gomeros – people from La Gomera
gran – great
guagua – bus
guanarteme – island chief
Guanches – the original inhabitants of the Canaries

Herreños – people from El Hierro
horario – timetable
hostal – commercial establishment providing accommodation in the one- to three-star range; not to be confused with youth hostels (of which there is only one throughout the islands)
hoteles – one- to five-star hotel

IGIC – Impuesto General Indirecto Canario (local version of value-added tax)
iglesia – church

jamón – cured ham

lagarto – lizard
laurisilva – laurel
librería – bookshop
lucha canaria – Canarian wrestling

malpaís – volcanic badlands
malvasía – Malmsey wine
marcha – action, nightlife, 'the scene'
mencey – Guanche king
menú del día – set menu
mercado – market
mesón – old-fashioned restaurant or tavern
mirador – lookout point
mojo – Canarian sauce made with either red chilli peppers, coriander or basil
montaña – mountain
Mudéjar – Islamic-style architecture
muelle – wharf or pier
municipio – town council
museo – museum, gallery

norte – north

Palmeros – people from La Palma
papas arrugadas – wrinkly potatoes
parador – chain of state-owned upmarket hotels
parque nacional – national park
paseo marítimo – seaside promenade
pensión – guesthouse (one-or two-star)
piscina – swimming pool
plateresque – silversmith-like
playa – beach
pozo – well
pueblo – village
puerto – port

GLOSSARY

ración – large tapas

romería – festive pilgrimage or procession

sabina – juniper

Semana Santa – Holy Week, the week leading up to Easter

señorío – island government deputising for the Spanish crown

s/n – *sin numero* (without number); sometimes seen in street addresses

sur – south

taberna – tavern

tapas – bar snacks originally served on a saucer or lid (*tapa*)

taquilla – box office

tasca – pub, bar

terraza – terrace; outdoor cafe tables

thalassotherapy – warm sea-water treatment designed to remove stress and physical aches

timple – type of ukulele and the musical symbol of the Canary Islands

Tinerfeños – people from Tenerife

valle – valley

vega – plain, flatlands

volcán – volcano

zumería – juice bar

Behind the Scenes

SEND US YOUR FEEDBACK

We love to hear from travellers – your comments keep us on our toes and help make our books better. Our well-travelled team reads every word on what you loved or loathed about this book. Although we cannot reply individually to your submissions, we always guarantee that your feedback goes straight to the appropriate authors, in time for the next edition. Each person who sends us information is thanked in the next edition – the most useful submissions are rewarded with a selection of digital PDF chapters.

Visit **lonelyplanet.com/contact** to submit your updates and suggestions or to ask for help. Our award-winning website also features inspirational travel stories, news and discussions.

Note: We may edit, reproduce and incorporate your comments in Lonely Planet products such as guidebooks, websites and digital products, so let us know if you don't want your comments reproduced or your name acknowledged. For a copy of our privacy policy visit lonelyplanet.com/privacy.

OUR READERS

Many thanks to the travellers who used the last edition and wrote to us with helpful hints, useful advice and interesting anecdotes:

A Andrea Cross, Anton Krivtsun, Armand Labat **B** Brad Kallenberger **C** Chantal Reijers, Christian Merz, Colin Molloy **D** David Lapointe **E** Elizabeth Crutchley, Elizabeth Reyes, Elke Belde **F** Florian Kruse **G** Graham Clement, Guntram Schroebler **H** Harry White **I** Irene Montaner **J** Jan Gray, Jo Beggs, John Read, Jonathan Wood, Juliet Challis, Jurgis Karpus **K** Karl Lamens, Kevin Nead, Kim Dorin **L** Laura Alcaraz, Leona Tuck **M** María Merino, Marie Boutin, Michael de Graaf **P** Patricia Hyder, Paul Clark, Paun Koutroumbas **R** Raquel Gómez

AUTHOR THANKS

Lucy Corne

Huge thanks to my mum, Joy, and dad, Dave, for acting as overseas au pairs. I had a lot of help from old friends – *muchísimas gracias* to Alejandro, Virginia, Iván, Héctor and especially Pepe Julio for all the suggestions. Thanks also to Thomas at Ventana Azul, my Las Palmas host Alberto for the insider tips, the lovely ladies at Arrecife tourism, my co-author Josephine for all her speedy responses, and above all my boys, Shawn and Kai – the best travel companions

you could ever ask for. Travelling with a toddler was tough, but what a blast!

Josephine Quintero

Josephine would like to thank all the helpful folk at the various tourist information offices, as well as Jorge Gonzalez, a valuable contact in Tenerife. Thanks too to Destination Editor Lorna Parkes, my charming co-author Lucy Corne and to all those involved in the title from the Lonely Planet offices, as well as to all my Spanish *malagueño* friends who provided endless advice, contacts and tips, and to Robin Chapman for looking after Marilyn (the cat).

ACKNOWLEDGMENTS

Climate map data adapted from Peel MC, Finlayson BL & McMahon TA (2007) 'Updated World Map of the Köppen-Geiger Climate Classification', *Hydrology and Earth System Sciences*, 11, 1633–44.

Cover photograph: Windmill near the village of Tefia, Fuerteventura; Marco Simoni/Alamy

THIS BOOK

This 6th edition of Lonely Planet's *Canary Islands* guidebook was researched and written by Lucy Corne and Josephine Quintero. The previous edition was also researched and written by Josephine, with Stuart Butler. This guidebook was produced by the following:

Destination Editors
Jo Cooke, Lorna Parkes
Product Editors
Anne Mason, Tracy Whitmey
Regional Senior Cartographer Anthony Phelan
Senior Cartographer
Diana Von Holdt
Book Designer
Wibowo Rusli

Assisting Editors Imogen Bannister, Melanie Dankel, Anne Mulvaney, Rosie Nicholson, Kristin Odijk, Chris Pitts, Vicky Smith, Ross Taylor
Cover Researcher
Naomi Parker
Thanks to Sasha Baskett, Andi Jones, Karyn Noble, Angela Tinson, Tony Wheeler

Index

NOTES

285

NOTES

NOTES

Map Legend

Sights
- Beach
- Bird Sanctuary
- Buddhist
- Castle/Palace
- Christian
- Confucian
- Hindu
- Islamic
- Jain
- Jewish
- Monument
- Museum/Gallery/Historic Building
- Ruin
- Shinto
- Sikh
- Taoist
- Winery/Vineyard
- Zoo/Wildlife Sanctuary
- Other Sight

Activities, Courses & Tours
- Bodysurfing
- Diving
- Canoeing/Kayaking
- Course/Tour
- Sento Hot Baths/Onsen
- Skiing
- Snorkelling
- Surfing
- Swimming/Pool
- Walking
- Windsurfing
- Other Activity

Sleeping
- Sleeping
- Camping

Eating
- Eating

Drinking & Nightlife
- Drinking & Nightlife
- Cafe

Entertainment
- Entertainment

Shopping
- Shopping

Information
- Bank
- Embassy/Consulate
- Hospital/Medical
- Internet
- Police
- Post Office
- Telephone
- Toilet
- Tourist Information
- Other Information

Geographic
- Beach
- Gate
- Hut/Shelter
- Lighthouse
- Lookout
- Mountain/Volcano
- Oasis
- Park
- Pass
- Picnic Area
- Waterfall

Population
- Capital (National)
- Capital (State/Province)
- City/Large Town
- Town/Village

Transport
- Airport
- Border crossing
- Bus
- Cable car/Funicular
- Cycling
- Ferry
- Metro station
- Monorail
- Parking
- Petrol station
- S-Bahn/S-train/Subway station
- Taxi
- T-bane/Tunnelbana station
- Train station/Railway
- Tram
- Tube station
- U-Bahn/Underground station
- Other Transport

Note: Not all symbols displayed above appear on the maps in this book

Routes
- Tollway
- Freeway
- Primary
- Secondary
- Tertiary
- Lane
- Unsealed road
- Road under construction
- Plaza/Mall
- Steps
- Tunnel
- Pedestrian overpass
- Walking Tour
- Walking Tour detour
- Path/Walking Trail

Boundaries
- International
- State/Province
- Disputed
- Regional/Suburb
- Marine Park
- Cliff
- Wall

Hydrography
- River, Creek
- Intermittent River
- Canal
- Water
- Dry/Salt/Intermittent Lake
- Reef

Areas
- Airport/Runway
- Beach/Desert
- Cemetery (Christian)
- Cemetery (Other)
- Glacier
- Mudflat
- Park/Forest
- Sight (Building)
- Sportsground
- Swamp/Mangrove

OUR STORY

A beat-up old car, a few dollars in the pocket and a sense of adventure. In 1972 that's all Tony and Maureen Wheeler needed for the trip of a lifetime – across Europe and Asia overland to Australia. It took several months, and at the end – broke but inspired – they sat at their kitchen table writing and stapling together their first travel guide, *Across Asia on the Cheap*. Within a week they'd sold 1500 copies. Lonely Planet was born.

Today, Lonely Planet has offices in Franklin, London, Melbourne, Oakland, Beijing and Delhi, with more than 600 staff and writers. We share Tony's belief that 'a great guidebook should do three things: inform, educate and amuse'.

OUR WRITERS

Lucy Corne

Gran Canaria, Fuerteventura, Lazarote Lucy's first introduction to the Canary Islands was a four-month stint entertaining kids in a Gran Canaria tourist resort. It did not show off the best that the island had to offer, but rare days off were spent discovering there was more to Gran Canaria than beaches and all-you-can-drink boat trips. She soon moved to Las Palmas and spent four years in the Canaries, teaching English, writing for a local newspaper and exploring hamlets, hiking trails and hidden beaches across all seven islands. She was thrilled to return for this book and was particularly excited to revisit Gran Canaria's mountainous centre, roam barefoot again on Isla Graciosa and attempt to eat her body weight in papas arrugadas. See more of Lucy's work at www.lucycorne.com. Lucy also wrote the Plan Your Trip, Island Cuisine, Canarian Arts & Culture, Life on a Volcano and Survival Guide chapters.

Read more about Lucy at:
http://auth.lonelyplanet.com/profiles/lucycorne

Josephine Quintero

Tenerife, La Gomera, La Palma, El Hierro Josephine has lived on mainland Spain for over 20 years and has visited the Canary Islands on several occasions, including researching two previous editions of this title. She finds that the islands continually throw up surprises, although there is one constant: the genuine friendliness of the locals. Highlights during this trip included gazing at evocative art at the magnificent TEA museum in Santa Cruz, listening to soul-stirring Silbo (whistling) in La Gomera, and hiking in the lush green hinterland in La Palma where there was (thankfully) no mobile signal and only the sound of birdsong. Josephine also wrote the Canary Islands Today and History chapters.

Read more about Josephine at:
http://auth.lonelyplanet.com/profiles/josephinequintero

Published by Lonely Planet Publications Pty Ltd
ABN 36 005 607 983
6th edition – Jan 2016
ISBN 978 1 74220 558 8
© Lonely Planet 2016   Photographs © as indicated 2016
10 9 8 7 6 5 4 3 2 1
Printed in China